EYEWITNESS TRAVEL GUIDES

WARSAW

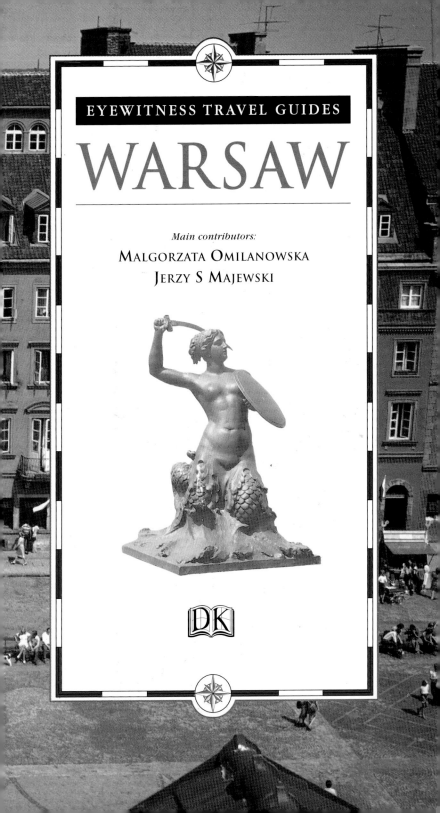

EYEWITNESS TRAVEL GUIDES

WARSAW

Main contributors:

MALGORZATA OMILANOWSKA

JERZY S MAJEWSKI

LONDON, NEW YORK,
MELBOURNE, MUNICH AND DELHI
www.dk.com

Produced by Wydawnictwo Wiedza i Życie, Warsaw
SERIES EDITOR Ewa Szwagrzyk
CONSULTANT Dr Hanna Faryna-Paszkiewicz
JACKET Krzysztof Stefaniuk
DESIGNERS Krzysztof Giedziński, Paweł Pasternak
EDITORS Joanna Egert, Anna Kożurno-Królikowska, Bożena Leszkowicz, Teresa Czerniewicz-Umer

Dorling Kindersley Ltd
CONSULTANT EDITOR Ian Wisniewski
SENIOR DESIGNER Dutjapun Williams
EDITORS Michael Ellis, Peter Preston, Jane Simmonds
RESEARCHER Bogdan Kaczorowski

CONTRIBUTORS
Małgorzata Omilanowska, Jerzy S Majewski, Piotr Bikont

PHOTOGRAPHERS
Hanna Musiał, Maciej Musiał, Agencja "Piękna", Mariusz Kowalewski

ILLUSTRATORS
Andrzej Wielgosz, Piotr Zubrzycki

Printed and bound by L. Rex Printing Company Limited, China

First published in Great Britain by Dorling Kindersley Limited, 80 Strand, London WC2R ORL

Reprinted with revisions 1999, 2000, 2001, 2003

A CIP CATALOGUE RECORD IS AVAILABLE FROM THE BRITISH LIBRARY.

ISBN 0-7513-4833-3

The information in this Dorling Kindersley Travel Guide is checked regularly.
Every effort has been made to ensure that this book is as up-to-date as possible at the time of going to press. Some details, however, such as telephone numbers, opening hours, prices, gallery hanging arrangements and travel information are liable to change. The publishers cannot accept responsibility for any consequences arising from the use of this book, nor for any material on third party websites, and cannot guarantee that any website address in this book will be a suitable source of travel information. We value the views and suggestions of our readers very highly. Please write to: Publisher, DK Eyewitness Travel Guides, Dorling Kindersley, 80 Strand, London WC2R 0RL, Great Britain.

◁ **View of the Old Town Market Square**

CONTENTS

King Zygmunt III Waza

INTRODUCING WARSAW

Flowers in the Botanical Gardens

Madonna and Child by Botticelli, in the National Museum

Warsaw Area by Area

Decoration from Wilanów Palace

Travellers' Needs

Palace on the Water in Łazienki Park

Survival Guide

Painted Easter eggs

Houses in the Old Town

Mead

How to Use this Guide

THIS EYEWITNESS Travel Guide enables you to make the most of your time in Warsaw, with the minimum difficulty. It offers knowledgeable recommendations for sights and areas to visit, places to stay and restaurants, as well as the most useful practical information. *Introducing Warsaw* locates the city geographically, sets modern Warsaw in its historical context and describes the changing lives of its inhabitants through the seasons of the year. *Warsaw Area by Area* is the main sightseeing part of the guide, covering all of the capital's major sights with maps, photographs and illustrations. It also includes the routes of three guided walks around the city and offers suggestions for day trips outside Warsaw. Specially selected information about hotels, restaurants, shops, cafés, bars, entertainment and sports events can be found in the *Travellers' Needs* section. The *Survival Guide* gives practical information on everyday needs, from making telephone calls to using the public transport system.

Visitors planning a tour of Warsaw

Warsaw Area by Area

The centre of Warsaw has been divided into seven sightseeing areas. Each area has its own chapter and is colour-coded for easy reference. Every chapter opens with a list of the sights described, which are numbered and plotted on an *Area Map*. Detailed information for each sight is presented in numerical order, making it easy to find within the chapter.

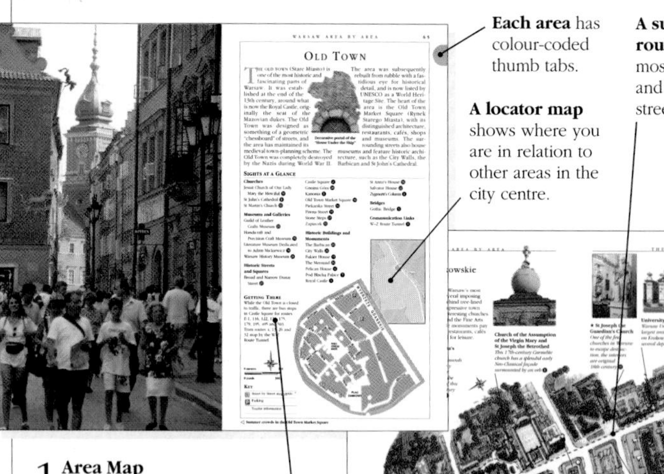

Each area has colour-coded thumb tabs.

A suggested route takes in the most interesting and attractive streets in the area.

A locator map shows where you are in relation to other areas in the city centre.

Locator map

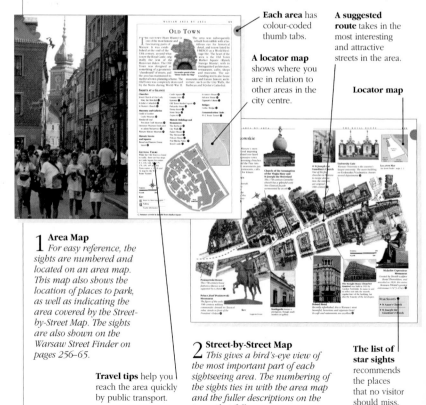

1 Area Map
For easy reference, the sights are numbered and located on an area map. This map also shows the location of places to park, as well as indicating the area covered by the Street-by-Street Map. The sights are also shown on the Warsaw Street Finder on pages 256–65.

Travel tips help you reach the area quickly by public transport.

2 Street-by-Street Map
This gives a bird's-eye view of the most important part of each sightseeing area. The numbering of the sights ties in with the area map and the fuller descriptions on the pages that follow.

The list of star sights recommends the places that no visitor should miss.

Warsaw Area Map

The colour-coded areas shown on this map *(see inside front cover)* are the seven main sightseeing areas – each covered by a full chapter in *Warsaw Area by Area (pp62–165)*. The seven areas are highlighted on other maps throughout the book. In *Warsaw at a Glance (pp32–51)*, for example, they help locate the top sights, including galleries and museums, palaces and parks, religious buildings and cemeteries. They are also used to show the location of the top restaurants, cafés and bars *(pp206–7)*, and Warsaw's best hotels *(pp198–9)*.

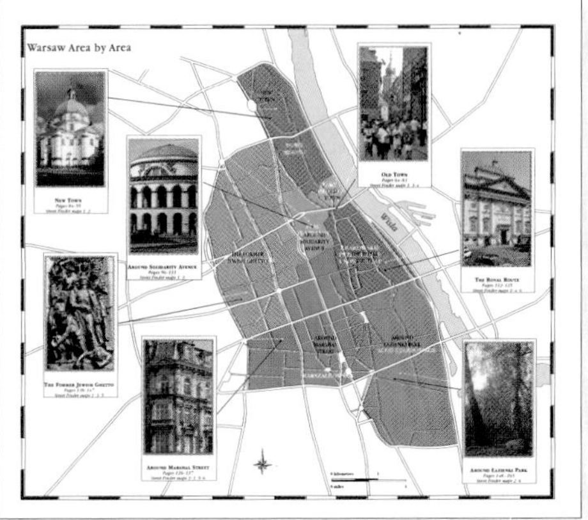

Façades of important buildings are often shown to illustrate their architectural style, and help you to recognize them quickly.

Practical information lists all the information you need to visit every sight, including a map reference to the *Street Finder (pp256–65)*.

Numbers refer to each sight's position on the area map and its place in the chapter.

The visitors' checklist provides all the practical information needed to plan your visit.

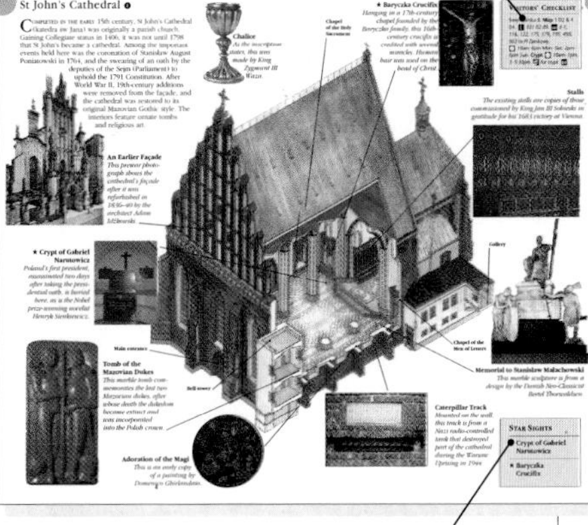

3 Detailed information on each sight

All the important sights in Warsaw are described individually. They are listed in order, following the numbering on the Area Map. Addresses and practical information are provided. The key to the symbols used in the information block is on the back flap.

4 Warsaw's top sights

Historic buildings are dissected to reveal their interiors; while museums and galleries have colour-coded floorplans to help you locate the most interesting exhibits.

Stars indicate the features no visitor should miss.

Introducing Warsaw

Putting Warsaw on the Map

WARSAW, THE CAPITAL CITY of Poland, has a population of around 1.6 million, and covers an area of 494 sq km (185 sq miles). The city, which is also capital of the historic district of Mazovia, is located within central Poland on the banks of the River Vistula (Wisła). Warsaw's location makes it an ideal base for visiting other important Polish cities, such as Kraków, Gdańsk, Wrocław and Poznań.

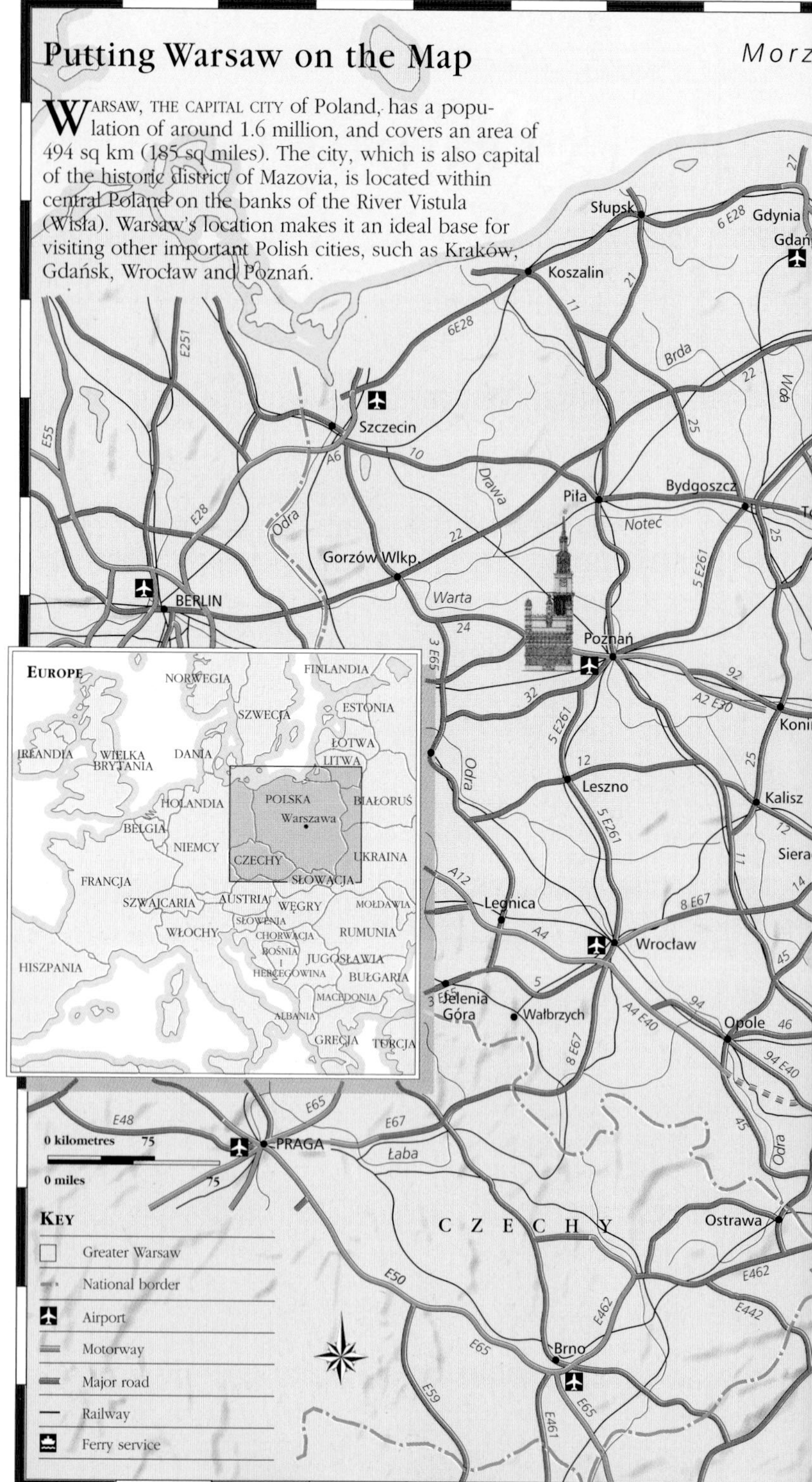

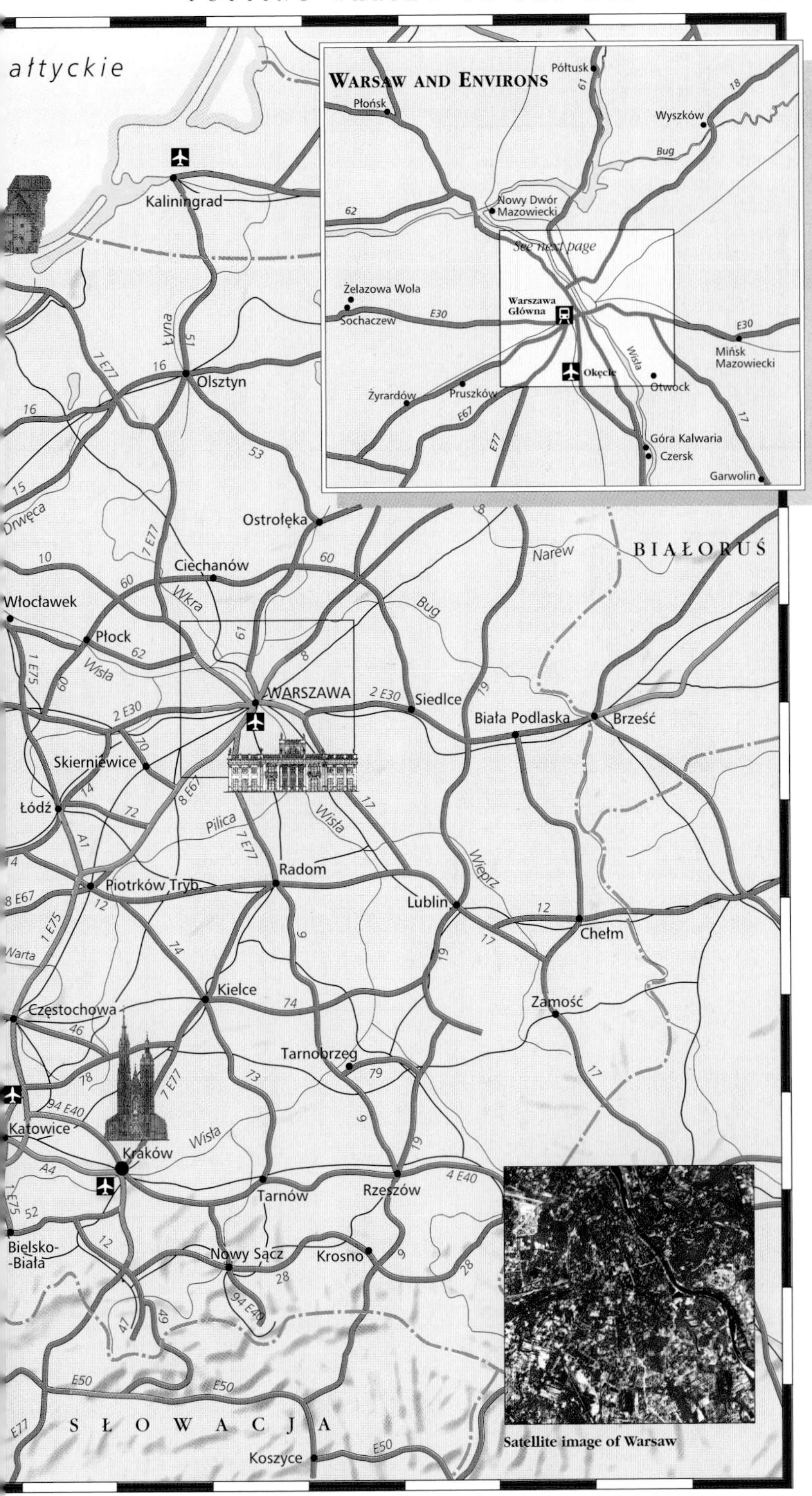

Satellite image of Warsaw

Greater Warsaw

THE MAJORITY of attractions listed in this guide are located within central Warsaw, and are easily reached either on foot or by public transport. Moreover, many of Warsaw's most attractive and historic sights are located along what is called the Royal Route, which consists of the main thoroughfares leading from the Royal Castle in the Old Town to Łazienki Park and Wilanów Palace. This book divides the city into seven districts, each of which is detailed within the *Warsaw Area by Area* section.

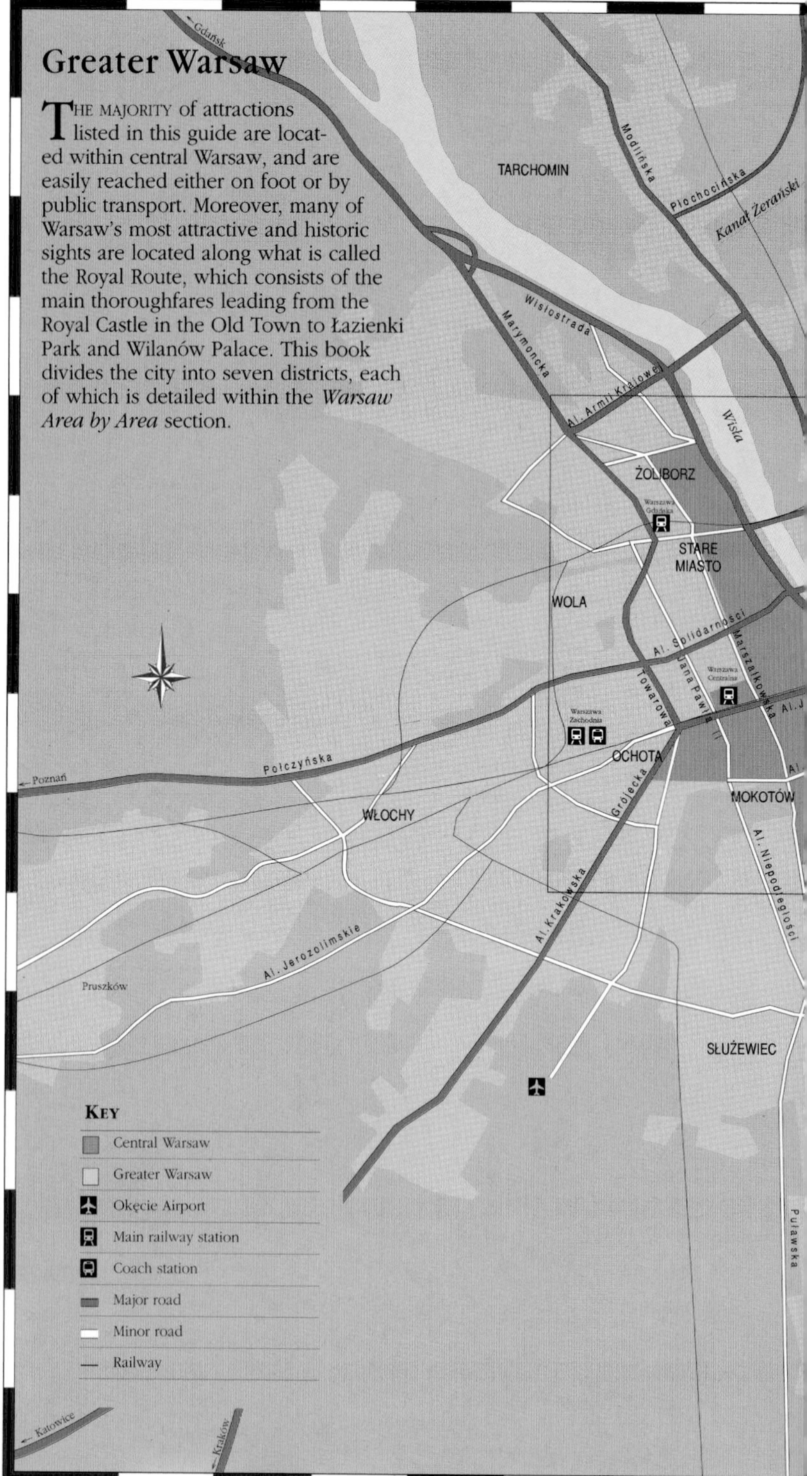

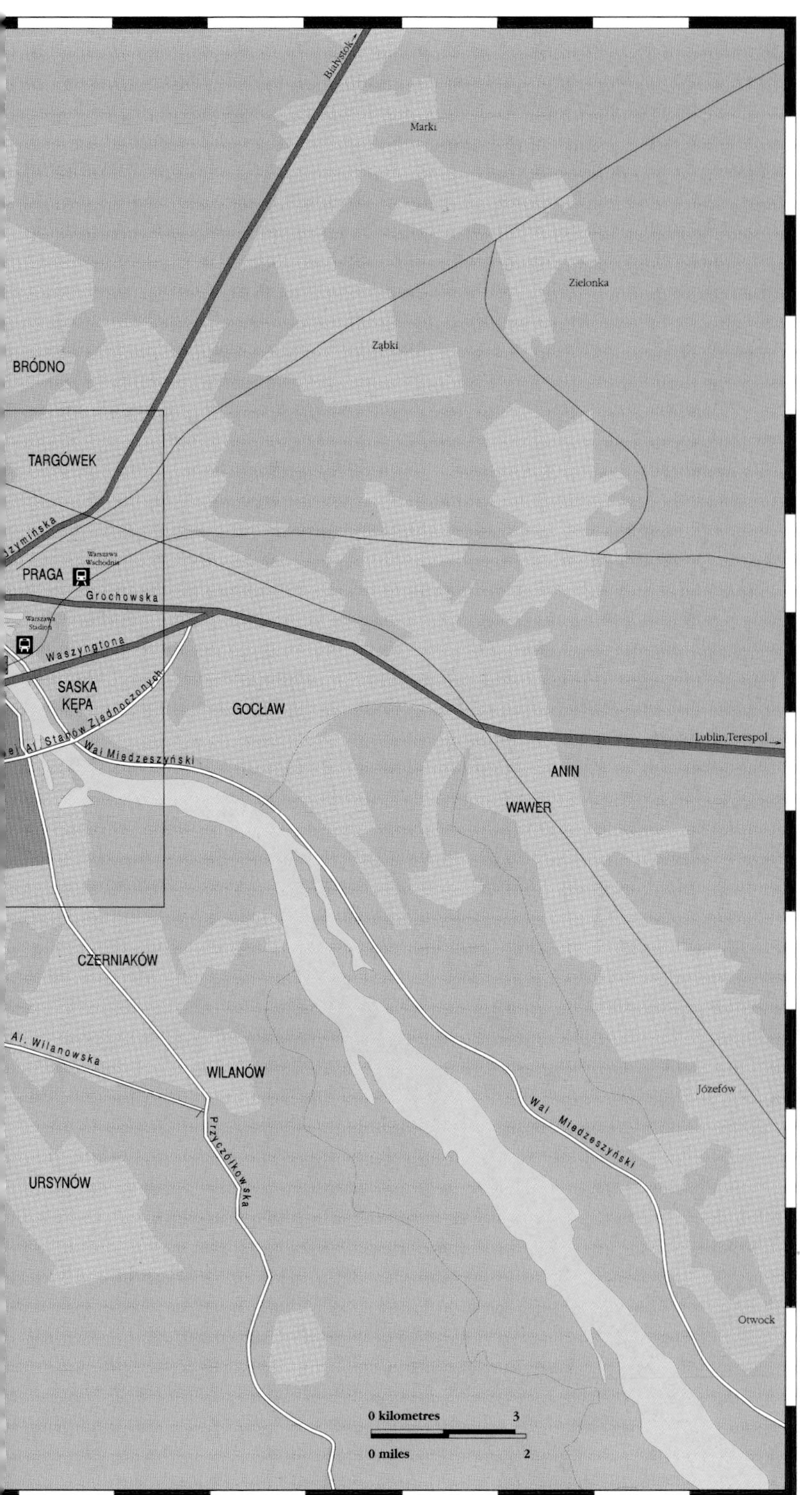
Białystok
Marki
Zielonka
Ząbki
BRÓDNO
TARGÓWEK
Warszawa Wschodnia
PRAGA
Grochowska
Warszawa Stadion
Waszyngtona
SASKA KĘPA
Al. Stanów Zjednoczonych
GOCŁAW
Wał Miedzeszyński
Lublin, Terespol
ANIN
WAWER
CZERNIAKÓW
Al. Wilanowska
WILANÓW
Józefów
Przyczółkowska
URSYNÓW
Otwock
0 kilometres 3
0 miles 2

The History of Warsaw

Warsaw is one of Europe's youngest capital cities; it became Poland's capital only in the 16th century, though early settlements existed from the 10th century. At the end of the 13th century, Bolesław II, Duke of Mazovia, established a residence and founded what is now known as the Old Town.

The crest of the City of Warsaw

At the beginning of the 15th century, Duke Janusz I Starszy also established his court in Warsaw, and the town developed rapidly in the late Middle Ages. Although Kraków was the capital, Warsaw remained the seat of the Mazovian dukes. When the dynasty died out in 1526, the king took control of the duchy.

Warsaw's growing status, and central position in Poland, resulted in Parliament being moved from Kraków to Warsaw in 1569. Warsaw became the capital in 1596, when King Zygmunt III Waza transferred his permanent residence there. In the 17th century, Warsaw continued to develop rapidly with various churches and palaces being built. But the city's evolution was halted by the Swedish invasion of 1655, known as "the Deluge".

Warsaw continued to grow in the late 18th century during the reign of Poland's last king, Stanisław August Poniatowski. However, the city was occupied by Prussia in 1795. In 1815 Warsaw came under Russian rule. Russian suppression of the 1830 and 1863 insurrections left Warsaw politically weak, but the city still saw rapid industrial growth in that century. Before World War I, Warsaw was Europe's eighth largest city.

When Poland regained independence after World War I, Warsaw was re-established as the capital. During World War II Warsaw experienced three dramatic events: the siege of September 1939, the 1943 uprising in the Jewish Ghetto, and the 1944 Warsaw Uprising. Following this last uprising, the Nazis systematically destroyed almost the entire city. Overall, 700,000 of Warsaw's inhabitants (almost half the total) were killed or displaced during the war.

The city came under Communist control in 1945, and a massive rebuilding programme restored many of Warsaw's historic monuments. In 1989 the city celebrated the first postwar democratic elections which ended the Communist era. The pages that follow outline the most important periods of Warsaw's history.

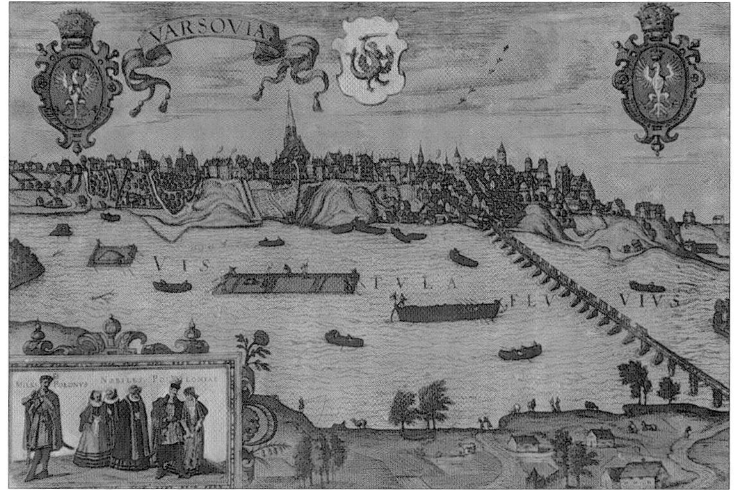

A late 16th-century panorama of Warsaw

◁ Portrait of King Stanisław August Poniatowski by Marcello Bacciarelli

Kings and Rulers

Warsaw was originally a seat of the dukes of Mazovia, who were descended from the Polish Piast dynasty. At the beginning of the 15th century, Duke Janusz I Starszy gave Warsaw the status of Mazovia's capital. In 1526, after the death of the last two dukes, Mazovia came under the direct rule of the king, and Warsaw was a royal residence of the Jagiellon dynasty. Warsaw became the capital of the Polish Commonwealth in 1596, under King Zygmunt III Waza, the third king to be elected after the hereditary system was abolished. He and his successors enriched Warsaw with various architectural works. The monarchy ended when Poland lost its independence at the end of the 18th century and, apart from the Napoleonic era, Warsaw was ruled by occupying powers. From 1918 to 1939, and since 1989, Poland's presidents have governed from Warsaw.

1587–163 Zygmunt I Waz (resident i Warsaw fror 159(

1294–1313 Bolesław II

1313–41 Trojden I

1341–55 Kazimierz I

1429–54 Bolesław IV

1488–92 Janusz II

1518–26 Janusz III

1573–5 Henryk Walezy*

1576–86 Stefan Batory*

1200	1300	1400	1500
DUKES OF MAZOVIA			JAGIELLONI
1200	1300	1400	1500

1355–74 Siemowit III

1374–1429 Janusz I Starszy

1471–88 Bolesław V

1492–1503 Konrad III Rudy

1503–18 Anna Radziwiłł (Konrad's widow)

1506–48 Zygmunt Stary* (who ruled Mazovia from 1526)

1518–24 Stanisław I

1548–72 Zygmunt August*

Mazovian Dukes

*Resident in Kraków

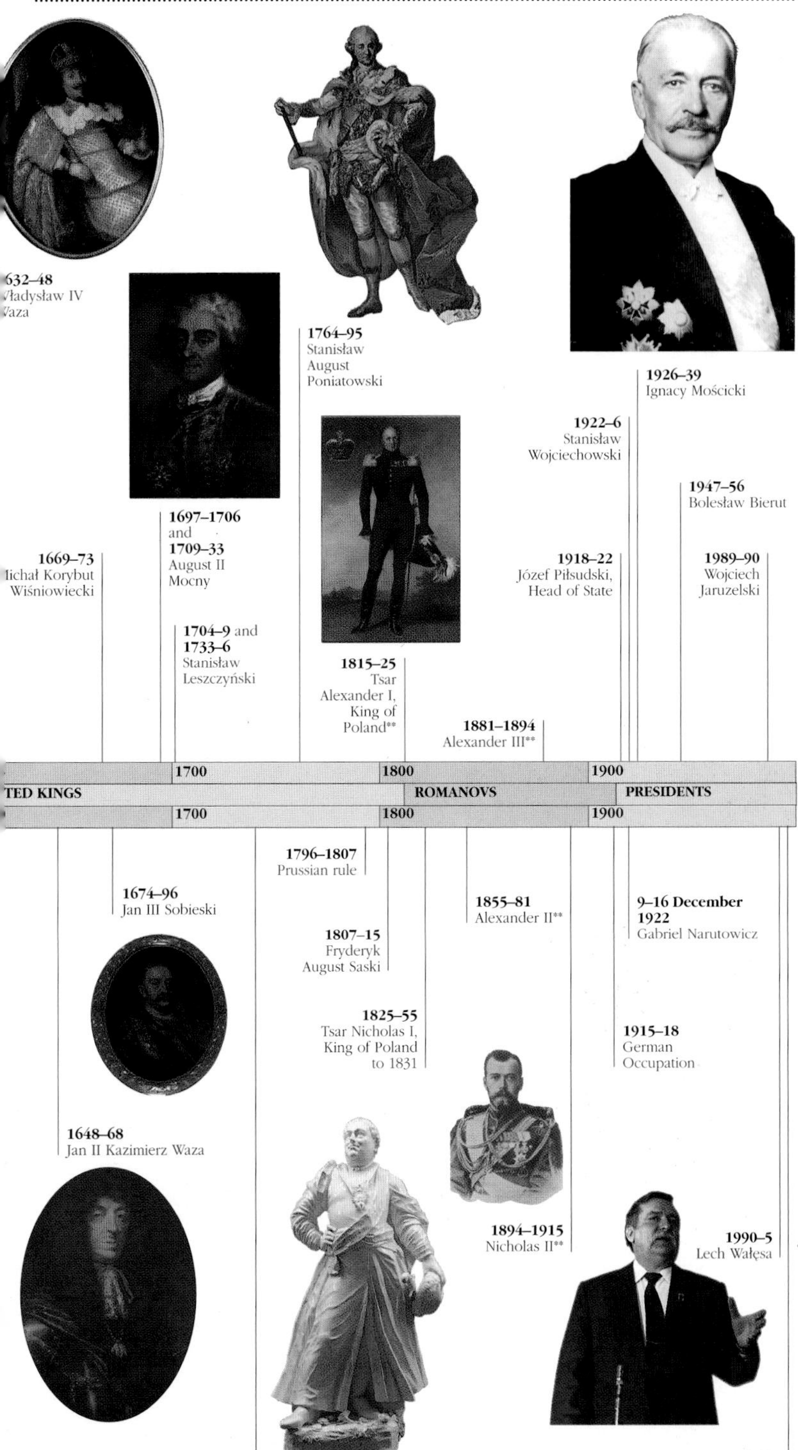

632–48
Władysław IV Waza

1764–95
Stanisław August Poniatowski

1926–39
Ignacy Mościcki

1922–6
Stanisław Wojciechowski

1947–56
Bolesław Bierut

1697–1706 and 1709–33
August II Mocny

1669–73
Michał Korybut Wiśniowiecki

1918–22
Józef Piłsudski, Head of State

1989–90
Wojciech Jaruzelski

1704–9 and 1733–6
Stanisław Leszczyński

1815–25
Tsar Alexander I, King of Poland**

1881–1894
Alexander III**

1700 | 1800 | 1900

TED KINGS | ROMANOVS | PRESIDENTS

1700 | 1800 | 1900

1796–1807
Prussian rule

1674–96
Jan III Sobieski

1855–81
Alexander II**

9–16 December 1922
Gabriel Narutowicz

1807–15
Fryderyk August Saski

1825–55
Tsar Nicholas I, King of Poland to 1831

1915–18
German Occupation

1648–68
Jan II Kazimierz Waza

1894–1915
Nicholas II**

1990–5
Lech Wałęsa

1995–
Aleksander Kwaśniewski

1733–63
August III

**Resident in St Petersburg

Warsaw's Origins

Although earlier settlements had existed on this site, Warsaw is believed to have been founded at the end of the 13th century, when Duke Bolesław II built a castle. The town expanded under Duke Janusz I Starszy (1374–1429), becoming the Mazovian region's cultural and political centre, and the parish church (now St John's Cathedral, *see pp76–7*) gained Collegiate status. Houses were initially built of timber, later replaced by stone. In the late 14th century the New Town started to develop to the north of the Old Town; it was granted separate status in 1408.

Warsaw's mermaid

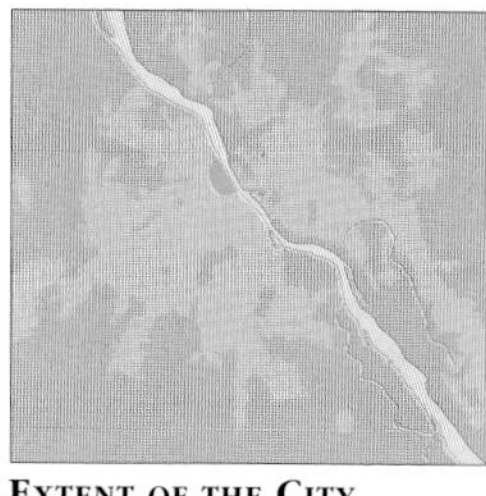

Extent of the City

c.1500 *Today*

Presbytery of St John's Cathedral
This is the city's oldest example of Gothic architecture, dating from the first half of the 14th century.

Warsaw Seen From the Vistula *(1581)*
The earliest surviving depiction of Warsaw, a woodcut, documents its Gothic skyline.

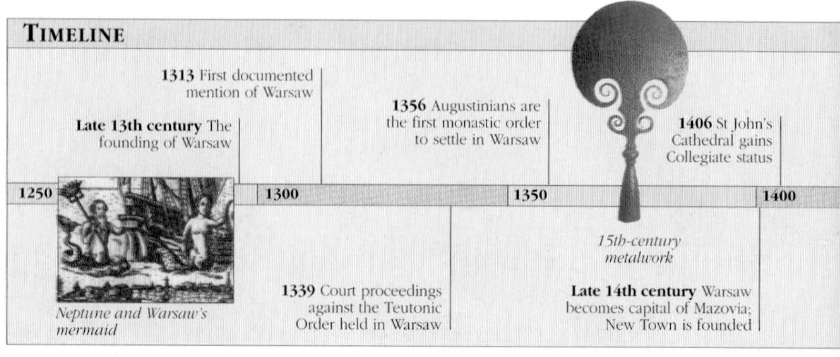

Timeline

1313 First documented mention of Warsaw

Late 13th century The founding of Warsaw

1356 Augustinians are the first monastic order to settle in Warsaw

1406 St John's Cathedral gains Collegiate status

1250 | 1300 | 1350 | 1400

Neptune and Warsaw's mermaid

15th-century metalwork

1339 Court proceedings against the Teutonic Order held in Warsaw

Late 14th century Warsaw becomes capital of Mazovia; New Town is founded

Gothic Portal
This is at No. 21 in the Old Town Market Square.

Duchess Anna Odrowąż
A Mazovian Duchess (1498–c.1557).

Warsaw's Legends

Numerous Varsovian legends were chronicled by the poet Artur Oppman (known as Or-Ot), who lived in the Old Town in the 19th century.

One tale attributes the town's name to the original landowners, Wars and Sawa. Another tells of a mermaid who lived in the Vistula and protected the town, while serenading its inhabitants. Meanwhile, a ferocious monster guarded treasure in the vaults of Zapiecek Square. One look from this monster was lethal, but it was eventually subdued by a cobbler's apprentice. A golden duck was also said to guard treasure in an underground lake beneath the Ostrogski Palace.

Dukes of Mazovia
This fragment of a miniature painted in 1449 shows 14th–15th-century Mazovian dukes.

Canon Stanisław of Strzelec
As tutor to the last Mazovian dukes, he was entombed in the Cathedral in 1532.

Silver Cockerel
This was a symbol of the Brotherhood of Marksmen. It was commissioned in the mid-16th century by a Varsovian aristocrat, Jan Baryczka.

Ducal Seal
Used by the Mazovian Duke Konrad II (1252–94), this seal is in the Raczyński Palace archives (see p92).

1429 Death of Duke Janusz I Starszy

1454 Construction of St Anna's Church and Bernardine monastery begins

Gothic door lock and key

1569 Parliament moves to Warsaw from Kraków

1573 First royal election held in Warsaw

1450 | 1500 | 1550 | 1600

1469 Autonomy granted to Jewish Council, which had been founded 100 years earlier

1526 Death of Janusz III, the last Duke of Mazovia

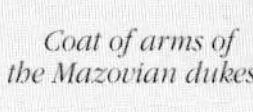

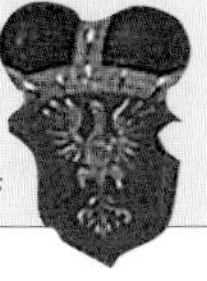

Coat of arms of the Mazovian dukes

Warsaw During the Waza Period

Portrait of King Władysław IV

A NEW ERA BEGAN IN 1596 when King Zygmunt III Waza transferred the royal residence from Kraków and made Warsaw the capital. Renowned Italian architects rebuilt the Royal Castle on a grand scale and added several early Baroque buildings. The court also became the intellectual heart of Central Europe, and brought numerous aristocratic families and several monastic orders to Warsaw. The Swedish invasion of 1655 took a heavy toll on the city, however, and was followed by considerable rebuilding work.

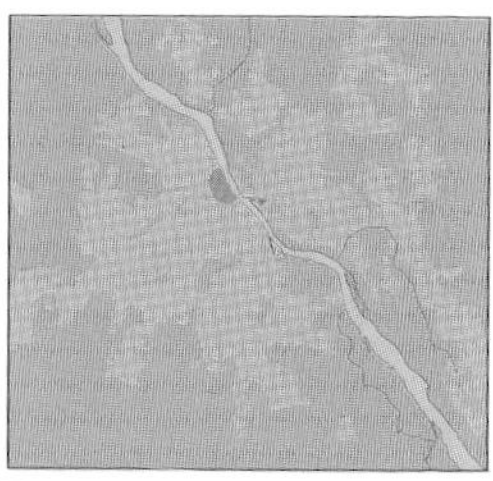

EXTENT OF THE CITY

1650 *Today*

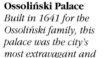

Ossoliński Palace
Built in 1641 for the Ossoliński family, this palace was the city's most extravagant and luxurious residence. It was destroyed in 1655.

Queen Cecylia Renata
Queen Cecylia (1611–44) was the first wife of King Władysław IV.

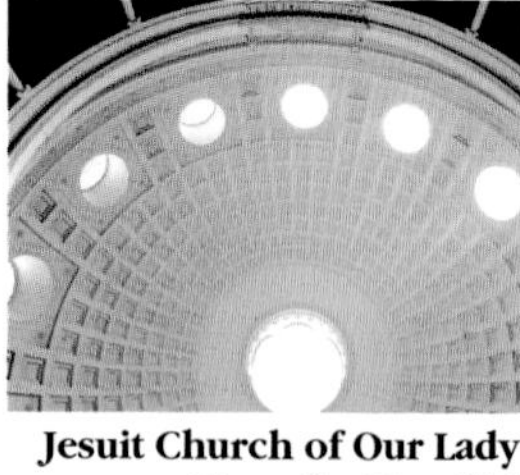

Jesuit Church of Our Lady Mary the Merciful
Built between 1609–26, it has a remarkable dome.

TIMELINE

Artillery of the Waza period in the Polish Military Museum (see p152)

Detail of No. 28 Old Town Market Square

1596 Royal residence moves from Kraków to Warsaw

1597 Jesuits settle in Warsaw

1598 Rebuilding of the Royal Castle begins

1600

1607 Devastating fire in the Old Town

1611 Zygmunt III Waza's triumphal arrival in Warsaw

1615

Stockholm Scroll
Several metres long, this 17th-century scroll shows the wedding procession of King Zygmunt III Waza.

Where to See the Wazas' Warsaw

The best example of this period's architecture is the Royal Castle *(see pp70–73)*. Rebuilt after being destroyed during World War II, the Royal Castle contains several royal portraits of the period *(see below)*. Ujazdowski Palace *(p159)*, and several burghers' houses in the Old Town, such as the "Little Black Boy House" *(p78)*, also date from this time. Early Baroque churches include the Jesuit Church of Our Lady Mary the Merciful *(p74)* and St Jacek's Church *(p88)*.

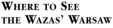

***Portraits of** Zygmunt III Waza, Władysław IV and Jan Kazimierz from the Royal Castle*

A Panorama of Warsaw

This mezzotint, first published in 1696 by Samuel Pufendorf, was based on drawings by Erik Jönsen Dahlbergh, court draughtsman of King Charles Gustav of Sweden. It shows Warsaw's Baroque buildings prior to the 1655 Swedish invasion.

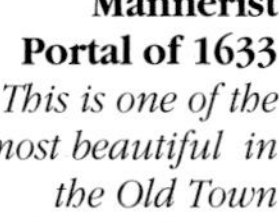

King Zygmunt III Waza
Zygmunt's Column, from 1644, is the oldest secular monument in Poland.

Mannerist Portal of 1633
This is one of the most beautiful in the Old Town Market Square.

1625–6 The worst period of the plague

1630

1632 King Zygmunt III Waza dies

1637 Opening of the first permanent theatre in the Royal Castle

1644 Zygmunt III Waza's Column is erected

1645

1648 Władysław IV dies

The Waza family's coat of arms

1655 Swedish invasion

1660

Typical Warsaw burghers

Warsaw After the Swedish Invasion

Warsaw was gradually rebuilt after the devastating Swedish invasion of 1655. The short reign of King Michał Korybut Wiśniowiecki, elected in 1669 after Jan II Kazimierz Waza abdicated, was followed by that of Jan III Sobieski. He was a great patron of the arts, whose election in 1674 inaugurated a new era. Poland's political standing rose, helped by the king's great victory over the Turks at Vienna in 1683.

Jan III Sobieski Monument

Extent of the City

1655–1700 Today

Krasiński Palace *(1677–82)*
It was designed by the royal architect, the Dutchman Tylman of Gameren, one of many renowned designers brought to Warsaw by Jan III Sobieski.

The Daybreak
This work was painted by Jan Reisner, on the ceiling of the queen's chamber at Wilanów.

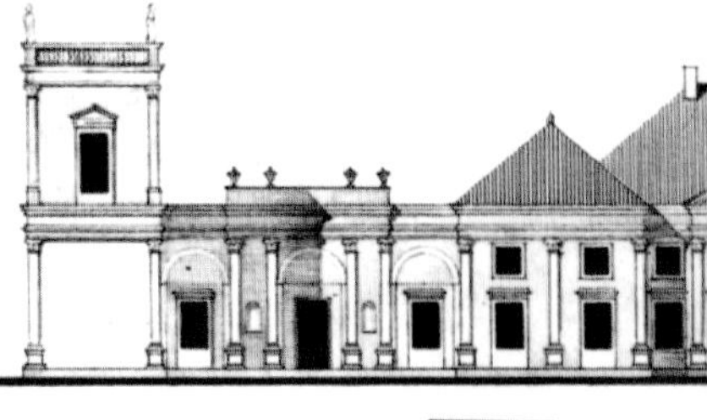

Field Hetman (Deputy Commander-in-Chief) Stefan Czarniecki
He helped lead Poland to victory over Sweden in 1655–7.

A Noble's Funeral Portrait
In 17th-century Poland such portraits were specially painted and attached to the coffin while it was displayed before a funeral.

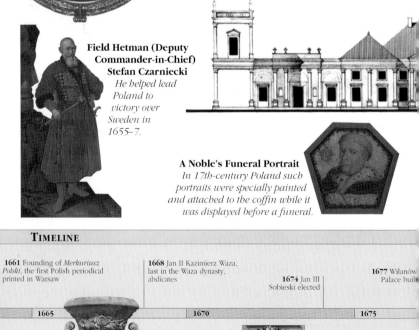

Timeline

1661 Founding of *Merkuriusz Polski*, the first Polish periodical printed in Warsaw

1665

1668 Jan II Kazimierz Waza, last in the Waza dynasty, abdicates

1670

1674 Jan III Sobieski elected

1675

1677 Wilanów Palace buil

Urn from Ostrogski Palace

Detail from the façade of Wilanów Palace

Queen Marysieńka
Pictured here, together with her children, Marysieńka was the beloved wife of Jan III Sobieski.

Capuchin Church of the Transfiguration
It was founded by Jan III Sobieski in gratitude for his victory over the Turks at Vienna in 1683.

Where to See Jan III Sobieski's Warsaw

In addition to Wilanów Palace *(see pp168–71)*, Warsaw has several other buildings from this period. They include the Krasiński Palace *(p102)*, Ostrogski Palace *(p123)* and St Casimir's Church *(p90)*, all of which were designed by the court architect Tylman of Gameren.

***Ostrogski Palace** now houses the Frederic Chopin Museum* (p123).

Dome of St Antony of Padua Church
Situated in Czerniakowska Street, this church was built in 1687–93 to a design by Tylman of Gameren.

Wilanów Palace (1677)

Serving as King Jan III Sobieski's summer residence, surrounded by picturesque gardens, this palace was not used for official functions.

Hussar's Armour
The Polish "winged hussars" won their greatest victories in the 17th century.

Main altar in St Antony of Padua Church

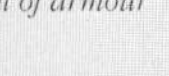

17th-century suit of armour

1680 | 1685 | 1690

1683 Victory over the Turks in the Battle of Vienna

1692 Construction begins of the Marywil, a covered market area founded by Queen Marysieńka

Saxon Warsaw

In the first half of the 18th century two of Poland's elected kings, August II Mocny and August III, were Saxons from the Wettin dynasty. From their court in Dresden, these kings brought the finest Saxon architects and craftsmen to Warsaw, where they created Baroque and Saxon Rococo-style buildings. Despite this, both monarchs spent most of their time in Dresden, and dragged Poland into a series of futile wars.

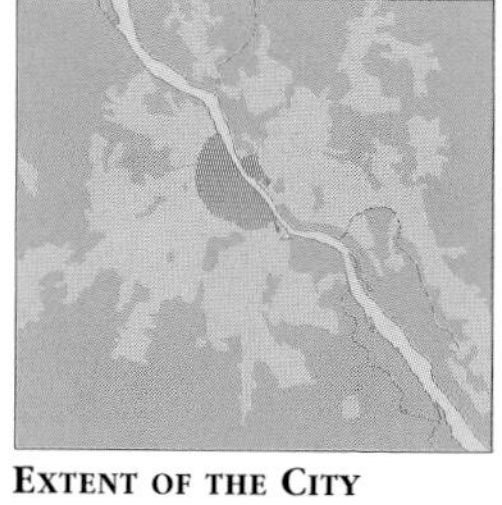

Extent of the City

1750 Today

Rococo Bureau-Secretaire
This fine 18th-century example from the National Museum (see pp154–7) *is painted with mythological scenes, and features a clock built into its crest.*

Meissen Porcelain
Saxon kings were the first to introduce Meissen porcelain to Poland; this figurine is in the Royal Castle (see pp70–73).

Dress Sash
Sashes were an essential element of the traditional dress code of Polish aristocrats. This sash can be seen in the National Museum.

Saxon Axis
August II Mocny was inspired by the Versailles of Louis XIV to build an extravagant residence surrounded by gardens. This was part of a town-planning scheme.

Timeline

1697 August II Mocny elected king of Poland

Cartridge box of a cavalry officer

1704 Stanisław Leszczyński elected king of Poland

1727 Saxon Gardens become Warsaw's first public park

1690 1700 1710 1720

1702 Northern War begins

1709 August II Mocny becomes king again

1713 Construction of the Saxon Axis begins

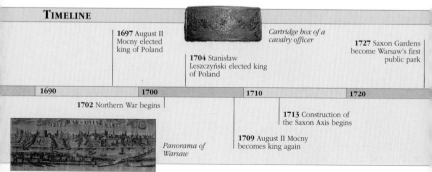

Panorama of Warsaw

Anna Orzelska
August II Mocny gave his daughter Anna a palace, known as the Błękitny (Blue) Palace, as blue was her favourite colour (see p106).

Where to See Warsaw's Saxon Architecture

Many of the Saxon buildings in Warsaw, including several palaces and churches on Krakowskie Przedmieście *(see pp112–25)* and Senatorska Street, have been rebuilt since World War II.

***Przebendowski-Radziwiłł Palace** was designed in 1728 by Jan Zygmunt Deybel for King August II's treasurer* (see p103).

Kulawka
A Kulawka *wine glass had no base, so that guests always had to drink each toast down in one.*

Pulpit in St Joseph the Guardian's Church
Designed in 1760 by Jan Jerzy Plersch, its boat-like shape symbolized the teaching role of the Church.

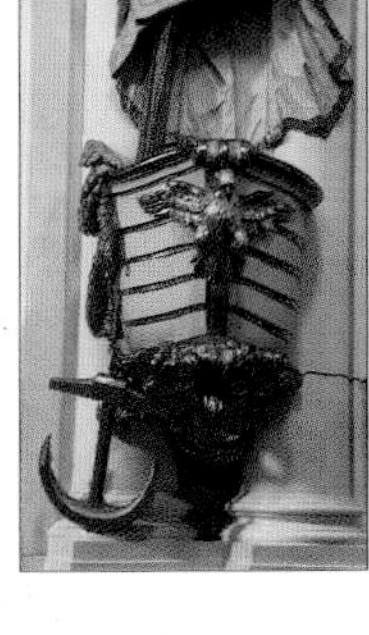

Standard-bearer opening the royal procession

Polish soldiers

Infantry and cavalry flags

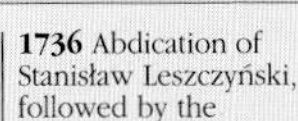

Polish and Saxon Regiments

The summer camp and military displays held on Czerniaków fields in 1732 were in honour of Anna Orzelska's return to Poland from her Grand Tour of Europe.

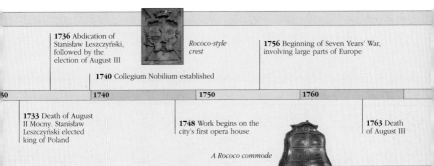

Personification of Poetry
This is one of many sculptures in the Saxon Gardens from the workshop of Jan Jerzy Plersch. Lactating breasts symbolized the fertility of poetic imagination.

1733 Death of August II Mocny. Stanisław Leszczyński elected king of Poland

1736 Abdication of Stanisław Leszczyński, followed by the election of August III

Rococo-style crest

1740 Collegium Nobilium established

1748 Work begins on the city's first opera house

1756 Beginning of Seven Years' War, involving large parts of Europe

1763 Death of August III

1730 | 1740 | 1750 | 1760

A Rococo commode

Warsaw Under the Last Polish King

POLAND'S LAST KING, Stanisław August Poniatowski, was a great aesthete and patron of the arts who made Warsaw a European cultural centre. However, he faced opposition from the aristocracy, making Poland vulnerable, while a lack of military strength meant that the rulers of Prussia, Russia and Austria were able to divide Poland among them.

The royal coat of arms

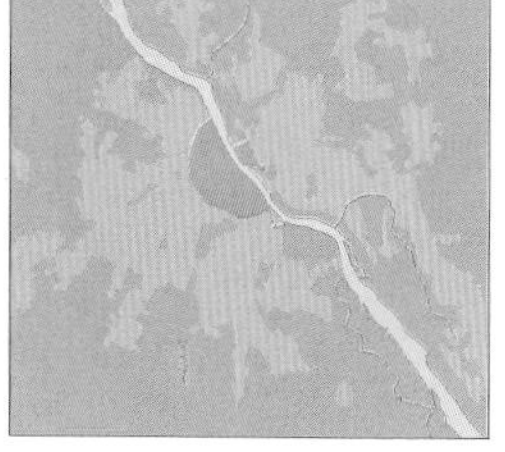

EXTENT OF THE CITY

1770 *Today*

Hugo Kołłątaj
A prominent intellectual and figure of the Enlightenment, he was also involved in drafting the Polish Constitution of 1791.

The election field contained the throne for the future king.

The Voivode (Lord Lieutenant) of the Płock region hands over his region's vote to the marshal of the Sejm (Parliament).

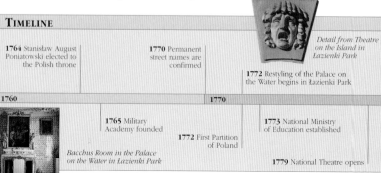

1791 Constitution
This bill of human rights, ratified on 3 May, was the first in Europe.

Knights' Hall in the Royal Castle
The king redecorated this hall, and the entire first floor of the Royal Castle, in an early Neo-Classical style.

TIMELINE

1764 Stanisław August Poniatowski elected to the Polish throne

1770 Permanent street names are confirmed

Detail from Theatre on the Island in Łazienki Park

1772 Restyling of the Palace on the Water begins in Łazienki Park

1760 | 1770 | 1

1765 Military Academy founded

Bacchus Room in the Palace on the Water in Łazienki Park

1772 First Partition of Poland

1773 National Ministry of Education established

1779 National Theatre opens

King Stanisław August Poniatowski
In this portrait the king is depicted deep in thought, contemplating Poland's fate a few months before the Second Partition of 1793.

Where to See Poniatowski's Warsaw

The Łazienki Park and Palace complex, including the Old Orangerie *(see pp162–5)* is a beautiful example of Neo-Classicism. Similar palaces can be seen on Krakowskie Przedmieście *(pp118–25)*, Długa Street *(p102)* and Senatorska Street *(pp106–7)*.

Royal theatre *in the Old Orangerie*

Each region had its own flag.

Royal Election

Polish kings had been elected by the aristocracy since 1573. Bernardo Bellotto painted the election of Stanisław August Poniatowski in 1764.

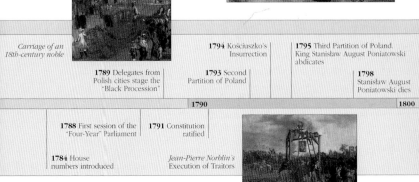

Theatre on the Island
The fashion for antiquities led the king to construct a theatre in Łazienki Park featuring Romantic ruins as a backdrop.

Tadeusz Rejtan
As a protest against the 1772 Partition, this member of Parliament barred the door to the Chamber of Deputies.

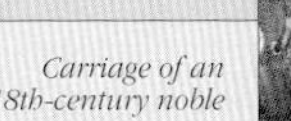

Carriage of an 18th-century noble

1784 House numbers introduced

1788 First session of the "Four-Year" Parliament

1789 Delegates from Polish cities stage the "Black Procession"

1790

1791 Constitution ratified

1793 Second Partition of Poland

1794 Kościuszko's Insurrection

1795 Third Partition of Poland. King Stanisław August Poniatowski abdicates

1798 Stanisław August Poniatowski dies

1800

Jean-Pierre Norblin's Execution of Traitors

Warsaw During the Partitions

One of the most difficult periods in Warsaw's history was during the partition of Poland, between Austria, Prussia and Russia, at the end of the 18th century. Hopes of regaining independence with Napoleon's support proved illusory. Moreover, insurrections resulted in tighter Russian control, with academic and cultural institutions being closed. It was a time, however, that saw rapid industrial growth.

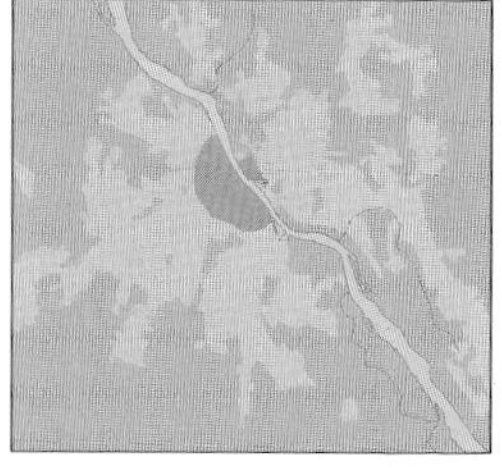

Extent of the City

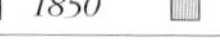

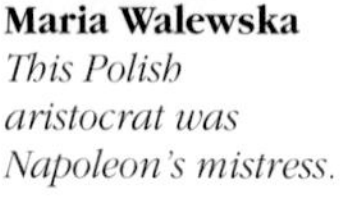

Maria Walewska
This Polish aristocrat was Napoleon's mistress.

Napoleon Granting a Constitution to the Grand Duchy of Warsaw
Napoleon briefly inspired Polish hopes of regaining national independence.

Poland Partitioned
Poland's three neighbouring powers, Russia, Prussia and Austria, divided up the Polish Commonwealth between them. In a contemporary caricature, Catherine the Great of Russia and Frederick Wilhelm II of Prussia quarrel over the spoils following the First Partition in 1772.

Personification of Poland

Catherine the Great of Russia

Piotr Wysocki
On 29 November 1830 he led fellow officer cadets in an attack on the residence of Grand Duke Constantine. This began the unsuccessful November Insurrection.

Timeline

- **1775**
- **1796** Prussian army enters Warsaw
- **1800** Inaugural session of the Society of the Friends of Science in Warsaw
- **1807** Grand Duchy of Warsaw created
- **1815** Warsaw becomes capital of a Polish kingdom under the Russian tsar
- **1816** Opening of the Royal University of Warsaw
- **1825** Work begins on building the Grand Theatre
- **1830** November Insurrection
- **1832** In retaliation for the 1830 Insurrection, the Russians build a citadel
- **1845** First section of the Warsaw–Vienna railway line opened

Soldiers of the Napoleonic era

Marshal Street
This broad street, with its multi-storey buildings, was the principal thoroughfare of 19th-century Warsaw.

Henryk Sienkiewicz
He won the Nobel Prize in 1905 for his novel about ancient Rome, Quo Vadis. *However, his novels on Polish history are more popular.*

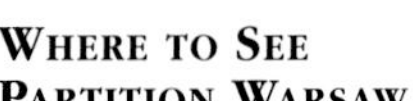

Where to See Partition Warsaw

While Marshal Street has lost its original appearance, the style of 19th-century Warsaw can still be seen in some of the city's streets. Lwowska Street *(p137)* and Aleje Jerozolimskie *(p136)* feature architecture from the Partition era, as do palaces and villas on Ujazdowskie Avenue *(p150)*.

Villa Sobański *is situated on Ujazdowskie Avenue.*

Advertisement for Okocim Beer
The original was painted by Wojciech Kossak, on tin.

King Frederick Wilhelm II of Prussia

Frederic Chopin
This great pianist and composer left Warsaw in 1830, never to return.

Mourning Jewellery
Poland was in mourning after the 1863 Insurrection failed. Women even wore special mourning jewellery.

Zachęta building

1863 January Insurrection begins

1881 Contract signed with Englishman William Lindley for the building of the city's sewerage and water systems

1905 Poles support the labourers' insurrection in Russia

Warsaw tramcar

1908 Electric tramways introduced

1850 | 1875 | 1900

Grand Theatre

1866 Warsaw's first horse-drawn trams

Insignia of the 1863 Insurrection

1900 Construction of the Philharmonic building begins

1915 Russian army withdraws from Warsaw

20th-Century Warsaw

Twenty years of independence ended when the Nazis and Soviets both invaded Poland in 1939. Warsaw was then occupied by the Nazis for more than five years. The Jewish population suffered huge losses within the ghetto area, and was finally exterminated in 1943 after the Ghetto Uprising; the next year, the Warsaw Uprising was also brutally suppressed. Eighty per cent of the city had been destroyed, but massive reconstruction during the Communist era revived much of Warsaw's architectural character. 1989 marked the end of Communist rule.

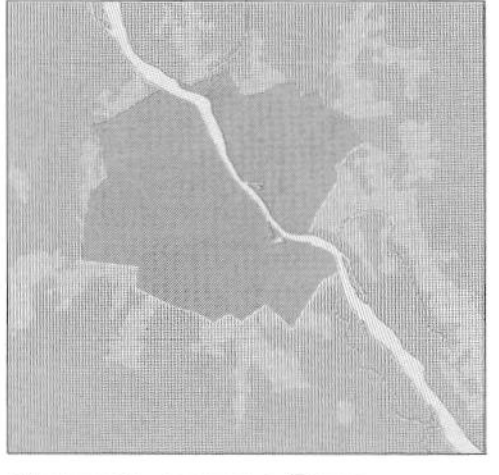

Extent of the City

1916 *Today*

A Warsaw Coffee House
The colourful life of Warsaw between the wars, seen in a painting by Józef Rapacki.

Tanks on Puławska Street
The Communist government's reaction to the rise of Solidarity was to declare martial law in December 1981.

Józef Piłsudski
Marshal Piłsudski led the Polish army that liberated the country in 1918. He was subsequently proclaimed the first head of state of an independent Poland.

Warsaw Uprising
The Polish Home Army attempted to liberate the city from the Nazis in 1944.

Timeline

1915 Warsaw University reopens

1918 Warsaw freed from German occupation

1920 Poland defeats Soviet Russia in the Battle of Warsaw in August

1926 Coup d'état by Marshal Piłsudski

The Airmen's Memorial

1939 The Nazis enter Warsaw on 28 September

1940 Jews are confined to the ghetto

1943 On 19 April the uprising begins in the Jewish ghetto

1944 On 1 August the Warsaw Uprising begins

1945 In January Warsaw is liberated by the Red Army

1955 World Festival of Youth

1956 Władysław Gomułka seizes powe after a rally Plac Defila

1915 1930 1945

Baśka Orwid
The 1930s film-star models an evening gown that won a prize at a society ball.

John Paul II's 1987 Visit
The Polish Pope celebrated mass by the Palace of Culture and Science.

The Miner
As well as Socialism, the Communist era introduced a new style in the arts, Socialist Realism.

Socialist Realism

The principles of Socialist Realism developed in the Soviet Union under Stalin. This style was imposed on architecture, the visual arts and literature in postwar Poland, and lasted until the mid-1950s. The imagery often verged on self-caricature. Its heroes were Communist Party workers, hearty wenches and muscular labourers, as in the painting below from the National Museum *(pp154–7)*. Architectural examples of Socialist Realism *(pp132–3)* include the Palace of Culture *(pp134–5)*, which combines monolithic architecture with sculptures and murals on the same colossal scale.

Youth Brigade on Rebuilding Work *by Helena Krajewska*

Warsaw in 1945

Scenes of massive devastation met the people of Warsaw when they returned after World War II.

Poster for the Fifth Chopin International Piano Competition
The Chopin Competition has been held in Warsaw every five years since 1927.

Church at Stegny
Modern churches are a ballmark of Polish avant-garde architecture.

Solidarity *emblem*

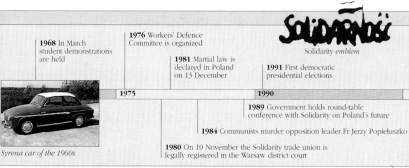

1968 In March student demonstrations are held

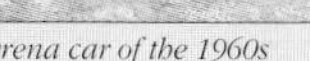

Syrena car of the 1960s

1975

1976 Workers' Defence Committee is organized

1980 On 10 November the Solidarity trade union is legally registered in the Warsaw district court

1981 Martial law is declared in Poland on 13 December

1984 Communists murder opposition leader Fr Jerzy Popiełuszko

1989 Government holds round-table conference with Solidarity on Poland's future

1990

1991 First democratic presidential elections

WARSAW AT A GLANCE

Warsaw's wide selection of palaces, museums, monuments and places of worship spans various periods and architectural movements. Gothic, Renaissance, Baroque, Rococo, Neo-Classical, Secession and Socialist Realist are all represented. Almost 140 attractions are listed in the *Area by Area* section of this guide, most of which are easily reached within the city centre. The following 18 pages summarize Warsaw's leading sights, which convey the diverse character of the city. This ranges from ornate and romantic to grand and imposing, as well as modern and metropolitan. Each sight mentioned is cross-referenced to its own full entry elsewhere in the guide. This section also features some of Warsaw's most celebrated natives, who went on to achieve international acclaim. Some of the city's foremost attractions are illustrated below.

WARSAW'S TOP TEN TOURIST ATTRACTIONS

St Anna's Church
See p116

Royal Castle
See pp70–73

National Museum
See pp154–7

St John's Cathedral
See pp76–7

Old Town Market Square
See pp78–9

Palace of Culture and Science
See pp134–5

Monument to the Ghetto Heroes
See p142

Grand Theatre
See pp110–11

Łazienki Park and Palaces
See pp162–5

Wilanów Palace and Park
See pp168–71

◁ **The Palace on the Water in Łazienki Park**

Famous Emigrés

WARSAW HAS BEEN HOME to many celebrated figures, including writers, musicians and scientists. However, the 18th-century partitions, two world wars and the Communist era have frequently created political situations hostile to the development of their talents. Many emigrated during these times, and went on to attain international success, though the world has often been unaware of their origins.

Helena Modrzejewska (1840–1909)
Prior to her departure for the United States, she triumphed at the Teatr Rozmaitości (Variety Theatre, see p111*).*

Isaac Bashevis Singer (1904–91)
This Polish Jewish writer lived for several years on Krochmalna Street. He won the 1978 Nobel Prize for Literature.

Ignacy Paderewski (1860–1941)
Composer, pianist and politician, he led the Warsaw Philharmonic's first concert (see p131).

Czesław Miłosz (b. 1911)
This poet, translator and Nobel Prize winner for Literature lived in Warsaw from 1937–44. For the first two years he worked for Polish Radio on Zielna Street.

The Former Jewish Ghetto

Joseph Conrad (1857–1924)
Conrad was the nom de plume of novelist Teodor Józef Korzeniowski. Before settling in England in 1884, he lived at No. 47 Nowy Świat (see p124).

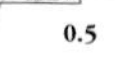

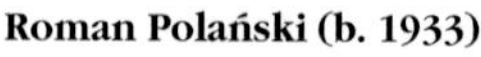

Roman Polański (b. 1933)
The actor and director was born in Paris and brought up in Poland. Best-known for films such as Rosemary's Baby *and* Tess, *he has also staged* Amadeus *in Warsaw's Wola Theatre.*

Marie Skłodowska-Curie (1867–1934)
Born in the New Town, she achieved international acclaim in Paris for her scientific discoveries and twice won the Nobel Prize (see p90).

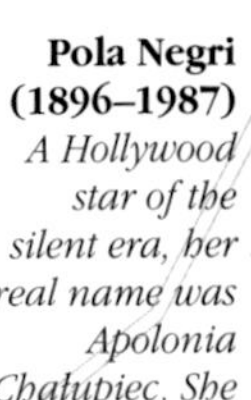

Pola Negri (1896–1987)
A Hollywood star of the silent era, her real name was Apolonia Chałupiec. She lived at No. 11 Browarna Street.

Jan Kiepura (1902–66)
This famous tenor began his career in Warsaw's Grand Theatre (see pp110–11).

Pope John Paul II (b. 1920)
Before leaving for Rome, where he was elected Pope on 16 October 1978, John Paul II would stay with the Ursuline Sisters at No. 2 Wiślana Street, whenever he was visiting Warsaw.

Tadeusz Kościuszko (1746–1817)
The leader of the 1794 insurrection conducted the defence of Warsaw, an event which was subsequently named in his honour. He was also a graduate of the Knights Academy (see p121).

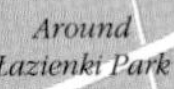

Frederic Chopin (1810–49)
One of the greatest composers and pianists, as a child he lived at No. 5 Krakowskie Przedmieście (see p121).

Arthur Rubinstein (1886–1982)
This world-famous pianist studied at the Warsaw Conservatoire, before emigrating in 1906 (see p123).

Warsaw's Best: Museums and Galleries

DESPITE THE DEVASTATIONS of World War II, Warsaw still enjoys a wide range of museums and art galleries. Their collections illustrate the city's history, and explore the works of its writers, artists and other historic figures. Many museum buildings are also of architectural merit. The Modern Art Centre (Centrum Sztuki Współczesnej), for instance, is housed in the 17th-century Ujazdowski Castle, while the Warsaw History Museum occupies several burghers' houses.

Warsaw History Museum
Various exhibits illustrate the history of the city together with its inhabitants.

Jewish History Institute Museum
The museum's collection details the cultural heritage of Poland's Jews.

The Former Jewish Ghetto

Zachęta (National Contemporary Art Gallery)
This is Poland's premier modern art venue housed in an impressive Neo-Renaissance building, which dates from 1903.

Museum of Mankind
The folk arts and crafts of Poland and other lands are featured here.

Around Marshal Street

National Museum
Warsaw's largest museum has a collection of Polish and other art, including the renowned painting by Józef Mehoffer, Strange Garden (1903).

Frederic Chopin Museum
The Chopin memorabilia includes personal possessions and the original manuscript for his Mazurka in F minor, *opus 68 no. 4.*

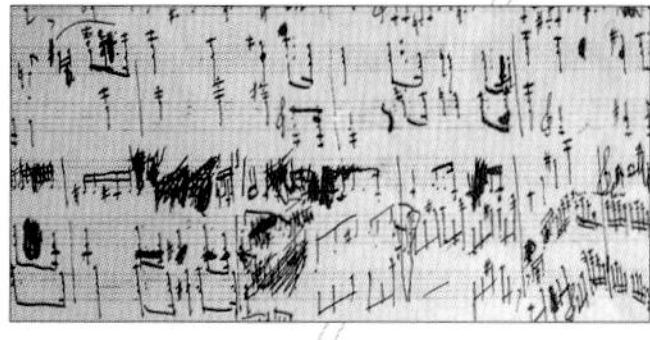

Literature Museum
The museum displays memorabilia, manuscripts and re-created room sets of Poland's most celebrated writers, including Melchior Wańkowicz's study.

Polish Military Museum
Founded in 1920, at the instigation of Poland's head of state, Marshal Józef Piłsudski, the museum's collection of arms and memorabilia details the history of Poland's military forces, from their origins to the present day.

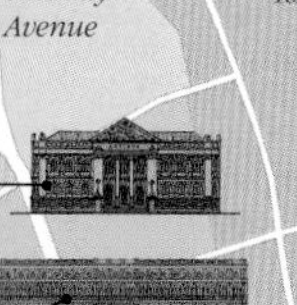

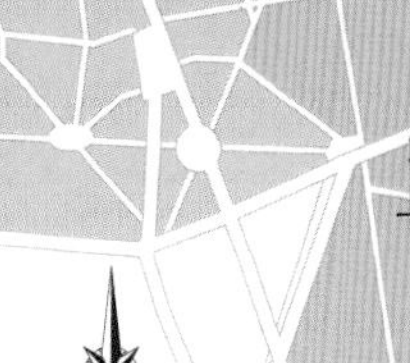

Warsaw Archdiocese Museum
A limited, though interesting, collection of sacred art and crafts includes this cross, which dates from the early 16th century, with 17th-century appliqué.

Modern Art Centre
In addition to exhibition space, the centre includes cinemas, a library and a modern art information centre.

Exploring the Museums and Galleries

Ammonite

The National Museum's extensive collection makes it the city's most interesting museum, though former royal residences such as the Royal Castle, and smaller, more specialized museums also have fascinating collections.

Polish Painting and Sculpture

Józef Simmler's *Death of Barbara Radziwiłł* in the National Museum

The largest collection of Polish paintings and sculpture is within the **National Museum** (Muzeum Narodowe). This includes one of the most famous Polish paintings, *The Battle of Grunwald* by Jan Matejko (1838–93), the country's finest historical painter. The modern and contemporary art gallery features work by leading artists such as Stanisław Wyspiański (1869–1907) and Jacek Malczewski (1854–1929).

The **Royal Castle** (Zamek Królewski) has a vast collection of furniture, sculpture, decorative art and paintings, including works by Jan Matejko. The collection is growing all the time, thanks to donations from Polish émigrés.

A fascinating display of Polish fine arts, paintings and sculpture can be seen in many buildings within **Łazienki Park**, particularly in the Palace on the Water (Pałac na Wodzie) and White House (Biały Dom). In the Old Orangerie, Classical sculptures and plaster casts are evocatively set among greenery.

Modern art can also be seen at the Neo-Classical Królikarnia Palace (a separate part of the National Museum). It houses the **Xawery Dunikowski Museum**, which is dedicated to the eponymous sculptor. Temporary modern art exhibitions are held at the **Modern Art Centre** (Centrum Sztuki Współczesnej) and **Zachęta**. The best modern art galleries include Test, Zapiecek, Foksal and Kordegarda.

European Painting and Sculpture

***The Raising of Lazarus* by Carel Fabritius in the National Museum**

Warsaw's most comprehensive collection of European art can be seen at the **National Museum**. This includes works by various Flemish, Dutch, Italian, French and German masters, such as Botticelli, Fabritius and Greuze.

The **Royal Castle** also has an extensive collection of European art. The Canaletto Room displays views of Warsaw by Bernardo Bellotto, pupil and nephew of Canaletto, who used his mentor's name.

Other nationalities represented include the Dutch painter Willem Claesz Heda, various French artists such as Claude Joseph Vernet and Elisabeth Vigée-Lebrun, while German artists include Hans Dürer, Joachim von Sandrart, and Angelika Kauffmann.

Mask in the Museum of Mankind

Various European masters can also be seen at **Wilanów** and **Łazienki** palaces. The **John Paul II Collection**, which includes Impressionist paintings, is housed within the former Bank of Poland and Stock Exchange building.

Archaeological Collections

Polish archaeologists have made significant contributions to archaeological discoveries around the world, and this is reflected in the wealth of the city's archaeological collections.

The **National Museum** has a wide range of ancient Egyptian, Greek and Roman art. The museum's most extraordinary gallery, however, displays early medieval wall paintings from Faras in the Sudan. This is the only collection of its kind in Europe.

Archaeological discoveries made in Poland are exhibited at the **Archaeology Museum** (Muzeum Archeologiczne).

***Portrait of St Anna* by an unknown artist in the National Museum**

Folk Art

Folk art can be seen at the **Museum of Mankind** (Muzeum Etnograficzne). The extensive collection includes Polish folk costumes from different regions, together with various artefacts that illustrate folklore, rural life and traditions. There are also works by internationally acclaimed Polish folk artists.

Additionally, Asian and Pacific folk art forms part of

the collection at the **Asia and Pacific Museum** (Muzeum Azji i Pacyfiku).

Arts and Crafts

Arts and crafts, both Polish in origin and international, are represented in the **National Museum**. Meanwhile, there are various exhibits associated with handicrafts on display within the **Warsaw History Museum** (Muzeum Historyczne m st Warszawy).

An interesting though limited collection can be seen in the **Handicraft and Precision Craft Museum** (Muzeum Rzemiosł Artystycznych i Precyzyjnych). Various leather objects and associated items are displayed in the **Guild of Leather Crafts Museum** (Muzeum Cechu Rzemiosł Skórzanych).

There are also major exhibitions at the Palace on the Water in Łazienki Park, at the Royal Castle and also at Wilanów Palace.

The **Pod Blachą Palace**, within the Royal Castle complex, has Europe's most comprehensive collection of Eastern rugs.

In Wilanów, the Orangerie houses an Arts and Crafts Gallery. Additionally, Wilanów's **Poster Museum** (Muzeum Plakatu) was the world's first museum of its kind, and is housed within a former stable. It contains posters by some of the finest artists of the 20th century, including Alphonse Mucha, Andy Warhol and Pablo Picasso. The Poster Museum also organizes the Warsaw Poster Biennale.

The **Warsaw Archdiocese Museum** (Muzeum Archidiecezji Warszawskiej) features a selection of Arts and Crafts exhibits alongside its collection of religious art.

History and Heritage

The **Warsaw History Museum** illustrates the evolution of Warsaw, and the heritage of the city's people. The **Polish Military Museum** (Muzeum Wojska Polskiego) is housed in the National Museum. Its collection of military memorabilia spans centuries of the armed forces' history.

The **Jewish History Institute Museum** (Muzeum Żydowskiego Instytutu Historycznego) traces the history of Warsaw's Jews, including the events of the Holocaust.

The **Independence Museum** (Muzeum Niepodległości) has a collection of documents detailing Poland's struggle for independence over the last three centuries.

Warsaw has many other specialist museums. The **Literature Museum** (Muzeum Literatury) has exhibits detailing the life and work of the Romantic poet Adam Mickiewicz. The collection of manuscripts and first editions includes works by Juliusz Słowacki and Henryk Sienkiewicz.

Samovar, the Warsaw History Museum

Museums have also been established in honour of some of Warsaw's famous inhabitants, such as Ignacy Paderewski (at Łazienki Park), Frederic Chopin (at Ostrogski Palace) and Marie Curie.

The history of Polish theatre is exhibited at the **Theatre Museum** (Muzeum Teatralne) within the Grand Theatre.

Science and Technology

The development of science and technology is detailed in the **Museum of Technology** (Muzeum Techniki). A branch of this is the **Industry Museum** (Muzeum Przemysłu), housed in a former metal plating factory. Its collection includes vintage cars.

Natural history is covered by three museums. The **Museum of Evolution** (Muzeum Ewolucji) features dinosaur skeletons found in the Gobi Desert by Polish palaeontologists. The **Geology Museum** (Muzeum Geologiczne) has rock and mineral specimens collected from all over Poland. While the **Earth Sciences Museum** (Muzeum Ziemi) has an impressive collection of amber.

Vintage cars on display in the Industry Museum

Finding the Museums and Galleries

Archaeology Museum *p102*
Asia and Pacific Museum *p 89*
Earth Sciences Museum *p153*
Frederic Chopin Museum *p123*
Geology Museum *p39*
Guild of Leather Crafts Museum *p82*
Handicraft and Precision Craft Museum *p75*
Independence Museum *p102* also branches at Al Szucha *p159*, Pawiak *p145*, X Citadel Pavilion *p95*
Industry Museum *p147*
Jewish History Institute Museum *p145*
John Paul II Collection at the former Bank of Poland *p104*
Łazienki Park and Palaces *pp162–3*
Literature Museum *p81*
Marie Skłodowska-Curie Museum *p88*
Modern Art Centre *p159*
Museum of Evolution *p39*
Museum of Mankind *p130*
Museum of Technology *pp134–5*
National Museum *pp154–5*
Pod Blachą Palace *p69*
Polish Military Museum *p152*
Poster Museum at Wilanów *p168*
Royal Castle *pp70–73*
Theatre Museum within the Grand Theatre *p110*
Warsaw Archdiocese Museum *p188*
Warsaw History Museum *p81*
Wilanów Palace and Park *pp168–71*
Xawery Dunikowski Museum at Królikarnia *p172*
Zachęta *p130*

Warsaw's Best: Sacred Buildings

Poland has been known historically for its religious tolerance. This is testified by Warsaw's magnificent range of sacred buildings, which form an important element of the city's character. While many of these buildings were destroyed during World War II, some survived intact, and retain their unique interiors and features. Others have been painstakingly restored in the postwar years.

Basilian Church of the Assumption of the Blessed Virgin Mary
This Byzantine-Ukrainian Orthodox church contains magnificent paintings by the 18th-century Polish artist Franciszek Smuglewicz.

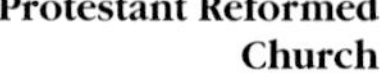

Protestant Reformed Church
This Neo-Gothic church, which was built in the 1860s, has an exquisite steeple.

The Former Jewish Ghetto

Nożyk Synagogue
The only synagogue to survive World War II intact was founded from 1898–1902 by the Nożyk family.

Augsburg Protestant Community Church
This architectural masterpiece by Szymon Bogumił Zug is in early Neo-Classical style.

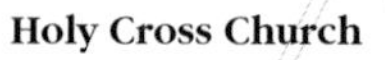

Holy Cross Church
Here you can see epitaphs to renowned Poles, and an urn containing Chopin's heart. This was placed here after his death in Paris, in accordance with his will.

Our Lady Mary's Church in the New Town
The oldest church in the New Town has retained its Gothic character, despite being damaged during the war.

St Mary Magdalene's Russian Orthodox Church
In 1969–70 restoration work was carried out on this principal Orthodox church. The conservation work restored Vinogradov's original 19th-century wall decorations.

St John's Cathedral
Many of the cathedral's monuments escaped wartime damage. Others were reconstructed, such as the tomb of the Speaker of the Sejm (Parliament), Stanisław Małachowski, which was designed by Bertel Thorwaldsen.

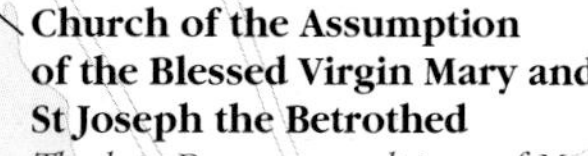

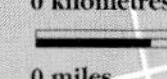

New Town
Old Town
Around Solidarity Avenue
The Royal Route
Around Marshal Street
Around Łazienki Park
0 kilometres 1
0 miles 0.5

Church of the Assumption of the Blessed Virgin Mary and St Joseph the Betrothed
The late Baroque sculpture of Mary and Joseph's wedding is one of the finest of its kind.

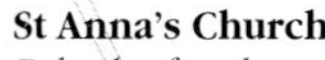

St Anna's Church
Rebuilt after the war, St Anna's stands adjacent to the Gothic vaulted Bernardine Monastery, which escaped wartime damage.

Exploring Warsaw's Sacred Buildings

Angel at St Joseph the Guardian Church

THE FIRST CHURCHES were built when the town of Warsaw was founded in the 14th century. However, the devastation of the 1655 Swedish invasion meant that none of Warsaw's earliest churches have survived in their original form. The greatest era of religious building was the late Baroque period, which remains the most typical style among Warsaw's churches.

Presbytery of St Anna's Church

Medieval Churches

WARSAW'S FIRST churches, built in the early 14th century, were wooden.

The city's oldest church is **St John's Cathedral** (katedra św Jana), which also dates from the 14th century. Originally a parish church built in the Gothic style, it underwent various alterations over the centuries. Following its destruction during World War II, the cathedral was restored to its original style, known as Mazovian Gothic.

Another fine example of Gothic is **Our Lady Mary's Visitation Church** (kościół Marii Panny) in the New Town. It was founded in the 15th century by Anna, the wife of Duke Janusz I Starszy of Mazovia. The **Bernardine Monastery**, by **St Anna's Church** in Krakowskie Przedmieście, features an early Gothic presbytery, as well as cloisters with late Gothic vaulting.

Renaissance and Mannerist Churches

RENAISSANCE and Mannerist styles enjoyed only a brief popularity in Warsaw. Moreover, there are few examples of these styles as they were fashionable at virtually the same period as late Gothic and early Baroque. The Bernardine Monastery, for example, was built in a Gothic style in the 16th century, and was almost contemporary with the beautiful early Baroque alterations which made to the Royal Castle (Zamek Królewski).

The finest example of Mannerism, albeit combined with Baroque, is the **Jesuit Church of Our Lady Mary the Merciful** (Sanktuarium Matki Bozej) in the Old Town. It has a fine Mannerist-Baroque façade, and unusual elliptical dome above the presbytery.

Baroque façade of St Martin's in the Old Town

Baroque Churches

OF THE CITY'S early Baroque churches, almost all were destroyed during the Swedish invasion. However, one of the most interesting Baroque interiors to survive is within **St Jacek's Church**. Its side aisles are an example of the Lublin style of ribbed vaulting.

Reconstruction following the Swedish invasion resulted in many new churches. Several were designed by the architect Józef Szymon Bellotti, featuring wall-and-pillar aisles. These include **Church of the Assumption of the Blessed Virgin Mary and St Joseph the Betrothed** (kościół Wniebowzięcia NMP i św. Józefa Oblubieńca), **Holy Cross** (św. Krzyża), **St Antony of Padua Reformed Church** (św Antoniego Padewskiego, Reformatów), and a recreated aisle of **St Anna's Church**.

The Dutch architect Tylman of Gameren designed the **St Antony of Padua Church** (św. Antoniego Padewskiego, Bernardynów), which was constructed in Czerniakowska

Domes and Spires

As in any city, church domes and spires provide good orientation points. They frame numerous perspectives from Warsaw's streets, and add variety to the panoramic view from the Vistula. A great number of churches were destroyed during World War II, but since then many have been rebuilt. Some were returned to their original form, which had been lost during previous refurbishments.

Gothic

Bell tower, Our Lady Mary's Visitation Church

Baroque

St Casimir's

Neo-Classical

St Alexander's Church

Neo-Renaissance façade of All Saints Church

Street, as well as **St Casimir's** (św. Kazimierza).

The **Capuchin Church of the Transfiguration** (kościół Przemienienia Pańskiego, Kapucynów) is also a Baroque masterpiece. Notable

Church of St Andrew of Bobola

late Baroque churches are **Church of the Holy Spirit** (św. Ducha) and **Holy Trinity** (Przenajświętszej Trójcy), but **St Joseph the Guardian** (Opieki św. Józefa) is considered the most beautiful. The façades of existing churches were also recreated in a late Baroque style, including **St Martin's**, the **Assumption of the Blessed Virgin Mary** and **Our Lady Queen of Poland** (NMP Królowej Korony Polskiej).

Neo-Classical and Revival Architecture

There are several outstanding examples of early Neo-Classical religious architecture in Warsaw. **Augsburg Protestant Community Church** (kościół Ewangelicko-Augsburgski), on Małachowskiego Square, was built by Szymon Bogumił Zug, in 1777–81. The **Basilian Church of the Assumption of the Blessed Virgin Mary** (kościół Wniebowzięcia NMP, Bazylianów), dating from the same period, was designed by Dominik Merlini.

Chrystian Piotr Aigner redesigned the façade of St Anna's church in a Neo-Classical style, modelling it on the Palladian façades of Venetian churches. Aigner also designed **St Alexander's Church**, built in 1818–25.

Many churches were built during the 19th-century Revival period, when historic styles were back in fashion. Henryk Marconi specialized in the Neo-Renaissance. This was exemplified by **St Anna's Church** in Wilanów, **St Karol Boromeusz** at Chłodna Street, and **All Saints** (Wszystkich Świętych) on Grzybowska.

The Neo-Gothic style was favoured by Józef Pius Dziekoński, who designed the **Church of the Saviour** (kościół Zbawiciela), **St Florian's** and **St Stanisław the Bishop** in Wola. The **Protestant Reformed Church** in Leszno is also Neo-Gothic.

Several Russian Orthodox churches were built in the 19th century, when Warsaw was under Russian rule. They were usually built in the Byzantine-Russian style, though only four have survived; **St Mary Magdalene's**

St Alexander's Neo-Classical altar

is one. Almost all the synagogues destroyed during World War II were 19th century. The only survivor is **Nożyk Synagogue**, built 1898–1902.

Warsaw's Churches

Augsburg Protestant Community Church *p130*
Basilian Church of the Assumption of the Blessed Virgin Mary *p100*
Bernardine Monastery and St Anna's Church *p116*
Capuchin Church of the Transfiguration *p101*
Church of the Assumption of the Blessed Virgin Mary and St Joseph the Betrothed *p118*
Church of the Holy Spirit *p88*
Church of the Saviour *p137*
Holy Cross Church *p122*
Holy Trinity Church *p188*
Jesuit Church of Our Lady Mary the Merciful *p74*
Nożyk Synagogue *p145*
Our Lady Mary's Church *p93*
Our Lady Queen of Poland *p92*
Protestant Reformed Church *p146*
St Alexander's Church *p152*
St Anna's Church *p116*
St Antony of Padua Church *p173*
St Antony of Padua Reformed Church *p107*
St Casimir's *p90*
St Jacek's Church *p88*
St John's Cathedral *pp76–7*
St Joseph the Guardian *p120*
St Karol Boromeusz *p177*
St Martin's *p74*
St Mary Magdalene's Russian Orthodox Church *p174*
St Stanisław Kostka *p175*

Revival

Bell tower, St Anna's Church

Eclectic

Church of the Saviour

Modernism

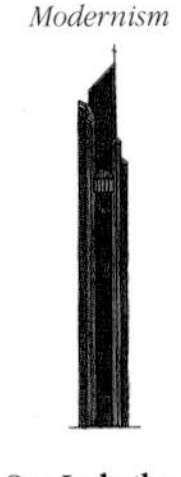

Our Lady the Merciful, in Stegny

Exploring Warsaw's Cemeteries

WARSAW'S OLDEST CEMETERIES were founded at the end of the 18th century. Fortunately, the majority of the city's cemeteries were spared the destruction of World War II, and even the Jewish cemetery survived unscathed. A walk around any of the Powązki cemeteries provides not only an historic, but also an artistic experience. These cemeteries feature mausoleums and tombs in a variety of architectural styles. They were designed by master craftsmen to commemorate some of Warsaw's most distinguished citizens.

The Communal Cemetery in Powązki
Originally a military cemetery, it also features a symbolic cross commemorating the Katyń victims.

Muslim Tartar Cemetery
This was the only cemetery to be almost completely destroyed during World War II. Few tombstones have survived intact.

Russian Orthodox Cemetery
St Jan Klimak, one of only two working Orthodox churches in Warsaw, is located here.

Warsaw Uprising Cemetery
This cemetery was established in 1945 for the victims of the 1944 Warsaw Uprising.

Augsburg Protestant Cemetery
Splendid tombs of the city's former bourgeoisie can be seen at this cemetery.

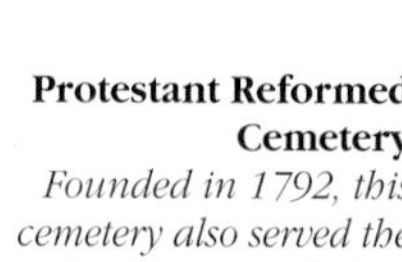

Protestant Reformed Cemetery
Founded in 1792, this cemetery also served the Anglican population.

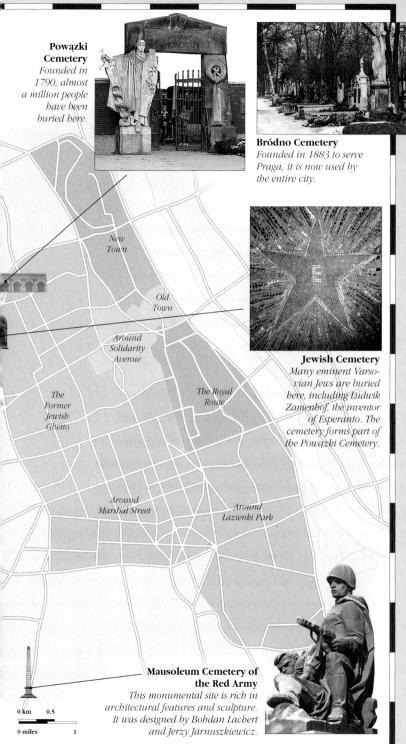

Powązki Cemetery
Founded in 1790, almost a million people have been buried here.

Bródno Cemetery
Founded in 1883 to serve Praga, it is now used by the entire city.

Jewish Cemetery
Many eminent Varsovian Jews are buried here, including Ludwik Zamenhof, the inventor of Esperanto. The cemetery forms part of the Powązki Cemetery.

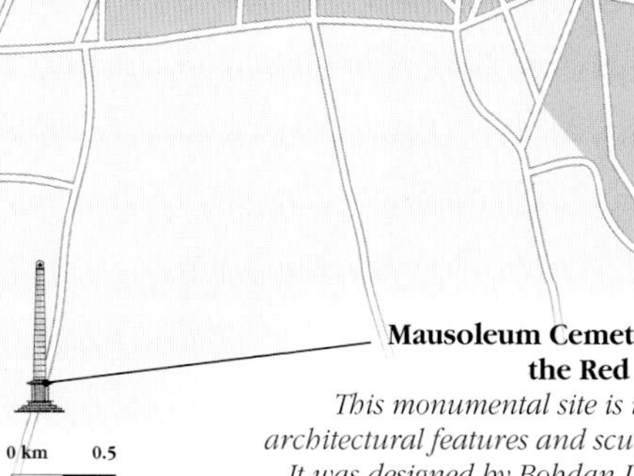

Mausoleum Cemetery of the Red Army
This monumental site is rich in architectural features and sculpture. It was designed by Bohdan Lachert and Jerzy Jarnuszkiewicz.

Exploring Warsaw's Cemeteries

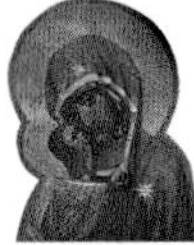
Painting at Wolski Cemetery

THE GREATEST CONCENTRATION of cemeteries is in the Powązki district, where there are seven, bearing witness to Warsaw's multi-religious and multinational history. As well as its large-scale cemeteries, Warsaw also has smaller, parish cemeteries, such as Wilanów, which are worth visiting.

Roman Catholic Cemeteries

POWĄZKI IS THE OLDEST of Warsaw's principal cemeteries. Since its establishment in 1790, approximately one million people have been buried here. The cemetery's tombs and mausoleums span the various artistic styles of the past 200 years.

Among the most historic sections of the cemetery are the St Karol Boromeusz Church and the catacombs. By this section is the Aleja Zasłużonych (Avenue of Merit). Along this thoroughfare many celebrated Polish figures are buried, including the authors Władysław Reymont and Bolesław Prus, the opera singer Jan Kiepura, the composer Stanisław Moniuszko and the film director Krzysztof Kieślowski, best known for his *Three Colours* trilogy.

Many of the tombstones on this avenue were designed by outstanding architects and sculptors. The finest examples include works by Jakub Tatarkiewicz, Pius Weloński and Wacław Szymanowski, whose Secessionist monument of Frederic Chopin stands in Łazienki Park.

Bródno is the largest cemetery in Poland. Originally it served the poorest inhabitants of the Praga district, but gradually the entire city and various social classes began to use it. By the 1920s even prominent citizens such as Roman Dmowski and Cardinal Aleksander Kakowski were buried here.

Roman Catholics were also served by a section of the **Communal Cemetery** (Cmentarz Kommunalny) in Powązki, as well as the **Wolski Cemetery** and large, new municipal burial grounds on the outskirts of the city.

Some of Warsaw's most historic districts have retained their "rural" cemeteries. Even though they are now surrounded by modern buildings, their unique, intimate atmosphere has not been lost. Among these are cemeteries at **Wilanów, Tarchomin** and **Służew**. At Służew cemetery, by the chapel of St Catherine (św Katarzyny), lie the remains of political prisoners murdered during the Stalinist era.

Powązki, the oldest of Warsaw's cemeteries

Secessionist tomb by Wacław Szymanowski at Powązki Cemetery

Military Cemeteries

THE CEMETERY with the longest military tradition is the Communal Cemetery in Powązki. Originally established for Russian soldiers, it has been used since 1918 by the Polish Army. This includes servicemen who died during World War I and the Polish-Soviet War. There is also a section for victims of the January insurrection of 1863.

At the outbreak of World War II, the cemetery was initially used to bury soldiers killed during the first month of the war, followed by members of the resistance and victims of the Warsaw Uprising. From 1941 the cemetery was also used to bury Nazi soldiers. After the war a symbolic tomb was established, dedicated to Polish officers murdered by the Red Army in Katyń.

Having been extended, the cemetery also incorporates Aleja Zasłużonych, where Polish politicians such as Bolesław Bierut and Władysław Gomułka are buried.

After the war, the ashes of Warsaw's resistance fighters were moved from the Communal Cemetery to the **Cemetery of the Warsaw Uprising** (Cmentarz Powstanców Warszawy).

The Jewish Cemetery, in the Powązki district

This was founded in 1945, near the **Russian Orthodox Cemetery** (Cmentarz Prawosławny). The ashes of an estimated 40,000 Varsovians were exhumed and reburied at the Cemetery of the Warsaw Uprising, following the liberation of Warsaw. A separate tomb was established in memory of Jews murdered between 1940–43.

Warsaw also has military cemeteries dedicated to other nationalities. The **Italian Army Cemetery** (Cmentarz Żołnierzy Włoskich) on Pułkowa Street dates from 1927. Soldiers killed on Polish soil during World War I, and the ashes of Italian prisoners of war killed by the Nazis, were buried there.

Soldiers of the Red Army killed during the liberation of Warsaw in 1944–5 are buried in a separate cemetery. Founded in 1949, it was the work of outstanding Polish architects, sculptors and designers.

Powązki Cemetery on All Souls' Day

Cemeteries Serving Other Religions

Almost all religions that have been practised in Poland have also established their own cemeteries in Warsaw.

The **Jewish Cemetery** is in Powązki. Ludwik Zamenhoff, the creator of the Esperanto language, is one of several eminent Jews who are buried here.

The **Augsburg Protestant Cemetery** holds the family tombs of Warsaw's great industrialists, including the Wedel family (whose chocolate cakes are legendary), together with celebrated figures from the arts world. Among these are the painter Wojciech Gerson, and Samuel Bogumił Linde, who compiled a renowned Polish dictionary. The **Protestant Reformed Cemetery** includes the biologist Marcel Nencki, the painter Józef Simmler and the popular singer Anna German.

During World War II, a section of the Powązki cemetery suffered considerable damage. However, the worst destruction was inflicted on two Muslim cemeteries, one of which is the **Tartar Cemetery**. These cemeteries include Russian soldiers, as well as merchants and diplomats.

Among those that escaped wartime destruction are the **Jewish Cemetery** in Bródno, and two in the Wola district.

Adamina Chołoniewska's ornate tombstone at Powązki Cemetery

They are the tiny **Karaite Cemetery** and a large **Russian Orthodox Cemetery**. In addition to Russians buried during the Partition of Poland (1772–1918), a number of Russian builders, accidentally killed during construction of the Palace of Culture, are also buried in this cemetery.

Finding Warsaw's Cemeteries

Augsburg Protestant *p179*
Bródno *p45*
Jewish *pp178–9*
Powązki *pp176–7*
Powązki Communal *p44*
Protestant Reformed *p179*
Russian Orthodox *p44*
Warsaw Uprising *p44*

Warsaw's Best: Palaces and Gardens

For centuries Warsaw's architectural style was dominated by the prevailing taste of the royal court and nobility. The Baroque era, from the late 16th to the early 18th century, saw many of Poland's wealthiest families establishing residences in Warsaw. The funds lavished on these private residences, which were designed by the finest architects, often exceeded the amounts spent on royal palaces. Their façades add an air of splendour to Warsaw's most prestigious streets, while many of the gardens that originally belonged to these houses are now attractive public parks.

Krasiński Gardens
Adjoining the Krasiński Palace, this park was laid out in the 17th century. After World War II the park was extended to incorporate the former Nalewki Street and part of the destroyed Jewish Ghetto.

Saxon Gardens
Open to the public since 1727, the gardens were originally part of the so-called "Saxon Axis", a Baroque town-planning scheme.

Botanical Gardens
These gardens were established in 1818, within the vicinity of Łazienki Park.

The Former Jewish Ghetto

Królikarnia
This small Neo-Classical palace was built in 1782–9 by royal architect Dominik Merlini, for the notorious gambler Karol de Valery Thomatis. The building now houses a museum dedicated to the Polish sculptor Xawery Dunikowski.

Wilanów Park
The gardens were laid out in two sections: the symmetrical French-style terraces, and the English-style landscaped garden, which runs along the lake.

Royal Castle
The ballroom, open to the public since 1988, was the final room to be reconstructed within the Royal Castle.

Ujazdowski Castle
Although the castle survived a fire during World War II, the ruins were demolished in 1954. Twenty years later it was rebuilt in the original Baroque style, and now houses the Modern Art Centre.

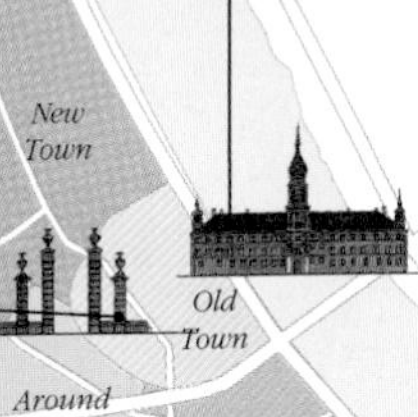

Łazienki Park
The park was established in the 17th century on the site of a former zoo. The palaces and pavilions were added later.

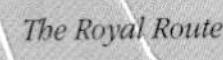

Palace on the Water
A copy of the Belvedere Apollo *adorns the ballroom's chimney-piece, which is supported by figures of Marsyas and Midas.*

Wilanów Palace
The interiors of this palace, built as King Jan III Sobieski's summer residence, retain their original 17th-century style.

Exploring the Palaces and Gardens

None of Warsaw's palaces survived World War II intact, and those that escaped structural damage had their interiors looted. Major postwar reconstruction was often limited to the façades of the palaces, while the interiors were frequently adapted to other uses. The most beautiful palaces, however, did have their interiors restored, and most are now open to the public as museums. Other palaces serve as exhibition venues, government offices or as the headquarters of various organizations. Warsaw is also proud of its parks and gardens, and is one of Europe's greenest capitals.

Putti on the terrace at Wilanów

Ujazdowski Park

Baroque Palaces

Warsaw's oldest palace is the **Royal Castle** (Zamek Królewski), which includes fragments of the Mazovian Dukes' original Gothic castle. Rebuilt for King Zygmunt III Waza (1587–1632), this is a unique early Baroque building, which was both a royal residence and the seat of the Polish Parliament. The **Ujazdowski Castle** (Zamek Ujazdowski) was also rebuilt in a Baroque style during the reign of Zygmunt III Waza. Other palaces from that period did not survive the 1655 Swedish invasion, and were rebuilt in later years.

The royal summer residence in **Wilanów** was built during the reign of Jan III Sobieski (1674–96). The royal architect, Tylman of Gameren, also designed other palaces for Warsaw's magnates. The most splendid are the **Krasiński Palace** (Pałac Krasińskich) and the **Gniński–Ostrogski Palace** (Pałac Gnińskich-Ostrogskich), usually referred to as the Ostrogski Palace, which contains the Frederic Chopin Museum.

The election of August II Mocny as king in 1697 led to architects from Dresden coming to Warsaw. They designed the Saxon Axis (Oś Saska) and Saxon Palace (Pałac Saski). New palaces were built, and existing ones restyled in Baroque and Rococo fashion. Among these are the **Kraków Bishops' Palace** (Pałac Biskupów Krakowskich), the **Blue Palace** (Pałac Błękitny) and **Czapski Palace** (Pałac Czapskich).

The **Branicki Palace** on Miodowa Street, **Radziwiłł Palace** in Leszno, **Sapieha Palace** in the New Town, and **Potocki Palace** on Krakowskie Przedmieście were rebuilt after World War II.

The exquisite Moorish Salon within the Neo-Classical Pac Palace

Neo-Classical Palaces

During the reign of King Stanisław August Poniatowski (1764–95), art and architecture continued to flourish. He commissioned new interiors for the Royal Castle and redesigned the **Łazienki Palace and Park.** Among the architects then working in Warsaw were Efraim Schroeger, Chrystian Piotr Aigner, Szymon Bogumił Zug, Jan Chrystian Kamsetzer and Dominik Merlini. They designed and refurbished several Neo-Classical palaces, drawing their inspiration from antiquity and from the then fashionable Andrea Palladio (1508–80). Palladian style is evident in the **Primate's Palace** (Pałac Prymasowski), and the **Królikarnia** (Rabbit Warren) mansion, based on Andrea Palladio's Rotunda. The **Raczyński, Mostowski, Belweder, Lubomirski, Pac** and **Tyszkiewicz** palaces are also Neo-Classical.

The Baroque Ostrogski Palace

The Neo-Classical Tyszkiewicz Palace

Namiestnikowski Palace, originally a 17th century building, was restyled in a Neo-Classical manner by Chrystian Piotr Aigner, after Poland came under Russian rule in the early 19th century. First used as a residence for the tsar's governor, it is now the official residence of the president of Poland.

PARKS AND GARDENS

WARSAW'S first gardens were laid out for the grand palaces. The oldest examples are the **Krasiński** and **Saxon Gardens** (Ogród Saski), with the Saxon Gardens the first to open to the public. Centrally located and close to the Old Town, the Saxon Gardens provide an ideal haven while sightseeing. The largest of the former palace gardens are Łazienki Park and Wilanów Park, on the edge of the city.

Fragments of the English landscaping style have also survived, such as Morskie Oko surrounding Szuster Palace, created in the 18th century for Princess Izabela Lubomirska. There are also several monastery gardens in Warsaw, situated on picturesque slopes. Among these are gardens which belong to the Order of the Holy Sacrament and the Reformation Brethren in the New Town, the Nuns of the Visitation, on Krakowskie Przedmieście, and the St Vincent de Paul Sisters of Mercy on Tamka Street. However, these gardens are not open to the public, and can only be seen from a distance.

More parks were laid out in the 19th century, including the **Botanical Gardens** and the **Ujazdowski Park**. At the beginning of the 20th century, the extensive **Skaryszewski Park**, dedicated to Ignacy Paderewski *(see p34)*, was created in the Praga district, which is located on the right bank of the River Vistula.

After Poland regained its independence in 1918, several parks were created on sites that were formerly occupied by fortifications. One example is **Traugutt Park**.

Following World War II, land was nationalized, which made it possible to transform several undeveloped and war-damaged demolition sites into parks and squares. This resulted in Podzamcze Park, which is close to both the Old and New Towns, and the vast Central Park of Culture (Centralny Park Kultury), in Powiśle. In 1992, the Park of Culture was dedicated to the pre-war Polish leader, Marshal Edward Rydz-Śmigły.

The Botanical Gardens, laid out in the 19th century

The Palace on the Water in Łazienki Park, designed by Domenik Merlini

FINDING THE PALACES AND GARDENS

Warsaw Through the Year

Warsaw has plenty to offer throughout the year, but is particularly enjoyable during spring and autumn, when the weather is sunny but mild, and there is a wealth of cultural and religious events. The summer means warmer weather and more visitors, as well as the annual Mozart Festival, among others. Music festivals continue in the autumn, with modern music celebrated in both the Warsaw Autumn and the Jazz Jamboree. The Chopin International Piano Competition is also held every five years. Winter is marked by Christmas preparations, followed by the carnival season. Details of festivals and continuous events can be obtained from tourist information offices *(see p237)* and local publications *(see p245)*.

Spring

The major religious festival in spring is Easter. It is as important for Poles as Christmas, and in Warsaw it dominates this time of the year. The season brings the first warm weather of the year; streets and parks come to life and the sunshine hails the start of the tourist season. Consequently, museums extend their opening hours and attractions such as the Botanical Gardens reopen their gates to visitors.

March

Palm Sunday, Niedziela Palmowa *(Sun before Easter)*. In the morning people go to Mass to have their "palm" branches blessed. Traditionally, these branches are made as colourful as possible, using blossoming spring flowers, and the procession to church is a delightful sight.
Easter Saturday, Wielka Sobota. Varsovians take a basket with foodstuffs *(święconki)* such as rye bread to church to be blessed. Various churches display a symbolic "Christ's Tomb", often beautifully decorated and carrying a social or political message.
Easter Monday, Poniedziałek Wielkanocny. A public holiday also known as *śmigus-dyngus* after the tradition of sprinkling people with water. This rustic custom has also become an urban institution and source of much amusement.
Drowning of Marzanna, Topienie Marzanny *(21 Mar)*. Stemming from a pagan tradition, an effigy of Marzanna (a witch symbolizing winter) is "drowned" on the first day of spring to mark the death of winter. Children make a Marzanna figure out of straw and rags and carry her to the banks of the River Vistula. There, they throw her into the water, while singing folk songs.

Easter palm

International Poster Biennale, Międzynarodowe Biennale Plakatu. Held every two years, this exhibition of posters is organized by the Poster Museum *(see p168)*.

April

April Fools' Day, Prima Aprilis *(1 Apr)*. People play practical jokes on each other.

Children throwing water on *śmigus-dyngus* (Easter Monday)

Guard by the Tomb of the Unknown Soldier

Newspapers and TV and radio stations run trick stories to catch out the unwitting.

May

Labour Day, Święto Pracy *(1 May)*. A public holiday in honour of the workers.
3 May Constitution Day, Święto Uchwalenia Konstytucji 3 maja *(3 May)*. A public holiday on the anniversary of the first Polish Constitution of 1791. Celebrations are in the Parliament and Royal Castle.
Warsaw International Book Fair, Warszawskie Międzynarodowe Targi Książki *(third week of May)*. This is held in the Palace of Culture and Science *(see pp134–5)*.
Festival of Latin-American Culture, Festiwal Kultury Latynoamerykańskiej. This week-long festival displays a range of Latin-American art.

Sunshine Chart
The largest number of sunny days in Warsaw is usually between the months of May and August. However, spring and autumn are also sunny and mild, particularly the months of April, September and the first half of October. During the winter, Warsaw's skies are mostly clouded over.

Enjoying the sunshine by Chopin's monument in Łazienki Park

SUMMER

Although Warsaw is not as hot as some other European capitals, many people still leave the city and head for their *działka* (small chalet in the country), swimming pools or the beach. In July and August most theatres and the Philharmonic are closed, but the Chopin Music Society organizes regular performances through the summer. Plenty of seasonal cafés and beer-houses open, offering live music and some food alfresco.

JUNE

Chopin Music Concerts, Koncerty Chopinowskie *(Sundays in Jun)*. Concerts are held (weather permitting) in Łazienki Park.
Garden Theatre Festival, Konkurs Teatrów Ogródkowych *(early Jun–mid-Sep)*. Street theatre troupes perform in Warsaw's squares, and the courtyard of the Dean's House.
Mozart Festival, Festiwal Mozartowski *(mid-Jun–end of Jul)*. *(See right.)*
Midsummer's Eve, Noc Świętojańska *(23 Jun)*. At this picturesque celebration, hundreds of wreaths bearing candles are set adrift on the River Vistula, accompanied by lively firework displays.

JULY

Organ Music Festival, Festiwal Muzyki Organowej *(Jul – until the end of the holidays)* in St John's Cathedral.
Warsaw Summer Jazz Days *(Jun)*. This is an annual 3-day series of performances held at various venues, with performances by Polish jazz players as well as guest artists from around the world.

AUGUST

Anniversary of the 1944 Warsaw Uprising, Rocznica Wybuchu Powstania Warszawskiego *(1 Aug)*. This anniversary is commemorated by all Varsovians.
Assumption of the Virgin Mary, Wniebowzięcie Matki Boskiej *(15 Aug)*. A public holiday, and an important religious festival celebrated throughout Poland. The object of particular veneration is an icon of the Black Madonna in Jasna Góra Monastery in Częstochowa, about 200 km (125 miles) southwest of Warsaw. Numerous pilgrims make the journey on foot from Warsaw and all over Poland to arrive in Częstochowa on this day.

MOZART FESTIVAL

This popular summer event provides a unique opportunity to hear all of Mozart's operas, including his early works, performed by the same group of artists. The Festival is organized by the Warsaw Chamber Opera *(see p146)*, whose director is Stefan Sutkowski. Concerts of Mozart's music are also performed by symphony and chamber orchestras in the Philharmonic *(see p131)* and the opulent surroundings of some of Warsaw's palaces. Additionally, choral works, such as masses, are performed in several churches around the city.

Performance of the *Magic Flute* during the Mozart Festival

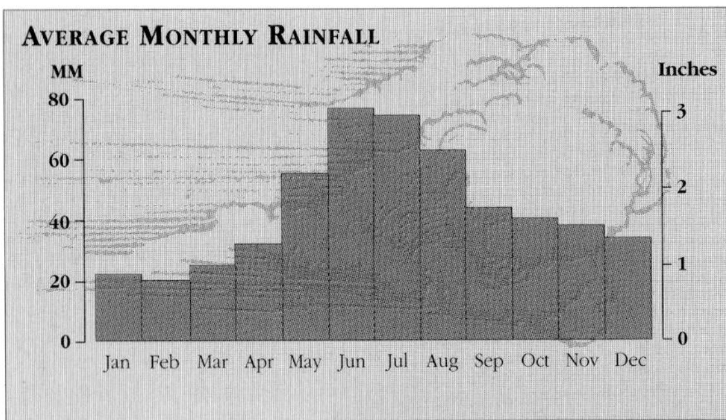

Rainfall Chart
Warsaw has a continental climate, so its weather is often fickle. The city can suffer from heavy summer rain, which can go on for days, though during some years Warsaw has experienced drought. Snow falls every winter, which creates a beautiful white landscape.

AUTUMN

ONE OF THE BEST times to visit Warsaw is in the autumn, between September and early October. There are fewer tourists, generally the weather is good and the parks are rich with autumnal tones.

The majority of Warsaw's cultural events take place in the autumn, the most important of which include the Warsaw Autumn, the Warsaw Film Festival and the Jazz Jamboree. Additionally, theatres and the National Philharmonic Orchestra reopen, following their summer break. Various ceremonies also mark the reopening of the universities.

A park lane in autumn

SEPTEMBER

Warsaw Autumn *(third and fourth weeks of Sep)*. This ten-day festival of contemporary music brings together composers and performers from around the world.
Warsaw Autumn of Poetry *(throughout Sep)*. Poets give readings in several venues around the city. One of the most historic and popular venues is the Old Gunpowder Depository (Stara Prochownia, *see p89*).

Concert in the annual Jazz Jamboree festival

OCTOBER

Warsaw Film Festival *(throughout Oct)*. An international festival of new and classic films, shown in several cinemas around the city.
Jazz Jamboree *(Oct)*. One of the most important jazz festivals in Europe, held annually in Warsaw since 1958.
Festival of Early Music *(throughout Oct and Nov)*. Focusing on Renaissance and Baroque music, performances are held in several venues. On Sundays concerts take place in the Royal Castle.

NOVEMBER

All Saints' Day *(1 Nov)*. A public holiday, celebrated as the Feast of the Dead. Many people visit cemeteries, tidy up family graves and decorate

CHOPIN INTERNATIONAL PIANO COMPETITION

One of the most important piano competitions in the world, this event has been held in October or November every five years since 1927. It is organized by the Frederic Chopin Society, and only music by this composer is performed. Concerts are held in the Philharmonic. The festival attracts the world's finest pianists and their peers, who sit on the competition jury or simply attend the competition to hear new performers. Among former winners of the competition, whose careers it has helped to launch, are Vladimir Ashkenazy, Maurizio Pollini, Martha Argerich and Krystian Zimerman.

Frederic Chopin

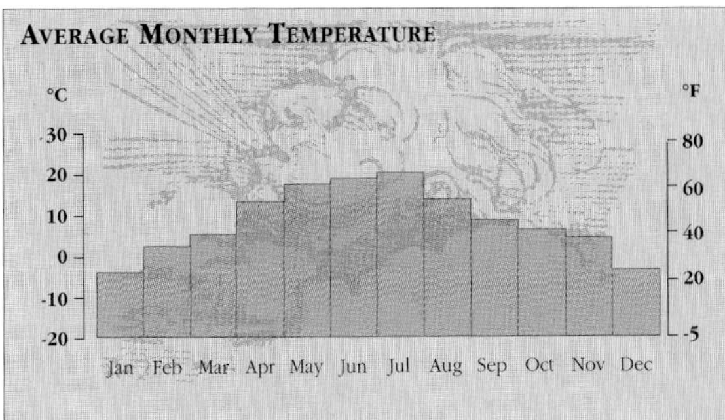

Temperature Chart
This chart shows the average temperatures for each month in Warsaw over the past 30 years. As the figures indicate, most summers are pleasantly warm, although sometimes there can be very hot spells. Winters are usually frosty, with temperatures frequently falling below freezing.

them with flowers and candles. At dusk the cemeteries glow with candlelight.

Independence Day *(11 Nov).* This commemorates the end of the German occupation of Warsaw in 1918. It is regarded as the date when Poland finally regained independence, following the partitions that began in the 18th century.

Candle illuminating a grave on All Saints' Day

Winter

Warsaw's winters are usually very cold and snowy. Seeing the city shrouded in snow makes a lasting impression on visitors; among the most romantic areas to stroll in are Łazienki Park and the Old Town.

December is taken up with preparations for Christmas, which most people celebrate in a traditional manner. This means a 12-course meatless dinner (one course for each apostle) on Christmas Eve, which begins when the first star appears. After this dinner Varsovians attend Midnight Mass, while Christmas carols are sung throughout the city.

New Year's Eve marks the beginning of the Carnival season of dances and parties, including masked balls. The Carnival celebrations culminate with a bout of revelry on Shrove Tuesday.

December

Christmas Fairs *(throughout Dec).* Plac Defilad, in front of the Palace of Culture and Science, and Plac Zamkowy are occupied by stalls where you can buy Christmas trees, decorations, and various foodstuffs for the Christmas Eve dinner.

Christmas Eve *(24 Dec).* Festivities begin with a meatless dinner after nightfall.

Christmas Day and Boxing Day *(25 and 26 Dec).* All churches hold special Masses.

New Year's Eve *(31 Dec).* Celebrations go on in style, with grand balls and private parties. Crowds also gather in Plac Zamkowy under King Zygmunt's Column.

January

Warsaw Theatre Meetings Poland's most outstanding theatre productions from the previous year are presented as an "encore" in January.

February

"Fat Thursday" *(end Feb).* In Poland the last day of indulgence before the fasting of Lent is the Thursday before Ash Wednesday. The traditional activity is to eat heartily, and patisseries sell more doughnuts than anything else on this day.

Shrovetide *(end Feb).* The last Saturday of the Carnival season before Ash Wednesday is a day of revelry, with balls and events like the Bill Haley Rock'n'Roll competition.

Public Holidays

New Year's Day (1 Jan)
Easter Monday *
Labour Day (1 May)
Constitution Day (3 May)
Corpus Christi *
Assumption of the Virgin Mary (15 Aug)
All Saints' Day (1 Nov)
Independence Day (11 Nov)
Christmas Eve, Christmas Day and Boxing Day (24, 25 & 26 Dec)
* Dates change according to the church calendar.

A display of typical Christmas decorations

A River View of Warsaw

The river Vistula has always played an important role in Warsaw's history, particularly in developing the city's trade. Providing a width of 225 m (750 ft) of navigable waters, the river was always the main waterway connecting Warsaw with other towns such as Kraków and Sandomierz in the south, and Toruń, Płock, Włocławek and Gdańsk to the north.

The first permanent bridge across the Vistula was built in the 16th century, but it lasted only about 30 years. It wasn't until the mid-19th century that the next permanent bridge was built, following the invention of caissons (watertight chambers used in underwater construction). Until that time the river could be crossed all year round by boat, while pontoon bridges were constructed in the summer. When the river froze over during the winter, people also walked across the ice. Warsaw still has too few bridges. Currently there are only six road and two railway bridges.The problem of flooding was solved only in the 19th century when dams were built. At the same time, boulevards were constructed on the Left Bank, though only the central sections were completed.

Unlike other European capitals, Warsaw has retained many undeveloped riverside sites, including Praga's marshy banks and several parks at the foot of the escarpment. Consequently, the river and river banks act as a viewing platform, providing wonderful panoramas of the city. These can be admired while strolling along the boulevards or when taking a boat trip.

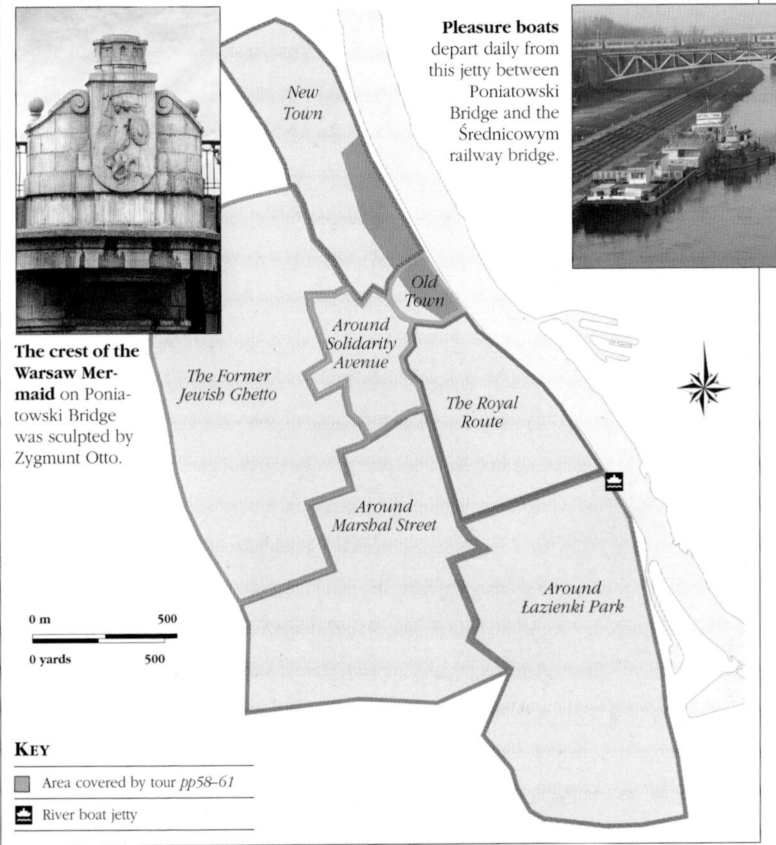

Pleasure boats depart daily from this jetty between Poniatowski Bridge and the Średnicowym railway bridge.

The crest of the Warsaw Mermaid on Poniatowski Bridge was sculpted by Zygmunt Otto.

Key

Area covered by tour *pp58–61*

River boat jetty

◁ **The Mermaid Monument by Ludwiki Nitschowej, on Wybrzeże Kościuszkowskie**

Old Town

THE PANORAMA OF THE OLD TOWN (Stare Miasto) is dominated by the magnificent Royal Castle, with its Gothic and Baroque architecture. The Gothic St John's Cathedral is also an imposing feature, together with the Jesuit Church of Our Lady Mary the Merciful. Burghers' houses form a backdrop to King Zygmunt's Column on Castle Square, while a cluster of steep, red roofs inset with skylights extends to the north.

St Martin's Tower
This is visible at the end of a charming alleyway connecting Świetojańska Street with Piwna Street, opposite St John's Cathedral (see p75).

Castle Square
Approached from Krakowskie Przedmieście, this square (Plac Zamkowy) is an impressive entrance to the Old Town (see p68).

Royal Castle
A feature of the castle is the late 16th-century Władysław Tower, which has an impressive stone portal (see p71).

Kubicki Arcades

Pod Blachą Palace
Originally built in the 1650s, its late Baroque façade dates from the 18th century. The tin roof added at the same time provided the name, which means "Under Tin" (see p69).

St John's Cathedral
The Gothic façade, including this arched portal, was reconstructed after World War II and designed by Jan Zachwatowicz (see pp76–7).

Jesuit Church of Our Lady Mary the Merciful
This Mannerist-Baroque church dates from the 17th century (see p74).

No. 2 Old Town Market Square
Once owned by the Jesuits, this house features a plaque dedicated to the preacher Piotr Skarga (see pp78–9).

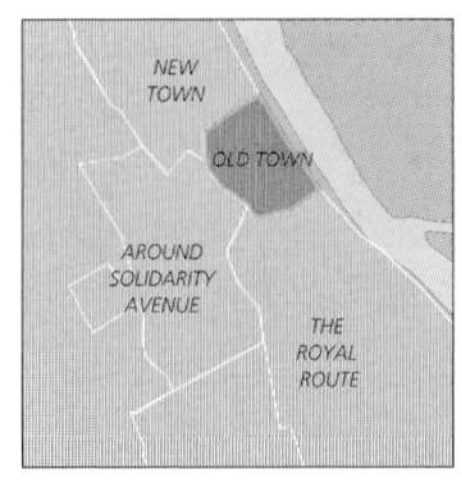

LOCATOR MAP
See Street Finder, maps 1–4

House "Under the Lion"
No. 13 in the Old Town Market Square, this house contains murals painted between 1928–9 by Zofia Stryjeńska (see p78).

Wąski Dunaj
This street owes its name (which means "narrow Danube") to a stream that flowed here during medieval times (see p82).

Kleinpoldt House
Part of the Warsaw History Museum, this house in the Old Town Market Square has the Old Town's only 18th-century painted ceiling (see p81).

Gnojna Góra
This was Warsaw's historic refuse dump (see p83).

Old Town Market Square
The square includes Baroque, Gothic and Neo-Classical buildings (see pp78–9).

Kamienne Schodki
Originally, this narrow and stepped street led up to a gate in the Old Town walls. The street's name means "Stone Steps" (see p83).

New Town

SEEN FROM THE RIVER VISTULA, the New Town (Nowe Miasto) panorama features many church towers and spires, together with magnificent cloistered gardens along the river embankments. Remarkably unchanged despite almost 45 years of Communist rule, these tranquil gardens are still tended by monks and nuns, only separated by a wall from the bustle of the New Town. One of the most popular tourist attractions, the New Town's attractive streets are lined with churches, restaurants and shops.

St Jacek's Church
This Baroque church was built by the Dominicans in the 17th century (see p88).

Barbican
Separating the Old Town and New Town, this gatehouse was built in the 16th century to a design by Venetian architect Giovanni Battista (see p83).

Freta Street
This charming, cobbled street is a favourite place for a promenade, with its many restaurants, cafés and shops (see p90).

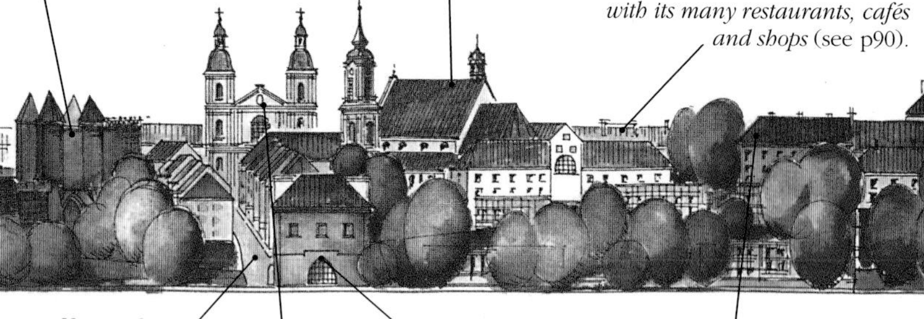

Mostowa Street

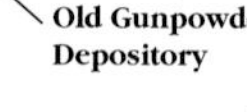

Old Gunpowder Depository

Marie Skłodowska-Curie Museum
Dedicated to Marie Skłodowska-Curie's life and work, the museum occupies her family home on Freta Street (see p89).

Church of the Holy Spirit
This Baroque church, originally built by the Pauline order in the early 18th century, was rebuilt from its wartime ruins (see p88).

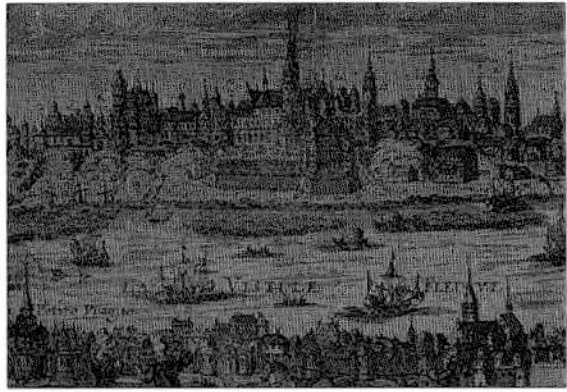

18th-century Warsaw is seen in this panorama of the Old Town and New Town, depicting various landmarks that are still recognizable today.

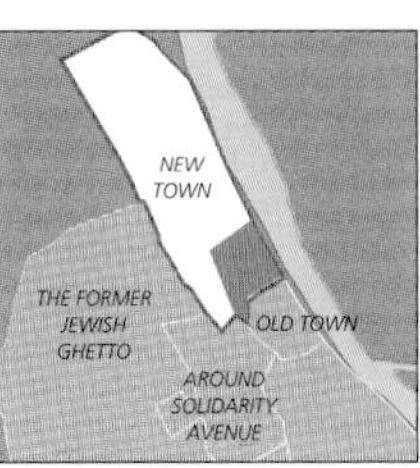

Locator Map
See Street Finder, maps 1–3

Nove Miasto Restaurant, one of several excellent restaurants in the New Town, is very popular with health food enthusiasts and vegetarians *(see p214)*. The restaurant's large terrace is ideal for alfresco dining during the summer.

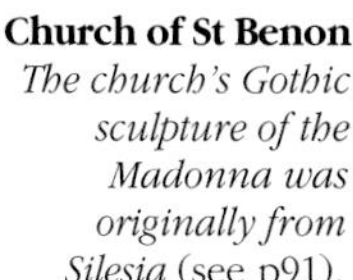

Church of St Benon
The church's Gothic sculpture of the Madonna was originally from Silesia (see p91).

New Town Market Square
This photograph, dating from 1917, shows St Casimir's Church. To its left is the characteristic belltower of Our Lady Mary's Church.

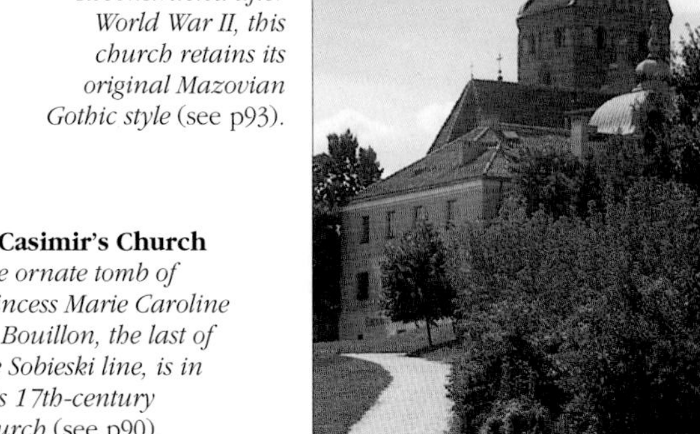

Our Lady Mary's Church
Reconstructed after World War II, this church retains its original Mazovian Gothic style (see p93).

St Casimir's Church
The ornate tomb of Princess Marie Caroline de Bouillon, the last of the Sobieski line, is in this 17th-century church (see p90).

Warsaw Area by Area

APTEKA

OLD TOWN

THE OLD TOWN (Stare Miasto) is one of the most historic and fascinating parts of Warsaw. It was established at the end of the 13th century, around what is now the Royal Castle, originally the seat of the Mazovian dukes. The Old Town was designed as something of a geometric "chessboard" of streets, and the area has maintained its medieval town-planning scheme. The Old Town was completely destroyed by the Nazis during World War II. The area was subsequently rebuilt from rubble with a fastidious eye for historical detail, and is now listed by UNESCO as a World Heritage Site. The heart of the area is the Old Town Market Square (Rynek Starego Miasta), with its distinguished architecture, restaurants, cafés, shops and museums. The surrounding streets also house museums and feature historic architecture, such as the City Walls, the Barbican and St John's Cathedral.

Decorative portal of the "House Under the Ship"

SIGHTS AT A GLANCE

Churches
Jesuit Church of Our Lady Mary the Merciful 10
St John's Cathedral 8
St Martin's Church 12

Museums and Galleries
Guild of Leather Crafts Museum 23
Handicraft and Precision Craft Museum 15
Literature Museum Dedicated to Adam Mickiewicz 19
Warsaw History Museum 20

Historic Streets and Squares
Broad and Narrow Dunaj Street 21
Castle Square 2
Gnojna Góra 28
Kanonia 9
Old Town Market Square 16
Piekarska Street 14
Piwna Street 11
Stone Steps 27
Zapiecek 13

Historic Buildings and Monuments
The Barbican 25
City Walls 24
Fukier House 17
The Mermaid 26
Pelican House 6
Pod Blachą Palace 7
Royal Castle 1
St Anna's House 18
Salvator House 22
Zygmunt's Column 4

Bridges
Gothic Bridge 5

Communication Links
W–Z Route Tunnel 3

GETTING THERE

While the Old Town is closed to traffic, bus stops in Castle Square serve routes E-1, E-3, 116, 122, 125, 160, 174, 175, 180, 192, 195, 303 and 503. Tram routes 4, 13, 26 and 32 stop by the W–Z Route Tunnel.

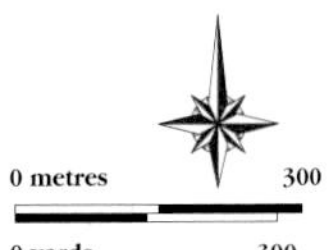

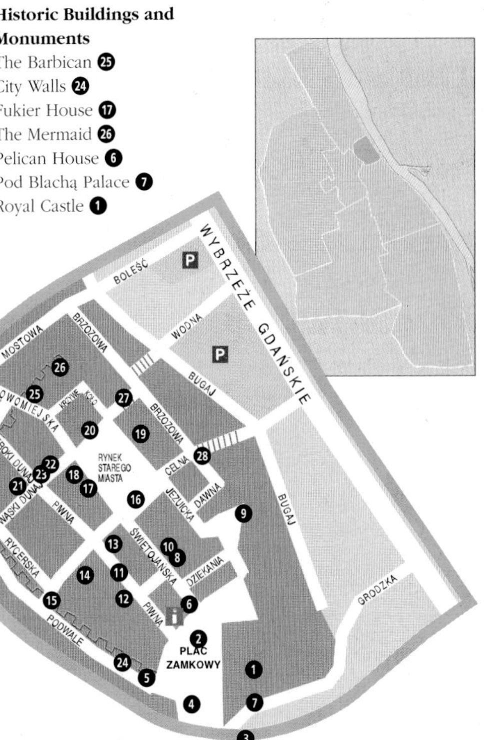

KEY

Street-by-Street map *pp66–7*
Parking
Tourist information

Summer crowds in the Old Town Market Square

Street-by-Street: Old Town

The Old Town is one of Warsaw's most beautiful and fascinating areas. Varsovians as well as tourists enjoy strolling along its historic streets. The Old Town Market Square, with authentically re-created burgher's houses, offers a range of restaurants, cafés, galleries, shops and museums. When the weather is warm, the square becomes full of café tables, various traders pitch their stalls and street artists abound. The adjacent streets, particularly Piwna and Jezuicka, also feature an array of historic attractions including monuments, churches, museums and palaces.

St Martin's Church
The lower floors of this church tower, a dominant feature of Piwna Street, are Gothic, while the top two floors are Baroque 12

Piwna Street
Sculpted pigeons above the entrance to No. 6 commemorate a woman who fed the birds among the postwar ruins of the Old Town 11

★ Royal Castle
This room, with magnificent interior features dating from 1777–81, currently serves as a venue for concerts and other important events 1

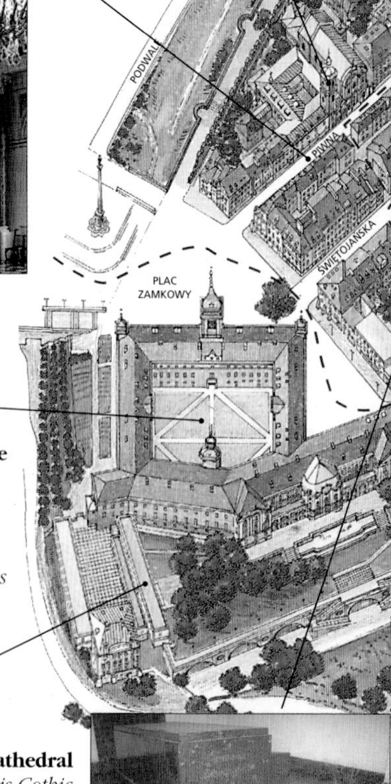

Pod Blachą Palace
The extensive collection of Oriental rugs and textiles in the palace includes this 17th-century "dragon" design Armenian rug 7

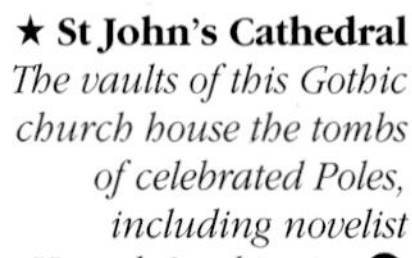

★ St John's Cathedral
The vaults of this Gothic church house the tombs of celebrated Poles, including novelist Henryk Sienkiewicz 8

City Walls
In places, it is still possible to see the double ring of defensive walls that surrounded the Old Town. The walls are best preserved by the Barbican ㉔

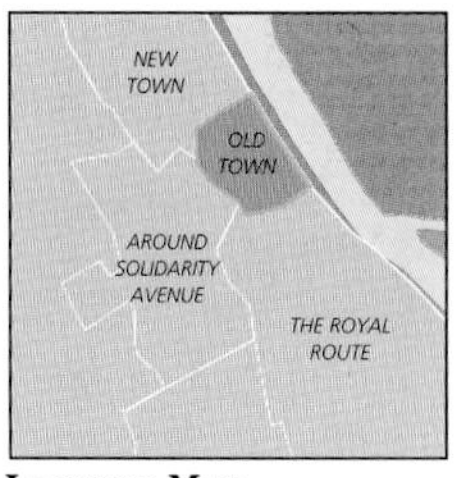

LOCATOR MAP
See Street Finder, maps 1, 4

PODWALE

RYNEK STAREGO MIASTA

Salvator House
Religious statues once stood atop the façade of this 17th-century house ㉒

This painting by Alexander Gierymski, which was completed in 1883, depicts the portal of a house in the Old Town Market Square, as well as the dress styles of the time.

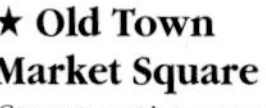

★ Old Town Market Square
Street artists are just one element of this beautiful and bustling square ⓰

KEY

– – Suggested route

0 metres 100

0 yards 100

Kanonia
A church bell dating from 1646 stands at the centre of this small square, the site of houses that were originally built for the cathedral canons ❾

STAR SIGHTS

- **★ Royal Castle**
- **★ St John's Cathedral**
- **★ Old Town Market Square**

Zygmunt's Column in the middle of Castle Square

Royal Castle ❶

Zamek Królewski

See pp70–73.

Castle Square ❷

Plac Zamkowy

Map 2 D2 & 4 D4. *E-1, E-3, 116, 122, 125, 160, 170, 174, 175, 180, 192, 195, 303, 503.* *4, 13, 26, 32.*

Castle square only dates from 1818–21, when it was laid out by architect Jakub Kubicki. Before then the area it covers was the outer courtyard, or bailey, of the castle, surrounded by houses and by sections of the city walls, including the important Krakowska Gate. This was the town's main gateway to the south, giving access to the road to Kraków.

The eastern side of the square is filled by the Royal Castle. To the north and west it is framed by houses. To the south the square opens up into Krakowskie Przedmieście, which forms the initial part of Warsaw's "Royal Route" *(see pp112–25)*, leading from the castle to the royal summer residence of the Wilanów Palace and Park *(see pp168–71)*.

Castle Square is one of the emblems of Warsaw, and symbolizes Poland's capital for the whole country. Crowds gather in the square for political demonstrations, and Varsovians greet the New Year here with the popping of champagne corks. This is also the favourite place in the city for lovers to arrange their rendezvous.

W-Z Route Tunnel ❸

Tunel Trasy W-Z

Map 1 C2, 2 D2, 3 C5 & 4 D5. *125, 170, 190.* *4, 13, 26, 32.*

This tunnel is a section of the east–west (W–Z) Route, running underneath Castle Square and Miodowa and Senatorska streets to take traffic between Solidarity Avenue and the Śląsko-Dąbrowski Bridge. The building of the tunnel in 1947–9 caused great concern among local people, as it was feared that the construction work was undermining the foundations of houses in the streets above. Escalators lead from Castle Square to the tunnel entrance. Since they were built at the height of the Communist era, the decor of these sections of the tunnel is in pure Socialist Realist style, reminiscent of the Metro stations in Moscow or St Petersburg.

Figure of the king from Zygmunt's Column

Zygmunt's Column ❹

Kolumna Zygmunta

Plac Zamkowy. **Map** 2 D2 & 4 D5.

The column standing in the centre of Castle Square is the oldest non-religious memorial monument in Warsaw. It is dedicated to King Zygmunt III Waza, who transferred his residence to Warsaw in 1596 *(see pp20–21)*. The column was erected in 1644, on the orders of the king's son, King Władysław IV.

A drawing to show how Zygmunt's column was first erected

The granite main column rises from a tall plinth, and supports a bronze figure of King Zygmunt holding a cross in one hand and a sword in the other. This impressive statue was the work of Clemente Molli, but the column and base were designed by two famous Italian architects who worked for many years for the kings of Poland: Agostino Locci the Elder and Constantino Tencalla.

The monument is 22 m (72 ft) high, and virtually unique in Europe because, with its large cross, it glorifies the monarch in a manner that was usually reserved for saints. It has been damaged in war and restored many times over the centuries, but the bronze figure of the king has managed to escape destruction. The present column, however, is actually the third one that has been built to support the statue. Parts of the second one can be seen lying nearby.

A cheerful tenement house in Warsaw's popular Castle Square

Gothic Bridge ❺
Most gotycki

Plac Zamkowy. **Map** 2 D2 & 4 D5.

Only a section remains of this two-arched brick bridge, built at the end of the 15th century, but in use again today. It once spanned the moat in front of the Krakowska Gate, on the main route out of the city to the south. At its southern end the bridge was protected by a fortified gatehouse. This, like the walls and main gate, was demolished in 1808, when the moat was filled in and the bridge buried. Its existence was forgotten for many years, and it was only discovered in 1977. After restoration it was opened to pedestrians in 1983.

The pelican on Pelican House

Pelican House ❻
Kamienica Pod Pelikanem

Plac Zamkowy 1/13. **Map** 2 D2 & 4 D4.

The large house that fills the corner where Piwna Street meets Castle Square was built in the late 17th century and completed in 1705. In the mid-18th century this was the home of the royal architect, Karl Friedrich Pöppelmann. It is one of seven houses that originally stood on the north side of what was then Bernardyńska Street, one of the historic streets of Warsaw's Old Town. The south side of Bernardyńska Street was demolished when Castle Square was opened up in the early years of the 19th century. Since then, this and the other houses on the former north side of the street have faced onto the square. The "Pelican House" takes its name from the sculpture of a pelican which can be seen on one corner of the building. The house also has a wooden porch, running the length of the ground floor windows, that is a typical feature of Warsaw houses of the 17th and 18th centuries.

This house, as with others on this side of Castle Square, was destroyed in 1944 during World War II. It was reconstructed in 1957, with new sgraffito by Edmund Burke. It now houses a tourist information centre.

Pod Blachą Palace ❼
Pałac Pod Blachą

Plac Zamkowy 2. **Map** 2 D2 & 4 D4. *657 2170.* *E-1, E-3, 116, 122, 125, 160, 170, 174, 175, 180, 190, 192, 195, 303, 503.* *Plac Zamkowy.* *10am–4pm Tue–Sat.* *included in Royal Castle, see* *pp70–73.*

Baroque in style, this palace was last "modernized" in 1720, on the initiative of its then owner Jerzy Dominik Lubomirski. Its ornate walls conceal the remains of an older house, built in the previous century.

The palace frequently changed hands. Its owners included Poland's last king, Stanisław August Poniatowski, and his nephew, the famous hero of the Napoleonic Wars Prince Józef Poniatowski. After years of neglect the building was partially restored in 1932. Rooms in the north wing were redecorated with original panelling designed for the Royal Castle by the royal architect Dominik Merlini in 1778–80. Since 1988 the palace has formed part of the Royal Castle Museum, and housed a collection of Oriental rugs and textiles. The bequest of Teresa Sahakian, it is the world's largest and most valuable collection of Caucasian rugs.

At the rear of the palace, built into the Castle hill, there is a vault that in the 17th century belonged to a Masonic lodge. Statues of Greek deities stand along its walls.

The grand Baroque frontage of Pod Blachą Palace

Royal Castle ❶

THE ROYAL CASTLE (Zamek Królewski) is a magnificent example of Baroque architecture. A castle was originally built on this site by the Mazovian dukes in the 14th century. After Warsaw became the seat of the Sejm (Parliament) in 1569, and King Zygmunt III Waza chose this castle as his royal residence in 1596, Warsaw replaced Kraków as the capital of Poland. Between 1598 and 1619 Italian architects restyled the castle into a polygon. In the 18th century, King Augustus III gave the east wing a Baroque style. In 1939, the castle was burned, and then blown up by the Nazis in 1944. Reconstruction, which was funded by public donations, lasted from 1971 to 1988. The castle is now a museum housing furniture, paintings and numerous *objets d'art*.

★ Zygmunt's Tower
A clock was first installed in the tower in 1622. It was rebuilt and the clock restarted in 1974.

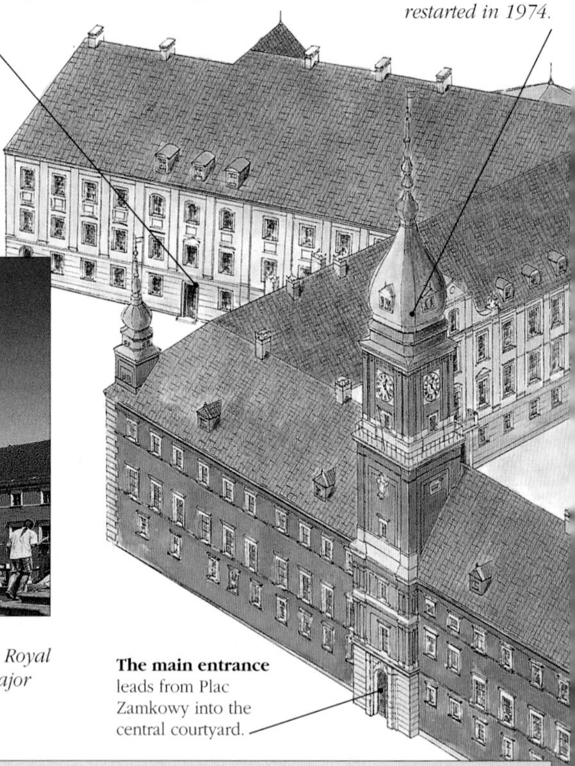

Bacciarelli Annexe
During the 18th century this was a studio and art school run by Marcello Bacciarelli. It is now a popular Registry Office.

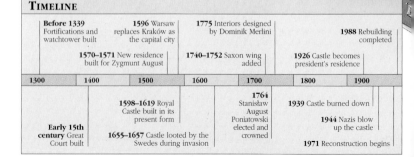

The Royal Castle
Since reconstruction, the Royal Castle is once again a major feature of the city.

The main entrance leads from Plac Zamkowy into the central courtyard.

TIMELINE

- **Before 1339** Fortifications and watchtower built
- **Early 15th century** Great Court built
- **1570–1571** New residence built for Zygmunt August
- **1596** Warsaw replaces Kraków as the capital city
- **1598–1619** Royal Castle built in its present form
- **1655–1657** Castle looted by the Swedes during invasion
- **1740–1752** Saxon wing added
- **1764** Stanisław August Poniatowski elected and crowned
- **1775** Interiors designed by Dominik Merlini
- **1926** Castle becomes president's residence
- **1939** Castle burned down
- **1944** Nazis blow up the castle
- **1971** Reconstruction begins
- **1988** Rebuilding completed

1300 | 1400 | 1500 | 1600 | 1700 | 1800 | 1900

★ Saxon Wing
Remodelled in a Baroque style during the reign of King August III in the 18th century, this wing faces east towards the River Vistula.

Visitors' Checklist

Plac Zamkowy 4. **Map** 2 D2 & 4 D4. *657 21 70.* **Ticket office** *657 23 38 (9am–2pm Tue–Fri).* *E-1, E-3, 116, 122, 160, 174, 175, 192, 195, 303, 460, 503.* *10am–4pm Tue–Sat, 11am–4pm Sun.* **Royal Apartments** *15 Apr– 30 Sep: 10am–6pm Mon–Sat, 11am–6pm Sun; 1 Oct–14 Apr: 10am–3pm Tue–Sat, 11am–3pm Sun.* *1 Jan, Easter, 1 May, Corpus Christi, 1 Nov, 24–25 Dec, 31 Dec.* *except Sun.* *www.zamek-krolewski.art.pl*

The Kubicki Arcade is a viewing terrace, supported by arcades, overlooking the re-created castle gardens.

Great Court
Rebuilt in its original Gothic style, this was the residence of the Mazovian dukes during the 15th century.

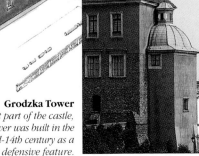

Władysław's Tower
Built in 1571, the tower was remodelled in 1637–43.

Grodzka Tower
The oldest part of the castle, the tower was built in the mid-14th century as a defensive feature.

Star Sights

- ★ Saxon Wing
- ★ Zygmunt's Tower

Exploring the Royal Castle

THE ROYAL CASTLE'S fascinating interiors are the result of its dual role: being a royal residence as well as the seat of the Sejm (Parliament). Meticulously reconstructed after World War II, the castle features royal apartments, as well as the Chamber of Deputies and the Senate. Many of the furnishings and *objets d'art* are original, with statues, paintings and even fragments of woodwork and stucco that were hidden from the Nazis. Among the paintings exhibited in the castle's rooms and galleries are works by Bernardo Bellotto and Marcello Bacciarelli.

Gallery of Decorative Arts
The 17th and 18th century exhibits on display here include donations by the Ciechanowiecki foundation.

Second floor

★ Ballroom
Seventeen pairs of gilt columns support the ceiling of this grand room. The ceiling painting is a reproduction of Bacciarelli's Dissolution of Chaos.

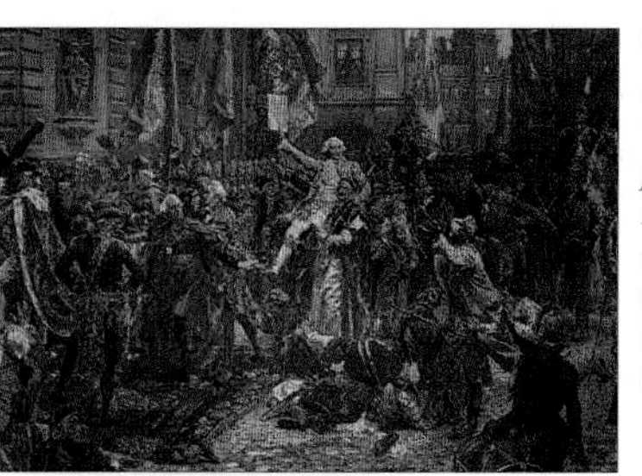

The Prince's Apartments
These rooms hold paintings by Jan Matejko, including The Ratification of the Constitution of 3 May.

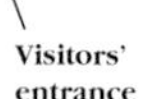

Visitors' entrance

★ Senate Chamber
The Constitution of 3 May was ratified here in 1791 (see p26).

Cellars

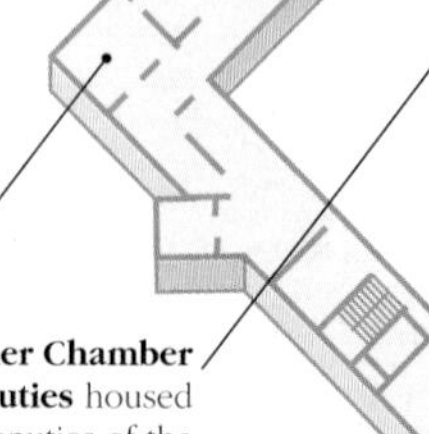

The Former Chamber of Deputies housed the deputies of the Sejm's Lower House in the 17th century.

KEY TO FLOORPLAN

- Royal apartments
- King Poniatowski's apartments
- Great apartment
- Sejm (Parliament)
- Prince's apartments
- Former Chamber of Deputies
- Permanent exhibitions
- Non-exhibition areas

Lanckoroński Gallery

★ Marble Room
This room's lavish decor and furnishings date from the reign of King Władysław IV Waza in the 17th century. The portraits of Polish monarchs by Marcello Bacciarelli are 18th century.

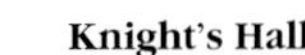

Knight's Hall
A statue of Chronos by Jakub Monaldi dominates this beautifully appointed room.

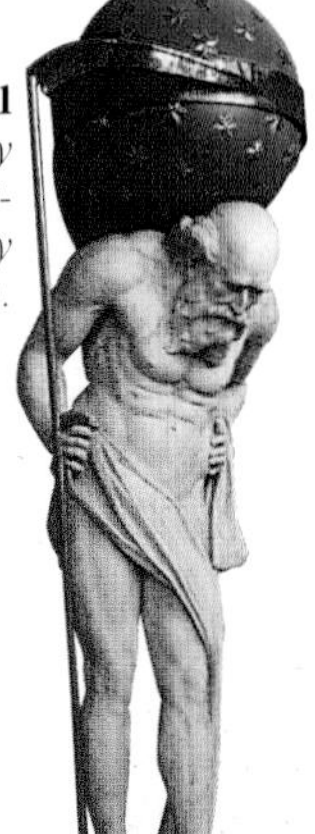

Gallery Guide

An archaeological exhibition is housed in the cellars. On the ground floor is the court of chambers, while the King's apartments and the Great apartments are on the first floor. The second floor includes the living quarters of S. Żeromski, the Gallery of Decorative Arts and the Lackoroński Gallery, as well as a hall for temporary exhibitions.

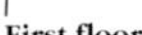

First floor

New Audience Room
In addition to its fine parquet floor, this room includes the original stucco work.

Ground floor

★ Canaletto Room
Bernardo Bellotto, who often used the name of his uncle Canaletto, painted the views of 18th-century Warsaw exhibited in this room.

King Stanisław August Poniatowski's Apartments
The Rococo panelling, from the destroyed Tarnowski Palace, is thought to be by Juste-Aurèle Meissonier.

Star Features

- ★ Ballroom
- ★ Marble Room
- ★ Canaletto Room

St John's Cathedral ❽

Katedra św. Jana

See pp76–7.

Kanonia ❾

Map 2 D2. *E-1, E-3, 116, 122, 125, 160, 170, 174, 175, 180, 190, 192, 195, 303, 503.* *4, 13, 26, 32.*

This small square (which is actually triangular in shape) is located behind St John's Cathedral. It is lined with attractive houses, which were built for the cathedral clergy on the site of a former graveyard. Dating from the1500s, these houses were reconstructed after the war.

In the centre of the square is a church bell, cast in 1646 by Daniel Tym. He also cast the original bronze figure of Zygmunt III Waza *(see p68).*

The covered footbridge originally connected the Royal Castle with the cathedral. It was built for royal use as a form of security, after Michał Piekarski attempted to kill Zygmunt III Waza (1587–1632) as he entered the cathedral.

Piekarski was tortured before being killed, and during his torture uttered nonsense. This resulted in the Polish saying: "muttering like Piekarski".

Between 1800 and 1823, the Society of the Friends of Science, established by the Enlightenment writer Stanisław Staszic, held its meetings in the square at Nos. 5 and 8.

One of Warsaw's most prominent poets, Artur Oppman (known as Or-Ot), lived at No. 8 from 1910 to 1925.

The Jesuit Church of Our Lady Mary the Merciful

Jesuit Church of Our Lady Mary the Merciful ❿

Sanktuarium Matki Bozej Łaskawej

Świętojańska 10. **Map** 2 D2. *831 16 75.*

Built together with a monastery, in a style that mixes Mannerism and Baroque, this church dates from 1621. After the dissolution of the monastery in 1773, the church remained largely unchanged until 1944, when it was almost completely destroyed. The original architectural records survived the war, which enabled this unique church to be accurately reconstructed.

Occupying a narrow site, the church has several interesting features. A lantern in the dome floods the presbytery with daylight. The building's Gothic vaults were formed from the cellars of houses that were demolished when the church was built. Among the tombstones in the vaults is the magnificent monument to Jan Tarło, which was designed by Jan Jerzy Plersch.

The entrance to the church features the figure of a bear, which formerly stood in the Piarist church in Długa Street.

Piwna Street ⓫

Ulica Piwna

Map 1 C2. *E-1, 116, 122, 174, 175, 195, 503.*

The longest street in the Old Town, Piwna Street connects Castle Square with Wąski Dunaj Street. Piwna Street was first mentioned in the 15th century, when it was also known as St Martin's (after the church on this street). Piwna Street was originally a fashionable address for aristocratic families, though it is now known for its fine restaurants.

An illustration of Piwna Street in 1865

Kanonia's historic houses, with the church bell displayed in the square

St Martin's Church ⓬

Kościół św. Marcina

Piwna 9/11. **Map** 1 C2. *831 02 21.*

Dating from the 15th century, St Martin's Church was built for the Augustinian Order, who came to Warsaw in

Crucifix in St Martin's Church

1352. Its present form is the result of two Baroque-style refurbishments: between 1631 and 1636, and in the mid-18th century. The latter was supervised by the renowned architect Karol Bay, whose designs included a "wave-like" façade. Unfortunately, this was destroyed in World War II.

Nevertheless, a modern interpretation of the Baroque interiors was re-created under the direction of Sister Anna Skrzydlewska. The only original artefact that remains is a partially burned crucifix, which has been hung on a pillar in the nave.

St Martin's church has long played an important role in the history of Warsaw. From the 16th century, it was used by the Mazovian gentry. In the 17th century, theological and philosophical debates were held at St Martin's.

In 1950 the church was taken over by a Franciscan order of nuns, the Servants of the Holy Cross. Their mission is to care for the poor.

During the 1980s, members of Solidarity and other anti-Communist movements held clandestine meetings here.

Adjoining St Martin's Church, there is a delightful cloistered courtyard, which is part of the nunnery.

Zapiecek ⓭

Map 2 D1. 🚌 *E-1, E-3, 116, 122, 160, 170, 174, 175, 180, 190, 192, 195, 303, 503.*

ORIGINALLY PART of Piekarska Street, this square is a thoroughfare in its own right.

During the 19th century it was the venue for Warsaw's most important bird market. A comprehensive choice ranged from racing pigeons to more exotic songbirds.

The surrounding attractions currently include a contemporary art gallery. There are several restaurants in the square that provide alfresco tables during the summer months.

A plaque on one of the walls of the square commemorates the fact that Warsaw's Old Town has now been added to UNESCO's esteemed list of World Heritage Sites.

Piekarska Street ⓮

Ulica Piekarska

Map 2 D1. 🚌 *E-1, E-3, 160, 116, 122, 174, 175, 192, 303, 503.*

THIS STREET was originally occupied by numerous bakers and millers, as its name suggests (*piekarz* is Polish for "baker").

Brick buildings were first constructed on this street in the 18th century. At the same time, a section of the Old Town's defensive walls was demolished to provide a direct link to Podwale Street.

At the junction of Piekarska and Rycerska streets was a square called Piekiełko – "little hell". During the 16th–17th centuries, executions were carried out in the square. These included the burning of witches and poisoners. Michał Piekarski, who attempted to kill King Zygmunt III Waza, was also executed here.

At the Podwale end of the street is the Jan Kiliński monument *(see p101)*. He was a heroic leader of the 1794 Kościuszko Insurrection.

Handicraft and Precision Craft Museum ⓯

Muzeum Rzemiosł Artystycznych i Precyzyjnych

Piekarska 20. **Map** 2 D1. ☎ *831 96 28.* ◯ *9am–3pm Mon–Fri.*

HOUSED IN an 18th-century building, which was restored after World War II, the collection includes jewels and watches. The earliest exhibits are from the 16th century. Other *objets d'art* include the "masterworks", which had to be presented to

Clock at Handicraft Museum

a craft's guild by engravers and goldsmiths, before they could work independently.

Old Town Market Square ⓰

Rynek Starego Miasta

See pp78–9.

Diners at one of the pavement restaurants on Zapiecek Square

St John's Cathedral 8

COMPLETED IN THE EARLY 15th century, St John's Cathedral (katedra św Jana) was originally a parish church. Gaining Collegiate status in 1406, it was not until 1798 that St John's became a cathedral. Among the important events held here was the coronation of Stanisław August Poniatowski in 1764, and the swearing of an oath by the deputies of the Sejm (Parliament) to uphold the 1791 Constitution. After World War II, 19th-century additions were removed from the façade, and the cathedral was restored to its original Mazovian Gothic style. The interiors feature ornate tombs and religious art.

An Earlier Façade
This prewar photograph shows the cathedral's façade after it was refurbished in 1836–40 by the architect Adam Idźkowski.

Chapel of the Holy Sacrament

★ Crypt of Gabriel Narutowicz
Poland's first president, assassinated two days after taking the presidential oath, is buried here, as is the Nobel prize-winning novelist Henryk Sienkiewicz.

Tomb of the Mazovian Dukes
This marble tomb commemorates the last two Mazovian dukes, after whose death the dukedom was incorporated into the Polish crown.

Bell tower

Main entrance

PRIMATE OF THE MILLENNIUM

Cardinal Stefan Wyszyński (1901–1981) became Primate of Poland in October 1948. Committed to defending the nation's Christian identity, he was arrested in 1953 and not released until 1956. Until his death he was the spiritual leader of Polish Catholics, which frequently brought him into conflict with the communist leaders. In 1980–81 he was a mediator between Solidarity and government.

★ Baryczka Crucifix
Hanging in Baryczka Chapel, this 16th-century crucifix is credited with several miracles. Human hair was used on the head of Christ.

Visitors' Checklist

Świętojańska 8.
Map 1 D2 & 4 D4.
831 02 89.
E-1, 116, 122, 175, 195, 503 to Pl Zamkowy.
10am–6pm Mon–Sat, 2pm–6pm Sun.
for crypt.

Stalls
The existing stalls are copies of those commissioned by King Jan III Sobieski in gratitude for his 1683 victory at Vienna.

Chapel of the Men of Letters

Gallery
leading to the Royal Castle *(see pp70–73)*.

Memorial to Stanisław Małachowski
This marble sculpture is from a design by the Danish Neo-Classicist Bertel Thorwaldsen.

Star Sights

- **★ Crypt of Gabriel Narutowicz**
- **★ Baryczka Crucifix**

Caterpillar Track
Mounted on the wall, this track is from a Nazi radio-controlled tank that destroyed part of the cathedral during the Warsaw Uprising in 1944.

Old Town Market Square 16

UNTIL THE END OF THE 18TH CENTURY, the Old Town Market Square was the most important public square in Warsaw. Here, regular fairs and municipal festivities were held and, on rare occasions, executions were carried out. The Town Hall occupied the centre until its demolition in 1817. The four sides of the 90 by 73 m (295 by 240 ft) square are named after prominent 18th-century parliamentarians. The houses, which lend the square its unique character, were built or restyled by wealthy merchant families in the 17th century. Today, café tables and stalls line the square, and horse-drawn carriages *(dorożkas)* await those who wish to tour the narrow streets of the Old Town. The sound of barrel organs often echoes round its ancient walls.

Sign for Bazyliszek restaurant

OLD TOWN MARKET SQUARE

- Zakrzewski Side
- Barss Side
- Dekert Side
- Kołłątaj Side

ZAKRZEWSKI SIDE

Majeran House (No. 11)

Bazyliszek House (No. 5), with the bankers' sign of the mythical reptile

Gilded House
Stanisław Baryczka, mayor of the Old Town, lived here in the 17th century. His initials can be seen in the lattice-work of the transom window.

At the Lion
A painting by Zofia Stryjeńska (1928) decorates the façade of this house. There is also a lion in gilded relief on the corner.

Orlemus House
This houses the Literature Museum (see p81). *Here you will find first editions and memorabilia relating to Adam Mickiewicz, Poland's beloved Romantic poet.*

BARSS SIDE

Troper House (No. 10)

Simonetti House
The plaque under the clock of this house commemorates the postwar reconstruction of the Old Town.

★ Fukier House
This once belonged to the Polish line of the medieval Fugger family. It now houses one of Warsaw's best restaurants (see p80).

Kołłątaj Side

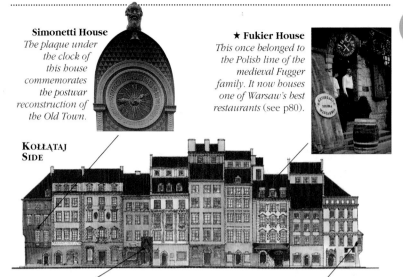

Wilczek House
From the original medieval house on this side, only the Gothic portal remains.

★ Statue of St Anna
A corner niche shows the figure of St Anna holding the Virgin Mary and Child (see p80).

★ House of the "Little Black Boy"
This is named after the sculpture of a young boy on the façade.

Falkiewicz House
The parapet wall is crested with the figure of the Virgin Mary, flanked by Saints Elizabeth and Stanisław.

Dekert Side

All the houses on this side are interconnected and form the Warsaw History Museum *(see p81)*.

Burbach House (No. 2)

Baroque Ceilings
Ceilings on the third floor of No. 34, Kleinpoldt House, are painted in the Baroque style.

Star Sights

- ★ **Statue of St Anna**
- ★ **Fukier House**
- ★ **House of the "Little Black Boy"**

Fukier House 17

Kamienica Fukierów

Rynek Starego Miasta 27. **Map** 2 D1 & 4 D4.

Now housing one of the city's most stylish restaurants, this building dates originally from the 15th century. Its present Neo-Classical style is from 1782, when architect Szymon Bogumił Zug is thought to have made major alterations.

The house retains the name of the Fukier family, who acquired it in 1810. The Fukiers were the Polish branch of the Fuggers, a German family who for centuries were among the most powerful bankers in Germany. Even German emperors were often in debt to them. The Fuggers were also merchants and dominated Europe's spice trade.

While the Polish branch of the family did not achieve quite the same level of commercial success, the Fukiers nevertheless amassed a considerable fortune as wine merchants. Up until World War II, the Fukiers were particularly renowned for their stocks of Hungarian wine and Polish mead.

During World War II, only the ground floor and cellar of Fukier House escaped destruction. Having been painstakingly restored, the ornate, gilded façade includes a frieze in the pattern of a gentleman's traditional dress sash. Above the portal is the Fukier family crest, comprising two crossed lilies, together with the letter F.

The Fukier restaurant now occupies the ground floor, the cellar (which is original 15th century), and a charming cloistered courtyard. It is run by the Gessler family, who are established restaurateurs in the city. The menu offers modern interpretations of classic Polish cuisine *(see p214)*.

The top floors of Fukier house are occupied by the Society of Art Historians.

Fukier House, now transformed into a renowned restaurant

St Anna's House 18

Kamienica Pod św. Anną

Rynek Starego Miasta 31. **Map** 2 D1 & 4 D4. ***Entrance Hall only*** *8am–4pm Mon–Fri.*

Dating from the 15th century, this building has changed hands and been altered many times. However, the house has retained some of its earliest features. Gothic arches span the entrance hall, as well as the façade which faces Wąski Dunaj Street. The house also includes a statue of its namesake, St Anna.

During the 18th century the house served as a renowned restaurant, owned by a Frenchman called Quellus. In 1913, the house was bought by public subscription for the Historical Society of Warsaw. It is currently occupied by the Polish Academy of Science, which shares the premises with the Polish Historical Society.

Portal at St Anna's House

Portals of Old Town Burgher's Houses

Among the Old Town's best preserved architectural features are its portals (doorways and other entrances). The portals are often highly decorative, and those in the Old Town Market Square exemplify a succession of architectural styles, ranging from Gothic to Renaissance, and from the Mannerist style to the Baroque.

Gothic

15th-century brick portals at No. 21 showing several stages of construction

Late Gothic

Elaborate Gothic portal at No. 31 exemplifies the genre

Julian Tuwim's study in the Literature Museum

Literature Museum Dedicated to Adam Mickiewicz ⓳

Muzeum Literatury im. A Mickiewicza

Rynek Starego Miasta 18/20. **Map** 2 D1 & 4 D4. *831 40 61.* *10am–3pm Mon, Tue & Fri; 11am–6pm Wed, Thu; 11am–5pm Sun & public hols.* *except Sun.*

THIS MUSEUM occupies two burgher's houses, Orlemus' and Balcer's, which date from the 15th century. Both houses have undergone changes over the centuries.

After World War II, they were reconstructed in a late Baroque style. However, the original Gothic arch and frescoes have been retained in the entrance hall of No. 20.

Ten of the museum's galleries are devoted to Poland's most renowned Romantic poet, Adam Mickiewicz *(see p117)*. On display are his original manuscripts, first editions and various memorabilia.

The lives and works of other Polish writers and poets, including Julian Tuwim, Leopold Staff, Melchior Wańkowicz and Kazimierz Wierzyński, are explored in separate galleries. Additionally, the museum collects works of art relating to the periods in which these writers worked. The museum's vast collection can also be seen in frequent temporary exhibitions.

The Literature Museum has a separate exhibition venue located at 40 Polna Street (in the vicinity of Łazienki Park). This branch celebrates the life and works of the Polish novelist Maria Dąbrowska.

Warsaw History Museum ⓴

Muzeum Historyczne m. st. Warszawy

Rynek Starego Miasta 28/42. **Map** 2 D1 & 4 D4. *635 16 25.* *11am–5:30pm Tue & Thu, 10am–3:30pm Wed & Fri; 10:30am–4:30pm Sat–Sun.* *one weekend per month.* **Cinema** *9:30am–3:30pm.* *except Sun.*

THE WARSAW HISTORY Museum occupies all the houses on the Dekert side of the Old Town Market Square, as well as three in the adjacent Nowomiejska Street. Houses on the Dekert side were less damaged in World War II, some retaining their façades and one or two keeping their interiors, which can be viewed via the museum. However, the museum's collection was totally destroyed during the war.

The existing collection is housed in 60 rooms, with Warsaw's history conveyed through paintings, drawings, illustrations, sculpture, arts and crafts, handicrafts and archaeological finds.

Models are used to illustrate buildings which no longer exist. Additionally, a few galleries feature re-created room sets and artisans' studios, from various periods.

A vast collection of photographs and postcards spans historic and contemporary Warsaw, as does the extensive library.

A film of the history of Warsaw, with commentary available in several languages, is shown in the museum cinema. This includes footage shot by the Nazis, documenting their systematic destruction of Warsaw. This was ordered by Hitler in response to the Warsaw Uprising of 1944. The film also covers the city's massive post-war rebuilding programme.

In the museum courtyard are fragments of historic stonemasonry and statuary, discovered during reconstruction work.

Printers' room reconstructed in the Warsaw Museum

Renaissance

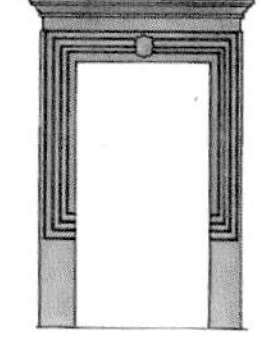

Interior doorway in typical Renaissance style at No. 1

Mannerist

Ornate portal dating from the early 17th century at No. 36

Early Baroque

Reconstructed early period sandstone portal at No. 7

Baroque

Portal with pediment dating from 1663, at No. 38

Broad (Szeroki) Dunaj Street

Broad and Narrow Dunaj Street ㉑

Szeroki i Wąski Dunaj

Map 1 C1.

Wąski (Narrow) Dunaj Street leads from the Old Town Market Square to the city walls, while adjoining it is Szeroki (Broad) Dunaj Street, which is effectively a small square. Both the names derive from the Dunaj stream, which originally had its source in this area.

During the Middle Ages, Wąski Dunaj Street was largely inhabited by Jews. Their place of worship was a synagogue on the corner of Wąski Dunaj Street and Żydowska (Jewish) Street. Neither the street nor the synagogue still exists.

Detail of portal at Salvator House

Historically, both the Dunaj streets were commercial areas. In the 17th century a fish market was held in Szeroki Dunaj Street, which became a vegetable and flower market in the 19th century.

The commercial importance of this area was underlined by the former Butcher's Gate (Brama Rzeźnicza), named after an abattoir by the city walls. Many cobblers also lived on Szeroki Dunaj Street, such as Jan Kiliński, who lived at No. 5. Esteemed in the trade, he was also a leader of the 1794 Kościuszko Insurrection.

Salvator House ㉒

Kamienica Salwator

Wąski Dunaj 8. **Map** 1 C1.

Built in 1632 for Jakub Gianotti, Salvator House took its name from the bas-relief of Jesus and St Veronica that was originally above the building's façade.

The house has retained an early Baroque style and the portal features the original owner's initials and monogram. However, the religious statues were omitted in the postwar Communist reconstruction, and replaced by more secular images: an obelisk and a pedlar girl.

A Boy Insurgent

Guild of Leather Crafts Museum ㉓

Muzeum Cechu Rzemiosł Skórzanych im. Kilińskiego

Wąski Dunaj 10. **Map** 1 C2. *831 96 37.* *10am–3pm Thu–Sat.*

The Guild of Leather Crafts Museum is within a building that is known locally as the Shoemakers' House. It is a 16th-century building, reconstructed in an 18th-century style after World War II.

The museum's collection includes the reconstructed workshop of a shoemaker and also that of a saddler. Both feature examples of their respective crafts. Exhibits also illustrate the life of Colonel Jan Kiliński, to whom the museum is dedicated. As well as a master of the Guild, he was also a hero of 1794's Kościuszko Insurrection.

City Walls ㉔

Mury miejskie

Podwale. **Map** 1 C2.

Warsaw is one of the world's few capital cities to have retained large sections of the original defensive walls. Constructed during the 14th and 15th centuries in the form of a double ring, they were additionally fortified by several towers, positioned at regular intervals. The Old Town was also protected by two main gates: the Krakowska (Kraków), to the south, of which the only remaining feature is the Gothic bridge *(see p69)*, and Nowomiejska (as well as the Barbican) to the north of the Old Town.

Eventually, however, the brick walls became obsolete as a means of defending the city, and some sections were incorporated into houses that were subsequently built there.

In 1937–8, a major initiative was launched to excavate the city walls. During this period, buildings that had encroached upon the city walls were demolished. This initiative continued after World War II, when more of the city walls were restored and certain fragments reconstructed.

Presently, the inner section of the city walls is far better

Saddlers' workshop in the Guild of Leather Crafts Museum

preserved than the outer walls, of which only mere fragments still remain.

On Wąski Dunaj Street, the rectangular Knights Tower (Baszta Rycerska) has been reconstructed, and towards Nowomiejska Street there is the partly reconstructed Gunpowder Tower (Baszta Prochowa). On the remains of one of the turrets of this tower stands the famous statue *A Boy Insurgent*, designed by Jerzy Jarnuszkiewicz.

The Barbican, part of the Old Town's fortifications

The Barbican ㉕
Barbakan

Nowomiejska. **Map** 1 C1.

Built in 1548 as the final part of the Old Town's fortifications, the Barbican was designed by the Venetian architect Giovanni Battista.

Constructed on the site of an earlier fortified building, the Barbican's principal role was to protect Nowomiejska Gate to the north of the Old Town. The remains of Nowomiejska Gate are now marked by a low wall and variously coloured flagstones.

The Mermaid ㉖
Pomnik Syrenki

Map 1 C1.

Mermaid images have been used as a symbol on the crest of Warsaw since the mid-14th century. Originally the Warsaw mermaid resembled a ferocious-looking monster, with overtones of a dragon, having claws and wings.

However, over the centuries, images of the mermaid gradually became more traditional (not to mention attractive), and took on the more recognizable form of the half human and half fish creature.

By the 19th century, artists such as the sculptor Konstanty Hegel also endowed the mermaid with great beauty. Nevertheless, she retained a ferocity, armed with a raised sword and shield. This image made her a perfect symbol for a city in which so many battles have been fought.

In 1855, Hegel's mermaid became the centrepiece of a fountain in the Old Town Market Square (on the site of the former Town Hall).

When the fountain was dismantled in 1929, the mermaid sculpture was initially transferred to the Solec sports club, and then, at a later date, to a park in Powiśle.

The mermaid finally returned to the Old Town in 1972, when it was decided to place the sculpture on the remains of the Marszałkowska Tower.

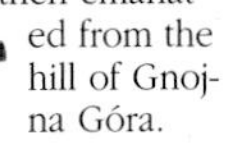

The mermaid

Stone Steps ㉗
Kamienne Schodki

Map 2 D1.

Widely regarded as the most picturesque street in the Old Town, Kamienne Schodki is effectively a series of steps. The steps run from the Old Town Market Square, cross Brzozowa Street, and continue on to Bugaj Street. Before Warsaw acquired a piped water supply, this route was used for carrying water from the River Vistula to supply the Old Town.

Enchanting views of the Vistula can be enjoyed from the top of Kamienne Schodki. It is a view that was much admired by Napoleon Bonaparte in the early 19th century, although he is said to have complained about the less enjoyable odours, which then emanated from the hill of Gnojna Góra.

Stone Steps by the Market Square

Gnojna Góra ㉘

Celna. **Map** 2 D1.

Located at the end of Celna Street, Gnojna Góra is an ideal vantage point from which

A 17th-century illustration of the mound of Gnojna Góra

to enjoy the panorama of the River Vistula and the views of Warsaw's right bank.

However, this site has a less picturesque heritage. Gnojna Góra, which translates as "Dung Mound", was used as a refuse dump by the Old Town for centuries.

Fragments of Gnojna Brama (Dung Gate), which provided access to the mound, can still be seen where it was attached to the house at the junction of Celna Street and Brzozowa Street. The gate is popularly abbreviated to Gnojna.

As strange as it may seem, Gnojna Góra was also thought to possess healing properties. Syphilis was one of many illnesses "treated" here, where the unfortunate patients were buried up to their necks in the mound. Regrettably, there is no record of how effective this treatment proved.

New Town

Nowe Miasto (New Town) was originally known as New Warsaw. The area began to develop at the end of the 14th century, alongside a thoroughfare leading from the Old Town to the village of Zakroczym, on the banks of the River Vistula. In 1408 Duke Janusz the Elder granted Nowe Miasto its own separate status, outside the jurisdiction of the mayor of the Old Town. The New Town established its own council and a Town Hall in the Market Square, as well as several churches and monasteries. Unlike the Old Town with its barbican, the New Town was not fortified. The peak of the New Town's evolution was the end of the 18th century. However, the New Town lost its independent status in 1791, when it was incorporated into the city of Warsaw. It then became known as the district of Nowe Miasto. After World War II, the New Town was carefully re-created, and it is now one of Warsaw's most popular districts.

An historic well in the Market Square

Sights at a Glance

Churches
Church of the Holy Spirit 2
Church of Jan Boży 18
Church of Our Lady, Queen of Poland 14
Church of St Benon 11
Church of St Francis 17
Our Lady Mary's Church 16
St Casimir's Church 10
St Jacek's Church 1

Historic Buildings
Old Gunpowder Depository 7
Raczyński Palace 13
Royal Well 20
Sapieha Palace 12
Warsaw's Smallest House 5

Museums and Galleries
Asia and Pacific Museum 6
Citadel Museum 21
Maria Skłodowska-Curie Museum 3

Historic Roads and Districts
Freta Street 8
Mostowa Street 4
New Town Market Square 9

Parks and Gardens
Traugutt Park 19

Monuments
Memorial of the Warsaw Uprising of 1944 15

Residential Districts
Żoliborz 22

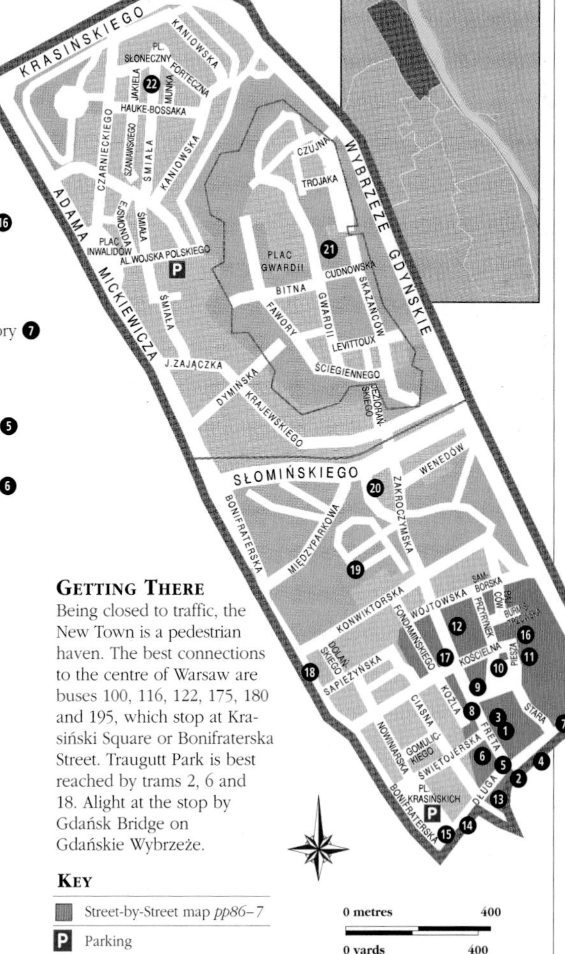

Getting There

Being closed to traffic, the New Town is a pedestrian haven. The best connections to the centre of Warsaw are buses 100, 116, 122, 175, 180 and 195, which stop at Krasiński Square or Bonifraterska Street. Traugutt Park is best reached by trams 2, 6 and 18. Alight at the stop by Gdańsk Bridge on Gdańskie Wybrzeże.

Key

Street-by-Street map *pp86–7*

P Parking

0 metres 400

0 yards 400

◁ **St Casimir's Church**

Street-by-Street: New Town

COLOURFUL HOUSES AND CHURCHES, which were rebuilt from ruins after World War II, feature among the attractions of the New Town. Here you can take a stroll along the steepest street in Warsaw, Mostowa Street. This leads to a tower which, in the 16th century, guarded the entrance to one of Europe's longest bridges.

Freta
The strange name of the New Town's main street originally meant "uncultivated field" and subsequently came to denote a suburb ❽

★ St Jacek's Church
The church's main feature – the magnificent 17th-century tomb of local burgher Adam Kotowski and his wife, Małgorzata – is the work of the celebrated Dutch architect, Tylman of Gameren ❶

Marie Curie
The house in which Marie Skłodowska-Curie was born in 1867 is now a museum ❸

Church of the Holy Spirit
Pilgrims travel from the steps of this Baroque church to the shrine of the Black Madonna at Częstochowa ❷

Old Gunpowder Depository
Once a bridge gate, later it became a gunpowder depository and then a prison; today it houses a theatre company ❼

★ New Town Market Square
A town hall once occupied the centre of this square ❾

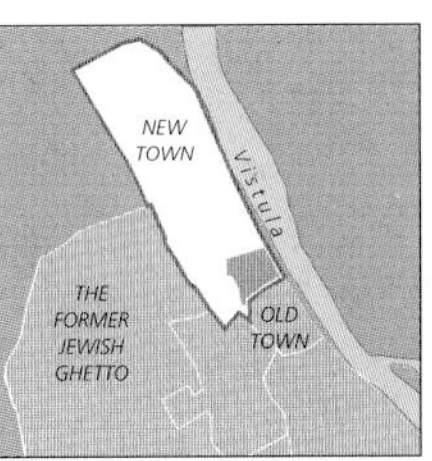

LOCATOR MAP
See Street Finder, maps 1, 3

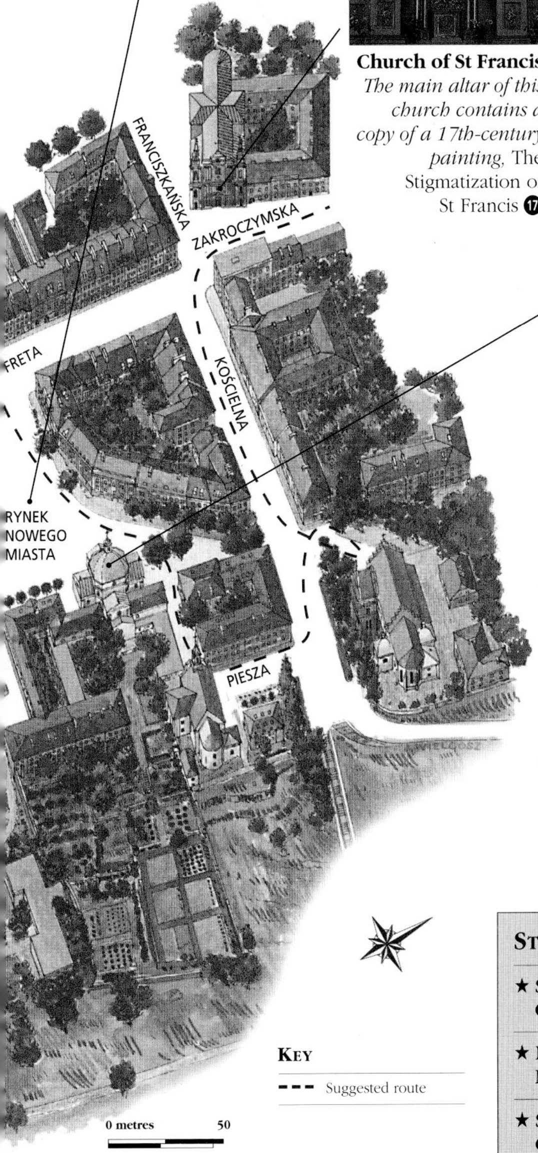

Church of St Francis
The main altar of this church contains a copy of a 17th-century painting, The Stigmatization of St Francis ⓱

★ St Casimir's Church
This Baroque church, designed by Tylman of Gameren, now has a modern interior ❿

A wooden bridge, the Zygmunt August Bridge, stretched across the River Vistula in the 16th century. It was one of the greatest engineering achievements of the Renaissance.

RYNEK NOWEGO MIASTA

KEY

- - - Suggested route

0 metres 50

0 yards 50

STAR SIGHTS

- ★ **St Jacek's Church**
- ★ **New Town Market Square**
- ★ **St Casimir's Church**

St Jacek's Church ❶

Kościół św. Jacka, Dominikanów

Freta 8/10. **Map** 1 C1. *635 47 00.* *116, 122, 174, 175, 180, 195, 303.*

At the beginning of the 17th century, while the Jesuits were building a Baroque church in the Old Town, the Dominicans began to construct a Gothic presbytery at St Jacek's church. The reason for choosing the Gothic style for

Church of St Jacek

their building may have been because of the order's conservative (even archaic) outlook. Alternatively it may have been an attempt to underline the Dominicans' ancient history, even though the order was only established in Warsaw in 1603.

Construction of St Jacek's Church was interrupted by a sudden outbreak of the plague in 1625. During this time the Dominicans would only hear confession and distribute

The Kotowski tombs in the Church of St Jacek

Holy Communion through small holes which were specially made in the church doors. The church was finally completed in 1639, next to the city's largest monastery.

St Jacek's has a side nave with a beautiful vaulted ceiling decorated in Lublin-style stucco work. This nave also features the tombs of Anna Tarnowska and Katarzyna Ossolińska who were the first of the four wives of Jerzy Ossoliński, the Voivode (Lord Lieutenant) of Podlasie region.

The magnificent chapel of Adam and Małgorzata Kotowski, which includes their portraits painted on a tin surface, was built in 1690–94 to the designs of Tylman of Gameren (the renowned Dutch architect who was exalted in Poland). Their black marble tombs are in the crypt. Adam Kotowski was the son of a Silesian peasant who moved to Warsaw, acquired vast wealth and became ennobled. Inscribed tablets within the church also commemorate Polish resistance leaders of World War II.

Pulpit in the Church of the Holy Spirit

Church of the Holy Spirit ❷

Kościół św. Ducha, Paulinów

Nowomiejska 23. **Map** 1 C1. *831 45 74.* *116, 122, 174, 175, 180, 195, 303.*

The original wooden Church of the Holy Spirit was built during the 14th century. Subsequently extended, it was razed in 1655 during the Swedish invasion. As the city lacked the funds to rebuild the church, King Jan Kazimierz donated the site to the Pauline Order of Częstochowa. This monastic order was famous for defending the Jasna Góra monastery in Częstochowa (Poland's holiest shrine) against the Swedes. The church was rebuilt in a Baroque style, between 1707–17, by Józef Piola and Józef Szymon Bellotti.

The Pauline monks constructed defensive walls around the church and adjoining the monastery, which were also integrated into the city's existing fortifications.

Since 1711, the church has served as a starting point for the annual pilgrimage to Jasna Góra monastery at Częstochowa, about 200 km (125 miles) south of Warsaw.

Marie Skłodowska-Curie (1867–1934)

Marie Skłodowska was 24 years old when she left Warsaw to study in Paris. Within seven years she had become internationally renowned as the co-founder of a new branch of science, radioactivity. Together with her French husband, Pierre Curie, she discovered two new radioactive elements: radium and polonium. In 1903 Marie Curie was the first woman to receive the Nobel Prize for physics. In 1911 she was awarded the Nobel Prize for chemistry. Marie Curie was also instrumental in establishing the Institute of Radiology in Paris. Following her death in 1934, she was interred in the family grave at Sceaux near Paris. In 1995 her remains were transferred to the Panthéon in Paris, which was a great tribute to Poland's foremost scientist.

The Church of the Holy Spirit seen from Mostowa Street

Marie Skłodowska-Curie Museum ❸

Muzeum Marii Skłodowskiej-Curie

Freta 16. **Map** 1 C1. *831 80 92.* *116, 122, 174, 175, 180, 195, 303.* *10am–4pm Tue–Sat, 10am–2pm Sun.*

THIS SMALL MUSEUM, established in the house where Marie Skłodowska-Curie was born, opened in 1967 on the centenary of her birth.

Various exhibits trace her successes and the challenges she faced. Films of Curie's life and the history of science can also be seen on request.

Mostowa Street ❹

Ulica Mostowa

Map 1 C1. *116, 122, 174, 175, 180, 195, 303.*

DESCENDING steeply towards the Vistula River, Mostowa Street (Bridge Street) is considered one of the most picturesque in Warsaw.

The street led to a wooden bridge which from 1575–1603 connected the New Town with the nearby village of Praga. By the 18th century, Mostowa Street featured brick buildings, with various inns and shops, as well as accommodation for craftsmen, shopkeepers, officials of the law courts and the police. Policemen were employed at the prison which was converted from the gate house by the bridge. Walking in the direction of the Vistula leads to the imposing Dominican church and monastery, which are situated adjacent to the junction with Freta Street.

Warsaw's Smallest House ❺

Najmniejszy Domek Warszawy

Długa 1. **Map** 1 C1. *116, 122, 174, 175, 180, 195, 303.*

THIS TINY HOUSE, which is attached to the Church of the Holy Spirit, is so small that it is now used merely as a newspaper kiosk. The house was built towards the end of the 18th century, and is Neo-Classical in style.

The kiosk which was originally Warsaw's smallest house

It always had the distinction of being the smallest house in Warsaw, occupying a site that only measures a few square metres. However, in spite of its size, the house always had an individual street number.

Asia and Pacific Museum ❻

Muzeum Azji i Pacyfiku

Freta 5. **Map** 1 C1. *635 28 11.* *116, 122, 174, 175, 180, 195, 303.* *11am–5pm Tue–Sun.*

THE MUSEUM has two exhibition venues, one on Freta Street and the other in Nowogrodzka Street, leading to the Asian and Nusantara collections respectively. Temporary exhibitions of Asian culture are also held in the museum.

Old Gunpowder Depository ❼

Stara Prochownia

Boleść 2. **Map** 2 D1. *116.*

ORIGINALLY this was a gatehouse by the wooden bridge that crossed the Vistula from 1575 to 1603. Designed and built by Erazm Cziotko of Zakroczym, the bridge was financed by King Zygmunt August and his sister Anna.

Destroyed in 1603 by ice-floes, some of the bridge's oak columns remained submerged in the river until salvaged in the mid-19th century. The Russian field marshal Paskiewicz used them to make furniture for his palace in Belarus.

From 1646, the gatehouse was used to store gunpowder. In 1767 it became a prison. Inmates included the 18th-century schemer Maria Dogrum, who falsely accused the king's valet of trying to poison Duke Adam Kazimierz Czartoryski. In 1831 the prison was converted into rented accommodation.

Burned in World War II and rebuilt in 1961–5, the gatehouse is now headquarters for a theatre company.

Triangular pediment on the façade of the Old Gunpowder Depository

Freta Street 8
Ulica Freta

Map 3 C4 & 1 C1. 🚌 *116, 122, 174, 175, 180, 303.*

Now the main thoroughfare of Nowe Miasto, Freta Street was originally laid out as a section of road to link Warsaw with the nearby village of Zakroczym.

The first houses were built on Freta Street during the 14th century, though it wasn't until a century later that Freta Street was incorporated into the town of Nowe Miasto.

Before World War II, Freta Street's shops were principally occupied by milliners and makers of artificial flowers.

Baroque window in Pod Opatrznością house in Freta Street

Now the choice includes antique shops, restaurants and cafés. Recommended are Pod Samsonem restaurant *(see p214)* and Pożegnanie z Afryką (Farewell to Africa) café, which serves some of the city's best coffee.

New Town Market Square 9
Rynek Nowego Miasta

Map 3 C4 & 1 C1. 🚌 *116, 122, 174, 175, 180, 195, 303.*

The market square is the heart of the New Town. It was formerly rectangular, but various redevelopments have produced an irregular triangular shape. The Town Hall (Ratusz) stood in the centre of the market square until 1818, when it was demolished. However, this also opened up a splendid view of St Casimir's Church.

Snow and sunlight on New Town Market Square in winter

The market square was reconstructed after the war, but not very accurately, and the façades of several houses were covered by murals in Socialist Realist style. Near the junction with Freta Street there is a charming 19th-century well.

St Casimir's Church 10
Kościół św. Kazimierza

Rynek Nowego Miasta 2. **Map** 3 C4 & 1 C1. ☎ *635 71 13.* 🚌 *116, 122, 174, 175, 180, 195, 303.* ***Convent*** ● *to the public.*

The church and convent belonging to the French order of the Sisters of the Blessed Sacrament was founded in about 1688 by King Jan III Sobieski and Queen Maria Kazimiera.

The church was designed by Tylman of Gameren in a late Baroque style. The interior, originally decorated with frescoes, is now plain white. The best feature is the tombstone of Princess Marie Caroline de Bouillon, the granddaughter of Jan III Sobieski. The tombstone was set in 1746 by Bishop Andrzej Załuski, along with Prince Michał Kazimierz Radziwiłł, who was suitor of the princess. The broken shield and toppling crowns which decorate the tomb are taken from the Sobieski coat-of-arms, but also refer to the end of the Sobieski family line.

The green-domed roof on St Casimir's Church

A splendid garden that lies behind the convent has remained unchanged since the 17th century. At its edge, terraces descend to the flowing waters of the River Vistula.

Church of St Benon ⓫

Kościół św. Benona

Piesza 1. **Map** 1 C1. 🚌 *116, 122, 174, 175, 303, 503.*

THIS DIMINUTIVE CHURCH was founded in 1787 by King Stanisław August Poniatowski on behalf of Redemptorist monks. These monks were in

The New Town's 18th-century Church of St Benon

the care of abbot Clement Dworzak, a Moravian, who was sent to Warsaw from Rome. He opened two orphanages, one for girls and one for boys, while also providing for the orphans' continued education.

In 1808, unfounded accusations that the monks were spying for the Austrians led the Napoleonic authorities to expel the abbot and 30 monks, and close the church. For the next 100 years it was used to manufacture knives and kitchen utensils. The Redemptorists returned after the war to rebuild the church. The modern interiors also include original sculptures.

Sapieha Palace ⓬

Pałac Sapiehów

Zakroczymska 6. **Map** 3 C4. ☎ *831 32 09.* 🚌 *174, 175, 503.* ***Not open*** *to the public.*

The Rococo façade of Sapieha Palace

THIS VAST former palace originally belonged to the princely Sapieha family. It was built in 1731–46 for Jan Fryderyk Sapieha, who was the Chancellor of the Grand Duchy of Lithuania. The powerful Polish-Lithuanian Commonwealth, which united the two countries, had been inaugurated in the 16th century, and by the mid-18th, it was Europe's largest empire.

The architect of the Sapieha palace, Jan Zygmunt Deybel, was also an officer in the Saxon Corps of Engineers. Designed in a Rococo style, the palace has an impressive façade which includes an ornamental triangular pediment, as well as urns, sculptures and a balcony.

Magdalena Sapieha, née Lubomirska, who was married to one of the later owners of the palace, was a lively character and renowned as a society beauty, which made her the toast of 18th-century Warsaw. When Stanisław August Poniatowski was still young (and before ascending the throne), he had been in love with Magdalena Sapieha.

The palace was converted for use as an army barracks in the 19th century, and its magnificent gardens were used, somewhat incongruously, for military exercises. The Fourth Polish Infantry regiment, which played an important and heroic role during the 1830–31 uprising, was stationed at the palace.

Having been burnt by the Nazis in 1944, the façade was restored in its original style. The interiors were converted for use as a school.

The Church of St Casimir in New Town Market Square

Raczyński Palace ⓭

Pałac Raczyńskich

Długa 7. **Map** 1 C1. 🚌 *116, 122, 174, 175, 180, 195, 303.*

THIS PALACE, which now serves as an archive for ancient documents, was completed in 1786. It was designed by the royal architect Jan Chrystian Kamsetzer.

An interesting feature of the palace is the reconstructed early Neo-Classical ballroom. This is decorated with stucco work and allegorical paintings representing Justice. Ironically, the life and deeds of the original owner, Kazimierz Raczyński, the chief marshal of the crown, were at odds with these allegorical paintings. Public opinion branded him corrupt and a traitor to his country.

In the 19th century, the palace was the seat of the Government Justice Commission, and during the interwar years it housed the Ministry of Justice.

The palace witnessed several tragic events during World War II. One wall retains bullet marks from the public execution of 50 men, who were stopped at random in the vicinity of the palace on 24 January 1944. On 13 August 1944, during the Warsaw Uprising, a German tank-trap loaded with ammunition exploded nearby, killing 80 resistance fighters. On 2 September 1944, when the palace was serving as a field hospital, the infamous SS arrived and murdered several hundred of the wounded.

The dignified, Neo-Classical façade of the Raczyński Palace

Church of Our Lady, Queen of Poland ⓮

Katedra Polowa Wojska Polskiego

Długa 13/15. **Map** 1 C2. ☎ *831 93 81.* 🚌 *116, 122, 174, 175, 180, 195, 303.*

Church of Our Lady, Queen of Poland

DESIGNED BY Tytus Boratini, this Baroque church was built in 1660–82. Its Palladian façade, designed by Jakub Fontana, was constructed in 1758–69.

The church features seven ornamental altars, with paintings by prominent artists of the time, including Szymon Czechowicz and Jan Bogumił Plersch. It also provided an office for Fr Stanisław Konarski (1700–73) of the Piarist order. He was equally a politician, educational reformer and founder of the Collegium Nobilium *(see p100)*.

Anchor from the Church of Our Lady

In 1835, tsarist authorities commandeered the building, converting it into a Russian Orthodox church. The steeples were replaced by onion domes, which remained in place until Poland regained independence in 1918. The church was then carefully restored to its original design.

Now serving as the cathedral church of the Polish Armed Forces, the walls are lined with plaques commemorating all the servicemen who fell during World War II.

Memorial of the Warsaw Uprising of 1944 ⓯

Pomnik Powstania Warszawskiego 1944

Plac Krasińskich. **Map** 1 C1 & 3 C4. 🚌 *100, 116, 122, 175, 180, 195, 303, 503.*

UNVEILED IN 1989, this memorial was designed by Wincenty Kućma, within an architectural setting devised by Jacek Budyn. It consists of two bronze groups: soldiers defending a barricade and others descending into the sewers. Many sewers were used during the Uprising as a means of communication between isolated combat groups. The manhole of one such sewer entrance has been preserved at the junction of Długa Street and Krasiński Square. During the 50th anniversary commemorations of the Uprising in 1994, the German President Roman Herzog visited the memorial and apologized to the Polish nation for what it suffered during World War II, and for the bloody means the Nazis used to quell the Uprising.

Our Lady Mary's Visitation Church ⓰

Kościół H Nawiedzenia NMP

Przyrynek 2. **Map** 3 C3. *175, 503.* *831 24 73.*

The parish church of the Virgin Mary is the oldest church in Nowe Miasto. It was founded by Anna, the wife of Duke Janusz the Elder, at the beginning of the 15th century. Legend has it that the church was built on a site where pagan rituals had been held.

During its 19th-century refurbishments, the church changed architecturally. Having been destroyed during World War II, the church was restored to its original 15th-century Gothic style. The presbytery was reconstructed solely using medieval methods, which precluded the use of pre-cast building materials.

The churchyard also includes a memorial to Major Walerian Łukasiński (1786–1868), who founded the National Patriotic Association during the tsarist occupation. A terrace by the church provides wonderful views across the rooftops of the Old Town, the River Vistula and the Praga district beyond.

Church of St Francis ⓱

Kościół św. Franciszka, Franciszkanów

Zakroczymska 1. **Map** 3 C3. *175, 503.* *831 20 31.*

Franciscans first settled in Warsaw in 1645, and construction of the Church of St Francis began in 1679.

A section of the Memorial to the Heroes of the Warsaw Uprising

However, completing the church was a slow process. While it was consecrated in 1737, the finishing touches to the façade weren't completed until 1788. Not surprisingly, several architects were involved in the design of the church. These included Jan Ceroni, Antoni Solari, Jakub and Józef Fontana as well as Józef Boretti.

Subsequently, the nave retained a Baroque manner, while the façade was topped with obelisks that have lent it a Neo-Classical appearance.

The church is also significant for its religious relics. A glass coffin, for instance, contains the bones of the former Roman legionnaire who became Saint Vitus. These bones were given to the Franciscans by Pope Benedict XIV in 1745.

Also worth seeing are the Baroque epitaphs of two of the church's benefactors, together with their portraits. One benefactor is depicted wearing Sarmatian armour; Sarmatia was an ancient province in southeast Poland.

A painting of St Anthony of Padua hangs in a side chapel of the church. Painted by Mateusz in 1664, it is considered to be one of the most valuable examples of 17th-century Varsovian art.

The Church of St Francis, with its dark, hard-edged towers

Church of Jan Boży ⓲

Kościół św. Jana Bożego

Bonifraterska 12. **Map** 1 B1 & 3 C4. *100, 116, 122, 174, 175, 180, 195, 303, 503.* *2, 15, 18, 35, 36.* *831 41 40.*

This modest church, built in 1726

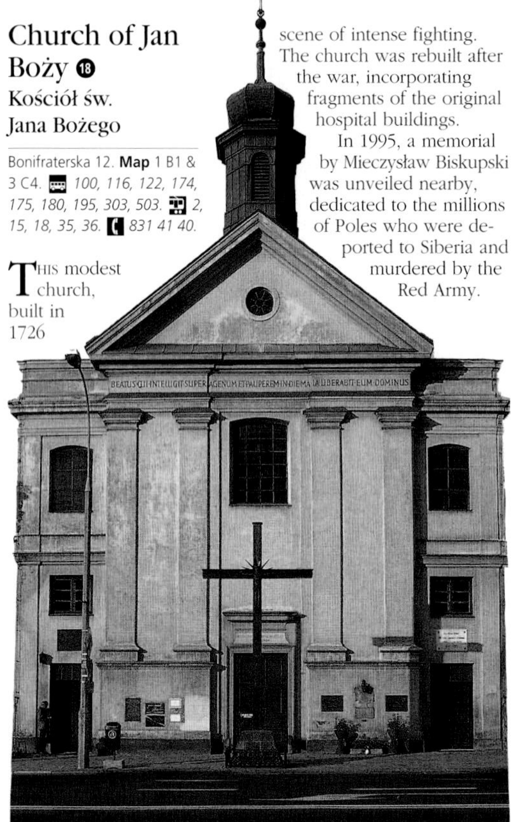

The modest façade of the Church of Jan Boży

and designed by Józef Fontana and Antoni Solari, belonged to the Bonifraters' monastic order. The order was established in the 16th century with the aim of caring for the ill and infirm. Next to the church was a hospital, which was among the first to care for the mentally ill. Unfortunately, until about the mid-19th century, doctors were poorly equipped to deal with mentally ill patients. Treatments were limited to doses of castor oil, poppy-seed potions, colonic irrigation, hot and cold baths, and bleeding the patients.

In 1760 the hospital was enlarged by the architect Jakub Fontana. At that time it was customary to hold an annual open day during Whitsuntide, when Varsovians could visit the hospital.

During the 1944 Warsaw Uprising, the hospital was the scene of intense fighting. The church was rebuilt after the war, incorporating fragments of the original hospital buildings.

In 1995, a memorial by Mieczysław Biskupski was unveiled nearby, dedicated to the millions of Poles who were deported to Siberia and murdered by the Red Army.

Traugutt Park ⓳

Park Traugutta

Zakroczymska. **Map** 3 C3. *103, 127, 175, 503.* *1, 2, 6, 18.*

The Traugutt Park was laid out in 1925, on the site of historic fortifications which surrounded the city's 19th-century citadel. The existing Legionnaire's Fort, with its preserved earth and brickwork fortifications, is where members of the Polish National Council were executed by a Russian firing squad, following the 1863 uprising. The park is named after the insurgents' leader, Romuald Traugutt, who was the last to be shot. The site of this execution is marked by a memorial, established in 1916.

In one of the park's more secluded spots, standing on a red granite plinth, is a statue of a mother and child. This allegorical, Secessionist statue represents Motherhood. Dating from 1902, it is the work of the accomplished Polish sculptor Wacław Szymanowski, whose statues can also be seen in Powązki cemetery *(see p46)*.

The park is extensive and well maintained. While it provides delightful walks, it is not advisable to wander there after dark.

Statue representing Motherhood in Traugutt Park

Royal Well ⓴

Zdrój Królewski

Zakroczymska. **Map** 3 C3. *103, 127, 175, 503.* *1, 2, 6, 18.*

The Royal Well was a source of exceptionally pure and palatable water. It was originally enclosed by a small pavilion built in the early 18th century. This pavilion was then redesigned in 1771, at the request of King Stanisław August Poniatowski.

Records of workmen who were employed on the rebuilding project show that they received an extra payment to buy cudgels, which were intended to protect them against thieves on their way home at night.

In 1832, when the Russians were constructing the nearby citadel, they covered the Royal Well with soil. A few years later it was uncovered, and a Neo-Gothic pavilion was built around it, designed by the Polish architect Henryk Marconi.

The Neo-Gothic pavilion that stands over the Royal Well

Warsaw Citadel and Independence Museum 21

Cytadela Warszawska i Muzeum Niepodległości

Museum, Pavilion X, Skazańców 25. **Map** 3 C2. *839 12 68.* *185, 318.* *2, 6, 18 (entails walking from Gdańsk Bridge).* *9am–4pm Wed–Sun.*

THE CITADEL is an enormous fortress, which was built by the Russians, not to defend the city from outside attack, but to intimidate its inhabitants.

Construction of the citadel was ordered by Tsar Nicholas II in 1832, following the November 1830 insurrection. Based on a design by General Ivan Dehn, the citadel was built in stages and finally completed in 1887. This entailed destroying the barracks of the former Royal Guards, as well as the Piarist monastery and the residential area of Żoliborz.

The citizens of Warsaw had to bear the astronomical cost of building the citadel. Meanwhile, Russian officials and army officers made their fortunes by investing money in this development.

The brick and earth fortress, encircled by a moat and defensive brick wall, stands on a hill close to the River Vistula, and dominates the surrounding area.

Four Neo-Classical gates lead to the interior, where a range of buildings include the so-called "tenth pavilion". This was a high security prison, used solely to house Polish political prisoners. Following World War II, this pavilion was refurbished to provide an exhibition venue. Currently it houses a branch of the Independence Museum, tracing Polish history since the 18th-century partitions. One of the museum's prized possessions is a *kibitka*, a carriage which was used to transport Polish political prisoners to the labour camps of Siberia.

Some of the citadel's other buildings are occupied by the European Academy of Arts.

Former Officers' Quarters in Żoliborz 22

Żoliborz Oficerski

Between Mickiewicza, Krasiński, pl Inwalidów and al Wojska Polskiego. **Map** 3 B2. *116, 122, 157, 195, 303.* *4, 6, 15, 36.*

A cannon on the citadel's ramparts

THIS AREA forms part of the large residential district of Żoliborz, developed between the wars. Much of Żoliborz incorporated the citadel's esplanade, an open area in front of the citadel, which left any attackers exposed.

Redeveloped in the 1920s as a housing estate for military personnel, the quiet streets were lined with charming villas, designed in a traditional country-house style. The façades were typically ornamented with columns and porticoes, and distinctive stepped roofs.

Neighbouring this area, which was then known as Officers' Żoliborz, was the Bureaucrats' Żoliborz, housing civil servants.

Following these developments, the Warsaw Housing Co-operative built blocks of flats to provide comfortable but inexpensive accommodation for the city's workers. However, this district remained separate from its grander neighbours, divided by Krasiński Street.

Construction of these housing projects provided architects with the opportunity to develop avant-garde concepts. The apartment blocks of particular interest are the so-called gallery flats, built in an open arch along Suzin Street in 1932, and designed by Stanisław and Barbara Brukalski. The blocks were separated by wide green spaces which were an innovation in Warsaw. The apartment blocks owned by the State Insurance Institution were built to the highest standards. The house at 34–36 Mickiewicz Street, designed by Juliusz Żórawski and built in the late 1930s, is an example of the influence of the renowned Modernist architect Le Corbusier.

A *kibitka* in the Independence Museum within the citadel

AROUND SOLIDARITY AVENUE

From the end of the 18th century to the mid-19th, Solidarity Avenue (Aleja Solidarności) and Plac Teatralny (Theatre Square) was Warsaw's commercial and cultural centre. The grand Neo-Classical buildings of the area, with their impressive colonnades, were constructed in the 1820s. These include the Grand Theatre (Teatr Wielki), which is one of the largest buildings of its kind in Europe. The area also features several large parks. The Krasiński Gardens (adjoining the magnificent Krasiński Palace) were first laid out in the late 17th century.

19th-century fountain by the Muranów cinema

The Saxon Gardens (Ogród Saski) were designed in a Baroque style, as part of a town planning scheme known as the Saxon Axis. The Saxon Gardens are all that remain of the former Royal Park, which encircled the residence of the Saxon King August II Mocny in the 18th century. A 19th-century colonnade originally divided the Saxon Gardens from Piłsudski Square, where official State functions are held. This is also where the Tomb of the Unknown Soldier, featuring a guard of honour and an eternal flame, was established in 1925.

SIGHTS AT A GLANCE

Churches and Monasteries

Basilian Church of the Assumption of the Blessed Virgin Mary 2
Capuchin Church of the Transfiguration 6
St Anthony of Padua Reformed Church 25

Historic Buildings

Arsenal 11
Collegium Nobilium 1
Former Bank of Poland 17
Former Landau Bank 23
Former State Bank 13
Grand Theatre 20
Kings' House 14
Mansions on Długa Street 10
Town Hall 16
Western & Discount Banks 19

Palaces

Blue Palace 22
Branicki Palace 3
Krasiński Palace 8
Morsztyn Palace 4
Pac Palace 7
Primate's Palace 26
Przebendowski-Radziwiłł Palace 12

Monuments

Jan Kiliński Monument 5
St John of Nepomuk Monument 24

Squares

Bank Square 15
Theatre Square 21

Historic Parks and Gardens

Krasiński Gardens 9
Saxon Gardens 18

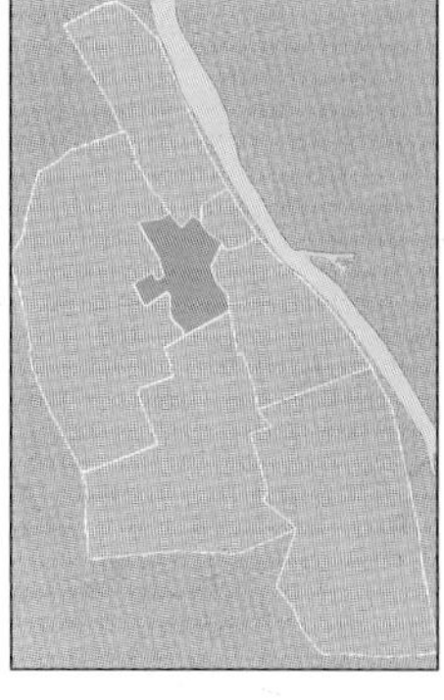

GETTING THERE

This area is adjacent to the city centre, and served by various tram and bus routes. Buses E-2, 107, 111, 119, 125, 166, 170, 171, 190, 406, 409, 410 and trams 2, 4, 15, 18, 26, 32, 35 and 36 all stop in Bank Square (Plac Bankowy). If you are travelling from the direction of Krakowskie Przedmieście and the south-central area, buses 116, 122, 174, 175, 185, 195, and 303 can all be taken from Nowy Świat and Krakowskie Przedmieście.

KEY

Map *see pp98–9*
P Parking

0 metres 400
0 yards 400

◁ **The former Bank of Poland and Stock Exchange in Bank Square**

Street-by-Street: Miodowa

As Miodowa street lies just outside the Old Town, it is often overlooked by visitors. However, the attractions of this elegant street include three Baroque churches and several palaces, set behind spacious courtyards. One of these, the Borch Palace, is now the seat of the Primate of Poland.

★ Capuchin Church of the Transfiguration
Founded in the 17th century by King Jan III Sobieski, it houses an urn containing his heart ❻

Borch Palace has been the seat of the Primate of Poland since 1843. However, its history is less pious. Built in the 17th century for Count Piotr Ricourt, this was the city's most notorious haven for gamblers. In the 1780s, the palace was refurbished by Dominik Merlini for the Deputy Crown Chancellor Jan Borch. The French-style garden has retained an exquisite pavilion.

Kraków Bishops' Palace was built as a residence by Bishop Kajetan Sołtyk in 1760–62. Having been largely destroyed in World War II, the palace was painstakingly restored to its original form.

Two stones stand outside the entrance of the Kraków Bishops' Palace. The stones have unusual openings that were originally used to extinguish burning torches.

Key

- - - Suggested route

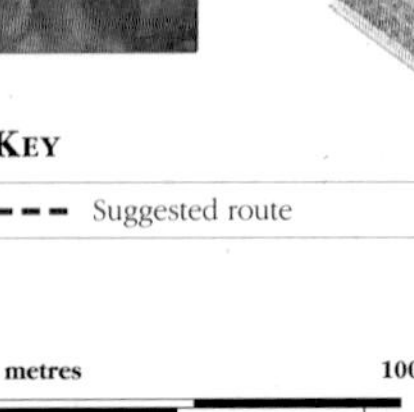

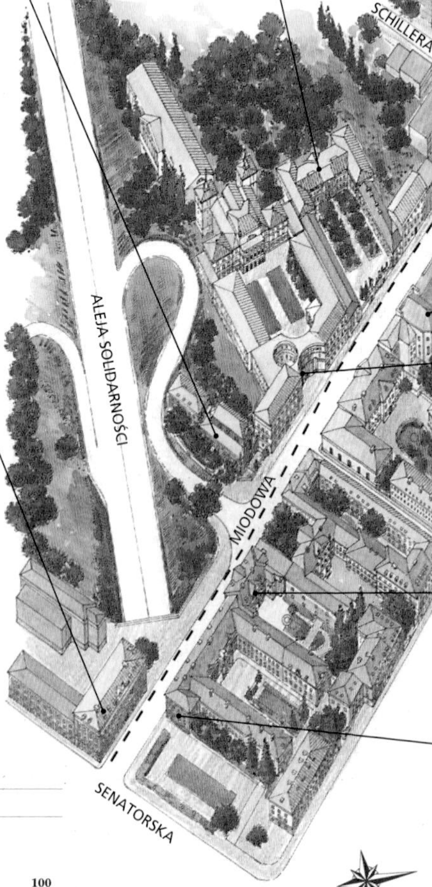

Krasiński Palace
One of two Neo-Classical wellheads of 1823–4 standing in front of the palace ❽

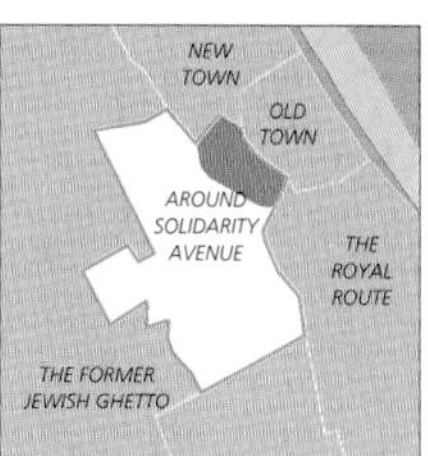

LOCATOR MAP
See Street Finder, maps 1, 3

Collegium Nobilium
The 18th-century building of the Collegium Nobilium now houses the Academy of Dramatic Arts ❶

Basilian Church of the Assumption of the Blessed Virgin Mary
This Ukrainian-Catholic church, which dates from the 18th century, boasts a grand and imposing façade ❷

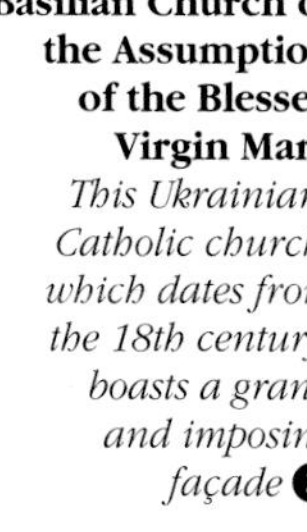

★ Pac Palace
The palace's finest feature is a emi-circular gateway, with Neo-Classical frieze by sculptor udwik Kaufmann ❼

Morsztyn Palace
This was once the Russian ambassador's residence, and was attacked during the 1794 insurrection ❹

Branicki Palace
The palace's Rococo façade is decorated with fine statues and sculptures ❸

STAR SIGHTS

- ★ **Pac Palace**
- ★ **Capuchin Church of the Transfiguration**

Collegium Nobilium ❶

Akademia Teatralna (Academy of the Dramatic Arts)

Miodowa 22/24. **Map** 1 C2 & 3 C4. *831 02 16.* *100, 116, 122, 160, 174, 175, 180, 192, 195, 303, 503.* ***Not open** to the public.*

THIS 18TH-CENTURY building originally housed the Collegium Nobilium, Poland's finest school for young nobles. It was established by Piarist monks, led by Father Stanisław Konarski, an academic and reformer during the Enlightenment. Built in 1743–1754 in a Rococo style, it was redesigned in 1786 in Neo-Classical style.

The school occupied the building until 1807, and was closed by the Russians after the insurrection of 1830–31. The building now houses the Academy of the Dramatic Arts, and is dedicated to the great Polish actor Aleksander Zelwerowicz.

Basilian Church of the Assumption of the Blessed Virgin Mary ❷

Kościół Wniebowzięcia NMP, Bazylianów

Miodowa 16. **Map** 1 C2 & 3 C4. *831 17 18.* *100, 116, 122, 160, 174, 175, 180, 190, 195, 303, 503.*

THE NEO-CLASSICAL façade looks palatial but in fact it belongs to the Basilian church. It was designed by Dominik Merlini and built in 1782–4. The interior is a postwar reconstruction and includes paintings by the 18th-century Polish artist Franciszek Smuglewicz.

Branicki Palace ❸

Pałac Branickich

Miodowa 6. **Map** 1 C2 & 3 C4. *100, 116, 122, 160, 174, 175, 190, 195, 303, 503.* ***Not open** to the public.*

FOLLOWING ALMOST complete destruction during World War II, this Rococo palace

Façade of the Basilian Church

was rebuilt between 1947 and 1953, using detailed historical research and 18th-century paintings for guidance.

Originally designed as a residence for the king's advisor, Jan Klemens Branicki, construction of the palace was first undertaken in 1740, by the architects Jan Zygmunt Deybel and Jakub Fontana.

Branicki was a distinguished soldier, but also a connoisseur of fine art, especially from France. He therefore travelled to Paris to acquire silver, porcelain, furniture and even marble fireplaces for his residences. His Warsaw palace was decorated with the advice of celebrated artists, such as the sculptor Jan Chryzostom Redler.

The palace faces Podwale Street, with the extensive forecourt entered through an ornamental gateway. Equally attractive is the façade overlooking Miodowa Street, which features Rococo sculptures. However, these are not original, having been fashioned in the 1950s.

Morsztyn Palace ❹

Pałac Morsztynów

Miodowa 10. **Map** 1 C2 & 3 C4. *100, 116, 122, 160, 174, 175, 180, 192, 195, 303, 503.* ***Not open** to the public.*

ORIGINALLY COMPLETED at the end of the 17th century, subsequent rebuilding gave this palace a late Baroque façade and Neo-Classical out buildings. In the early 18th century it was owned by the Voivode (Lord Lieutenant) of the Sandomierz region, Stefan Bidziński. He was a fearless soldier, famous for donating a vast sum to release the noblemen of Sandomierz from their Muslim captors.

Subsequent owners of the palace included J Massalski, the bishop of Vilnius, a distinguished man of letters. But as he was also a gambler and a rake, and expropriated former Jesuit estates, he was hanged during the 1794 Kościuszko Insurrection. On 17–18 April 1794, the palace (which had been the Russian ambassador's residence since 1790) was the scene of a fierce battle between Russian troops and Varsovians. Apparently, when the Russians finally ran out of shot, in desperation they used coins and buttons instead.

Attack on the Morsztyn Palace

The façade of Branicki Palace from Miodowa Street

Jan Kiliński Monument ❺

Pomnik Jana Kilińskiego

Podwale. **Map** 1 C2 & 3 C4. *116, 122, 174, 175, 195, 303.*

COMPLETED IN 1936 by Stanisław Jackowski, this monument honours Jan Kiliński, a hero of the 1794 Kościuszko Insurrection. Originally a cobbler, Kiliński became a colonel in the army. During the insurrection he led a successful attack on Morsztyn Palace *(see p100)*, which was then the Russian ambassador's residence.

Originally erected in Krasiński Square, the monument was removed in 1942 by the Nazis and hidden in the vaults of the National Museum (Muzeum Narodowe). Graffiti soon appeared on a wall of the museum, painted by boy scouts from the Szare Szeregi division of the Resistance, saying: "People of Warsaw, I am in here, Jan Kiliński." Reconstructed in 1945, the monument was moved to its present site a few years later.

Jan Kiliński Monument

Capuchin Church of the Transfiguration ❻

Kościół Przemienienia Pańskiego, Kapucynów

Kapucyńska 4. **Map** 1 C2 & 3 C5. *831 31 09. 116, 122, 174, 175, 179, 180, 195.*

THIS BAROQUE CHURCH, built by Izydor Affaita between 1683 and 1692, is thought to have been designed by Tylman of Gameren and Augustyn Locci, then completed by Karol Ceroni. Founded by King Jan III Sobieski, in gratitude for his victory over the Turks at Vienna in 1683, the church has a modest façade modelled on the Capuchin church in Rome. The somewhat ascetic interior also features unusual epitaphs.

The king's chapel contains a Rococo urn with the ashes of King August II Mocny, and a 19th-century sarcophagus containing the heart of King Jan III Sobieski. Another chapel houses an 18th-century marble urn, by Jan Redler, dedicated to Anna (née Kolowrath), wife of Henryk Brühl, a hated minister at the court of King August II Mocny.

Since 1948 the church vaults have housed a nativity scene with moving figures, of particular interest to children.

A limited use of colour, and an absence of gilt, is a feature of the altars in the Capuchin Church, as monastic rules insist on the pursuance of poverty.

Pac Palace ❼

Pałac Paca

Miodowa 15. **Map** 1 C2 & 3 C4. *116, 122, 174, 175, 180, 195, 303.* *by arrangement.*

ORIGINALLY A RESIDENCE of the Radziwiłł family, this Baroque palace was designed by Tylman of Gameren, and built between 1681 and 1697.

The palace was the scene of an historic event, on the night of 3 November 1771, when a rival royalist group kidnapped King Stanisław August Poniatowski, in front of the palace gates. However, this disorganized plot soon failed, and by the following morning the king had returned to his castle.

Between 1824 and 1828 the architect Henryk Marconi completely redesigned the palace, on behalf of the new owner, Ludwik Pac. The interiors featured Gothic, Renaissance, Greek and Moorish styles, while the façade was refashioned in a Palladian manner.

The impressive semi-circular gateway, which opens onto Miodowa Street, was modelled on a triumphal arch. The gateway's Neo-Classical reliefs depict the Roman Counsel Fleminius, granting freedom to the Greek cities. This was the work of Ludwik Kaufmann, a pupil of the celebrated sculptor Antonio Canova. The building currently houses the Ministry of Health.

Neo-Gothic style in Pac Palace

Krasiński Palace ❽
Pałac Krasińskich

Plac Krasińskich 5. **Map** 1 C2 & 3 C4. *635 62 09.* *100, 116, 122, 174, 175, 180, 195, 303, 503, 518.* *by prior arrangement.*

THIS BAROQUE PALACE is regarded as one of the most beautiful buildings in Warsaw. Constructed between 1687 and 1700, it was designed by Tylman of Gameren for the mayor of Warsaw, Jan Dobrogost Krasiński.

A triangular pediment features ornamental reliefs, depicting the heroic deeds of the legendary Roman patrician, Marcus Valerius (known as Corvinus), an ancestor of Jan Dobrogost Krasiński. The reliefs are the work of Andreas Schlüter, an outstandingly gifted sculptor and architect who later designed the Arsenal and Royal Castle in Berlin.

The Krasiński residence was originally furnished with great opulence. It included a gallery featuring the works of Rembrandt, Rubens, Dürer and Correggio. The palace was owned by the Krasiński family until 1765. Thereafter it housed the royal treasury, followed by various legal departments throughout the 19th century.

Rebuilt after World War II, the Krasiński Palace now houses a collection of antique prints and manuscripts from the National Library (Biblioteka Narodowa).

Triangular pediment with ornamental reliefs at the Krasiński Palace

Krasiński Gardens ❾
Ogród Krasińskich

Map 1 B2 & 3 C4. *100, 116, 122, 174, 175, 180, 195, 303.* *2, 15, 18, 35.*

TYLMAN of Gameren designed the 17th-century Krasiński Palace gardens and the Baroque gateway, as well as the palace itself. The gardens have been open to the public since 1776, when Krasiński Palace was taken over by the royal treasury.

The gardens were redesigned several times during the 19th century. From around 1900 until the start of World War II, the gardens were very popular with Jewish residents from northern Warsaw, which had few open spaces. Since the war the gardens have been greatly enlarged, and are now divided into several sections by avenues.

Summer in Krasiński Gardens

Mansions on Długa Street ❿
Pałacyki przy Długiej

Map 1 C2, 1 B2, 3 C4 & 3 C5. *116, 122, 174, 175, 180, 195, 303.*

DŁUGA STREET contains several mansions, and uniformly they each feature a courtyard enclosed by ornamental railings.

The façade of the 18th-century house at No. 26, formerly owned by Maria Radziwiłł, née Lubomirska, includes a triangular pediment featuring the Lubomirski family crest. Opposite, at Nos. 23–25 is a Neo-Classical mansion, which has an unusual, irregular forecourt.

Długa Street's most interesting building is the Baroque Four Winds Palace (Pałac Pod Czterema Wiatrami) at Nos. 38–40. Its ornamental gateway features statues which personify the four winds: Notus, Boreas, Eurus and Zephyrus.

Following their reconstruction after World War II, all of the buildings on Długa Street now house a wide range of public offices.

Statue at The Four Winds Palace

Arsenal ⓫
Arsenał

Długa 52. **Map** 1 B2 & 3 C5. *831 15 37.* *E-2, 107, 111, 116, 170, 190, 307.* *2, 4, 13, 15, 18, 32, 36.* *9am–4pm Mon–Fri, 10am–4pm Sun.* *Sat, every third Sun & July.* *free on Sun.*

THIS EARLY BAROQUE arsenal was built between 1638–47 on the orders of King Władysław IV Waza. One of Warsaw's fortified buildings, it now houses the Museum of Archaeology.

The exhibits have been collected from archaeological digs within Poland's prewar borders, as well as the current Polish Republic. There are also exhibits from other European countries, Asia, the Americas, and Africa. The exhibition of prehistoric Poland is also highly recommended. By prior arrangement, visitors can also make clay pots using prehistoric methods.

Przebendowski-Radziwiłł Palace ⓬
Pałac Przebendowskich-Radziwiłłów

Al. Solidamości 62. **Map** 1 C2 & 3 C5. *826 90 91.* *E-2, E-4, 107, 111, 119, 127, 171, 190, 406, 409, 410, 512.* *2, 4, 13, 15, 18, 32, 35, 36.* **Independence Museum** *10am–5pm Tue–Fri, 10am–4pm Sat & Sun.* *www.muzeum.zk.pl*

One of Warsaw's most beautiful palaces, it was built in 1728 for Jan Jerzy Przebendowski, who was

Przebendowski-Radziwiłł Palace

King August II's treasurer. The design, by Jan Zygmunt Deybel, features mansard roofs (with two slopes on both sides and both ends), as well as a bow front.

From 1760, for two years the palace was occupied by the Spanish envoy, Count Pedro Aranda. A fierce opponent of the Spanish Inquisition, he founded the Spanish Masonic Lodge and instigated the banishment of Jesuits from Spain. During his spell in Poland, the count also held magnificent parties.

The palace's quiet location in a narrow shopping street changed after the East–West tunnel was constructed in 1948–9. That resulted in the palace being surrounded by a major traffic artery. After the war the palace became the Lenin Museum. Since 1990 it has housed the Independence Museum (Muzeum Niepodległości), with a collection of documents relating Poland's history from the 18th-century partition to the present day.

Former State Bank ⓭
Dawny Bank Państwa

Bielańska 16. **Map** 1 C2 & 3 C5. *107, 111.* ***No admission*** *during redevelopment.*

Formerly occupied by the Russian State Bank, this building was built in 1906–11. Designed by the tsar's court architect from St Petersburg, Leontij N Benois, it included yellow and red sandstone slabs.

For over 50 years the building's battered walls bore witness to the battles of the Warsaw Uprising, when it was used as a military post defending access to the Old Town. The ruins have been included in the façade of a modern office building, which will also house the Museum dedicated to the Warsaw Uprising.

King Zygmunt III Waza

Kings' House ⓮
Dom Pod Królami

Daniłowiczowska 14/Hipoteczna 2. **Map** 1 C2 & 3 C5. *827 60 61.* *107, 111.* *8am–4pm.*

Despite its name, this was never a royal residence. The building owes its name to the gallery of Polish monarchs on the façade. These range from Mieszko I to Stanisław August Poniatowski. These stone portraits were discovered during refurbishment carried out in 1821, and built into the façade 80 years later. The building, however, is much older; it was constructed from 1617–24 as a seat of Mikołaj Daniłowicz of Żurów.

Following its reconstruction, from 1740–7, this building housed the first public library in Poland, which was established in 1761 by the Załuski brothers. In 1795 the library's entire collection was removed to St Petersburg, where it formed a foundation for the tsar's library. Part of the collection was retrieved in 1921, after Poland had regained independence. However, this important collection was burned during the 1944 Warsaw Uprising. The building currently houses the Polish Association of Authors (ZAIKS).

The ruined walls of the Former State Bank, now part of an office building

The Dzierżyński monument being pulled down in Bank Square

Bank Square ⓯
Plac Bankowy

Map 1 B3 & 3 C5. *100, 107, 111, 127, 171, 190, 406, 409, 410, 512.* *2, 4, 15, 18, 32, 35, 36.*

While the west side of this square has retained an imposing Neo-Classical appearance, the rest of the square was completely altered during postwar reconstruction. It was originally triangular in shape, and featured an ornamental fountain and an arrangement of flower beds in the centre.

After World War II the square was extended, and its name changed in honour of Feliks Dzierżyński, who became infamous for establishing the Soviet security service. A statue of him was also erected in the square. After the 1989 democratic elections the square regained its former name. When the monument of the loathed Dzierżyński was pulled down it smashed on the ground and fell apart, and pieces were snatched up by collectors.

Town Hall ⓰
Ratusz

Plac Bankowy. **Map** 1 B3 & 3 C5. *100, 107, 111, 127, 171, 190, 406, 409, 410, 512.* *2, 4, 15, 18, 36.*

This imposing group of Neo-Classical buildings dates from 1824–30. They were designed on a grand scale by Antonio Corazzi, who also designed the Grand Theatre *(see pp110–11)*, Staszic Palace *(p122)* and Mostowski Palace *(p146)*. The Town Hall originally housed the Administrative Commission for Revenues and Treasury, the ministerial palace of Duke Ksawery Drucki Lubecki and the Bank of Poland, as well as the Stock Exchange.

The buildings have impressive porticoes and arcades, with the former ministerial palace including a triangular pediment by Paweł Maliński. This features Trade, Wisdom and Industry, personified by Minerva, Jason and Mercury, together with allegories of the Vistula and Bug rivers. The ornamental borders and reliefs are the work of the sculptor Vincenti. From 1829 to 1831 one of Poland's most famous Romantic poets, Juliusz Słowacki, was a clerk at the Administrative Commission for Revenues and Treasury.

The palace was rebuilt in 1947, using Corazzi's original drawings. It now houses the Town Hall (Ratusz).

Former Bank of Poland and Stock Exchange (John Paul II Collection) ⓱
Dawny Bank Polski i Giełda

Elektoralna 2. **Map** 1 B3 & 3 C5. *620 27 25.* *107, 111, 171, 190, 406, 409, 410, 512.* *2, 4, 13, 15, 18, 26, 32, 35, 36.* *10am–5pm Tue–Sun.*

An outstanding example of Polish Neo-Classicism, the former Bank of Poland and Stock Exchange were both designed by Antonio Corazzi. Initially built from 1825–8, the building had already been extended by 1830, according to designs by Jan Jakub Gay.

The façades form two-storey arcades, with a dome over the original dealing room. The design includes minimally decorated spaces to underline its functional role. Currently, the building houses a collection of European paintings, dedicated to Pope John Paul II, and donated by Janina and Zbigniew Porczyński. These include over 450 works which are arranged thematically: Mother and Child, the Bible and saints, mythology and allegory, still life, landscape, and Impressionism.

The building also provides a venue for classical music concerts and poetry recitals.

The Former Bank of Poland and Stock Exchange building, now housing an art gallery

The grand, Neo-Classical buildings of Warsaw's Town Hall, rebuilt to the original plans of 1824

Modern Architecture in Warsaw

During the first decade following the fall of the Polish People's Republic and the first democratic elections in 1989 *(see pp30–31)*, hundreds of residential homes, shops and office buildings, both large and small, were built in Warsaw. A few prestigious public buildings were also commissioned. Although these early designs were rarely impressive architecturally, they were at least built to Western European standards, using materials of a higher standard than had been the norm during the communist regime. After 1996 original architecture of a much higher standard began to be designed and built, some of the most interesting emerging out of architectural competitions. A few of the most striking examples have been the subject of considerable controversy in recent years.

***Holland Park**, with its Modernist architecture, shows influences from the Modernism of the Netherlands. The Warsaw Stock Exchange building, at Plac Trzech Krzyży, is the most interesting office building in the city.*

***The University Library** is particularly noteworthy for its cathedral-like proportions and the inclusion of a botanical garden, which is located in the roof space. The façade represents a series of open books. The Neo-Classical buildings to either side were reconstructed in accordance with the style of Andrzej Kiciński. The juxtaposition of the two contrasting styles is highly successful.*

***The Daewoo Tower,** at the junction of Chłodna and Towarowa streets, has interesting modern interiors as well as a spacious atrium.*

The former Town Hall *buildings reconstructed at Plac Teatralny are merely a façade for the ultra-contemporary office buildings tucked behind. The complex also includes an interior atrium.*

Saxon Gardens ⓲
Ogród Saski

See pp108–9.

Former Western and Discount Banks ⓳
Dawny Bank Zachodni i Dyskontowy

Fredry 8. **Map** 1 C3 & 3 C5. *106, 111.* *8am–7pm Mon–Fri, 8am–noon Sat.*

UNTIL the devastation that was wreaked by World War II, Fredry Street was a heavily built-up commercial neighbourhood, the site of banks such as the Western and Discount, shopping arcades and hotels. One of the best known establishments was the Angielski (meaning "English") Hotel, which formerly stood at the junction of Fredry Street and Wierzbowa Street. It was at the Angielski Hotel that Napoleon Bonaparte stayed, during the time of his retreat from Moscow in 1812.

However, the former Western and Discount Banks, dating from 1896, provide the area's only original architecture. The Western Bank, designed by Józef Pius Dziekoński, has a magnificent staircase and Neo-Rococo interiors on the first floor. A notable feature of the Discount Bank is the skylight crowning the original trading room. The building's upper floors, designed by Kazimierz Loewe, are also worth visiting, and currently house a music library.

Grand Theatre ⓴
Teatr Wielki (Narodowy)

See pp110–11.

Theatre Square ㉑
Plac Teatralny

Map 1 C3 & 3 C5. *100, 111.*

THEATRE SQUARE was at the very heart of Warsaw until the outbreak of World War II. It was laid out in the first half of the 19th century, when the Grand Theatre was erected on the south side. The theatre replaced a trading and hotel complex known as Marywil, which was established in the 17th century.

Surrounding Theatre Square, there were once smart shops, arcades and elegant restaurants. In 1848 the Russian composer Mikhail Glinka lived and worked in one of the square's neighbouring houses, at No. 2 Niecała Street.

On the north side of the square, opposite the Grand Theatre, stood the small Church of St Andrew and the rambling Jabłonowski Palace. Between 1817–19 the palace was refashioned into the Town Hall (Ratusz). Close by was Blank's Palace, a late Baroque building, which was owned by Piotr Blank, an 18th-century Warsaw banker. At the beginning of the Nazi occupation, Warsaw's mayor, Stefan Starzyński was arrested in the palace. In 1944 during the Warsaw Uprising, the poet Krzysztof Kamil Baczyński died amid the ruins of the palace. After World War II, Blank's Palace was the only building to be reconstructed on the north side of Theatre Square. However, the remainder of this side is currently being recreated. Period-style buildings will house various financial institutions.

Monument to the Heroes of Warsaw

The Monument to the Heroes of Warsaw 1939–45 (known as simply as "Nike"), has been moved to the entrance of the W-Z route tunnel, from the site of the former Town Hall, which has finally been rebuilt.

A prewar view of Theatre Square and the Town Hall

Blue Palace ㉒
Pałac Błękitny

Senatorska 37. **Map** 1 C3 & 3 C5. *E-2, 100, 107, 111, 127, 171, 190, 409, 410, 512, 522.* *2, 4, 15, 18, 35, 36.* ***Not open** to the public.*

THE BLUE PALACE, which dates from the 17th century, was acquired by King August II Mocny in 1726 as a Christmas present for the king's beloved daughter, Anna Orzelska. This entailed refurbishing the palace in a Rococo manner, as this was Anna Orzelska's favourite architectural style. The designers were Joachim Daniel Jauch, Jan Zygmunt Deybel and Karol Fryderyk Pöppelmann. Moreover, as there wasn't much time before

Bernardo Bellotto's 18th-century painting of the Blue Palace

the Christmas in question, the alterations had to be completed in a great hurry. A total of 300 masons and craftsmen worked day and night for six weeks. Anna Orzelska subsequently named the palace after her favourite colour.

In the late 18th century the palace passed into the Czartoryski family. In 1811 it was acquired by the Zamoyskis, who refurbished it in a late Neo-Classical style, designed by Fryderyk A Lessel. The exquisitely furnished apartments were used to entertain royalty, such as the Saxon King Fryderyk August and Tsar Alexander I. Frederic Chopin also visited the palace and gave several concerts. The palace was reconstructed over two years, from 1948–50.

Former Landau Bank ㉓

Dawny Bank Landaua

Senatorska 38. **Map** 1 C3 & 3 C5.
826 62 71. *100, 107, 111, 119, 125, 127, 170, 171, 190, 409, 512, 520.* *2, 4, 15, 18, 35, 36.*
9am–6pm Mon–Fri.

While the exterior of the former Landau Bank appears unimpressive, having lost its original dome, the interiors are the best preserved examples of Secessionism in Warsaw dating from the late 19th century. The bank's former dealing room is crowned by a beautiful skylight.

Established by the renowned financier Wilhelm Landau, the bank was built between 1904–6. The bank was designed by two architects: Stanisław Grochowicz and Gustaw Landau-Gutenteger. After World War II, the Landau Bank gained a new use as the Communist Party's Propaganda Centre. Various political documents were stored in the bank's safe.

Currently, the Landau Bank building houses several French cultural institutions.

St John of Nepomuk monument

The Primate's Palace, one of Poland's finest Neo-Classical buildings

St John of Nepomuk Monument ㉔

Figura św Jana Nepomucena

Senatorska. **Map** 1 C3 & 3 C5.
100, 107, 111, 119, 125, 127, 170, 171, 190, 409, 410, 522. *2, 4, 15, 18, 35, 36.*

This rococo figure, by Giovanni Cievorotti, was commissioned in 1731 by the Marshal Józef Wandalin Mniszech. The plinth depicts St John's life (c.1345– 93). He died opposing Wenceslas IV's attempt to disband an abbey.

St Antony of Padua Reformed Church ㉕

Kościół św Antoniego Padewskiego Reformatów

Senatorska 31. **Map** 1 C3 & 3 C5.
107, 111, 127, 171, 409, 410, 413, 414, 415, 514, 515, 516, 522, 524. *2, 4, 15, 18, 35, 36, 45.*

King Zygmunt III Waza founded this tiny church in 1623, in gratitude to God for the recapture of the town of Smolensk from Russia. The laying of the foundation stone was witnessed by the king and queen, as well as two future kings of Poland (Władysław IV and Jan Kazimierz) and the Papal Nuncio Giovanni Altieri (later Pope Clement X). Originally wooden, the church acquired its present form in 1671–81. The nave has epitaphs to both wives of Marshal Józef Wandalin Mniszech, dated 1747 and 1772.

The 19th-century cloisters bear commemorative plaques and epitaphs. One is dedicated to Jerzy Iwanow Szajnowicz, a British agent in World War II. Revered as a hero in Poland and Greece, he was executed by the Nazis in Athens in 1943.

Primate's Palace ㉖

Pałac Prymasowski

Senatorska 13/15. **Map** 1 C3 & 3 C5.
E-1, 100, 111, 116, 122, 160, 174, 175, 195, 303, 503.
***Not open** to the public.*

When the bishop of Płock, Wojciech Baranowski, became Poland's primate in 1601, he gave the palace to Warsaw's Cathedral Chapter (a committee of the city's bishops) in exchange for "the anniversaries", or daily prayers for the souls of the clergy. Nevertheless, the palace continued as the Warsaw residence of Poland's primates.

The palace was extended in 1777–84 for primate Antoni Ostrowski with two semicircular wings culminating in attractive pavilions. The next primate, Michał Poniatowski, also extended the palace, using designs by Szymon B Zug after Andrea Palladio. Cited as the first Neo-Classical building in Poland, it was extensively reconstructed after damage during World War II.

Saxon Gardens ⓲

THE SAXON GARDENS were part of the Baroque town planning project known as the Saxon Axis, undertaken by August II Mocny between 1713–33. Its designers were Jan Krzysztof Naumann and Mateusz Daniel Pöppelmann. Adjoining the royal residence of Morsztyn Palace, the Saxon Gardens initially served as a royal garden, loosely based on those at Versailles. In 1727 the gardens became Warsaw's first public park, and nearly a century later, were redesigned by James Savage in the English style. Until World War II the gardens served as an alfresco "summer salon" for Varsovian society. However, the park has since lost many of its original attractions, such as the wooden summer theatre from 1870, which was destroyed at the outbreak of World War II.

The 19th-century watertower

Watertower (Wodozbiór)
Set by the lake and modelled on the Temple of Vesta in Tivoli, this relic of Warsaw's first water supply system was designed by Henryk Marconi.

★ Garden Statuary
This Baroque personification of Wisdom *was carved in sandstone by Jan Jerzy Plersch in the 1730s. The gardens now contain 21 statues, a fraction of the original total. Many were removed to St Petersburg by Marshal Suvorov. He recaptured Warsaw after the 1794 insurrection led by Tadeusz Kościuszko.*

Fountain
Designed by Henryk Marconi in 1855, the fountain appears in a song inspired by a Viennese waltz: "In the Saxon Gardens, by a flowing fountain, a young man sat next to a fair maiden."

★ Tomb of the Unknown Soldier
A triple arch is all that remains of the Saxon Palace colonnade, destroyed in World War II. It houses the Tomb of the Unknown Soldier. On 2 November 1925 an unknown victim of the defence of Lvov (1918–19) was interred here.

Maria Konopnicka Monument
Designed by Stanisław Kulon, this monument was erected in 1965 to honour the Polish poet and writer Maria Konopnicka (1842–1910).

Visitors' Checklist

Map 1 C3. *107, 111, 127, 171.* *2, 4, 15, 18, 36.*

Lake
Wild ducks enjoy the lake, which originally held carp and turtles, and served as a skating rink in winter.

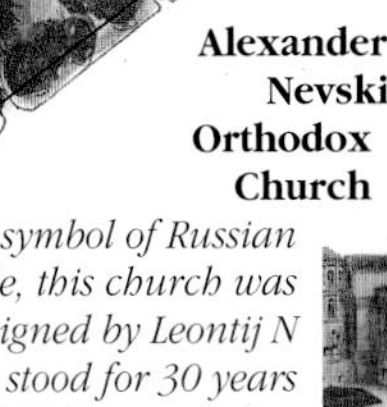

Alexander Nevski Orthodox Church
A symbol of Russian rule, this church was designed by Leontij N Benois. It stood for 30 years in Piłsudski Square, before being demolished in 1926.

Saxon Gardens
Before World War II, the gardens featured a 19th-century colonnade of the Saxon Palace.

Piłsudski Square was originally a courtyard of the Saxon Palace, though it has been used for various State ceremonies and parades since the early 19th century. It is named after Marshal Józef Piłsudski.

Józef Piłsudski Monument
Marshal Józef Piłsudski (1867–1935) was one of the most outstanding Polish statesmen of the 20th century (see p30).

Star Sights

- ★ **Tomb of the Unknown Soldier**
- ★ **Garden Statuary**

Grand Theatre (National Theatre) 20

Teatr Wielki (Narodowy)

ONE OF THE CITY'S LARGEST buildings before World War II, the Grand Theatre was built in 1825–33, to a design by Antonio Corazzi and Ludwik Kozubowski. Renowned craftsmen also contributed to the sublime interiors. Initially the building was to be named the National Theatre, but the defeat of the 1830 November Uprising forced a change of name. At one time it was even planned to convert the building into an Orthodox church. Ravaged during World War II, the theatre retained only its façade and several rooms. Greatly enlarged in the course of reconstruction, it also acquired modern interiors designed by Bohdan Pniewski. The theatre currently houses the National Opera and Ballet.

National Theatre
Since 1924, the National Theatre has been housed in the building's west wing, which burned down for the third time in 1985, but was re-opened in autumn 1996.

Stage
In total, the stage is 50 m (160 ft) high, and 54 m (180 ft) deep.

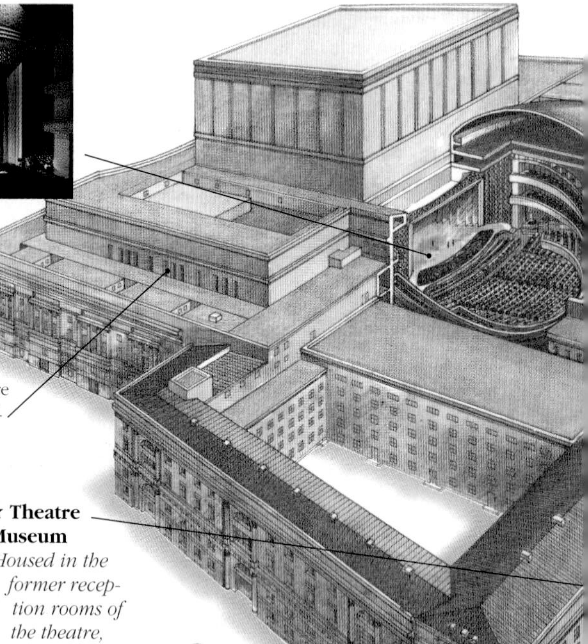

Backstage facilities were added after World War II.

★ Theatre Museum
Housed in the former reception rooms of the theatre, its exhibits include many period costumes from notable performances.

Moniuszko Monument
The statue of Stanisław Moniuszko (1819–72), who established the Polish National Opera, was created by Jan Szczepkowski and erected in 1965.

STAR SIGHTS

- ★ Façade
- ★ Theatre Museum

Triangular Pediment
The work of Tomaso Acciardi, this depicts the Muses crowning a bust of the ancient poet Anacreon with a wreath.

Visitors' Checklist

Plac Teatralny. **Map** 1 C3, 3 C5 & 4 D5. **Reception** *9am–4pm Mon–Sat.* **Box office** 692 07 53, 826 32 88. *9am–7pm Mon–Sat; 10am– 7pm Sun.* **Theatre Museum** *10am–2pm Tue–Fri, intervals.* *not Thu.*

Bogusławski Monument
The father of the Polish National Theatre, and driving force behind the construction of the Grand Theatre, Wojciech Bogusławski (1757–1829), was honoured with this monument by Jan Szczepkowski in 1936. Destroyed during World War II, it was reconstructed in 1965. In front of the monument is a pillar dating from 1880. It marks Warsaw's latitude and longitude.

Emil Młynarski Auditorium

The foyer, which was inspired by the ballroom in the Royal Castle, was designed by Bohdan Pniewski as part of the theatre's reconstruction after World War II.

★ Façade
A Neo-Classical covered market building, designed in 1819 by Chrystian Aigner, was incorporated into the façade of the theatre. This is all that survives of the traditional market area of Marywil, established in the late 17th century and demolished when the theatre was built.

Neo-Classical Frieze
Designed by Paweł Maliński, this frieze depicts Oedipus together with his entourage, returning home after competing at the Olympic Games.

ANNO RESTAVRATAE SALVTIS
STANISLAO AVGVSTO REGE
RELIGIONIS STVDIO
SVO AERE FRONTE ORNAVIT

The Royal Route

The Royal Route (Trakt Królewski) starts by Castle Square (Plac Zamkowy), and runs along Krakowskie Przedmieście and Nowy Świat. These thoroughfares originally developed in the late Middle Ages. Their rural setting, adjacent to the banks of the River Vistula, attracted Warsaw's wealthiest citizens, who built summer residences that were surrounded by gardens. Religious orders also established a number of monasteries here. Although the area suffered enormously during the Swedish invasion (1655), it was soon rebuilt. Krakowskie Przedmieście now features many buildings from the 17th and 18th centuries, particularly churches and palaces. The route extends into Nowy Świat (literally "New World"), which has buildings that are predominantly Neo-Classical in style, although the street's origins are medieval. These include town houses and palaces, together with exclusive cafés, restaurants, shops and fashionable boutiques.

Railings at the Adam Mickiewicz Monument

Sights at a Glance

Historic Buildings
Blikle 27
Bristol Hotel 12
Czapski Palace 17
Dean's House 5
Kossakowski Palace 26
Namiestnikowski Palace 10
Polish Theatre 22
Potocki Palace 9
Prażmowski House 1
Staszic Palace 20
Tyszkiewicz Palace 14
Uruski Palace 15
Warsaw University 16
Zamoyski Palace 29

Monuments
Adam Mickiewicz Monument 4
Nicholas Copernicus Monument 19
Prince Józef Poniatowski Monument 11
Warsaw's Mermaid 24

Churches
Church of the Assumption of the Blessed Virgin Mary 8
Holy Cross Church 18
St Anna's Church 2
St Joseph the Guardian's Church 13

Museums and Galleries
Caricature Museum 7
Ostrogski Palace 23

Historic Streets and Squares
Bednarska Street 3
Chmielna Street 30
Foksal 28
Kozia Street 6
Mariensztat 21
Nowy Świat 25

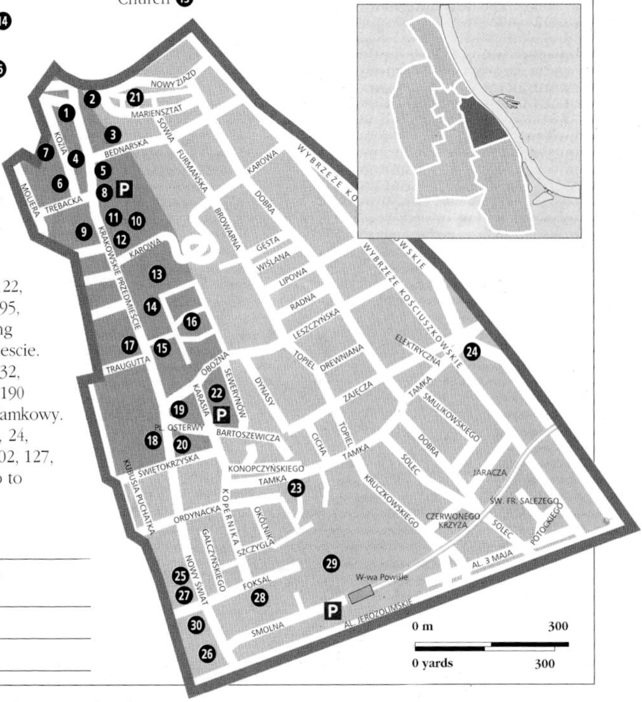

Getting There

Buses E-1, E2, 116, 122, 174, 175, 180, 192, 195, 303, and 503 go along Krakowskie Przedmiescie. Trams 4, 13, 26 and 32, and buses 125, 170, 190 and 307, go to Plac Zamkowy. Trams 7, 8, 9, 12, 22, 24, 25, and buses E-5, 102, 127, 158, 517 and 521, go to Rondo de Gaulle.

Key

Street-by-Street map *pp114–115*

P Parking

Railway line

0 m 300

0 yards 300

◁ **Neo-Classical façade of St Anna's Church**

Street-by-Street: Krakowskie Przedmieście

Krakowskie Przedmieście is one of Warsaw's most historic and beautiful streets. Several imposing palaces stand back from the road, behind tree-lined squares and courtyards, alongside impressive town houses and some of the city's most interesting churches. Warsaw University's main building and the Fine Arts Academy are also located here, while monuments pay tribute to eminent Poles. A range of restaurants, cafés and shops also make this street ideal for leisure.

★ St Anna's Church
Baroque murals by Walenty Żebrowski decorate the interior of this 16th-century church 2

Prince Józef Poniatowski Monument
The figure of this 19th-century military commander is in front of the President's Palace 11

Kordegarda houses a prestigious, though small, modern art gallery.

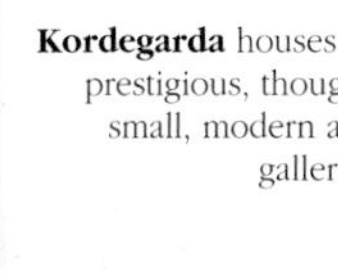

Church of the Assumption of the Blessed Virgin Mary
This 17th-century Carmelite church's façade is surmounted by an orb 8

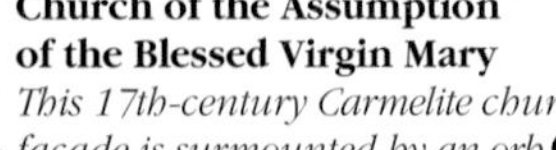

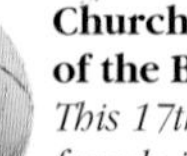

Bristol Hotel
Recently refurbished, this is Warsaw's most beautiful, luxurious and expensive hotel. Its café and restaurants are excellent 12

★ St Joseph the Guardian's Church
One of the few churches in Warsaw to escape destruction, the interiors are original 18th century ⓭

University Gate
Warsaw University is the country's largest university. The main building, on Krakowskie Przedmieście, houses several departments ⓰

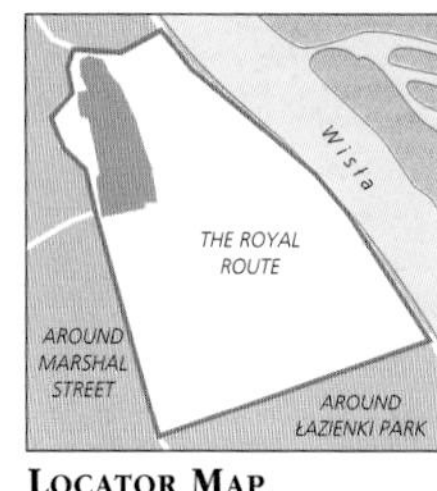

LOCATOR MAP
See Street Finder, maps 1, 3

Nicholas Copernicus Monument
Unveiled in 1830, this statue honours Poland's greatest astronomer (1473–1543) ⓳

0 m 75
0 yards 75

The Straight House (Dom bez Kantów) was built in 1933 by Czesław Przybylski. Its name is said to reflect not only the smooth, regular lines of the building, but also the honesty of the developers.

KEY

– – – Suggested route

STAR SIGHTS

- **★ St Anna's Church**
- **★ St Joseph the Guardian's Church**

Prażmowski House ❶

Kamienica Prażmowskich

Krakowskie Przedmieście 87.
Map 2 D3 & 4 D5.

PRAŻMOWSKI HOUSE was built in the second half of the 17th century for Dr Pastorius, the Royal Physician. It is now considered one of Warsaw's most beautiful buildings, but, throughout its history, frequent changes of ownership have led to substantial changes in style.

The existing Rococo style of the house dates from 1754. The refurbishment was designed by Jakub Fontana on behalf of the Leszczyński family, whose monogram features on the grille above the main entrance.

When it was again restored, after the devastation of World War II, the house was given to the Polish Literary Society. It was a frequent venue for lively meetings, which decided the fate of many a Polish writer, if not the entire cannon of Polish literature. A bohemian atmosphere can still be enjoyed in the building's café.

Prażmowski House

St Anna's Church ❷

Kościół św. Anny

Krakowskie Przedmieście 68.
Map 2 D2 & 4 D5. ☎ *826 89 91.*

THIS IMPOSING Gothic church was founded by Anna, the widow of Duke Bolesław III, and built in the late 15th century, together with a Bernardine monastery. The church was extended between 1518 and 1533, but then destroyed during the Swedish invasion of 1655.

The organ at St Anna's Church

Following this turbulent period, St Anna's was refurbished in a Baroque style. This was designed by Józef Szymon Bellotti, who preserved the original Gothic presbytery and façade. However, the façade was subsequently redesigned in a Neo-Classical style in the 18th century, by Chrystian Piotr Aigner and Stanisław Kostka Potocki.

The free-standing bell tower is another, though later, Neo-Classical feature, dating from the 1820s.

In 1864 St Anna's became (and remains) the University Church. Additionally, the side chapel of St Ładysław of Gielniów contains relics of this saint, who is also a patron saint of Warsaw.

The church has magnificent interiors, with several Rococo altars and frescoes by Walenty Żebrowski. Although the vaulted nave was destroyed during World War II, the Żebrowski frescoes have been restored.

St Anna's is the most popular choice for wedding ceremonies among Warsaw's students. This is partly due to superstition, as it is said that any marriage celebrated at St Anna's will be a happy one.

By the church are the remains of the 16th-century Bernardine monastery, which was closed in 1864. Cloisters in the monastery's east wing have retained their original vaulted ceilings. Behind St Anna's church is an attractive Neo-Classical colonnade, called Odwach. This colonnade is the city's best location for second-hand booksellers, and is an interesting place to browse.

Bednarska Street ❸

Ulica Bednarska

Map 2 D2 & 4 D5.

THIS STEEP, narrow street connecting Krakowskie Przedmieście with Powiśle was originally a dirt track, running alongside one of the numerous streams flowing into the River Vistula.

Between 1775 and 1864 the street was an important thoroughfare, as it led to a pontoon bridge, which was the only road link with the district of Praga. Bednarska Street acquired a certain notoriety in the 18th century, after "Kasztelanka", a bathhouse with an adjoining brothel, was built by a chatelain, Franciszek Jezierski.

The cobbled Bednarska Street

The fine Neo-Classical houses along Bednarska Street were designed by architects such as Antonio Corazzi and Jan Jakub Gay. In 1832, Alfons Kropiwnicki built the Majewski Bathhouse at Nos. 2–4, near the river. This is currently a school building.

In 1840–41 Jan Jakub Gay built a house for the Warsaw Charitable Society, situated at the street's junction with

Krakowskie Przedmieście. During World War II many houses suffered severe damage, but have been accurately rebuilt in keeping with the period character of this cobbled street.

The Dean's House, with its elegant rounded niche

Adam Mickiewicz Monument ❹

Pomnik Adama Mickiewicza

Krakowskie Przedmieście. **Map** 2 D3 & 4 D5.

WARSAW'S MONUMENT to the country's greatest Romantic poet was unveiled in 1898, on the centenary of his birth. As this took place during the Russian occupation of Poland, it was considered a great achievement by the Founding Committee, chaired by Michał Radziwiłł and Nobel-prize winning author Henryk Sienkiewicz. The statue was designed by Cyprian Godebski, while the plinth was by Józef Pius Dziekoński and Władysław Marconi.

Adam Mickiewicz Monument

The monument occupies a square that was cleared in the mid-19th century. Only the Baroque statue of the Madonna of Passau remains from the original square. Completed in 1683 by Józef Szymon Bellotti, the statue was commissioned by King Jan III Sobieski, in gratitude to God for victory over the Turks at Vienna, and for saving his family from the plague.

Dean's House ❺

Dziekanka

Krakowskie Przedmieście 56. **Map** 2 D3 & 4 D5.

DZIEKANKA, MEANING "the Dean's House", gained its name from the site it occupies. This was formerly owned by the deans of St John's College. Built in 1770–84, this Neo-Classical building was converted into an inn during the 19th century. Having been restored after World War II, it became a student hall of residence.

The façade features a large rounded niche, while the picturesque courtyard is surrounded by wooden balconies. In summer this is used for al fresco discos and theatrical performances.

Kozia Street ❻

Ulica Kozia

Map 2 D2 & 4 D5.

THIS NARROW, picturesque street connects Krakowskie Przedmieście with Miodowa Street. While the street dates from the 14th century, the existing buildings did not appear until the 17th century. Kozia Street acquired greater status in the 19th century, due to the Saski Hotel and the "Kawa u Brzezińskiej" café, frequented by Frederic Chopin and various writers. Studio M café and gallery, at the junction with Krakowskie Przedmieście, continue this tradition.

Kozia Street

In the adjacent Trembacka Street is the magnificent Rococo Saska Poczta (Saxon Post Office), which is also called Wessel Palace. Built in the mid-18th century for General Załuski, it became the main post office in 1780. It now houses the State Prosecutor's Office.

Caricature Museum ❼

Muzeum Karykatury

Kozia 11. **Map** 2 D3 & 4 D5. *827 88 95.* *11am–5pm Tue–Sun.*

FOUNDED IN 1978 at the instigation of cartoonist Eryk Lipiński, this is the world's first museum of its kind. The museum is housed in Dom Ogrodnika (The Gardener's House), which is part of the Primate's Palace *(see p107)*. The museum's collection includes satirical drawings, images and magazines from all over the world. Two rooms house temporary exhibitions, which change every two to three months.

The Caricature Museum's sign

Neo-Classical façade of the Church of the Assumption of the Blessed Virgin Mary

Church of the Assumption of the Blessed Virgin Mary and St Joseph the Betrothed 8

Kościół Wniebowzięcia NMP i św. Józefa Oblubieńca

Krakowskie Przedmieście 52/54. **Map** 2 D3 & 4 D5. *826 05 31.* *100, 111, 116, 122, 174, 175, 180, 192, 195, 303, 503.*

ORIGINALLY BUILT for the Discalced (barefooted) Carmelite Friars between 1661–82, this late Baroque church is thought to have been designed by Józef Szymon Bellotti. However, the Neo-Classical façade was designed by Efraim Schroeger in 1782, which makes the church one of the earliest examples of Neo-Classicism in the country.

Despite the devastation inflicted during World War II, the church has retained many of its original features. These include an impressive transept with rows of interconnecting side chapels. The beautiful main altar features a number of sculptures by Jan Jerzy Plersch. He also sculpted the Romantic grouping known as *Mary's Betrothal*, which stands in a side altar and came from the Dominican Church of the Observants, which is no longer standing.

Other notable features of this church include Baroque altar paintings, and two small canvasses by Szymon Czechowicz in the side altars. The friary buildings by the church were closed in 1864 and taken over by a theological seminary. Following recent refurbishment they have become part of the Archdiocese Museum.

Potocki Palace 9

Pałac Potockich

Krakowskie Przedmieście 15. **Map** 2 D3 & 4 D5. *100, 111, 116, 122, 174, 175, 180, 192, 195, 303, 503.* ***Not open*** *to the public.*

DATING FROM THE 1760s, this late Baroque palace is one of Warsaw's most imposing buildings. It was built for August Aleksander Czartoryski and his wife Maria Zofia, née Sieniawska, on the site of a former 17th-century residence that was owned by the influential Denhoff family.

The palace was inherited by August Czartoryski's daughter Izabela, who was married to Stanisław Lubomirski. She employed the prestigious architects Szymon Bogumił Zug and Jan Chrystian Kamsetzer to restyle the interiors in an extravagant manner.

Izabela Lubomirska was a renowned society figure, not only as the wife of the Grand Marshal, but also as a patron of the arts. Moreover, being something of a *grande dame*, she was actively involved in political life and intrigues during the reign of King Stanisław August Poniatowski.

During the 19th century the palace declined, and rooms were sublet. A pavilion in the courtyard was used to exhibit notable 19th-century paintings, such as Jan Matejko's *Battle of Grunwald* and the *Prussian Oath of Allegiance*.

At the end of the 19th century, the palace regained some of its former splendour, due to restoration work undertaken by Władysław Marconi. Reconstructed after World War II, the palace is now part of the Ministry of Arts and Culture.

Entrance to the late Baroque Potocki Palace

Namiestnikowski Palace 10

Pałac Namiestnikowski

Krakowskie Przedmieście 46/48. **Map** 2 D3 & 4 D5. *100, 111, 116, 122, 160, 174, 175, 180, 192, 195, 303, 503.* ***Not open*** *to the public.*

THE NEO-CLASSICAL style of this palace dates from Chrystian Piotr Aigner's refurbishment, in 1818–19. Aigner restyled an existing palace built during the mid-17th century.

The Namiestnikowski Palace has had a turbulent history, belonging to several important families, including the Koniecpolskis and Lubomirskis. From 1685 the palace was owned by the Radziwiłł family, who sold it in 1818 to the Russian government of Poland. Subsequently the palace became the official residence of the tsar's governors in Warsaw. A flamboyant resident in the

Namiestnikowski Palace, the official presidential residence

19th century was the prima ballerina Mrs Zajączek. She maintained a staggering beauty into old age, and scandalized society with her romances. It was rumoured that her vitality stemmed from a strict regime: bathing in icy water, sleeping in unheated rooms and eating cold food.

After World War II, the palace became the Council of Ministers' Office, and was the setting for important political events. The Warsaw Pact was signed here in 1955, as was a treaty in 1970 to promote relations with Germany. The round-table negotiations between the government and opposition groups were also held here in 1989.

Since 1994 the palace has been the official residence of the president of Poland.

Prince Józef Poniatowski Monument ⓫

Pomnik Księcia Józefa Poniatowskiego

Krakowskie Przedmieście.
Map 2 D3 & 4 D5.

VARSOVIANS were not enthusiastic about this fine sculpture when it was first unveiled to the public. Instead of portraying the prince in his uniform, the Danish sculptor Bertel Thorwaldsen depicted him as a barefooted Classical hero, clad in a tunic. The prince, who was one of Napoleon Bonaparte's marshals, perished in the River Elster in 1813 during the Battle of Leipzig, and quickly became a national hero in Poland. The statue was commissioned in 1816 by the Monuments Founding Committee, but its official unveiling was interrupted by the insurrection of November

The Classical-style portrayal of Prince Józef Poniatowski

1830. The sculpture was transferred to the Modlin Fortress, and in 1840 was moved to a palace in Homel, Belarus. This palace was the private residence of Russian general Ivan Paskiewicz.

The monument was returned to Poland in 1922 and put in Saxon Square, but it was destroyed during World War II. A new casting from the original mould was presented to the city of Warsaw by the citizens of Copenhagen in 1965.

Bristol Hotel ⓬

Krakowskie Przedmieście 42/44.
Map 2 D3 & 4 D5. *625 25 25.*
100, 111, 116, 122, 160, 174, 175, 180, 192, 195, 303, 503.

THE BRISTOL was originally one of Europe's grandest hotels, although the choice of architect provoked a scandal. A competition was held and prizes duly awarded, but the prize-winning design was then abandoned in favour of a scheme by one of the judges, Władysław Marconi. He was an outstanding architect, and despite the resulting furore, Marconi's essentially Neo-Renaissance plans met with widespread approval.

The specially formed building consortium, which included Ignacy Paderewski *(see p34)* among its members, also commissioned Otto Wagner the Younger to design the Secessionist interiors.

The Bristol was quickly established as a society venue, hosting parties and receptions that were regarded as the most stylish in Warsaw. It was also used to celebrate special occasions, including Marie Skłodowska-Curie's Nobel Prize, and the triumphs of the renowned operetta singer Lucyna Messal. During the 1930s, the painter Wojciech Kossak kept a studio on the 5th floor. He offered his paintings as payment; they can still be seen in one of the hotel's restaurants.

After World War II, the hotel continued to receive notable guests, but fell into some disrepair. Following huge refurbishment, the hotel reopened phoenix-like in 1992, having regained all of its former style and prestige.

The refurbished Bristol Hotel

Tabernacle in St Joseph The Guardian's Church

St Joseph the Guardian's Church ⓭

Kościół Opieki św. Józefa

Krakowskie Przedmieście 34. **Map** 2 D3 & 4 D5. *100, 111, 116, 122, 174, 175, 180, 192, 195, 303, 503.*

Construction of the church began in 1654. However, it was soon abandoned, and building did not resume until the 18th century, under Karol Bay. The façade was completed in 1763, having been designed by Efraim Schroeger. Fortunately, the church has never been damaged, and retains its original decor.

Among the church's most outstanding works of art are the Rococo pulpit, in the shape of a boat, and sculptures by the main altar. The ebony tabernacle, dating from 1654, was commissioned by Queen Ludwika Maria, and is decorated with silver plaques by Herman Pothoff.

The church also features several renowned paintings: *The Visitation* by Tadeusz Kuntze-Konicz, *St Luis Gonzaga* by Daniel Szulc and *St Francis of Sales* by Szymon Czechowicz.

On the church forecourt, stands a monument to cardinal Stefan Wyszyński, erected in 1987. Adjacent to the church is the Baroque convent of the Nuns of the Visitation. This order was invited to settle in Poland by Queen Ludwika Maria. Behind the convent is a magnificent garden, which is used by the nuns but unfortunately is closed to visitors.

The Visitation by Tadeusz Kuntze-Konicz

Tyszkiewicz Palace ⓮

Pałac Tyszkiewiczów

Krakowskie Przedmieście 32. **Map** 2 D3 & 4 D5. *E-2, 100, 111, 116, 122, 174, 175, 180, 192, 195, 303, 503.*

Regarded as one of the city's most beautiful Neo-Classical residences, this palace was originally built for Ludwik Tyszkiewicz. Construction began in 1785, following a design by Stanislaw Zawadzki. However, the palace was completed by the architect Jan Chrystian Kamsetzer in 1792.

The northern elevation of Tyszkiewicz Palace

The relatively modest façade of the palace is decorated with some fine stucco work, and the central balcony is supported by four elegant stone Atlantes *(see p51)*.

In 1840 the palace was acquired by the Potocki family, whose family crest now forms the central cartouche of the façade.

The most flamboyant owner of the palace was Count August Potocki, who was fondly known in Warsaw's aristocratic circles as Count Gucio. Renowned for his lavish lifestyle, he also figured in various scandals. However, this did not dispel his popularity, which he gained through his famous generosity and general *joie de vivre*.

The palace has been restored to its former glory, having been obliterated during World War II. It is currently part of Warsaw University.

Uruski Palace ⓯

Pałac Uruskich

Krakowskie Przedmieście 30. **Map** 2 D3 & 4 D5. *E-2, 100, 111, 116, 122, 174, 175, 180, 192, 195, 303, 403, 503.*

The late Baroque palace that originally occupied this site belonged to the father of Poland's last king. Moreover, it was in this palace that Stanisław August Poniatowski learned that he had been elected to the Polish throne in 1764. There is a monument situated in the courtyard which commemorates this event.

In 1844–7, the palace was restyled by Andrzej Gołoński for the new owner, Seweryn Uruski. Not only was Uruski considered nouveau riche, but he also had the brand new title of Count, granted by the Austrian authorities in 1844. This may explain why the family crest on the façade of the palace is so ostentatious.

Uruski family crest in a cartouche style

Restored after World War II, the palace also became part of the Warsaw University buildings.

Warsaw University ⓰

Uniwersytet Warszawski

Krakowskie Przedmieście 26/28. **Map** 2 D3 & 4 D5. *100, 111, 116, 174, 175, 180, 192, 195, 303, 503.*

The present site of Warsaw University was originally occupied by a summer

Kazimierzowski Palace, part of the University of Warsaw

palace, which belonged to the Waza dynasty in the 17th century. This building, the Kazimierzowski Palace, was used as the Knights School from 1765. In 1816 it became part of the newly established Warsaw University. Rebuilt in the Neo-Classical style, the palace currently houses the rector's offices.

The university's other Neo-Classical buildings include two annexes: Porektorski and Poseminaryjny. Built in 1814–16, they were designed by Jakub Kubicki. The Main School building (Szkoła Główna), designed by Antonio Corazzi, was completed in 1841. Meanwhile, Michał Kado designed the main auditorium and the former Fine Arts Academy in 1818–22.

Condottieri Monument in the courtyard of Czapski Palace

Following the 1863 January Uprising, the University came under the control of the Russian authorities. A new library was built in 1894, designed by Stefan Szyller and Antoni Jabłoński..

When Poland regained independence in 1918, the University acquired a new auditorium building, called the Audytorium Maximum.

Warsaw University is now Poland's largest academic institution and has expanded into buildings around the city.

Czapski Palace ⓱
Pałac Czapskich

Krakowskie Przedmieście 5. **Map** 2 D3 & 4 D5. ☎ 826 6251. **Chopin family salon** ◯ *10am–2pm Mon–Fri.* 🚌 *111, 116, 122, 174, 175, 192, 195, 303, 503.*

The Czapski palace has a fascinating heritage, having been owned by several of the most distinguished Polish families, and variously restyled by outstanding architects. The former owners of the palace include the Radziwiłł, Radzijowski, Sieniawski and Czartoryski families, who commissioned a host of architects, such as Tylman of Gameren, Augustyn Locci and Kacper Bażanka. The current style of the palace is late Baroque, dating from 1752–65, when the palace became the seat of the Czapski family. In 1795 the architect Jan Chrystian Kamsetzer added Neo-Classical wings to the palace.

The south wing was occupied by Frederic Chopin's family in 1826. Their former drawing room (salon) has been reconstructed, and is open to the public. The room features elegant period furniture, *objets d'art,* and memorabilia of the composer.

By the end of the 19th century, the palace was owned by the Krasiński family, whose members included the Romantic poet Zygmunt Krasiński.

After substantial restoration following World War II, the palace was incorporated into the Fine Arts Academy.

The 18th-century Czapski Palace

Warsaw University

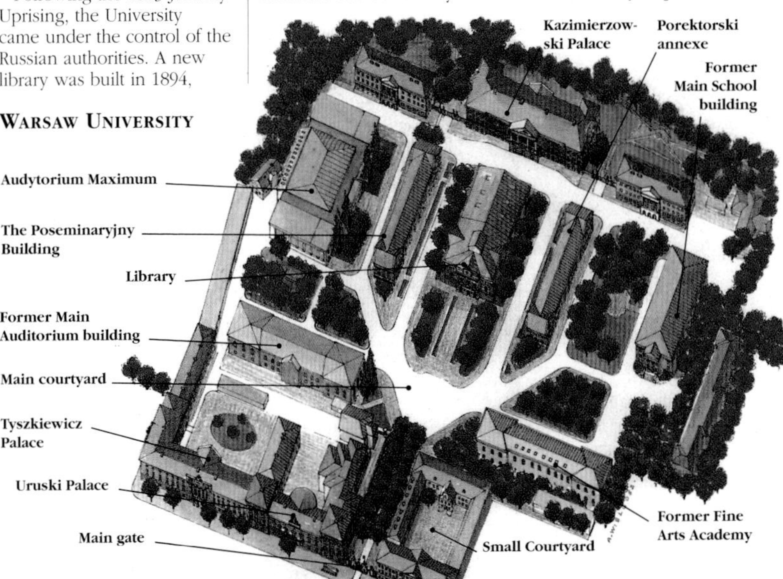

The magnificent twin towers of the Holy Cross Church

Holy Cross Church ⓲

Kościół św. Krzyża

Krakowskie Przedmieście 3. **Map** 2 D4. *826 89 10.* *111, 116, 122, 174, 175, 195, 303, 503.*

THIS SUPERB example of late 17th-century Varsovian architecture was designed by Józef Szymon Bellotti. Built in 1679–96, the Holy Cross Church replaced an earlier church, destroyed during the 1655 Swedish invasion. The present building includes a wall-and-pillar basilica.

The late-Baroque façade, featuring twin towers, was completed in 1760 under Jakub Fontana, several decades after the main building.

An extraordinary feature of the church is a "lower church" in the vaults, damaged with the main building in World War II. Among the surviving features, the most interesting is the altar in the south aisle, designed by Tylman of Gameren.

The church has been venue for many patriotic and religious ceremonies, including the funerals of statesman Stanisław Staszic, composer Karol Szymanowski and painter Leon Wyczółkowski. The hearts of composer Frederic Chopin and Nobel prize-winning novelist Władysław Reymont are in a side pillar of the nave. Mass is broadcast from the church on national radio each Sunday.

Nicholas Copernicus Monument ⓳

Pomnik Kopernika

Krakowskie Przedmieście. **Map** 2 D4. *111, 116, 122, 175, 195, 303, 503.*

STATESMAN Stanisław Staszic began raising funds for a monument to Poland's greatest astronomer in 1810. Created by the Danish sculptor Bertel Thorwaldsen, it was unveiled in 1830. During World War II, the Nazis covered the monument's inscriptions with plaques in German. These were removed by Alek Dawidowski, a member of the Szare Szeregi ("Grey Ranks") Resistance group. However, the monument suffered much wartime damage and was nearly dismantled for scrap in 1944. Fortunately it was restored instead. A monument cast from the same mould can also be seen in Chicago.

Staszic Palace ⓴

Pałac Staszica

Nowy Świat 72. **Map** 2 D4. *826 99 45.* *111, 116, 122, 175, 195, 303, 503.* *by arrangement.*

A FOUNDATION established by the statesman Stanisław Staszic funded this Neo-Classical palace, which was designed by Antonio Corazzi in 1820–23 for the Royal Society of the Friends of Science. Taken over by the Russians after the defeat of the 1830 November Uprising, it was rebuilt in the Russian-Byzantine style in 1892–3.

The palace was returned to its original style in 1926, by the architect Marian Lalewicz.

Façade of the Neo-Classical Staszic Palace

Mariensztat ㉑

Map 2 D2. *100, 128, 150, 318.*

MARIENSZTAT is named after a street that formerly ran alongside the Bernardine monastery gardens, between Krakowskie Przedmieście and Dobra Street.

Mariensztat's postwar buildings, influenced by 18th-century architecture

This area also housed the Powiśle market, destroyed during World War II.

The Powiśle site was redeveloped in 1948–9 to act as a "showpiece" of Socialist housing. Designed by Zygmunt Stępiński, in a style that was based on 18th-century Varsovian architecture, the estate was named Mariensztat.

The project was extolled in various songs, and even featured in the film *Przygoda na Mariensztacie* ("Adventure in Mariensztat"). Ironically, this necessitated building a mock-up of the estate, as it had not been completed.

The front of Warsaw's modernist Polish Theatre

Polish Theatre ㉒

Teatr Polski

Karasia 2. **Map** 2 E4. *826 79 72.* *116, 122, 175, 195, 303, 503.*

When the Polish Theatre was built in 1912, it was the country's most modern theatre, featuring a revolving stage and iron safety curtain. Designed by Czesław Przybylski, in a contemporary version of Empire style, the project was initiated by Arnold Szyfman, who became the theatre's first director. His opening production was *Irydion*, by Zygmunt Krasiński.

Szyfman reopened the theatre after World War II, when Juliusz Słowacki's *Lilla Weneda* was staged by the legendary director Juliusz Osterwa. The Polish Theatre remains one of the city's most popular theatrical venues.

Ostrogski Palace ㉓

Pałac Gnińskich-Ostrogskich

Okólnik 1. **Map** 2 E4. *826 59 35.* **Chopin Museum** *10am–5pm Mon, Wed & Fri; 12–6pm Thu; 10am–2pm Sat–Sun.* *for concerts.* *www.chopin.pl*

Ostrogski Palace was built in about 1681, as a pavilion to a much grander, but never completed project by Tylman of Gameren. The pavilion was erected close to the Vistula, on an elevated terrace above a cellar. According to legend, this cellar was inhabited by a Golden Duck, which stood guard over a treasure trove. The palace was frequently refurbished, but is now a postwar re-creation of its late 18th-century form.

In 1859 the palace became the home of the Warsaw Conservatoire. It then became the headquarters of the International Frederic Chopin Society after World War II and a Chopin Museum has since been established within the palace. It includes portraits, letters and manuscripts, and the grand piano on which Chopin composed during the last two years of his life.

The palace has a concert hall, where regular performances of Chopin's music are organized by the Society.

Chopin Museum within the Ostrogski Palace

Warsaw's Mermaid ㉔

Pomnik Syreny

Wybrzeże Kościuszkowskie. **Map** 2 F3. *162, 185, 362.*

Warsaw's Mermaid

This is the second monument devoted to Warsaw's mermaid, a mythical half woman half fish, which was believed to protect the city. The mermaid has appeared in the city of Warsaw's crest since the 14th century. Erected in 1939, this monument was designed by Ludwika Nitsch. The mermaid was modelled on Krystyna Krahelska, a renowned poet, who also composed the march that was sung by the Polish Resistance during the Warsaw Uprising of 1944, entitled: *Hej chłopcy, bagnet na broń* (Hey lads, place a bayonet on your weapon). Krahelska was killed during the uprising.

The mermaid figure was originally designed to be 20 m (62 ft) high, made of glass and placed on a pillar in the bed of the River Vistula. It was later decided to cast the mermaid in bronze at 2 m (6 ft) high, and erect the monument on Wybrzeże Kościuszkowskie, along the banks of the Vistula.

Warsaw's other mermaid monument is situated in the Old Town *(see p83)*.

Nowy Świat, **painted in 1892 by Władysław Podkowiński**

Nowy Świat ㉕

Map 2 D4 & 6 D1. 🚌 *111, 116, 122, 175, 195, 303, 503.*

CONTINUING ON from Krakowskie Przedmieście, Nowy Świat (meaning "New World") is the next stage of the Royal Route. The street's origins are medieval, when it became established as the main route to the towns of Czersk and Kraków.

It wasn't until the end of the 18th century that the first stone buildings were built on Nowy Świat. They were Neo-Classical palaces, with several late Neo-Classical town houses added in the early 19th century. At the end of that century Nowy Świat was renowned for its smart restaurants, cafés, shops, summer theatres and hotels.

After World War II, the Neo-Classical buildings were authentically reconstructed, with the remaining buildings also restyled in a Neo-Classical manner, to create uniformity.

This is still one of Warsaw's smartest streets, with its cafés and chic boutiques.

Kossakowski Palace ㉖

Pałac Kossakowskich

Nowy Świat 19. **Map** 2 E5 & 6 D1. 🚌 *111, 116, 122, 175, 195, 303, 503.*

THIS PALACE was originally built at the end of the 18th century for Izaak Ollier, a wealthy merchant, but the present Italian Renaissance style dates from 1849–51, when the new owner, Władysław Pusłowski, commissioned the renowned architect Henryk Marconi to renovate and restyle the building.

Kossakowski Palace

The palace was later acquired by Count Kossakowski. He established it as one of the city's most fashionable venues, where the intellectual elite attended glamorous balls and a literary salon every Friday. Guests could also admire the count's art collection. This was one of the finest private collections in Poland, including works by many foreign artists.

In 1892 the palace's belvedere (summer house) was used as a studio by the painter Władysław Podkowiński, who painted some outstanding views of Nowy Świat.

Blikle ㉗

Nowy Świat 33. **Map** 2 D5 & 6 D1. 🚌 *111, 116, 122, 175, 195, 503.*

ANTONI KAZIMIERZ BLIKLE established his eponymous patisserie in 1869, when he opened a shop and café in Nowy Świat. Until World War II, the Blikle Café was a popular meeting place for actors and artists. During the war actresses were employed here as waitresses.

During the Communist era the Blikle family managed to retain the patisserie (but not the café), producing the finest doughnuts in Warsaw. Since the democratic elections in 1989, the current owner, Andrzej Blikle, has opened other shops in Warsaw. In 1993 he also opened a café next door to the patisserie located on Nowy Świat.

Foksal ㉘

Map 2 E5 & 6 D1. 🚌 *111, 116, 122, 175, 195, 503.*

FOKSAL STREET was named after the pleasure garden that was established in this area during the 18th century. Modelled on the fashionable Vauxhall Pleasure Gardens in London, it was laid out at the urging of a banker, Fryderyk

Tenement block on Foksal Street

Kabryt. Included among the most popular attractions of the garden were the first balloons ever seen in Warsaw.

During the mid-19th century the garden was redeveloped, and one of its lanes was converted into a cul-de-sac, which connected with Nowy Świat. At about the same time, some palaces, including the Przeździecki, and tenement flats were constructed along this road, as well as the magnificent building for the Warsaw Rowing Society, which is located at No. 19.

The Przeździecki Palace can be found at No. 6 Foksal Street. The building, with its distictive narrow columns, was designed by Marceli Berent and constructed in 1878–9. It was originally owned by the Przeździecki family. The palace is now home to the Diplomatic Club of the Polish Ministry of Foreign Affairs.

Zamoyski Palace ㉙

Pałac Zamoyskich

Foksal 2. **Map** 2 E5 & 6 E1. *827 87 12, 827 87 14.* *100, 111, 116, 122, 175, 180, 195, 303, 503.*

Set in a magnificent landscaped park, this palace was built in 1878–9. It was designed by Leandro Marconi, who was from a family of distinguished architects. He created Baroque interiors, while ensuring the palace was comfortable as a private residence. Its façade exemplified the then fashionable "French Costume" manner (inspired by the Renaissance style of Henry IV and Louis XIII).

Entrance to Zamoyski Palace

The palace was occupied by the Zamoyski family until World War II. One of the many distinguished guests was, in 1923, the French World War I hero, Marshal Ferdinand Foch. The palace was then taken over by the state for the Society of Polish Architects. Since 1965 the left wing has housed Foksal Gallery, a modern art collection.

The delicate columns of Przeździecki Palace on Foksal Street

Musicians on Chmielna Street

Chmielna Street ㉚

Ulica Chmielna

Map 2 D5 & 6 D1. *111, 116, 175, 180, 303, 503, 522.* *2, 4, 7, 22, 24, 25, 35, 36.* **M** *Centrum.*

Before World War II Chmielna Street was renowned for its range of shops, street theatre and cafés.

During the Communist era, the street was renamed Henryk Rutkowski Street, and became a centre for private enterprise and retailing. It was here that Varsovians came to order outfits for weddings and other special occasions, and to buy accessories such as gloves and shoes. Second-hand shops offered what were known locally as "things from foreign parcels", meaning goods sent by relatives from the West. These would include fragrances, jeans and other clothes, and items such as Barbie dolls, which were impossible to buy in State-run shops in Poland.

Shops and cafés on Chmielna Street

Chmielna Street's renown has declined since its heyday, but it remains a charming pedestrianized shopping street with numerous cafés.

1893

AROUND MARSHAL STREET

DURING THE MID-19th century the commercial centre of Warsaw began to move away from the area around Krakowskie Przedmieście and Theatre Square, and towards Marshal Street (Marszałkowska). This was prompted by a new railway station serving the Warsaw–Vienna line, which opened in 1845 by the junction of Jerozolimskie Avenue and Marshal Street. The following decades saw Marshal Street established as the city's principal shopping area. Despite being destroyed during World War II, and subsequently redeveloped, Marshal Street has maintained its traditional status. However, the city's commercial centre has continued moving westwards, towards the Central Railway Station.

Plaque bearing the date of the Palace of Culture and Science

SIGHTS AT A GLANCE

Churches

Augsburg Protestant Community Church 2
Church of the Saviour 15

Historic Buildings and Streets

Central Railway Station 11
Engineers' Society 4
Filtering Plant 14
Former Bracia Jabłkowscy Department Store 8
Historic Buildings on Aleje Jerozolimskie 10
Lwowska Street 13
Palace of Culture and Science 9
Philharmonic 7
PKO SA Bank 5
Warsaw Technical University 12
Warszawa Hotel 6

Museums and Galleries

Museum of Mankind 3
Zachęta (Fine Art Society) 1

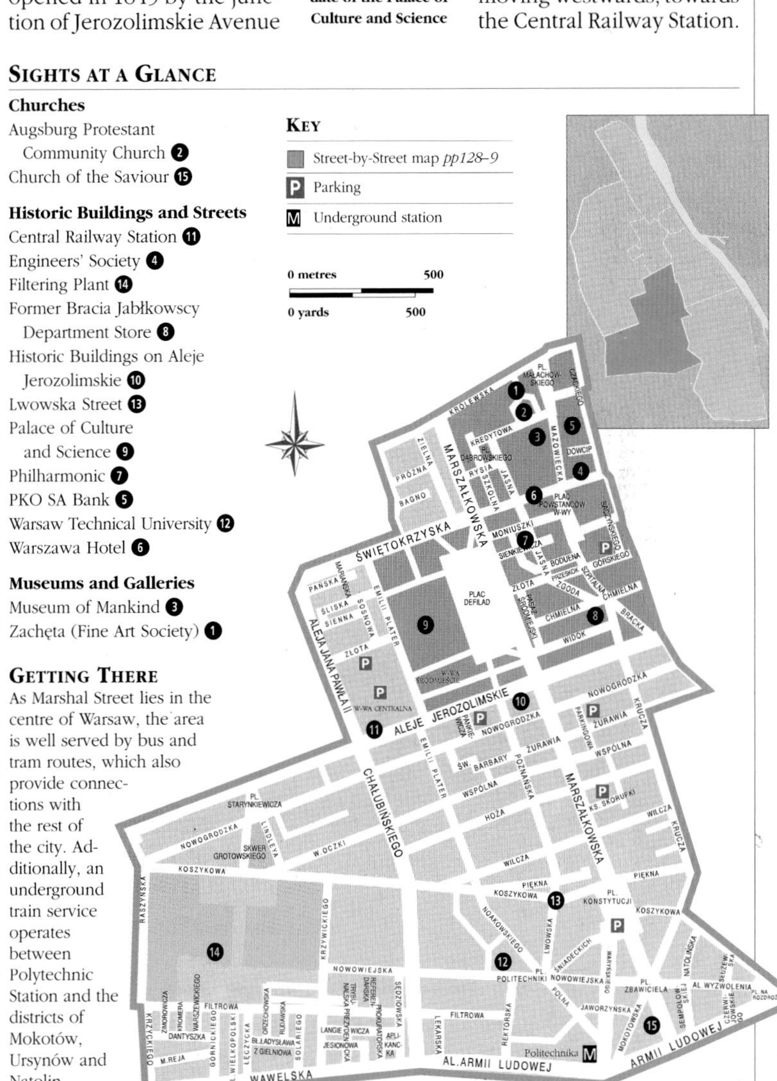

GETTING THERE

As Marshal Street lies in the centre of Warsaw, the area is well served by bus and tram routes, which also provide connections with the rest of the city. Additionally, an underground train service operates between Polytechnic Station and the districts of Mokotów, Ursynów and Natolin.

◁ **Ornate building in Szpitalna Street housing the Wedel confectionery shop**

Street-by-Street: Marshal Street

MARSZAŁKOWSKA (Marshal Street) is one of the city's main locations for banks, hotels and shops. The 1950s saw construction on a major scale in this street, including the building of Warsaw's tallest building, the Palace of Culture and Science. However, there are also some impressive turn-of-the-century buildings featuring particularly ornate interiors.

Zachęta (Fine Art Society)
Designed by Stefan Szyller and built in 1899–1903, it has recently been greatly extended ❶

★ Augsburg Protestant Community Church
This 18th-century church is renowned for its excellent acoustics ❷

Museum of Mankind
The museum has a wide range of Polish folk art, including this nativity scene ❸

★ Palace of Culture and Science
Statues of astronomer Nicholas Copernicus (left) and poet Adam Mickiewicz are distinctive features of the main entrance. The façade includes other sculptures in Socialist Realist style ❾

Marks & Spencer, the well known British store, recently opened here.

KEY

▬ ▬ ▬ Suggested route

Philharmonic Hall
This is the venue for the renowned Chopin Piano Competition, held every five years ❼

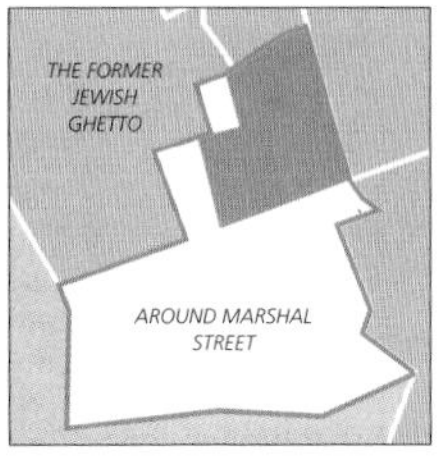

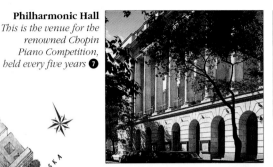

Locator Map
See Street Finder, maps 1, 2

The Bank Under the Eagles takes its name from the stone eagles, by Zygmunt Otto, on the roof. The bank was designed by Jan Heurich Jr in 1912–17.

The Wedel Pâtisserie in Szpitalna Street has retained its ornate turn-of-the-century decor. It is home to the renowned confectionery company Emil Wedel.

0 m 150

0 yards 150

★ Former ŚBracia Jabłkowscy Department Store
Built in 1913–14, Warsaw's oldest departmetnt store has recently been restored ❽

A new metro station, built on two storeys underground, has also been designed to accommodate a commercial center.

Star Sights

- **★ Augsburg Protestant Community Church**
- **★ Place of Culture**
- **★ Former ŚBracia Jabłkowscy Deparment Store**

Zachęta 1

Plac Małachowskiego 3. **Map** 1 C4. *827 58 54.* *106, 160.* *10am–6pm Tue–Sun (8pm Thu).* *free on Thu.*

This monumental building was constructed between 1899–1903, on behalf of the Society for the Promotion of Fine Art (Towarzystwo Zachęty Sztuk Pięknych, though usually it is simply abbreviated to Zachęta).

The Neo-Renaissance design was by Stefan Szyller, the leading architect of Warsaw's Revival period. His design included an imposing central staircase, a glass-roofed inner courtyard and plans for four wings. However, these wings were only fully completed as recently as 1995.

The aim of Zachęta was to promote contemporary Polish art. This included organizing exhibitions, competitions and annual salons. The society also purchased works of art for its own collection.

In 1922, Zachęta was the scene of a major political assassination. At an exhibition opening, the first president of the newly independent Republic of Poland, Gabriel Narutowicz, was shot dead.

Ornate façade of the Neo-Renaissance Zachęta building

His assassin was a Polish painter and art critic, named Eligiusz Niewiadomski.

More recently the Zachęta collection has been transferred to the National Museum, or Muzeum Narodowe as it is known in Warsaw *(see pp154–7)*. The building currently serves as a venue for temporary exhibitions of modern and contemporary Polish art.

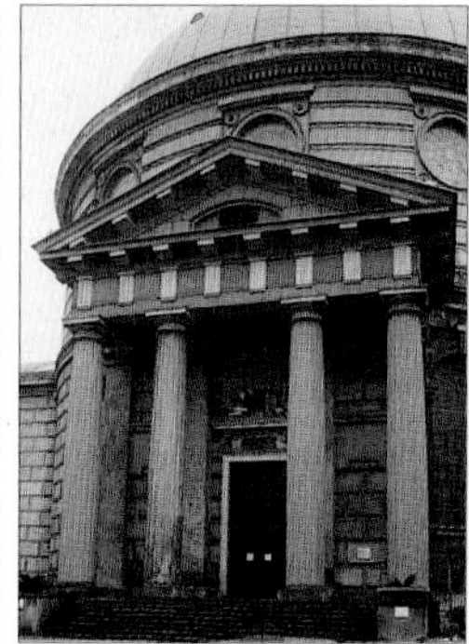

Portico of the Augsburg Protestant Community Church

Augsburg Protestant Community Church 2

Kościoł Ewangelicko Augsburski (Zbór św.Trójcy)

Kredytowa 4. **Map** 1 C4. *827 68 17.* *106, 160.* *Sun.*

Regarded as one of the most outstanding examples of Neo-Classical architecture in Poland, this church was built especially for the Lutheran community of Warsaw, in 1777–91. It also bears witness to the country's religious tolerance during the reign of Stanisław August Poniatowski, Poland's last king.

Designed by the architect Szymon Bogumił Zug, the church is reminiscent of the Pantheon in Rome, which the Romans built as "a temple of all the Gods". However, this source of inspiration was merely a starting point, from which Zug developed a unique architectural design.

There is an impressive Doric portico, which emphasizes the severity of the façade. It is crowned by a 58-m (189-ft) high dome. This feature originally made the church the tallest building in Warsaw.

The interior of the church features a vast cylindrical nave with rectangular transepts, and two-tier galleries supported by columns. The church is renowned for excellent acoustics, and is frequently used for concerts by church choirs of various denominations.

Museum of Mankind 3

Muzeum Etnograficzne

Kredytowa 1. **Map** 2 D4. *827 76 41.* *106, 160.* *9am–4pm Tue, Thu & Fri, 11am–6pm Wed, 10am–5pm Sat & Sun.* *free on Wed.*

One of the city's most beautiful 19th-century buildings, this museum was built in a Neo-Renaissance style, partly inspired by the Libreria Sansoviniana in Venice. It was originally built as the head office of the Land Credit Union, in 1854–8, and designed by Henryk Marconi, an Italian settled in Warsaw.

Within the Museum of Mankind's collection, there are permanent displays of

The Museum of Mankind

Polish folk costumes, folklore and arts and crafts. Also, the museum has a collection of ethnic and tribal art from around the world, including Africa, Australia, the Pacific and Latin America.

Temporary exhibitions are also put on, and the museum shop has a varied choice of items. Near the museum on Mazowiecka Street is "The Artist's House" (Dom Artysty). This contains a modern art gallery, and a well-stocked bookshop on the first floor.

Triangular pediment at the Engineers' Society

Engineers' Society ❹

Dom Stowarzyszenia Techników

Czackiego 3/5. **Map** 2 D4. *826 74 61.* *150, 155, 174, 192, 506.* *8am–4pm daily.*

THIS BUILDING'S lavish Neo-Baroque façade was designed by Jan Fijałkowski in 1903. It is embellished with allegorical figures by Zygmunt Otto, together with sculptures and other decorative details by Józef Gardecki.

The inscription on the portico is *Artibus Technicis* (meaning "Art and Engineering"). Below this are two figures: one is Archimedes holding a lever, and the other a "modern" woman, bearing luminous radium in her hand.

PKO SA Bank ❺

Bank PKO SA

Czackiego 21/23. **Map** 2 D4. *661 27 18.* *150, 155, 174, 192, 506.* *8am–6pm Mon–Fri, 10am–2pm Sat.*

Head office of the PKO SA Bank

THE BUILDING'S eclectic design was the work of Julian Ankiewicz. It was constructed in stages between 1878–94, and was later extended by Władysław Marconi in 1909–11. He added a triangular pediment above the portico, decorated with an allegory of Prosperity by Pius Weloński.

Formerly housing the Urban Credit Union, the building now serves as the head office of the PKO SA bank. The main hall, which is decorated with scenes of 18th-century Warsaw, has a fine skylight.

Warszawa Hotel ❻

Plac Powstańców Warszawy 9. **Map** 2 D4. *826 94 21.* *102, 148, 150, 155, 174, 180, 192, 506.* *2, 4, 15, 18, 35, 36.*

UNTIL THE Palace of Culture and Science was completed in 1955, this was the tallest building in Warsaw.

Built in 1934 on behalf of Prudential, the British insurance company, it was in the heart of the city's prewar banking district. The designers were Marcin Weinfeld and the mathematician Stefan Bryła. The latter was responsible for the steel frame, which enabled the building to withstand heavy shelling during the Warsaw Uprising in 1944.

Rebuilt in the Socialist Realist style during the postwar period, the building was then converted into a hotel.

Philharmonic ❼

Filharmonia

Jasna 5. **Map** 1 C5. *826 57 12.* *E-4, 107, 119.* **Box office** *10am–2pm, 3–7pm Mon–Sat.*

THE ORIGINAL style of the Philharmonic building was one of the city's most eclectic. Embellished with allegorical figures and statues of great composers, it was designed by the firm of Kozłowski and Pianka, and financed by private subscription. It was also built in record time. Construction began in 1900, with the inaugural concert held on 5 November 1901, led by Ignacy Paderewski *(see p34)*.

Rebuilt in the Socialist Realist style after World War II, the Philharmonic bears only a vague resemblance to its original form. The Chopin Piano Competition has been held here since 1927.

The Philharmonic at the beginning of the century

Warszawa Hotel, rebuilt after the war in the Socialist Realist style

Former Bracia Jabłkowscy Department Store ❽

Dawny Dom Towarowy Bracia Jabłkowscy

Bracka 25. **Map** 2 D5. *692 14 00.* *102, 107, 117, 128, 158, 171, 175.* *7, 8, 9, 22, 24, 25.* *10am–8pm Mon–Fri, 10am–5pm Sat, 10am–4pm Sun.*

ORIGINALLY WARSAW'S largest department store, this early Modernist building is considered to be one of the best examples of early 20th-century Polish architecture.

Designed by Franciszek Lilpop and Karol Jankowski, it was built in 1913–14 around a reinforced concrete framework. Nationalized after World War II, it initially traded as the Central Department Store (Centralny Dom Towarowy), before becoming the city's principal shoe shop (Dom Obuwia). The building fell into disrepair, but was restored recently and now houses chic boutiques. The ornate lobby features a Post-Secessionist stained-glass window (the largest in Warsaw), and humorous reliefs by Edmund Bartłomiejczyk.

Stained glass in Bracia Jabłkowscy store

Socialist Realism in Warsaw

THE REBUILDING OF WARSAW coincided with the emergence of Socialist Realism. This style of architecture presented an idealized version of reality, championing the achievements of Communism and its growing power with buildings and developments constructed on a monumental scale. The Marshal Street Residential Area (Marszałkowska Dzielnica Mieszkaniowa) is a symbol of this Socialist Realist era, inspiring the praise of writers and poets. Known as MDM, it was built in 1950–52, and replaced the partially destroyed houses on Marshal Street. The focal point of the development was at Constitution Square (Plac Konstytucji). While the façades of the buildings do show architectural merit, they are not as original as proclaimed in the propaganda of the day. Ironically, some recall the 1913 tenement building originally owned by Count Krasiński in Małachowski Square. And houses on Wyzwolenia Avenue resemble Place Vendôme in Paris. During Stalin's regime architects were banned from visiting Paris, so this was a way of enjoying a "small fragment" of that city in Warsaw.

A Socialist Realist style lamppost

The distinctive office block at No. 36 Krucza Street

The mainly glass façade of Smyk Department Store

KRUCZA STREET

AT THE END OF the 1940s and beginning of the 1950s, plans were drawn up to develop an office district in the area around Krucza, Wspólna and Żurawia streets. Large buildings with stone façades were subsequently constructed on the sites of burned down 19th-century tenement buildings. These were used to house government ministries, offices and industrial organizations.

Some buildings were also given unusual façades. The ministry building at No. 36 Krucza Street is reminiscent of a turn-of-the-century Chicago-style office block. The ten-storey Grand Hotel at No. 28 Krucza Street has a flat roof, intended to serve

SMYK ("THE BRAT")

BUILT OF GLASS and reinforced concrete, the materials associated with Modernism, this department store was officially condemned as "ideologically alien, cosmopolitan" architecture, when it was completed in 1952.

During the 1950s, the press frequently pictured the building's interiors and former café as the meeting place of Warsaw's "decadent youth".

The store suffered a major fire in 1977, but has subsequently been rebuilt.

The monumental colonnade of the Ministry of Agriculture

as a helicopter landing pad. By the hotel, on Three Crosses Square (Plac Trzech Krzyży), stands a group of buildings, originally housing the State Planning Committee, and featuring a large dome-covered conference hall.

The Ministry of Agriculture

Built in the Socialist Realist style, between 1951–5, the Ministry of Agriculture features Warsaw's tallest colonnade (on the Wspólna Street side), which is several floors high. In the 1950s plans were also drawn up to establish a large square situated opposite the ministry. This was intended to feature a cultivated field, where State farm workers who were visiting the ministry could be acquainted with the best farming methods.

Office Building at Wspólna Street

In the 1950s, the architect of this office building, Marek Leykam, was at the forefront of a particular architectural "resistance movement". While other architects were drawing up designs in accordance with the Socialist Realist "gospel", he was working in the International Style, creating buildings that were known as "razor blades", which were characterized by façades composed of repeated, prefabricated elements.

Among the examples of this style are the Budimex building at No. 82 Marshal Street, and the Mining Institute at No. 4 Rakowiecka Street.

In the first few years of the 1950s, Leykam planned to build a multi-storey "razor blade" building at No. 62 Wspólna Street. However, the authorities rejected his design, which prompted him to create a building on this site whose architectural style is actually a veiled parody of Socialist Realist principles.

The façades are variations on the theme of a 15th-century Florentine banker's palace, while the interior features a huge circular courtyard, which is covered over by a concrete dome and surrounded by several tiers of open galleries.

A dome-covered courtyard of the office block at No. 62 Wspólna Street.

The Banking and Finance Centre

This building, essentially influenced by Modernism, but with detailing in the style of Socialist Realism, was built in 1948–51 to a design by Wacław Kłyszewski, Jerzy Mokrzyński and Eugeniusz Wierzbicki. It was originally the seat of the ruling Communist Party Central Office.

It now serves as the Banking and Finance Centre, while housing the Stock Exchange (Eastern Europe's largest).

Housing Estates

Many of Warsaw's housing estates dating from the 1940s and 1950s display Socialist Realist architecture. Among these, the oldest is the small and very attractive estate at Mariensztat *(see pp122–3)*.

Larger estates were built on the site of the former Jewish Ghetto. One in this area is Muranów, which was designed by Bohdan Lachert. Its buildings were constructed on mounds of rubble, created from the postwar ruins of the district, which had been completely destroyed by the Nazis. The estate is full of tranquil squares and colonnades, as well as arched gateways leading to courtyards.

More monumental is the architecture of an estate built along Generał Anders Avenue and John Paul II Avenue, between Elektoralna Street and Solidarity Avenue. In addition, the basement of No. 36 John Paul II Avenue houses the Time shop, which still retains well-preserved 1950s decor.

The Banking and Finance Centre, housing Poland's Stock Exchange

Palace of Culture and Science ❾

THIS MONOLITHIC BUILDING was a "gift" from Soviet Russia to the people of Warsaw, and intended as a monument to "the inventive spirit and social progress". Built in 1952–5 to the design of a Russian architect, Lev Rudniev, it resembles Moscow's Socialist Realist tower blocks. Although the palace has only 30 storeys it was Europe's second tallest building when completed. Measuring just over 230 m (750 ft) including the spire, it has a volume of more than 800,000 cubic m (28 million cubic ft) and contains 40 million bricks. The interiors are said to feature many architectural and decorative elements, which were removed from stately homes after World War II. Although the palace is nearly half a century old, it still inspires extreme emotions among Varsovians, ranging from admiration to demands for its demolition. With the recent end of Soviet domination, the building's role has changed, and it now provides office space. However, the palace has remained a cultural centre with its two theatres, cinema, puppet theatre and excellent bookshop.

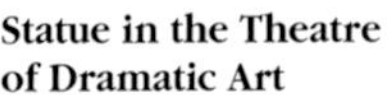

Statue in the Theatre of Dramatic Art
There are 28 such figures around the building. As Socialist Realist allegories, they represent themes such as Science, Art and the Collective Economy.

The Youth Palace contains a swimming pool, gymnasiums and a winter garden.

Lampposts, forming a semi-circle in front of the palace, are almost identical to their Muscovite prototypes.

★ Congress Hall
This is where Communist Party Congresses were formerly held. The hall continues to serve as a venue for various conferences, concerts and festivals. The best known festival is the Jazz Jamboree, which has been attended by such jazz legends as Louis Armstrong, Ray Charles and Miles Davis.

The Museum of Technology's main attractions are a planetarium and the Glass Girl, which is a model of the human body.

Plac Defilad

Almost 1 million people gathered here on 24 October 1956 to celebrate more enlightened government policies, and the appointment of Władysław Gomułka as First Secretary of the Polish Communist Party. The next great occasion here was the mass celebrated by Pope John Paul II in 1987, attended by hundreds of thousands of people.

Visitors' Checklist

Plac Defilad 1. **Map** 1 C5 & 5 C1. ☎ *656 62 01.* **Viewing Terrace** *Nov–Apr: 10am–4pm Mon–Sat, 10am–4pm Sun; May–Oct: 9am–midnight daily.*

The Viewing Terrace provides magnificent panoramas across the city.

Renaissance Attics
In Renaissance architecture, an ornamental wall above a cornice is known as an attic. The attics here were inspired by those on buildings in Kraków, Baranów and Krasiczyn.

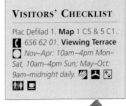

Stone obelisk in front of the palace

The Theatre of Dramatic Art is one of Poland's finest theatres.

Kinoteka is a new cinema complex. Other cinemas have been converted into the BAS Department Store.

Marble Interiors
Marble corridors and staircases link the Congress Hall with the first-floor reception rooms.

Dolphin Fountains
Within the squares surrounding the palace are four cast-iron fountains featuring dolphins. Nearby there are also three large stone fountains, and two smaller fountains.

Star Sight

★ **Congress Hall**

Historic Buildings on Aleje Jerozolimskie ⑩

Kamienice w Alejach Jerozolimskich

Map 5 C1 & 5 C2.

THE AREA ENCLOSED by Aleje Jerozolimskie and the neighbouring Nowogrodzka, Poznańska and Emilii Plater streets, features several outstanding buildings that date from the turn of the century.

The Polonia Hotel, at No. 45 Jerozolimskie Avenue, has a Parisian Beaux-Arts façade. Built between 1909 and 1913, it was commissioned by Count Konstanty Przeździecki. The hotel's flamboyant dining room has also retained its original Louis XVI style.

Buildings in Aleje Jerozolimskie

The adjacent building, at No. 47, has Secessionist interiors. There is also an impressive dome on one corner of the building. The eclectic façade of No. 51 was designed for the Hoser Brothers, a renowned landscape-gardening firm.

Through the main entrances of Nos. 49 and 51, there are two consecutive courtyards, known locally as "well shafts". These adjoining courtyards are typical of building in prewar Warsaw. Another example of this kind is at at No. 53, where the inter-connected courtyards have been converted into a glazed atrium, with galleries and glass-fronted lifts.

Nearby, in Nowogrodzka Street, there is a massive building, which was designed as the headquarters of the former Agricultural Bank. The architect was Marian Lalewicz, a Pole who returned to Warsaw after having worked in St Petersburg. Consequently, the building's Neo-Classical style resembles numerous buildings erected in St Petersburg before the Russian Revolution. The entrance hall was subsequently refurbished with various colourful Art Deco features.

Central Railway Station

Central Railway Station ⑪

Dworzec Centralny

Aleje Jerozolimskie 54. **Map** 5 C1. *9436.* *102, 105, 109, 128, 158, 160, 175, 505, 507, 519.* *7, 8, 9, 10, 12, 16, 17, 22, 24, 25, 33, 130, 151, 157.*

BUILT BETWEEN 1972 and 1976 to the design of Arseniusz Romanowicz, this is the principal railway station in Warsaw. Most trains stop here, arriving at the station's underground platforms via a tunnel under Aleje Jerozolimskie. The platforms are joined by several passageways, which run beneath the main concourse. In recent years these passages have gained a great number of shops, effectively becoming shopping arcades.

Warsaw Technical University ⑫

Politechnika Warszawska

Plac Politechniki. **Map** 5 C2. *660 72 11.* *Politechnika.* *2, 4, 15, 18, 35, 36.* *7am–9pm daily.*

WARSAW TECHNICAL UNIVERSITY is a complex of six buildings, built between 1899 and 1901, and designed by Stefan Szyller and Bronisław Brochwicz-Rogóyski. For the main building, Szyller devised a pentagonal layout arranged around a four-storey galleried courtyard. Known as the "Aula" (Assembly Hall), this spacious, glass-covered courtyard provides a popular venue for the staging of events, with smaller galleries surrounding the main area that showcase new work.

The glass-roofed Assembly Hall at Warsaw Technical University

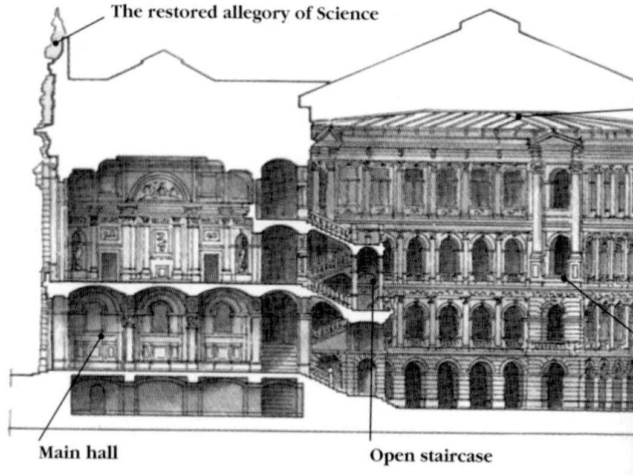

Lwowska Street ⓭
Ulica Lwowska

Map 6 D2 & 6 D3. *Politechnika.* *159.* *2, 15, 36.*

An atmosphere of turn-of-the-century Warsaw can best be enjoyed in Lwowska Street. This is the only street from that period in the city centre to escape the destruction of World War II.

A picturesque example of early Modernism, inspired by Scandinavian architecture, can be seen at No. 15/17. This building was designed in 1910 by Artur Górney.

The courtyard of No. 13 even features a small palace, which was built in 1912. The vast Secessionist/Modernist building on the corner of Lwowska and Koszykowa streets was originally the Russian College. It now houses the Architecture Department of Warsaw Technical University.

Buildings at the corner of Lwowska and Koszykowa streets

Filtering Plant ⓮
Stacja Filtrów

Starynkiewicza 5. **Map** 5 B2 & 5 B3. *628 80 61.* *159.* *2, 15.* *by arrangement.*

The water-filtering plant, which occupies a large site in central Warsaw, is one of the city's most important examples of 19th-century industrial architecture.

Part of the Filtering Plant

In the 1880s, Warsaw was the first city in the former Russian Empire to acquire a modern water and sewage system, thanks to the initiative of the city's president, General Sokrates Starynkiewicz.

However, the project had many opponents, particularly among landlords, who did not want to bear the expense of a sewage plant. One argument they cited was that the new system would damage agriculture in the surrounding region, by depriving farmers of the city's natural fertilizer.

The principal designers of the system were from England: William Lindley and his son William H Lindley, who had designed water-supply systems for other European cities. River and canal pumping stations were also built at various points by the Filtering Plant.

The Filtering Plant's most interesting features are within its underground structure. There, water filters consisting of inter-connected, vaulted brick chambers can be seen. They are supported by large granite pillars.

The former engine room now includes a small museum, which demonstrates the process of the Filtering Plant and illustrates the history of the project to build this water and sewage system.

Warsaw Technical University

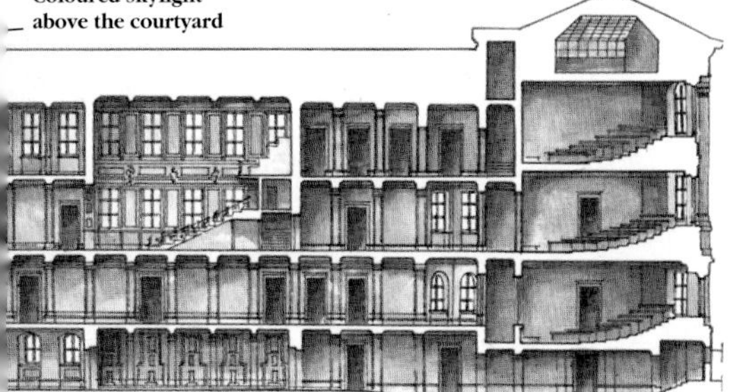

Church of the Saviour ⓯
Kościół Zbawiciela

Marszałkowska 37. **Map** 6 D3. *Politechnika.* *117, 131, 206.* *2, 4, 15, 18, 35, 36.*

Church of the Saviour

Built in 1901–11, the overall design of this church was based on a medieval cathedral. However, the façade and interiors were also inspired by Polish Renaissance and Baroque styles. The side chapels were modelled on the Zygmunt Chapel in Kraków's Wawel Castle, the royal residence until 1596.

The architects of this church, which is one of the city's largest, were Józef Pius Dziekoński, Ludwik Panczakiewicz and Władysław Żychiewicz.

THE FORMER JEWISH GHETTO

Before World War II, the northwest part of Warsaw's city centre comprised a large and mainly Jewish district known as Nalewki. Warsaw's Jewish population was then about 450,000, the largest after New York. In 1940 the Nazis turned Nalewki into the Jewish Ghetto and by 1942 over 300,000 people had been transported to death camps. A further 100,000 died or were killed in the Ghetto. Following the Ghetto Uprising in 1943, Nalewki was completely razed to the ground by the Nazis.

In the postwar years, redevelopment transformed the area into housing estates, while today, the Monument to the Ghetto Heroes is just one of the many important memorials to those that perished. A new museum, celebrating 800 years of Jewish civilisation in Poland, is due to open here in 2006.

SIGHTS AT A GLANCE

Historic Streets
Bohaterów Getta Street 13
Chłodna Street 7

Historic Buildings
Courts of Justice 18
Lubomirski Palace 20
Mostowski Palace 14

Monuments
Bunker Monument 3
Monument to the Ghetto Heroes 1
Monument to 300 Victims 6
Umschlagplatz Monument 4

Museums
Jewish History Institute 11
Norblin Factory 19

Sites of Remembrance
Path of Remembrance 2
Pawiak Prison 5
Remains of the Ghetto Wall 8

Churches and Synagogues
Church of the Nativity of the Virgin Mary 17
Nożyk Synagogue 9
Protestant Reformed Church 16

Modern Architecture
Blue Tower 12

Theatres
Jewish National Theatre 10
Warsaw Chamber Opera 15

GETTING THERE

The former Jewish Ghetto area is a sprawling district served by an extensive network of public transport. From the centre, you can take any tram or bus running along John Paul II Avenue or Marshal and Andersa streets heading towards Żoliborz.

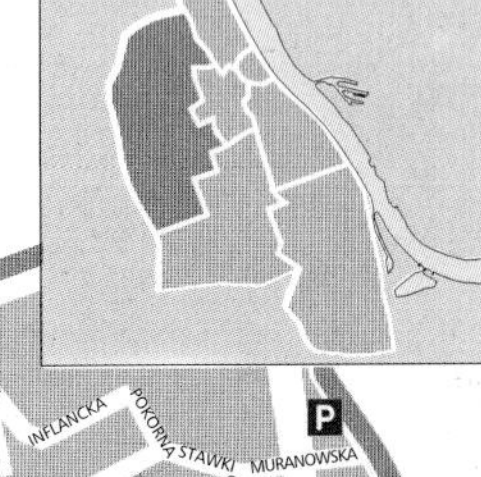

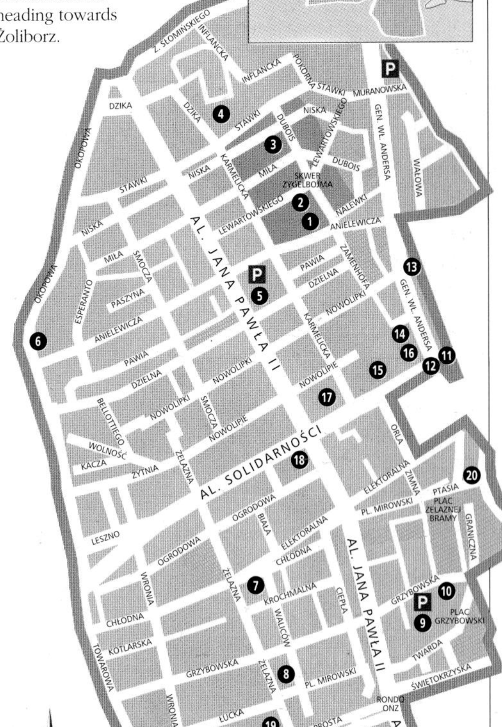

KEY

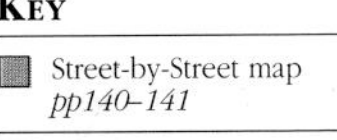

Street-by-Street map *pp140–141*

P Parking

◁ **Monument to the Ghetto Heroes**

Street-by-Street: Path of Remembrance

THE PATH OF REMEMBRANCE was laid out in the centre of the former Jewish Ghetto, where the fiercest fighting occurred in April 1943 during the Ghetto Uprising – an act of desperation instigated by the Jewish Fighters Organisation. The Ghetto, where hundreds of thousands of Jews lived in appalling conditions, was used as a source of free labour for the Nazis. The Germans suppressed the Uprising, then demolished the entire neighbourhood, using the area to torture prisoners from Pawiak *(see p143)*. The Jews who survived the Ghetto were murdered in the extermination camp at Treblinka. Monuments along the path commemorate the courage of the Ghetto's inhabitants.

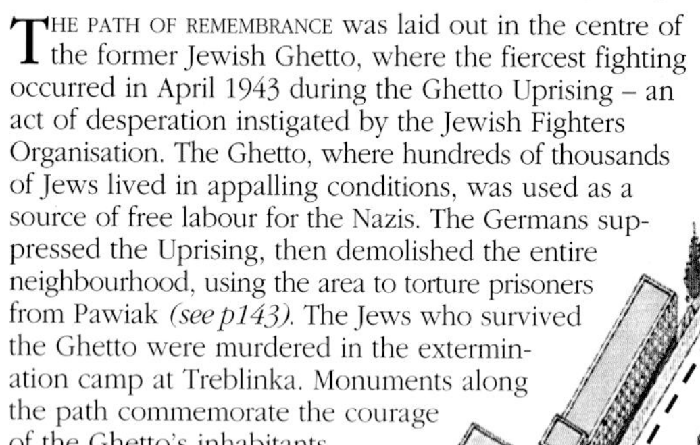

★ Umschlagplatz Monument
From this spot the Nazis deported 300,000 Jews to the death camps. The design recalls the cattle trucks used for transportation ❹

Bunker Monument
This marks the site of the bunker from which Mordechaj Anielewicz commanded the Ghetto Uprising ❸

El-Mole-Rachim
Bronisław Linke's painting, in the National Museum, expresses the despair of the jewish people.

KEY

– – – Path of remembrance

STAR SIGHTS

- ★ **Monument to the Ghetto Heroes**
- ★ **Path of Remembrance**
- ★ **Umschlagplatz Monument**

★ Path of Remembrance
This series of granite blocks was erected in the late 1980s. Each is dedicated to an event or hero of the Ghetto, with an inscription in Polish and Hebrew ❷

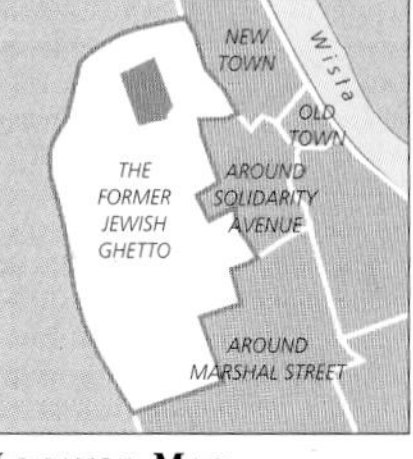

LOCATOR MAP
See Street Finder, maps 1, 3

★ Monument to the Ghetto Heroes
Erected in 1948, this powerful sculpture commemorates the Ghetto Uprising. It overlooks the centre of the former Jewish Ghetto ❶

0 m 50
0 yards 50

Mordechaj Anielewicz Street was once called Gęsia.

THE WARSAW GHETTO

The Ghetto was created in November 1940, and was inhabited principally by Jews. Initially, it extended to 307 ha (760 acres), enclosing the Jewish population of Warsaw and the surrounding towns – a total of around 450,000 people – but the area was quickly reduced by the Nazis. A reign of terror was imposed, and more than 100,000 of the inhabitants died of starvation and disease. From March 1942 mass deportations of Jews from the Ghetto to the extermination camp at Teblinka took place. The ultimate extermination of the Ghetto's inhabitants took place after the suppression of the Uprising, in May 1943.

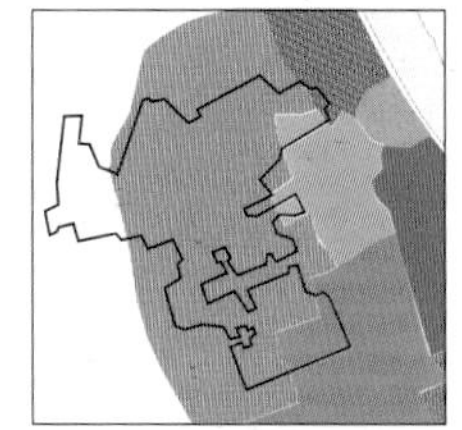

Border of the ghetto in 1940

The flattened area of the Warsaw Ghetto after its destruction in 1944

Monument to the Ghetto Heroes ❶

Pomnik Bohaterów Getta

Zamenhofa. **Map** 1 A2, 3 B4.
107, 111, 180.

ERECTED in 1948 when the city of Warsaw still lay in ruins, this monument was created by the sculptor Natan Rapaport and the architect Marek Suzin. The work symbolizes the heroic defiance of the Ghetto Uprising in 1943 *(see pp140–41)*, which was planned, not as a bid for liberty, but as an honourable way to die.

Reliefs carved on to the monument depict men, women and children struggling to flee the burning ghetto, together with a procession of Jews being driven to death camps under the threat of Nazi bayonets.

The monument was created from labradorite stone, quarried in Sweden. It is the stone that the Nazis intended to use for victory monuments in the countries that they conquered.

Path of Remembrance ❷

Trakt Męczeństwa i Walki Żydów

Zamenhofa, Stawki. **Map** 1 A1, 3 B4.
107, 111, 157, 180. *35.*

THE PATH of Remembrance, unveiled in 1988, is a route laid out between the Monument to the Ghetto Heroes and the Umschlagplatz Monument. The Path is marked by 16 granite blocks, commemorating the 450,000 Jews who were murdered in the Warsaw Ghetto and the heroes of the 1943 Uprising. Among those named on the blocks are Szmul Zygielbojm (1895–1943), a member of the Polish National Council in London, who committed suicide as an act of protest against the liquidation of the Warsaw Ghetto; Emanuel Ringelblum (1900–44), who founded the Ghetto archives which detail the resistance movement; Mordechaj Anielewicz (1917–1943), the commandant of the Jewish Resistance Organisation; Doctor Janusz Korczak who went to the death camps with the orphans in his charge *(see p143);* and Poet Icchak Kacenelson (1886–1944). Each of the granite blocks is engraved with Polish, Hebrew and Yiddish inscriptions, together with the dates 1940–43.

One of the granite blocks on the Path of Remembrance

Bunker Monument ❸

Pomnik Bunkra

Dzielna. **Map** 1 A2, 3 B5.
107, 111, 180.

BETWEEN THE STREETS of Miła and Niska, a small mound and boulder commemorate the the bunker in which Mordechaj Anielewicz (1917–43) led the Uprising. He blew up the bunker, committing suicide.

Umschlagplatz Monument ❹

Pomnik Umschlagplatz

Stawki. **Map** 1 A1, 3 B4.
148, 157, 170. *16, 17, 33, 35.*

THE UMSCHLAGPLATZ Monument was completed in 1988, on the site of a former

Marble wall of the Umschlagplatz Monument

railway siding (called Umschlagplatz) where Jews were loaded on to cattle cars and sent to almost certain death in the concentration camps.

The monument was a collaboration between the architect Hanna Szmalenberg and the sculptor Władysław Klamerus. The names of hundreds of people from the ghetto are inscribed on to the surface of the monument, including Janusz Korczak and his group of Jewish orphans.

Pawiak Prison ❺

Wiezienia Pawiak

Dzielna 24. **Map** 1 A2, 3 B5. *831 13 17.* *107, 111, 148, 157, 170.* *16, 17, 33.* *9am–5pm Wed, 9am–4pm Thu, 10am–5pm Fri, 9am–4pm Sat, 10am–4pm Sun.*

PAWIAK WAS BUILT as a prison by the Russians in 1830–35, following a design by Henryk Marconi, a member of a renowned family of architects.

The building became notorious during World War II, when it was used to imprison Poles and Jews arrested by the Nazis. Now in ruins, Pawiak serves as a museum. By

Obituaries on a tree at Pawiak

the entrance gates stands a "silent witness", in the form of a long-dead tree, covered with obituary notices for prisoners who died here during the war.

The Monument to 300 Victims, designed as a symbolic funeral pyre

Monument to 300 Victims ❼

Pomnik 300 Pomordowanych

Gibalskiego 21. *107, 111, 180.* *22, 27, 29.*

DURING BUILDING WORKS in 1988, the remains of 300 Jewish and Polish people were unearthed near the Jewish Cemetery. The victims had been murdered by Nazis on the playing fields of the Skra Sports Club.

This site is now a small cemetery, and is marked by a monument in the form of a funeral pyre. The monument was designed and built by two of Warsaw's well-known architects, Tadeusz Szumielewicz and Marek Martens.

Chłodna Street ❽

Ulica Chłodna

Map 5 A1. *125, 148, 157, 410, 522.* *16, 17, 20, 22, 24, 29, 32, 33.*

BEFORE WORLD WAR II, this was one of Warsaw's busiest streets. Its tenement blocks housed shops and several cinemas. Now, the only remnants of the street's original character are sections of tram rails and a few houses that survived the war.

Among these is the Neo-Baroque house at No. 20, known as the "House under the Clock" (dom Pod Zegarem). Designed by Wacław Heppen and Józef Napoleon Czerwiński, it was built in 1912. During the Nazi occupation, the house was within the ghetto area, and inhabited by Adam Czerniaków, chairman of the Judenrat (Jewish administration within the ghetto). Through his diaries, Czerniaków related the tragedy of Poland's Jews.

Chłodna street was an important thoroughfare and to make it accessible to the Nazis and prevent Jews from using it, a wall was built along both sides of the road. A wooden bridge then linked the two sides of the ghetto. There is a replica of the bridge in Washington's Holocaust Museum.

Wooden footbridge over Chłodna Street

JANUSZ KORCZAK

Janusz Korczak (born Henryk Goldszmidt, 1878 or 1879–1942) was a doctor, writer and educator, who devoted his life to children. He worked as a paediatrician, and from 1912 was the director of the Jewish orphanage in Warsaw. Throughout his life he fought tirelessly for children's rights, and even wrote children's books. In 1940 his orphanage was transferred to the ghetto, and in August 1942 Korczak voluntarily went to the death camps with the children from his orphanage. All perished at Treblinka.

Remains of the Ghetto Wall ❾

Fragmenty murów getta

Sienna 55, Waliców. **Map** 5 A2.
155, 157.

THE JEWISH GHETTO was created by the Nazis in 1940. The area was initially surrounded by a 3-m (10-ft) wall, with an additional metre (3 ft) of barbed wire subsequently added. When the boundaries were redrawn in 1941, to reduce the size of the ghetto, additional walls had to be built, many down the middle of streets.

The wall also ran along both sides of Chłodna Street, allowing it to be kept open for the Nazis, while preventing it from being used by Jews. This separated the ghetto into two parts, connected by a wooden pedestrian bridge across Chłodna Street.

Unauthorized crossing of the wall was punishable by death but many tunnels and concealed holes were dug out, and used to smuggle people and goods in and out.

Only a few fragments of the ghetto wall survive. A section can be seen in the courtyard at No. 55 Sienna Street, where there is a memorial plaque. Another fragment stands at the junction of Pereca and Waliców streets.

The façade of Nożyk Synagogue

Nożyk Synagogue ❿

Synagoga Nożyków

Twarda 6. **Map** 1 B4. *620 43 24.*
100, 160.

THE FOUNDERS of this synagogue were Zelman and Ryfka Nożyk, who in 1893 donated the land on which it was built, and left half of their estate to the Orthodox Jewish community. Building work lasted from 1898–1902, with the synagogue effectively concealed within a courtyard that was surrounded by tenement blocks. The synagogue was closed during World War II and used by the Nazis as a warehouse. It was reopened in 1945, and is currently the only active synagogue in Warsaw.

From 1977–83 the building was renovated, and the synagogue restored to its original condition. However, few of the tenement buildings which originally surrounded the synagogue have survived.

The synagogue has an impressive portico crowned by a metal dome bearing the Star of David. The interiors feature the Ark, the cabinet that contains the Torah scrolls, on which The Pentateuch (the first five books of the Bible) is written. The galleries that surround the nave were intended for the seating of women.

Jewish National Theatre ⓫

Państwowy Teatr Żydowski

Plac Grzybowski 12/16. **Map** 1 B4.
620 70 25. *100, 160.*
10am–2pm, 3pm–6pm Mon–Fri; noon–7pm Sat, 2:30pm–6pm Sun.

PERFORMING plays steeped in Jewish traditions, the Jewish National Theatre was founded in Łódź in 1949, when that city's theatre merged with another Jewish theatre company from Lower

Reading from a fragment of the Pentateuch at Nożyk Synagogue

A scene from a performance by the Jewish National Theatre

Silesia. The company moved to Warsaw in 1955, and this building dates from 1970. Performances are in Yiddish, with translations into Polish. The theatre also runs a Mime Theatre and an actors' studio.

A Torah shield, displayed at the Jewish History Institute

Jewish History Institute ⓬

Żydowski Instytut Historyczny

Tłomackie 3/5. **Map** 3 C5. ☎ 827 92 21. 🚌 *E-2, 107, 111, 125, 127, 170, 171, 190, 307, 406, 409, 512.* 🚋 *2, 4, 13, 15, 18, 26, 32, 35, 36.* ◯ *8am–4pm Mon–Fri.* **Museum** ◯ *9am–4pm Mon–Wed & Fri; 11am–6pm Thu.* *last admission 30mins before closing.*

THE Jewish History Institute's Neo-Classical building was designed by renowned architect, Edward Eber and was completed in 1936. When designing this building, Eber aimed to harmonize the façade with that of the neighbouring Great Synagogue (which was destroyed by the Nazis seven years later). The building served as both the Judaic Library and the Judaic History Institute. One of the Judaic History Institute's lecturers was the outstanding historian Dr Majer Bałaban.

Restored after World War II, the building became the Jewish History Institute. Its extensive archives include, amongst other things, documentation of synagogues and other Jewish buildings which no longer exist. The Institute also houses a library and a museum with relics from Jewish ghettos and Nazi death camps, and German collections of Judaica. There is also a large collection of work by Jewish artists including Leopold Gottlieb, Eliasz Kanarek, Jan Gotard and brothers Menasz and Ephraim Seidenbeutel.

The Blue Tower ⓭

Błękitny Wieżowiec

Plac Bankowy 2. **Map** 1 B3, 3 C5. 🚌 *E-2, 107, 111, 119, 127, 170, 171, 190, 409, 410, 415, 420, 508, 512, 515, 522, 524.* 🚋 *2, 4, 13, 15, 18, 26, 32, 35, 36.*

WITH ITS shimmering aquamarine glass walls, this tower is one of the city's most attractive buildings. It was completed in the early 1990s, after the fall of the Communist regime, by converting a tower block that had stood unfinished for over 25 years. The partially built façades of the tower block featured gold-coloured aluminium, and it became known as "the golden tooth of Warsaw." The structure was also said to be cursed, as it had been built on the former site of the Great Synagogue, once the largest Jewish temple in Warsaw. On 16 May 1943, the synagogue was blown up on the orders of the Nazi "butcher of the ghetto", General Jürgen Stroop, in retaliation for the Ghetto Uprising *(see p140)*. It represented the final, barbaric liquidation of the Jewish quarter. All that remains of the synagogue is a fragment of one of the stone columns and a cloak-room ticket. Both can now be seen in the Jewish History Institute Museum.

The Blue Tower

The Great Synagogue before it was destroyed by the Nazis

Bohaterów Ghetta Street 14

Ulica Bohaterów Ghetta

Formerly Nalewki Street. **Map** 3 C5. *111, 180, 516.* *2, 4, 15, 18, 35, 36.*

BEFORE WORLD WAR II, this was the area's main commercial street, and was principally occupied by Jews. Among the numerous shops and offices, the largest was Simons Arcade, at the junction with Długa Street. Several storeys high, it was built of glass and reinforced concrete over a four-year period from 1900 to 1904. The arcade housed shops, a hotel, small Jewish theatres and the Makabi Sports Club.

Nalewki Street was completely destroyed during World War II, and it is difficult to envisage its former appearance. However, part of the original street runs through Krasiński Gardens. There are bullet marks on fragments of remaining walls, and sections of tram lines among the cobbles.

Mostowski Palace 15

Pałac Mostowskich

Andersa 15. **Map** 1 B2 & 3 B4. *to Plac Zamkowy.*

THIS BEAUTIFUL Neo-Classical building was originally a Baroque palace that was the property of the Voivode (marshal) of Minsk, Jan Hilzen. From 1823 the palace housed the Administrative Commission for Internal Affairs. The Minister of the Interior, Tadeusz Mostowski, commissioned architect Antonio Corazzi to redesign the palace. The ornamental façade also includes some Neo-Classical reliefs by Paweł Maliński and Jan Norblin.

Following the Russian suppression of the November Uprising in 1830, the palace was converted into barracks for the Russian army.

After World War II the building was greatly extended, and served as the headquarters for the city's militia. For years rumours circulated in the city that the cellars beneath its offices were crowded with political prisoners. The palace now houses the Warsaw police headquarters.

The imposing Neo-Classical façade of Mostowski Palace

Warsaw Chamber Opera 16

Warszawska Opera Kameralna

Aleja Solidarności 76b. **Map** 1 B3 & 3 B5. *831 22 40.* *125, 170, 171.* *13, 23, 26, 32.*
Box office *Sep–Jul: 10am– 2pm, 4–7pm Mon–Fri, 4–7pm Sat–Sun.*

ORIGINALLY BUILT as a Protestant church between 1770–80, this building now houses the Warsaw Chamber Opera. It is also the venue that hosts an annual Mozart Festival held at the end of June and beginning of July. Designed by Szymon Bogumił Zug, the church was founded by the inhabitants of Leszno, a small town established and owned by the aristocratic Leszczyński family. Leszno was originally home to settlers from Germany, who managed to maintain their Protestant faith.

Warsaw Chamber Opera building

The tall, Neo-Gothic spire of the Protestant Reformed Church

Protestant Reformed Church 17

Kościół Ewangelicko Reformowany

Aleja Solidarności 76. **Map** 1 B3 & 3 B5. *831 23 83.* *E-2, 119, 125, 170, 171.* *13, 23, 26, 32.*

DESIGNED BY Adolf Adam Loewe, this Neo-Gothic church with its distinctive open-work tower was built between 1866 and 1882.

Unlike churches of other Christian denominations, notice that this church does not have a main altar. In its place, it contains a pulpit from which biblical stories are read to the churchgoers.

The Baroque Church of the Nativity of the Virgin Mary

Church of the Nativity of the Virgin Mary ⓲
Kościół Narodzenia NMP

Aleja Solidarności 80 (formerly Leszno Street). **Map** 1 A3 & 3 B5. *E-2, 119, 125, 170, 171.* *13, 16, 17, 19, 26, 32, 33.*

Built over a lengthy period from 1638 to 1731, this modest Baroque church has a courtyard, which originally held a pillory used to punish "promiscuous youths, notorious rogues and thieves".

During the partitions of Poland *(see pp28–9)*, the church was used as a prison for political activists.

It was within the Warsaw Ghetto in World War II, and used to help smuggle Jews out of the ghetto via tunnels under the crypt.

After World War II, when Leszno Street was widened to make way for the W–Z Route, the church found itself more than a little stranded in the middle of the new traffic system. In a feat of amazingly ambitious engineering mobility the entire building was subsequently transported 20 m (65 ft) in 1962, by means of what was then absolutely state-of-the-art technology.

Courts of Justice ⓳
Gmach Sądów

Aleja Solidarności 127. **Map** 1 A3 & 3 B5. 620 03 71. *8:30am– 4pm Mon–Fri* *119, 125, 171, 410, 522.* *13, 23, 26, 32.*

This monumental building, designed by Bohdan Pniewski, was constructed between 1935–9. A notable feature, extending across the full width of the façade, is the inscription: "Justice is the foundation of the strength and stability of the Republic".

During the Nazi occupation Polish Jews, and also Christians, used this building to smuggle themselves in and out of the Warsaw Ghetto.

After World War II, show trials of clergymen and political opponents of Communism were held here. However, in 1980 the Solidarity Trade Union was officially registered in the building, which was an unprecedented act in Communist bloc countries.

Steps up to the Courts of Justice

Norblin Factory ⓴
Fabryka Norblina

Żelazna 51/53. **Map** 5 B1. *620 47 92.* *105, 109, 150, 155, 157.* *10.* **Industry Museum** *9am–4pm Tue–Sat, 10am–4pm Sun.*

Currently housing the Industry Museum, part of the Museum of Technology *(see p134)*, this was formerly the Norblin, Buch Bros & T Werner Joint Stock Co, which was renowned for producing silver and silver-plated items, sheet metal and wire.

The museum comprises the original production halls, complete with equipment used there, such as stamping presses and forging machines.

Additional temporary exhibitions illustrate the intriguing history of the Norblin plant, and the evolution of the motorcycle. This includes a pre-war Sokół ("Falcon") motorcycle, which the majority of connoisseurs put on a par with the Harley-Davidson.

Lubomirski Palace ㉑
Pałac Lubomirskich

Plac Żelaznej Bramy. **Map** 1 B4. *107, 119, 127, 171, 508, 512.* *2, 4, 15, 18, 35, 36.* ***Not open*** *to the public.*

The most extraordinary event in the history of this 17th-century palace occurred in 1970, when the entire building was turned 78 degrees. The façade now completes the Saxon Axis (a Baroque town-planning scheme).

Originally Baroque, the palace was rebuilt and updated to the Rococo style. It also acquired Neo-Classical features, including a colonnade, in 1791–3. The architect was Jakub Hempel, hired by Prince Aleksander Lubomirski, whose wife Aleksandra was one of the few Poles guillotined in the French Revolution. Legend has it that Aleksandra was killed for rejecting the advances of the revolutionary Maximilien Robespierre.

The monumental colonnade of the Lubomirski Palace

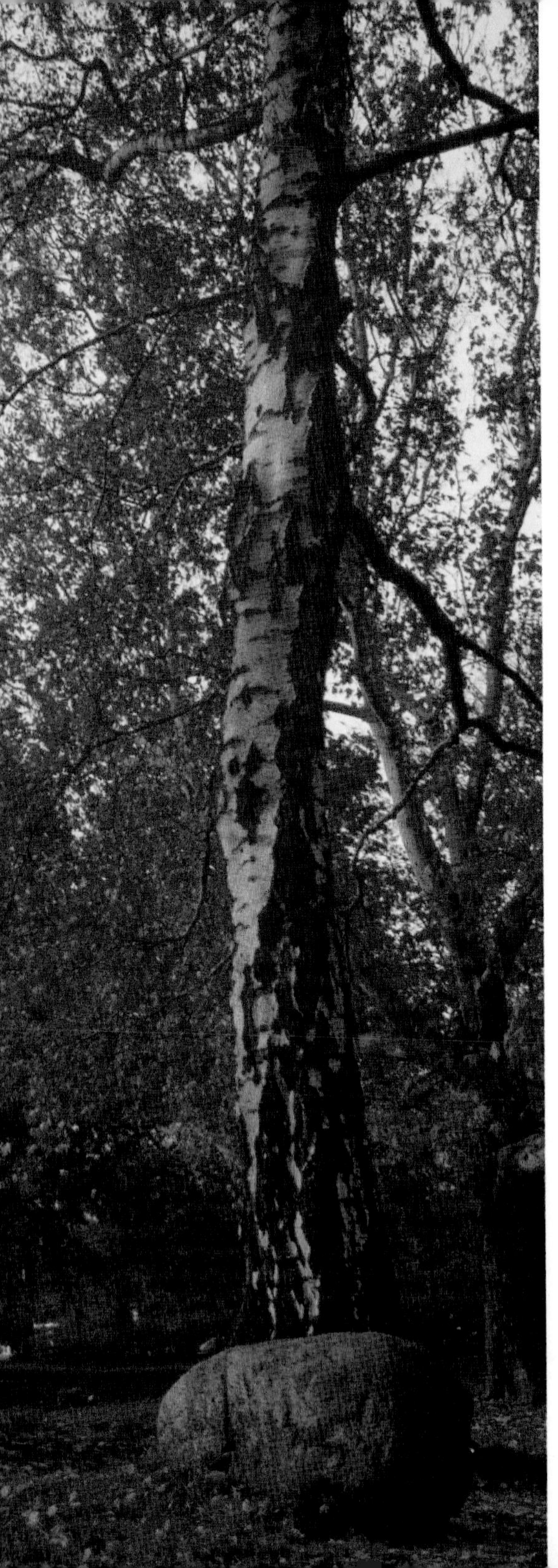

Sights at a Glance

Getting There

Various buses to Ujazdowskie Avenue, Ujazdowski Park and Łazienki Park pass along the Royal Route. Buses and trams running along Jerozolimskie Avenue pass the National Museum and Polish Army Museum. By these museums is the suburban railway station, Powiśle.

Key

Street-by-Street map *pp150–51*

P Parking

◁ **A pretty corner in Ujazdowski Pa**

AROUND ŁAZIENKI PARK

This part of Warsaw includes parks, palaces and other historic buildings, museums and government departments. Extending south from Three Crosses (Trzech Krzyży) Square, the main thoroughfare is Ujazdowskie Avenue, along which the former residences of Polish aristocrats and the city's wealthy merchant families can be seen. In addition to several government departments, the two chambers of the Polish Parliament occupy a large complex on the adjacent Wiejska Street.

Statue of a satyr in Łazienki Park

At the far end of Ujazdowskie Avenue is Belweder Palace, until 1994 the residence of Poland's president. A number of foreign legations are also on Ujazdowskie Avenue, including the embassies of Spain, the UK, Canada and the US.

However, Łazienki Park is the most popular attraction. This romantic, landscaped park includes the Palace on the Water, together with various other palaces, pavilions, an amphitheatre and two orangeries.

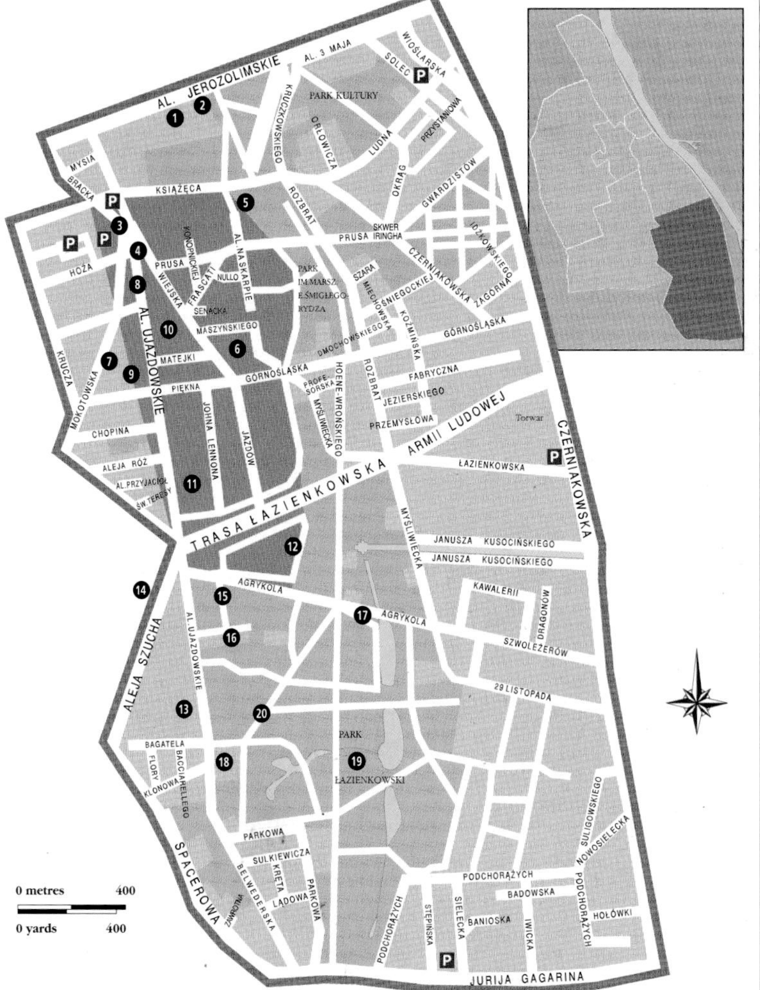

Street-by-Street: Along Ujazdowskie Avenue

THE AREA AROUND Ujazdowskie Avenue and Three Crosses Square is Warsaw's political and diplomatic district. It includes Belweder Palace, which was occupied by the head of state Józef Piłsudski *(see p30)* before World War II, and by Lech Wałęsa until 1994 when he transferred the president's official residence to Namiestnikowski Palace *(see pp118–9)*.

Parliament
The complex of parliamentary buildings includes the semi-circular Debating Hall, built in 1928 and decorated with Art Deco bas-reliefs 6

Hotel Sheraton
This modern hotel overlooks a monument to peasant activist Wincenty Witos (see p152).

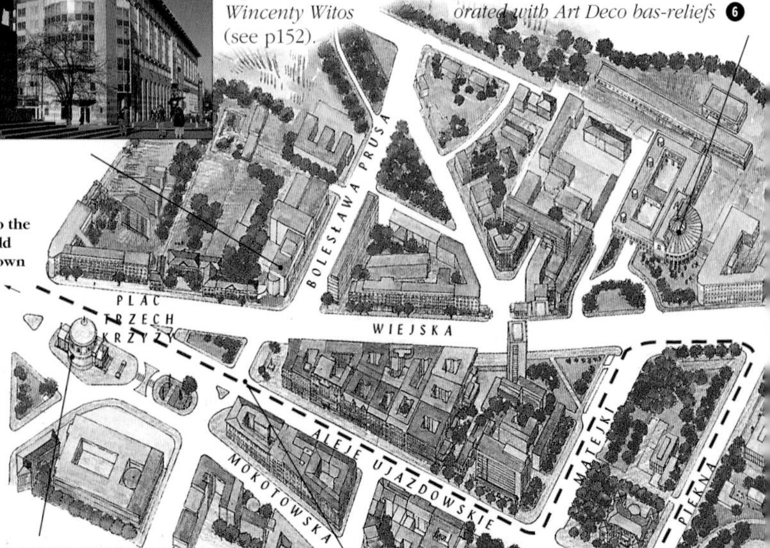

Three Crosses Square
Small 18th-century houses and St Alexander's Church nestle between modern 20th-century buildings 3

St Alexander's Church
This Neo-Classical church was remodelled and much enlarged in 1886–95, but after its destruction during World War II it was restored to its 18th-century form 4

Villas on Ujazdowskie Avenue
Villa Rau, like several other period buildings on this street, is occupied by a foreign legation 9

STAR SIGHTS

★ **Modern Art Centre**

★ **Łazienki Park**

KEY

— — — Suggested route

★ Ujazdowski Park
Created at the end of the 19th century, this small park is an oasis of greenery among the surrounding embassy buildings ⓫

THE ROYAL ROUTE
AROUND MARSHAL STREET
AROUND ŁAZIENKI PARK

LOCATOR MAP
See Street Finder, maps 2, 6

★ Modern Art Centre
Ujazdowski Castle, rebuilt after World War II in its original early Baroque style, now houses the Modern Art Centre ⓬

★ Łazienki Park
One of the city's most beautiful parks, it was laid out in the late 18th-century ⓳

Botanical Gardens
The gardens feature an observatory and a specialized plot for medicinal plants ⓯

National Museum ❶
Muzeum Narodowe

See pp154–7.

Suit of armour from the Polish Military Museum

Polish Military Museum ❷
Muzeum Wojska Polskiego

Aleja Jerozolimskie 3. **Map** 2 E5 & 6 E1. *629 52 71. 102, 111, 117. 7, 22, 24, 25. Powiśle. 10am–4pm Wed–Sun (11am–4pm during summer). Exhibition in park open until dusk, admission free.*

ESTABLISHED BY the statesman and military leader Marshal Józef Piłsudski *(see p30)*, the Polish Military Museum was opened in 1920. The museum has occupied its present site since 1933, and is Warsaw's second largest museum.

The collection grippingly manages to illustrate the history and development of Polish weapons, firearms and armour over the last thousand years, particularly from the early Middle Ages to the 18th century. This includes full tournament armours and an extremely rare gilded helmet, which belonged to a Polish chieftain in the early Christian era (Poland became a Christian country in 966).

The collection of hussars' armour is unique in Europe, and there is also a fine life-size mounted figure of a hussar on display. During the 17th century, Polish hussars were widely acknowledged as being the finest heavy cavalry in Europe, and their ultimate victory was at Vienna in 1683, when their charge mercilessly broke the mighty Turkish army. During that encounter, a splendid Turkish officer's tent was part of the booty taken by the hussars. Weapons, tanks and many aircraft from World War II can also be seen in the museum's park.

Three Crosses Square ❸
Plac Trzech Krzyży

Map 6 E1. *108, 116, 119, 122, 128, 151, 171, 180, 195, 404, 503, 509, 513, 518.*

THE NAME of this square does not quite tally with the fact that there are only two columns topped with gilded crosses in the square. These crosses were erected in 1731 by Joachim Daniel Jauch, on the order of King August II Mocny, and they marked the beginning of the Calvary Road (Stations of the Cross).

However, a third cross is held by the figure of St John of Nepomuk. This was erected in the square in 1752, founded by the Grand Court Marshal Franciszek Bieliński, to commemorate the completion of Warsaw's paving scheme. A fourth cross can be seen on the dome of nearby St Alexander's Church.

The two oldest houses on the square are both 18th century. The house on the corner of Nowy Świat Street has a very attractive early Neo-Classical façade, while the house at No. 2 is part of a complex belonging to the Institute for the Deaf and Blind, founded in 1817 by the parish priest, Father Jakub Falkowski. The institute's main office occupies a Neo-Renaissance house, which was built in the mid-19th century.

Figure of St Joh of Nepomuk

The area around the Wincenty Witos monument (Witos was Poland's prime minister in the early 1920s) is now a favourite haunt of young skateboarders.

St Alexander's Church ❹
Kościół św. Aleksandra

Plac Trzech Krzyży. **Map** 6 E1. *628 53 35. 100, 108, 116, 119, 122, 151, 171, 180, 195, 503, 509, 513.*

CHRYSTIAN PIOTR AIGNER designed this church, which was built between 1818–25. While the church was modelled on Rome's Pantheon, it is far more modest in size.

The most remarkable features of the church are two monumental porticoes, set in an otherwise plain façade.

Modernist Holland Park development, by St Alexander's Church

Warsaw in 1773, looking from the terrace of the Royal Castle. The series of 18th-century portraits by Marcello Bacciarelli includes a portrait of King Stanisław August Poniatowski, which symbolically shows the king with an hourglass.

Highlights from the Romantic section are two paintings by Piotr Michałowski: one of his daughter on horseback, and another of Napoleon Bonaparte, also on horseback. Other Romantic painters whose works are represented in the collection include Józef Simmler and Henryk Rodakowski. The former is famous for his painting *The Death of Barbara Radziwiłł*.

Leading the collection of paintings of historical subjects is Jan Matejko's great work *The Battle of Grunwald*. Among his other works is *Stańczyk*, which depicts the famous Polish court jester.

The Academic style can be seen in Henryk Siemiradzki's, work, particularly *Christian Dirce*, with Realism represented by the Gierymski brothers and Józef Chełmoński.

Impressionist paintings include works by Leon Wyczółkowski, Władysław Podkowiński and Józef Pankiewicz.

Symbolism and Modernism are represented by artists such as Józef Mehoffer, who painted *The Strange Garden*, as well as through Stanisław Wyspiański's pastel works.

20th-Century Polish Art

Between 1918–39, Polish art reflected all the main schools and genres of European art, with numerous examples among the National Museum's collection.

Important works include a number by Gauguin's disciple, Władysław Ślewiński, and a large collection by the Cubist artist Tadeusz Makowski.

Expressionist painters whose works can be seen in the museum's collection include Tytus Czyżewski, Leon Chwistek and Bolesław Cybis.

Works by Abstract painters such as Władysław Strzemiński and Henryk Stażewski, who were members of the "Blok" and "Praesens" artistic circles, are also exhibited.

More traditional styles of painting were followed by a number of Polish artists who worked in Paris, such as Jan Cybis, Józef Czapski and Tamara Łempicka, who became internationally acclaimed for her striking portraits.

There is also an interesting and varied selection of works by modern Polish sculptors. These include examples by Bolesław Biegas and the renowned Xawery Dunikowski *(see p172)*.

Primavera **(1936) by Polish artist Bolesław Cybis.**

Foreign Art

The foreign art collection embraces a wide range of artistic styles and schools, including works by Italian, French, Dutch, German and Flemish masters.

In the Italian collection, the most significant canvas is undoubtedly Sandro Botticelli's *Madonna and Child*. Other masterpieces include *Jesus Teaching in the Temple* by Cima de Conegliano and the splendid *Venus and Amor* by Paris Bordone. Baroque art is represented by several painters such as Crespi and Tiepolo, together with some outstanding works by Bernardo Bellotto.

A comparatively modest French collection includes *The Guitar Player* by Jean-Baptiste Greuze, as well as works by Natier and Largillière.

The Guitar Player **(1757) by Jean-Baptiste Greuze**

The German and Dutch collections include a polyptych of St Reinold by Joos van Cleve, a triptych known as *Ecce Homo* by Maerten van Heemskerck and a painting entitled *Beautiful Princess*, the work of Lucas Cranach.

Other Flemish and Dutch artists represented include Jan Brueghel, Jacob Jordaens, Jan Steen and Hendrick Terbrugghen. However, the most impressive painting from the Flemish and Dutch school is the *Resurrection of Lazarus* by Carel Fabritius.

Also on display are several works by Gustave Courbet, Maurice Vlaminck and Paul Signac, dating from the late 19th and early 20th century.

Polish Decorative Art

The second floor of the National Museum houses Polish arts and crafts. One gallery displays embroideries and a selection of other textiles together with some Gobelin tapestries. Another gallery features glass, porcelain and faïence, and gold artefacts from the workshops maintained by Polish aristocrats.

There are also displays of furniture of the 19th and 20th centuries, fashion and many other objects of applied art.

European Decorative Art

Around 500 items of decorative art are exhibited, dating from the medieval era to the 19th century.

"Under the Artichoke" villa in Ujazdowskie Avenue

Ujazdowskie Avenue ❽

Aleje Ujazdowskie

Map 6 E2 & 6 E3. *107, 116, 119, 122, 138, 151, 180, 182, 195, 503, 513.*

THIS TREE-LINED STREET is one of Warsaw's most beautiful, attracting crowds of people during the summer months.

The street was originally known as Calvary Road. It was designed by Joachim Daniel Jauch for King August II Mocny, and laid out on land belonging to Ujazdów village. In the late 18th century, Ujazdów became part of an urban development and the street was lined with lime trees. On the west side stand elegant villas and houses, built for Warsaw's ruling classes, while the eastern side is bordered by parks and gardens running from Piękna Street to Belweder Palace.

Villas on Ujazdowskie Avenue ❾

Pałacyki w Alejach Ujazdowskich

Map 6 E2. *107, 116.*

AMONG the avenue's most interesting villas is one that stands at Nos. 12–14. It was built in the 19th century, and owned by the Marconi family. Restyled in 1869 by Leandro Marconi, it is known as "Under the Artichoke" after the decorative artichoke on its façade. At No. 27 is the Neo-Classical Rau villa, which was also designed by Marconi.

Town Houses on Ujazdowskie Avenue ❿

Kamienice w Alejach Ujazdowskich

Map 6 E2. *107, 116, 119, 122, 195, 501, 503, 509, 513.* ***Not open*** *to the public.*

GILT STUCCO WORK, marble walls and roof gardens typified Ujazdowskie Avenue's chic houses. Nos. 17 and 19, designed by Grochowicz, have survived in their original form. The eclectic No. 17 was built in 1904 for the caviar importer Nicholas Szelechow. No. 19 was built in 1912 for Henryk Kołobrzeg-Kolberg, who produced optical instruments. Among the magnificent interiors were gilded balcony balustrades and Rococo-style bedrooms, complete with white marble fireplaces imported from Paris.

Gladiator **by Pius Weloński in Ujazdowski Park**

Ujazdowski Park ⓫

Park Ujazdowski

Aleje Ujazdowskie. **Map** 6 E2. *107, 116, 119, 122, 195, 503, 509, 513, 520.* *dawn–dusk.*

ONE HUNDRED years ago, this area was a venue for folk dancing and other types of popular entertainment. The most famous celebration held here was in 1829, when Tsar Nicholas I was crowned king of Poland. Crowds drank mead from special fountains, while beer and wine flowed from "natural springs".

The park's present form, with a lake, waterfall, bridges and various trees, was laid out in 1896, following a design by Franciszek Szanior. Within the park can be found two bronze statues: *Gladiator* by Pius Weloński (1892) and *Eve* by Edward Wittig. A set of scales for public use date from 1912.

Modern Art Centre ⓬

Centrum Sztuki Współczesnej

Aleje Ujazdowskie 6. **Map** 6 E3. *628 12 71.* *116, 119, 122, 195, 503, 509, 513.* *11am–4:30pm Tue–Thu & Sat–Sun, 11am–8:30pm Fri.* *free Thu.*

UJAZDOWSKI CASTLE, which now houses the Modern Art Centre, was built at the beginning of the 17th century for King Zygmunt III Waza and his son Władysław IV. The castle featured a courtyard, four towers and richly decorated interiors. Its splendour, was not long-lived, as the castle was looted by Swedish soldiers during the invasion of 1655. Between 1809 and 1944, it was used as a military hospital. Burnt out after the war, the ruins were detonated by the Communists in 1953. The castle was rebuilt in the 1970s, and houses a major collection of works by many of the greatest 20th-century artists. The Qchnia Artystyczna restaurant is also here, and offers the opportunity to enjoy views over the Royal Canal from its windows.

Ujazdowskie Avenue's wide, shaded walkways

Ujazdowski Castle, reconstructed in the 1970s and home to the Modern Art Centre

Cabinet Office ⑬

Urząd Rady Ministrów

Aleje Ujazdowskie 1. **Map** 6 E3. *116, 119, 122, 195, 503, 513.* ***Not open*** *to the public.*

The polish cabinet holds its regular meetings in this imposing office, situated on Ujazdowskie Avenue.

The building was constructed in 1900, following a design by architects Wiktor Junosza Piotrowski and Henryk Gay, and originally it served as the barracks for the Suvorov Cadet School. The Infantry Officers' School was also housed here up until 1926, after which the building became the headquarters of the Inspector General of the Polish Armed Forces.

During the interwar years one wing was used to house the Military Library and the Rapperswil Museum collection. Both the library and the museum collection were destroyed by fire in 1939, which was caused by Nazi bombardment.

Between 1984 and 1990, part of the building was occupied by the Communist Party's Academy of Social Sciences, which was commonly called "The First of May Academy".

These days the Cabinet Office is often the scene of anti-government demonstrations. Protesting miners have been known to spread heaps of coal outside the main entrance. Similarly, farmers have followed the miners' example by dumping mounds of potatoes.

The impressive main entrance to the Cabinet Office

Ministry of Education ⑭

Ministerstwo Edukacji Narodowej

Aleja Szucha 25. **Map** 6 E3. *629 49 19. 116, 119, 122, 151, 180, 195, 503.* **Museum of Struggle and Martyrdom** *9am–5pm Wed, 9am–4pm Thu, 10am–5pm Fri, 9am–4pm Sat, 10am–4pm Sun.*

The design of this building, which was constructed in 1925–30, is notable for the striking contrast between its façades and the interiors.

The modernist façade, with its impressive Neo-Classical columns, was designed by the architect Zdzisław Mączeński. Meanwhile, the Art Deco interiors were completed by Wojciech Jastrzębowski. The monumental proportions of this building must have pleased the Nazis, who used it as the Gestapo headquarters. The building's cellars were turned into torture chambers, and thousands of Poles died here during World War II.

Since then, the cellars have been transformed into the Museum of Struggle and Martyrdom (Mauzoleum Walki i Męczeństwa). Within this museum, one of the cells, which the prisoners called "the tramcar", has been preserved exactly as it was left by the Nazis. Prisoners waiting to be tortured had to sit behind one another, as in a tram, with their backs to the door. There they remained, motionless and silent, awaiting their fate.

Botanical Gardens ⓯

Ogród Botaniczny

Aleje Ujazdowskie 4. **Map** 6 E3. *553 05 11.* *116, 118, 119, 195, 403.* *Apr–Aug: 9am–8pm Mon–Fri, 10am–8pm Sat & Sun; Sep: 10am–6pm daily; Oct: 10am–5pm daily.*

Warsaw's first botanical gardens were laid out in 1811 behind Kazimierzowski Palace for the Medical School, which five years later became part of Warsaw University *(see pp120–21)*. The present gardens were laid out in 1818, when Tsar Alexander I endowed the University of Warsaw with a 22-ha (54-acre) site in Łazienki Park. The garden's director, Michał Szubert, published the first catalogue of plants growing in the gardens in 1824, listing more than 10,000 species, and at the time it was thought to be Europe's finest botanical garden.

Following the November Uprising of 1830, Russian acts of reprisal included reducing the size of the gardens by around two-thirds. Varsovians did not initially respect the gardens. As late as the 1850s, society ladies would arrive in horse-drawn carriages and steal specimens from the cacti collection.

During the same period, the gardens were also used as a rendezvous for clandestine patriotic meetings. On this site in 1792, foundations were laid for a Temple of Providence to commemorate the May

Tulips blooming in the spring

A quiet section of the historic Botanical Gardens

Constitution of 1791. Although the temple was never completed, traces of the foundations can still be seen in the gardens.

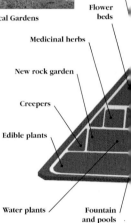

Azaleas and roses

Flower beds

Medicinal herbs

New rock garden

Creepers

Edible plants

Water plants

Fountain and pools

The Observatory

The Observatory ⓰

Obserwatorium Astronomiczne

Aleje Ujazdowskie 4. **Map** 6 E3. *629 40 11.* *116, 119, 195, 503.*

The observatory was built for the University of Warsaw in 1824, from a design by Michał Kado and Hilary Szpilowski, and supervised by the architect Chrystian Piotr Aigner.

In the 19th century, the society ladies of Warsaw used to gather on the observatory's terrace to view the botanical gardens and various alternative entertainments held in Ujazdowski Square. During the 1944 Warsaw Uprising, the observatory was burned, but was subsequently rebuilt following the war.

Jan III Sobieski Monument ⓱

Pomnik Jana III Sobieskiego

Agrykola. **Map** 6 E3. *100, 108, 116, 119, 162, 195, 503.*

This monument was erected by Poland's last king, Stanisław August Poniatowski, in 1788. It stands on the

Jan III Sobieski Monument

Botanical Gardens

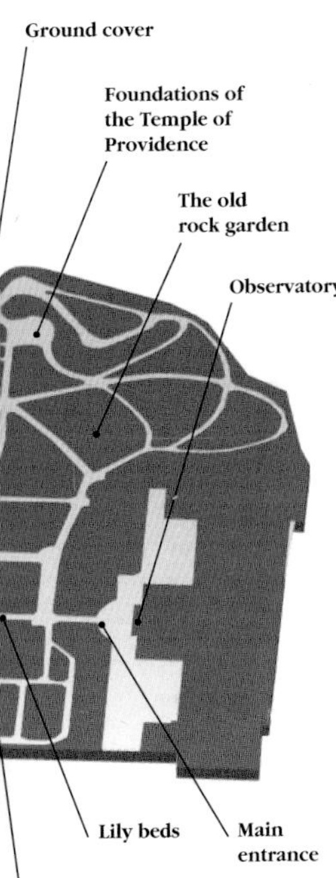

Agrykola Bridge and can be seen from the Palace on the Water, across the lake.

The monument was probably designed by André le Brun, and sculpted by Francis Pinck. The king is wearing Roman-style armour, according to the artistic conventions of the time, and his horse is trampling a Turk.

Apart from honouring Jan III Sobieski for defeating the Turks at Vienna in 1683, the monument also had a political motive. King Stanisław August Poniatowski aimed to incite anti-Turkish feelings, before joining a Russo-Austrian coalition in the war against the Ottoman Empire.

Belweder Palace 18

Pałac Belweder

Belwederska 52. **Map** 6 E4. *116, 119, 195, 503.*
by arrangement only.

Although this palace dates from the 17th century, it acquired a certain notoriety in 1818, when it became the residence of Warsaw's Russian viceroy, Grand Duke Constantine (the loathed brother of Tsar Alexander I).

The palace was refurbished and extended before the grand duke and his wife (a Polish aristocrat) took up residence, with the grounds also laid out to provide a landscaped park. Several romantic pavilions in Greek, Egyptian and Gothic styles were set around a pool and canals. These grounds are now part of Łazienki Park.

On 29 November 1830, an initial action of the November Insurrection saw a detachment of cadet officers, together with a number of students, attacking Belweder Palace. However, the grand duke managed to escape.

Since 1918, the palace has belonged to the state. Marshal Józef Piłsudski *(see p30)* occupied it from 1926 to 1935. It was then the official residence of Poland's president from 1945 to 1952 and 1989 to 1994.

One of the wide variety of plants in the Botanical Gardens

The beautiful Neo-Classical palace is best seen from the foot of the escarpment.

Łazienki Park 19

See pp162–3.

Magnolias in Łazienki Park

Palace on the Water 20

Pałac Na Wodzie

See pp164–5.

The elegant portal and columns at the entrance of Belweder Palace

Łazienki Park and Palaces ⓲

Łazienki Królewskie

The Łazienki Park dates from the Middle Ages, when it belonged to the Mazovian dukes. By the early 17th century, it belonged to the Polish crown, and housed a royal menagerie. In 1674 the Grand Crown Marshal Stanisław Herakliusz Lubomirski acquired the park, and Tylman of Gameren designed its hermitage and bathing pavilion. The pavilion gave the park its name, as *łazienki* means "baths". In the 18th century, the park was owned by King Stanisław August Poniatowski, who commissioned Karol Agrykola, Karol Schultz and Jan Schuch to lay it out as a formal garden. Dominik Merlini redesigned the pavilion as a residence. The Łazienki Palace is now a museum.

Peacock in Łazienki Park

★ Old Orangerie
In 1788 Dominik Merlini created a theatre in the east wing of this building. It is now one of the few remaining 18th-century court theatres.

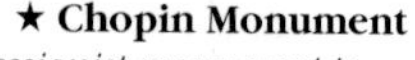

★ Chopin Monument
This Secessionist monument to Frederic Chopin was sculpted in 1908 by Wacław Szymanowski, but not unveiled until 1926. Positioned at the side of a lake, it depicts Poland's most celebrated composer sitting under a willow tree, seeking inspiration from nature.

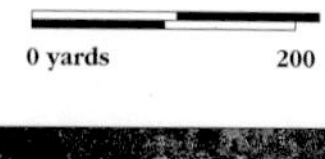

Sibyl's Temple
This Neo-Classical building, inspired by an ancient Greek temple, was constructed in the 1820s.

Water Tower
Built in 1778 to a design by Dominik Merlini, this water tower was restyled in 1827 by Chrystian Piotr Aigner.

Visitors' Checklist

Łazienki Królewskie, Agrykola 1. **Map** 6 E3, 6 F3, 6 E4, 6 F4. *621 62 41.* *100, 107, 108, 116, 119, 195, 503, 513.* **Łazienki Park** *daily till dusk.* **Palace on the Water** *9:30am–4pm Tue–Sun.* *free Sat.*

Hermitage
Designed by Tylman of Gameren as a retreat for Stanisław Herakliusz Lubomirski, it was completed in 1690. During the reign of Stanisław August Poniatowski, Henrietta Lhullier, a soothsayer and the king's confidante, lived here.

Sobieski Monument

Palace on the Water

Officer's School
It was from this building that officer cadets marched to attack the Belweder Palace (see p161)*. This incident started the 1830 Insurrection, on 29 November.*

Myślewicki Palace
Dominik Merlini designed this Neo-Classical palace in 1784 for Stanisław August Poniatowski's nephew, Prince Józef Poniatowski.

★ Theatre on the Island
A moat separates the auditorium from the stage, which has the form of a ruined temple in Baalbek.

★ White House
Designed by Dominik Merlini in 1774–7, it was used by Stanisław August Poniatowski for romantic rendezvous. In 1801 it was occupied by the future King Louis XVIII of France, then in exile.

New Orangerie
Constructed in 1861 using cast iron and glass, the new orangerie was designed by Józef Orłowski and Adam Loewe.

Star Sights

- ★ Theatre on the Island
- ★ White House
- ★ Old Orangerie
- ★ Chopin Monument

Palace on the Water ⓳

THIS PALACE is one of the finest examples of Neo-Classical architecture in Poland. King Stanisław August Poniatowski commissioned Dominik Merlini to refashion an existing 17th-century bathing pavilion into a royal summer residence. The task was completed between 1772–93. Unfortunately the king was only able to enjoy the palace for a few years. After the Third Partition of Poland he was forced to abdicate, and left Warsaw on 7 January 1795, watched by tearful crowds. He died three years later in St Petersburg. The Nazis planned to blow up the palace but, lacking time during their withdrawal from Warsaw, set fire to it instead. Rebuilding was completed in 1965.

18th-century jardinière

Personifications of The Four Elements by André le Brun

Bridge with a pillared gallery

Detail of Hercules in the Ballroom
Figures of Hercules, a centaur and Cerberus (the dog that guarded Hades), support the ballroom chimneypiece, symbolizing man's triumph over the forces of darkness.

Terrace

★ Bas-reliefs in the Bathing Room
17th-century bas-reliefs from the original bathing pavilion depict scenes from Ovid's Metamorphosis.

★ Ballroom
The highly decorated ballroom was designed by Jan Chrystian Kamsetzer.

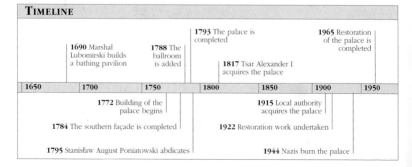

TIMELINE

- **1690** Marshal Lubomirski builds a bathing pavilion
- **1772** Building of the palace begins
- **1784** The southern façade is completed
- **1788** The ballroom is added
- **1793** The palace is completed
- **1795** Stanisław August Poniatowski abdicates
- **1817** Tsar Alexander I acquires the palace
- **1915** Local authority acquires the palace
- **1922** Restoration work undertaken
- **1944** Nazis burn the palace
- **1965** Restoration of the palace is completed

1650 | 1700 | 1750 | 1800 | 1850 | 1900 | 1950

Thursday Dinners

Every Thursday the king invited artists, writers and intellectuals to dinner. During the summer these dinners were held in the Palace on the Water, and in the Marble Room of the Royal Castle during the winter. A frequent guest was the poet, Bishop Ignacy Krasicki. The men-only dinners served as an artistic and political forum. But this did not prevent a tradition of "dessert poetry" – the writing of indecent verses during dessert which diners left under their dessert plates. The end of the meal was indicated by the serving of a dish of plums.

Bishop Ignacy Krasicki

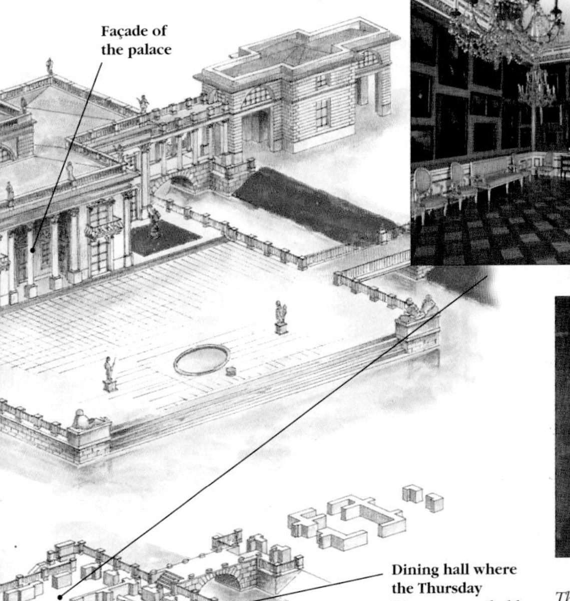

Façade of the palace

★ Picture Gallery
The gallery was designed by Jan Chrystian Kamsetzer in 1793, to exhibit the king's extensive collection. Each wall is hung with up to three rows of pictures, creating an impressive effect.

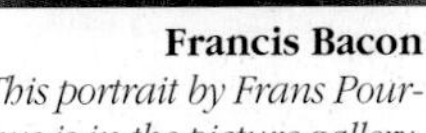

Francis Bacon
This portrait by Frans Pourbus is in the picture gallery.

Dining hall where the Thursday Dinners were held

Solomon's Hall
This was the main reception room. The ceiling was originally painted by Marcello Bacciarelli; destroyed in World War II, it has since been re-created.

Rotunda
This circular room was designed by Dominik Merlini as an equivalent of the Pantheon, for Poland's great monarchs. It includes sculptures of kings such as Kazimierz Wielki, Zygmunt Stary, Stefan Batory and Jan III Sobieski.

Star Sights

- ★ **Ballroom**
- ★ **Bas-reliefs in the Bathing Room**
- ★ **Picture Gallery**

Further Afield

While central Warsaw's most historic buildings were generally reconstructed after the devastation of World War II, other parts of the city feature many historic buildings which survived the war intact. Along the escarpment on the Left Bank of the River Vistula, for example, are several delightful residences set in their own parks. Most of these can easily be reached by public transport, or even on foot. On the outskirts of the city is Wilanów Palace and Park, originally the residence of King Jan III Sobieski. There is also the church and former Camaldolese hermitage, both situated within Bielański Forest. For leisurely day trips beyond the city boundaries, there are several options, including the romantically landscaped Arkadia Park and the neighbouring Nieborów Palace. There is also Żelazowa Wola, birthplace of Frederic Chopin and now a museum, as well as a scattering of historic towns, such as Łowicz, Pułtusk and Płock.

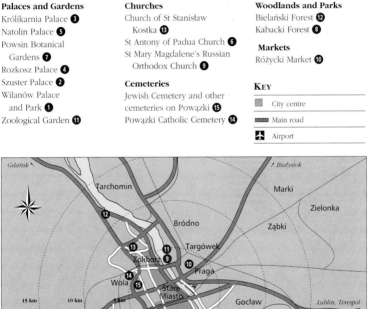

Airmen's Memorial by Wawelska Street

Sights at a Glance

Palaces and Gardens
- Królikarnia Palace 3
- Natolin Palace 5
- Powsin Botanical Gardens 7
- Rozkosz Palace 4
- Szuster Palace 2
- Wilanów Palace and Park 1
- Zoological Garden 11

Churches
- Church of St Stanisław Kostka 13
- St Antony of Padua Church 6
- St Mary Magdalene's Russian Orthodox Church 9

Cemeteries
- Jewish Cemetery and other cemeteries on Powązki 15
- Powązki Catholic Cemetery 14

Woodlands and Parks
- Bielański Forest 12
- Kabacki Forest 8

Markets
- Różycki Market 10

Key
- City centre
- Main road
- Airport

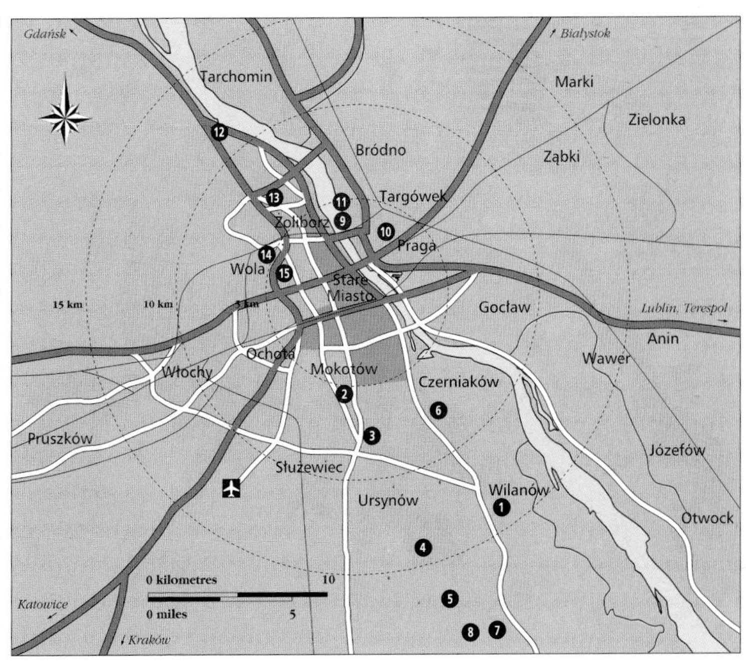

The Neo-Classical entrance gates to Wilanów Palace and Park

Wilanów Palace and Park ❶

ALTHOUGH IT WAS a royal residence, Wilanów Palace was actually designed as a private retreat for King Jan III Sobieski, who valued family life above material splendour. The original property, known as Villa Nova, was purchased in 1677 and within two years had been rebuilt into a mansion, designed by royal architect Augustyn Locci. Subsequently, two wings, towers and a first-floor banqueting hall were added, with the interiors decorated by some of Europe's finest craftsmen. Sculptures on the façades are by Andreas Schlüter, while a series of murals includes work by the 17th- and 18th-century artists Michelangelo Palloni, Claude Callot and Jerzy Eleuter Szymonowicz-Siemiginowski.

Detail of putti

Orangerie
This currently serves as a venue for arts and crafts exhibitions.

Tomb of Stanisław Kostka Potocki
Ironically, Poland's foremost Classical expert lies under a Neo-Gothic, rather than a Neo-Classical canopy, just outside the main gate.

Main Gateway
Dating from the 17th century, this impressive entrance features two allegorical figures representing War and Peace.

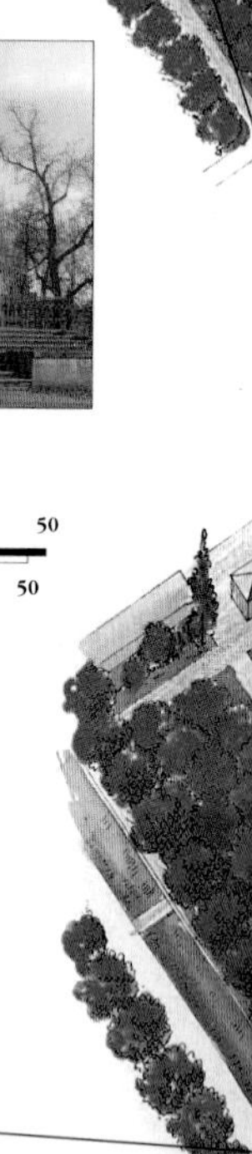

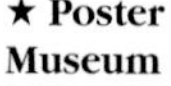

★ Poster Museum
Wilanów's former riding school now houses the fascinating Poster Museum (Muzeum Plakatu).

Gazebo
This Chinese gazebo is situated within the English-style garden, laid out during the 19th century, on the north side of the palace.

Visitors' Checklist

S.K. Potockiego 10–16. ☎ 842 07 95. 🚌 116, 130, 164, 180, 410, 522. **Palace** ○ 9:30am–2:30pm Mon, Wed– Sat; 9:30am–2:30pm Sun. ● Jan. **Park** ○ 9:30am–dusk. free Thu.

★ Baroque Park
The most historic section of Wilanów's grounds, laid out in the Baroque style, are behind the palace.

Palace Façade
The gardens were laid out to provide open perspectives, with this façade visible across the park, and even across the adjoining fields of Morysin.

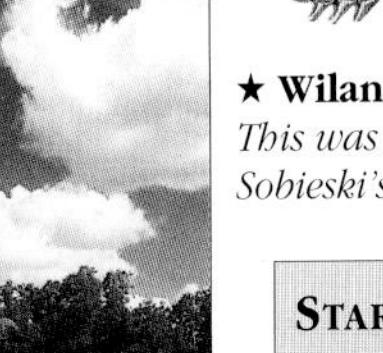

Stucco Pediment
Symbolizing King Jan III Sobieski's courage, this pediment is on the façade above an entrance to the park.

★ Wilanów Palace
This was King Jan III Sobieski's favourite "retreat".

Star Sights

- ★ **Wilanów Palace**
- ★ **Poster Museum**
- ★ **Baroque Park**

Exploring Wilanów Palace

The most interesting apartments, originally occupied by King Jan III Sobieski and his wife Marysieńka, are on the ground floor of Wilanów's main building, which has retained many of its original 17th-century features. The north wing comprises 19th-century rooms. These were formerly used to house the Potocki family's art collection, while also serving as living quarters for subsequent owners. The south wing includes the late Baroque Great Dining Room, designed for King August II Mocny, as well as Princess Izabela Lubomirska's apartments, which include a bathroom dating from 1775. The nursery and governesses' rooms are situated on the first floor, together with a fascinating portrait gallery.

Decorative detail from the façade

Florentine Bureau
This magnificent 17th-century bureau is in the king's antechamber.

Great Crimson Room
Taking its name from the coloured fabric that covers the walls, this room contains a giant table and serves as a venue for entertaining VIPs.

Sobieski Family Portrait
The marriage of King Jan III Sobieski and Marysieńka was a genuine love-match, which was then rare among royal couples.

Timeline

- **1667** Building of Wilanów begins
- **1681** Towers and galleries added
- **1692** Great Dining Room completed
- **1696** King Jan III Sobieski dies
- **1720** Palace acquired by Elżbieta Sieniawska
- **1723** Work commences on the wings
- **1730** King August II Mocny takes a lease on Wilanów
- **1775** Bathroom built for Izabela Lubomirska
- **1805** Stanisław Kostka Potocki creates a museum
- **1850** North wing extended and new pavilions built
- **1855–6** Chapel furnished
- **1945** Wilanów becomes a museum

1600 | 1650 | 1700 | 1750 | 1800 | 1850 | 1900

North Gallery
This gallery includes a portrait of Stanisław Kostka Potocki, painted by the French artist Jacques-Louis David (1748–1825).

Queen's Antechamber
The walls are still covered with the original Baroque fabric, dating from the 17th century, when Queen Marysieńka was in residence.

★ Great Hall
Szymon Bogumił Zug's Neo-Classical redesign retained some Baroque details, such as an Allegory of the Four Elements.

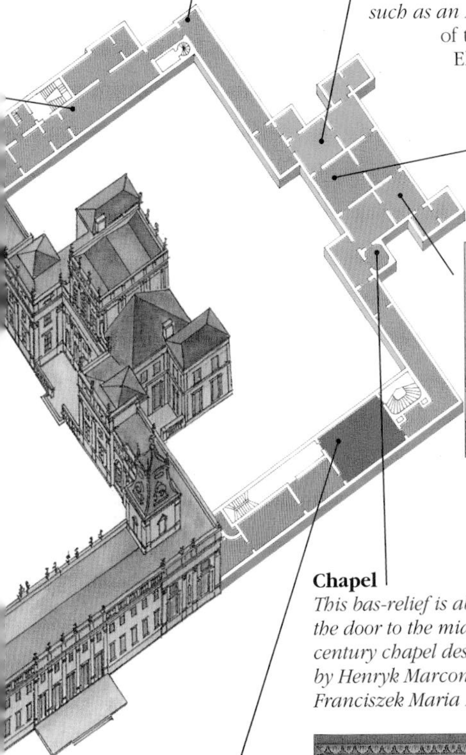

★ King's Bedchamber
The canopy over the bed is of 17th-century Turkish fabric.

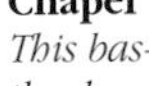

Chapel
This bas-relief is above the door to the mid-19th-century chapel designed by Henryk Marconi and Franciszek Maria Lanci.

The Great Dining Room, completed between 1730–33, was designed by Jan Zygmunt Deybel for King August II Mocny, who held a lease on Wilanów at that time.

Key to Floorplan

- Queen's apartments
- King's apartments
- Great Dining Room
- Princess Lubomirska's apartments
- Other rooms open to the public

Star Sights

- ★ **King's Bedchamber**
- ★ **Great Hall**

Szuster Palace ❷
Pałacyk Szustra

Szuster Palace

Morskie Oko 2. **Map** 6 E5. *849 68 56.* *122, 130, 167, 206, 505, 514, 515, 524.* *4, 18, 19, 35, 36.*

Efraim Schroeger originally designed this small palace as a "picturesque villa" for Princess Izabela Lubomirska (née Czartoryska). Built in 1774 and set in a landscaped park, the palace occupies an enchanting site, standing on an escarpment in Mokotów, an area on the outskirts of Warsaw. The park, which is known as Morskie Oko, was laid out in 1776–8 by Szymon Bogumił Zug, who went on to redesign Szuster Palace during the 1780s.

In 1820 the palace was acquired by Anna Wąsowicz-Potocka (née Tyszkiewicz). She commissioned Henryk Marconi to refurbish it in a Neo-Gothic style, which was undertaken between 1822–5.

The German scientist Alexander von Humboldt was received here in 1830. He described the palace and park as "richly adorned with flowers, marbles and ancient Greek artefacts". This was, however, a disappointment for Anna Potocka who was used to more effusive praise. Moreover, hurt by this remark she is reputed to have said: "I try talking to him about many interesting things and all he does is drone on about some Siberian grasses. A typically dense Prussian!"

From 1845 (for almost the next 100 years) the palace was owned by the Szuster family. After a fire in 1944 it was rebuilt as the headquarters of the Warsaw Music Society. The park, which was recently restored, includes a Moorish house, a dovecote, a late 18th-century gateway designed by Szymon Bogumił Zug, and the Szuster family mausoleum.

Królikarnia Palace ❸
Pałacyk Królikarnia

Puławska 113a. *843 15 86.* *167, 505, 514, 515, 524.* *4, 18, 19, 35, 36.* *10am–4pm Tue–Sun.* *free on Thu.*

The unusual name of this exquisite palace (literally meaning "rabbit hutch") stems from the fact that it occupies the site of a rabbit farm and hunting grounds, which belonged to King August II Mocny in the 18th century.

Designed in a Neo-Classical style by Dominik Merlini, the square shape and dome recall Andrea Palladio's masterpiece the Villa Rotonda, situated near Vicenza.

The palace was built between 1782 and 1786 for Karol de Valery Thomatis, director of King Stanisław August Poniatowski's Royal Theatre. In a park in Mokotów, the palace holds the Xawery Dunikowski Museum, containing works by this renowned Polish sculptor.

Falum **by Xawery Dunikowski in Królikarnia Palace**

Rozkosz Palace ❹
Pałac Rozkosz

Nowoursynowska 166. *515.*

Built between 1775 and 1780 for Izabela Lubomirska, the wife of the renowned army marshal, the palace is idyllically set on an escarpment in Ursynów, by the River Vistula. The name of the palace literally means "Delight". Ten years after being built, it was greatly refurbished, according to a joint design by Chrystian Piotr Aigner and Stanisław Kostka-Potocki (the subsequent owner).

Between 1822 and 1831 the palace belonged to the politician and writer Julian Ursyn Niemcewicz, who served as aide-de-camp to Tadeusz Kościuszko, the leader of the 1794 Insurrection. In 1858, the palace's new owner, Ludwik Krasiński, commissioned Zygmunt Rospendowski to redesign Rozkosz in a Neo-Classical style. The façade was then decorated with busts of military leaders, including Stefan Czarniecki, Paweł Sanguszko, Władysław Koniecpolski and Jan Tarnowski. There were also busts of several Polish queens, such as Barbara and Jadwiga.

Nowadays, Rozkosz Palace serves as the headquarters of the Agricultural College.

Neo-Classical façade of Rozkosz Palace in the snow

Natolin Palace, set in an ornate landscaped park

Natolin Palace ❺

Pałac w Natolinie

Nowoursynowska. *412, 505, 513.* *Natolin.* ***Closed.***

Decorated ceiling by Vincenzo Brenna at Natolin Palace

When this Neo-Classical residence was built in 1780–82, Natolin was several kilometres outside Warsaw's southern boundary. Today, however, urban housing estates encroach on the palace surroundings.

Natolin's architect, Szymon Bogumił Zug, was recommended to its owners by Prince August Czartoryski and his daughter Izabela Lubomirska, who owned the neighbouring palace and estate of Wilanów *(see pp168–71)*.

Natolin Palace has several notable features, including ornate wall and ceiling paintings by Vincenzo Brenna, an Italian architect and painter. The palace was significantly modified in 1808 by Chrystian Piotr Aigner, who added the distinctive dome and an unusual summer drawing room, which opens onto the garden.

The palace is set in a landscaped park, which extends along an escarpment. The park has a great many buildings and decorative features, among them a bridge, a Doric temple, an aqueduct and a Moorish gateway.

As neither the palace nor the gardens are open to the public, the only feature that can be readily admired is a remarkable oak tree, named Mieszko (as were several of the early Polish kings), which is situated by the palace on Nowoursynowska Street. This is the oldest tree in the whole of Warsaw. It is also thought that it is the sole surviving tree of the Mazovian Forest, which at one time covered the entire area.

The green-domed Baroque St Antony of Padua Church

St Antony of Padua Church ❻

Kościół św. Antoniego Padewskiego

Czerniakowska 2/4. *842 03 71.* *131, 159, 162, 180, 185, 187, 362.*

This baroque church, built between 1687 and 1693 by the Bernardine Order, was designed by the renowned architect Tylman of Gameren. The church stands on the site of the former village of Czerniaków, which belonged to Stanisław Herakliusz Lubomirski, the crown marshal.

The relatively plain façade of this church belies its highly ornate interior. This includes stucco work and murals illustrating the life of St Antony of Padua, which were principally painted by Antonio Giorgioli.

The altars include Baroque designs by the renowned German architect and sculptor Andreas Schlüter (1664–1714). Additionally, the main altar features a glass coffin which contains the relics of St Boniface (a 5th-century pope). These sacred relics were given to Stanisław Herakliusz Lubomirski in 1687 by Pope Innocent XI.

Powsin Botanical Gardens ❼

Ogród Botaniczny w Powsinie

Prawdziwka 2. *648 09 51.* *139.* *Apr–Oct: 10am–6pm daily.*

Powsin Botanical Gardens were established by the Polish Academy of Science in 1974 as a research and educational establishment. Since 1990, the gardens have been open to the public.

The 16-hectare (40-acre) site, located by the River Vistula, includes an arboretum, a collection of rare and endangered plants and trees, various medicinal plants and spices. There are also glasshouses that contain decorative plants.

Various pot plants, flowers and seedlings are on sale here, while fairs are held throughout the winter months.

Walking in the Kabacki Forest, to the south of Warsaw

Kabacki Forest 8

Las Kabacki

M *Kabaty.* Bus *412, 504, 505, 519.*

The Kabacki Forest, by the Botanical Gardens, on Prawdziwka Street, is a favourite with Varsovians for day trips. Comprising 920 ha (2,275 acres), the forest offers a wide variety of deciduous species, such as its fine oak trees, while other areas consist mainly of evergreen pines.

Before the outbreak of World War II, the forest was saved from developers by Stefan Starzyński, the mayor of Warsaw. He purchased the forest from its owners, on behalf of the City Council.

In the vicinity of Powsin, on the southeastern edge of the forest, is a holiday centre set among trees. This includes a swimming pool and other sports facilities, as well as chalet accommodation.

St Mary Magdalene's Russian Orthodox Church 9

Cerkiew św. Marii Magdaleny

Aleja Solidarności 52. **Map** 4 E3. Tel *619 08 86.* Bus *120, 125, 135, 160, 162, 170, 192, 362, 402, 512, 517, 718.* Tram *3, 6, 13, 21, 25, 26.*

Situated in the district of Praga on the right bank of the River Vistula, St Mary Magdalene's Church was built in 1868–9. The work of Nikolai Sychev, the building is topped with distinctive onion-shaped Byzantine domes.

The interiors feature murals by several Russian artists, together with an interesting iconostasis. This elaborate screen, which includes doors and icons arranged in tiers, divides the nave from the sanctuary. The church is not usually open to the public, apart from during services. One of the best times to visit is on Orthodox feast days when you can also listen to the superb church choirs.

Domes of St Mary Magdalene's Russian Orthodox Church

Różycki Market 10

Bazar Różyckiego

Targowa 54. **Map** 4 F4. Bus *101, 103, 120, 125, 135, 138, 169, 302, 509.* Tram *3, 6, 13, 21, 25, 26, 32.* Open *6am–6pm Mon–Fri.*

As a long established institution, the Różycki market is an ideal example of "old Warsaw". The market is located in the heart of Praga, to the south of St Mary Magdalene's Russian Orthodox Church.

However, with ongoing economic reforms and the redevelopment of Praga, the market has lost its position as Warsaw's most important shopping venue but has kept its traditional and highly individual atmosphere.

The market was established at the turn of the century by a Warsaw chemist, A Różycki, on the site of an even older market. Squeezed in between dilapidated tenement buildings, the market comprises hundreds of wooden stalls, mainly selling clothing and food. A local speciality is a hot tripe dish called *flaki*, which is eagerly recommended by street vendors.

The market has always been a haunt for pickpockets, and visitors should be attentive and guard valuables carefully.

The streets directly behind the market, Ząbkowska and Brzeska, are lined with old brick tenements, whose walls are still scarred with bullet marks, dating from World War II. Brzeska Street was, until recently, the place to obtain illicit drink. It is best avoided, especially at night or if you are alone.

Zoological Garden 11

Ogrod Zoologiczny

Ratuszowa 1/3. **Map** 4 D3 & 4 D4. Tel *619 40 41.* Bus *125, 160, 162, 170.* Tram *4, 6, 13, 21, 26, 32.* Open *9am–6pm daily.*

Warsaw's zoo, on the Right Bank of the River Vistula, opened in 1928. However, the city has a much longer zoological tradition, dating back to the 17th century, when wealthy magnates established private zoos. The original Warsaw zoo, established in the Praski

Mother and baby baboon in the Zoological Garden

Garden, was constantly evolving up until the outbreak of World War II. During the first few weeks of the war, much of the zoo was destroyed, the animals being slaughtered by Nazis.

The zoo was re-established after the war, in 1948, and currently occupies about 40 ha (100 acres), which is largely open-air. The zoo has about 3,000 animals in total, including 91 species of mammals, 87 species of birds, 49 of reptiles and about the same number of fish species.

The Małe Zoo ("Small Zoo") is a section where animals can be fed and petted. Additionally, there is a bear run, surrounded by a moat, that is located a few minutes' walk away from the main zoo in Solidarity Avenue.

Bielański Forest ⓬

Las Bielański

Dewajtis. 🚌 *121, 181.* 🚋 *6, 15, 17, 27.*

Situated on the banks of the River Vistula, to the north of the city, the Bielański Forest occupies an area of 150 ha (370 acres). This is all that remains of the prehistoric Mazovian Forest. The Bielański Forest comprises a wide range of plantlife and trees, including 700-year-old oaks.

The forest is now a protected National Park, although even as recently as a few decades ago, it was a popular venue for fairs and picnics, with people arriving in their thousands in pleasure boats.

The highest point of the forest is Pólkowska Hill, where the Church of the Immaculate Conception can be seen, by the banks of a river. This church was built by the Camaldolese monks between 1669 and 1710, and features an oval-shaped nave with Rococo-style stucco work. The monastery's benefactors included the Polish royal family and various other wealthy patrons. Their family crests can still be seen on the portals of the hermitages, at the rear of the church. These tiny dwellings were inhabited by monks until 1904. In the adjoining cemetery is the tomb of Stanisław Staszic (1755–1822), a famous political writer, philosopher and scientist, who co-founded the Royal Society of the Friends of Science.

Close to the church is the Cardinal Stefan Wyszyński University and the Warsaw Seminary. Both these buildings were constructed in the 1980s.

In Pułkowa Street, on the edge of the Bielański Forest, there is a small military cemetery for Italian soldiers. It was established in 1927, and designed by the Chief Technical Commissioner for Military Cemeteries, in Rome.

Buried here are the remains of Italian soldiers who were killed on Polish soil during World War I. There are also approximately 1,200 prisoners of war, who were murdered by the Nazis during World War II. The cemetery gateway is in the form of a triumphal arch. The railings are decorated with laurel leaves and Roman shield motifs.

Father Jerzy Popiełuszko's tomb at the Church of St Stanisław Kostka

Church of St Stanisław Kostka ⓭

Kościół św. Stanisława Kostki

Hozjusza 1. **Map** 3 A2. 🚌 *110, 116, 121, 122, 157, 181, 185, 195, 303, 409, 508, 514, 515.* 🚋 *6, 15, 36.*

This modernist church, with its open-work twin-tower, is a centre for Polish pilgrims, who come to visit the tomb of the late Father Jerzy Popiełuszko. He was famed for his sermons in defence of Poland's freedom during the Communist era. He was murdered in 1984 by Communist security agents. The Church of St Stanisław Kostka is set among the villas of Żoliborz.

Powązki Cemetery ⓮

Katolicki Cmentarz Powązkowski

See pp 176–7.

Candles and flowers decorating Powązki Cemetery on All Saints' Day

Powązki Catholic Cemetery ⓮

Katolicki Cmentarz Powązkowski

This is Warsaw's oldest and most beautiful cemetery. It forms part of a vast complex divided into separate areas, according to religious denominations, which includes Jewish and Protestant sections *(see pp178–9)*. Before the Catholic cemetery was established in 1790, the neighbouring site was occupied by Izabela Czartoryska's Rococo palace, modelled on the Trianon at Versailles and set in a romantic park. Close to the cemetery are streets with names such as Spokojna (quiet) and Smętna (sad). However, as the cemetery expanded, the system of indexing plots became ever more complicated. Locating specific tombs usually requires patience and a good map. By the main entrance (St Honorata Gate) is the church of St Karol Boromeusz. Originally founded in the 18th century by King Stanisław August Poniatowski and his brother Michał, Primate of Poland, this church was refurbished in 1891–8.

Lilpop Family Tomb
This Neo-Gothic cast-iron spire, designed by Józef Manzel in 1866, rises above the tomb of the Lilpop family (plot B) who were co-owners of a large metalworks.

Wacław Szymanowski
Szymanowski (1821–86) was a journalist and editor-in-chief of the Kurier Warszawski *newspaper. His tomb (plot 40) was carved by his son Wacław Jr in 1905, and is an outstanding example of Secessionist style.*

Edward Rydz-Śmigły
The Polish army's Supreme Commander during the September 1939 campaign, Rydz-Śmigły subsequently left the country and was interned in Romania. He escaped to Hungary then returned to occupied Warsaw where he died. He was buried under the pseudonym of Adam Zawisza, in a modest grave (plot 139) marked by a white birch cross.

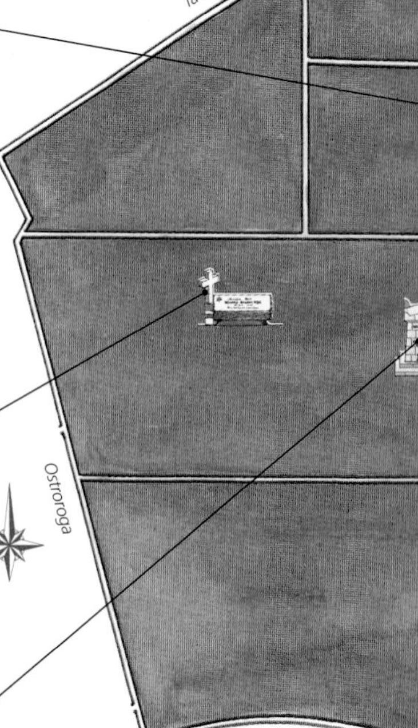

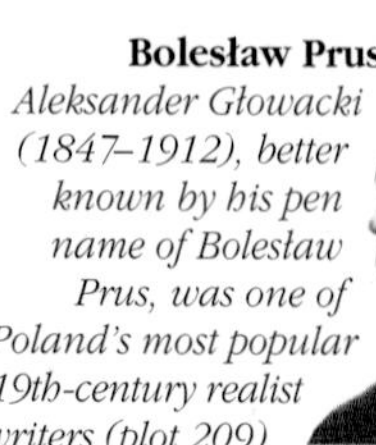

Bolesław Prus
Aleksander Głowacki (1847–1912), better known by his pen name of Bolesław Prus, was one of Poland's most popular 19th-century realist writers (plot 209).

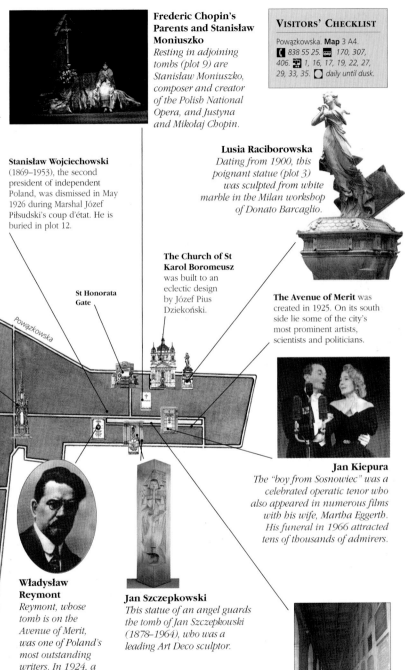

Frederic Chopin's Parents and Stanisław Moniuszko
Resting in adjoining tombs (plot 9) are Stanisław Moniuszko, composer and creator of the Polish National Opera, and Justyna and Mikołaj Chopin.

VISITORS' CHECKLIST

Powązkowska. **Map** 3 A4. *838 55 25.* *170, 307, 406.* *1, 16, 17, 19, 22, 27, 29, 33, 35.* *daily until dusk.*

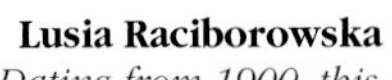

Lusia Raciborowska
Dating from 1900, this poignant statue (plot 3) was sculpted from white marble in the Milan workshop of Donato Barcaglio.

Stanisław Wojciechowski (1869–1953), the second president of independent Poland, was dismissed in May 1926 during Marshal Józef Piłsudski's coup d'état. He is buried in plot 12.

The Church of St Karol Boromeusz was built to an eclectic design by Józef Pius Dziekoński.

St Honorata Gate

Powązkowska

The Avenue of Merit was created in 1925. On its south side lie some of the city's most prominent artists, scientists and politicians.

Jan Kiepura
The "boy from Sosnowiec" was a celebrated operatic tenor who also appeared in numerous films with his wife, Martha Eggerth. His funeral in 1966 attracted tens of thousands of admirers.

Władysław Reymont
Reymont, whose tomb is on the Avenue of Merit, was one of Poland's most outstanding writers. In 1924, a year before he died, Reymont received the Nobel Prize for his novel Chłopi (The Peasants).

Jan Szczepkowski
This statue of an angel guards the tomb of Jan Szczepkowski (1878–1964), who was a leading Art Deco sculptor.

Catacombs
Built in 1792 and enlarged in 1851, the catacombs became the burial place for King Stanisław August Poniatowski's family and other renowned Poles.

Jewish Cemetery and other cemeteries at Powązki ⑮

Cmentarz Żydowski

THE JEWISH CEMETERY on Okopowa Street was established between 1799 and 1806. Now deserted, it is a very poignant area, with trees and thick undergrowth among tombstones making it difficult even to reach certain sections. Religious dictates ban human forms from appearing on tombstones, so they are decorated mainly with symbols and ornaments. Most tombs are marked by a simple stone *(masebas)*. However, there are also more elaborate features, such as marble obelisks, sarcophagi and chapels bearing memorial plaques *(obeles)*.

Wedel Family Mausoleum
This tomb of the renowned chocolate producers (Ave A, No. 31) is adorned with a bronze statue of Christ made in 1931 by Stanisław R Lewandowski.

Halpert Chapel
This large Empire-style chapel (Ave E) was commissioned by Maria Halpert and dedicated to the memory of her husband, Salomon, who died in 1832.

Braeunig Chapel
The oldest cast-iron chapel in Warsaw, this was constructed in 1821. It can be found on Ave D No. 55a.

Jenike Family Tomb
Made of red sandstone, this Secessionist tomb (Ave 54) was designed by Zygmunt Otto in 1903.

Młynarska

Żytnia

The Protestant Reformed Cemetery (Cmentarz Ewangelicko-Reformowany) is a well maintained cemetery used by the Lutheran and Protestant Reformed communities. Their respective burial grounds have been separated by a wall but before being relocated here, the two communities shared a cemetery in Mylna Street.

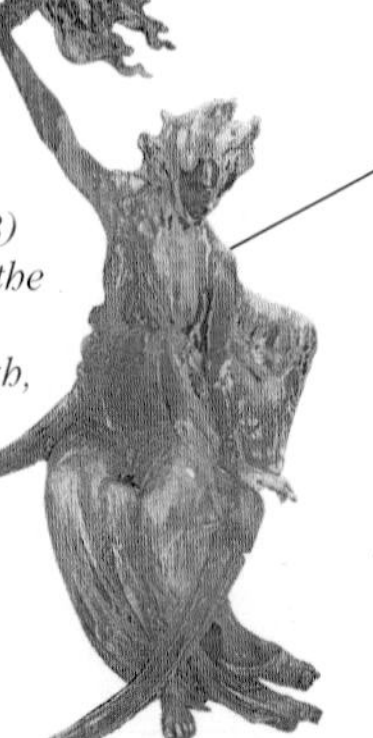

Laskowicki Family Tomb
This tomb (plot B) is crowned with the sculpture of an angel with a torch, designed by Bolesław Jeziorański.

Stefan Żeromski
Żeromski was one of the best-loved early 20th-century Polish writers, author of many short stories and novels such as Ludzie Bezdomni (Homeless People). *His tomb is situated in plot F.*

Estera Rachela Kamińska
This stage and film actress was known as the "mother of Jewish theatre". In 1915 she founded the Warsaw Jewish Theatre dedicated to her husband, Abraham Kamiński. Her tombstone (plot 39) was designed by Feliks Rubinlicht.

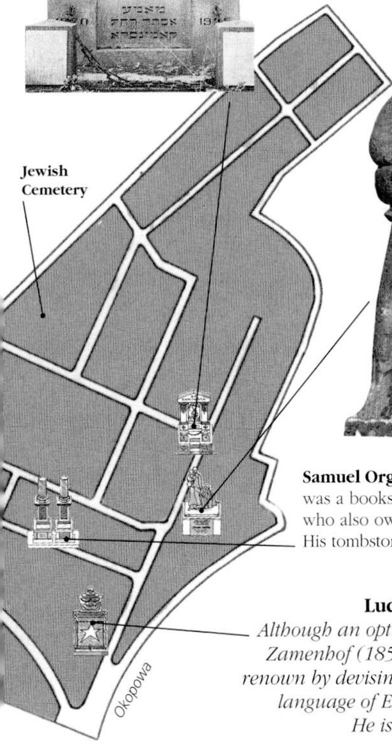

Jewish Cemetery

Janusz Korczak Monument
This monument (in plot 72) stands over a symbolic grave of Janusz Korczak (1878–1942). It depicts him accompanying the Jewish orphans, who were under his care, to a Nazi death camp.

Samuel Orgelbrand (1810–66) was a bookseller and publisher, who also owned a printing house. His tombstone is in plot 20.

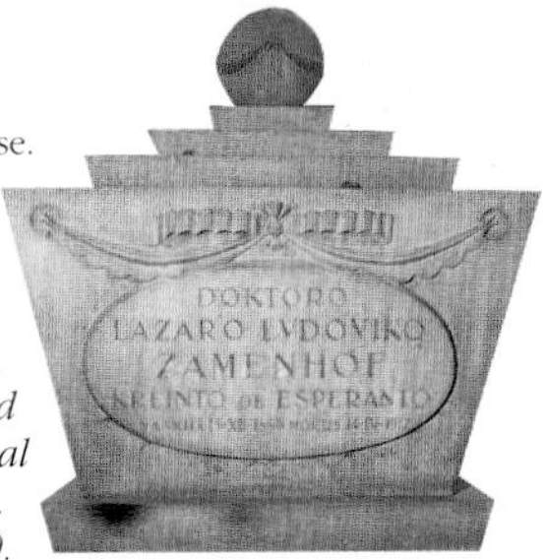

Ludwik Zamenhof
Although an optician by training, Zamenhof (1859–1917) achieved renown by devising the international language of Esperanto in 1887. He is buried in plot 10.

Okopowa

The Ausberg Protestant Cemetery (Cmentarz Ewangelicko-Augsburski), in Młynarska Street, has served as the resting place for various distinguished people since 1792. The cemetery was designed by Szymon Bogumił Zug, who was buried here in 1807.

Wojciech Gerson (1831–1901) was a popular 19th-century painter from Warsaw. His tomb can be found on Ave 19.

Anna German
This great performer (1936–82) had a wonderful voice and was one of Poland's most popular stars.

Symbols on Tombstones

The *masebas* at the Jewish Cemetery are decorated with symbols representing either the family, the surname or the profession of the deceased.

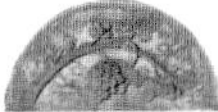

Day Trips from Warsaw

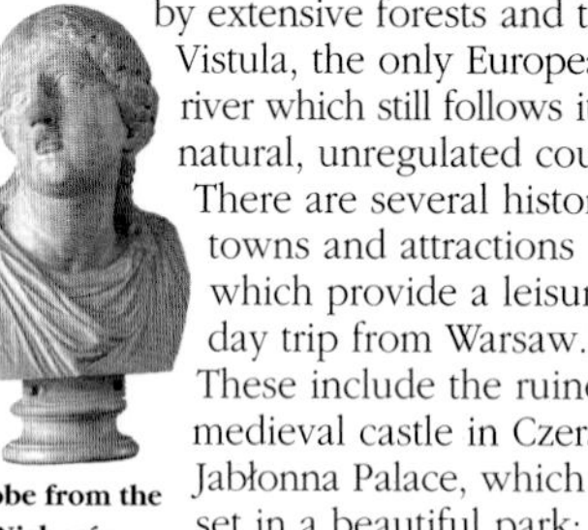

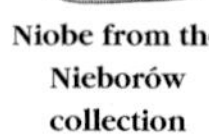

Niobe from the Nieborów collection

Warsaw is surrounded by the flat plains of Mazovia, which are varied by extensive forests and the Vistula, the only European river which still follows its natural, unregulated course. There are several historic towns and attractions which provide a leisurely day trip from Warsaw. These include the ruined medieval castle in Czersk; Jabłonna Palace, which is set in a beautiful park; and Żelazowa Wola, the manor house where Chopin was born. Some travel agents also offer organized tours *(see p237)* to these places.

Sights at a Glance

Palaces and Castles
Czersk 1
Jabłonna 2
Nieborów 3
Opinogóra 11

Historic Towns
Łowicz 5
Płock 10
Pułtusk 9

Historic Buildings
Żelazowa Wola 6

Cemeteries
Palmiry 7

Parks
Arkadia 4
Kampinos National Park 8

Key

- Central Warsaw
- Greater Warsaw
- Major road
- Airport

25 km = 16 miles

Łowicz costume

Czersk 1

39 km (24 miles) S of Warsaw. *from Mokotów Station, at the junction of Puławska and Nowoursynowska streets.*

The village of Czersk was originally the capital of the Mazovian region. In 1413 Czersk was succeeded by Warsaw as the Mazovian capital, when the route of the River Vistula apparently turned away from Czersk.

The village includes the ruins of a medieval castle, reached via a Gothic bridge spanning a moat. The ruins still standing date from the 14th–16th centuries, including three towers enlarged in the 16th century.

In the 13th century, Prince Konrad Mazowiecki, who brought the Teutonic Knights to Poland in 1226, imprisoned the infant prince Bolesław Wstydliwy (future Prince of Kraków) and Prince Henryk Brodaty, the Prince of Wrocław, in the south tower.

Jabłonna 2

20 km (12 miles) N of Warsaw. *628 16 75.* *723, 801.* **Park** *6am–10pm.*

Since the 15th century, there has been a palace on this site. Following the death of King Władysław IV Waza in 1648, the original palace became Karol Ferdynand Waza's headquarters when he contested the Polish throne.

The present Neo-Classical style dates from 1775–9, and is the result of Dominik Merlini's design for the Polish primate Michał Poniatowski.

In 1837 the palace was refurbished by Henryk Marconi. One significant change to the façade was the addition of a tower that has an unusual spherical roof.

The palace is set in a park, designed by Szymon Bogumił Zug in the 18th century.

During the summer, concerts and various other events are held in the park and the palace.

Nieborów 3

81 km (50 miles) W of Warsaw. *(046) 838 56 20, (046) 838 56 23.* *to Łowicz, then local bus.* ***Palace*** *Feb–Apr: 10am–4pm Tue–Sun; May–Jun: 10am–6pm Tue–Sun; Jul–Oct: 10am–4pm Mon–Fri, 10am–6pm Sat–Sun.* ***Park*** *until dusk daily.*

Designed in a Baroque style by Tylman of Gameren, Nieborów was built between 1690 and 1696, and set in a symmetrical garden. The palace was commissioned by the archbishop of Gniezno, Michał S Radziejowski, who was a generous patron of the arts.

Around 1766 Prince Michał K Ogiński had the pediment decorated in a Rococo style. It featured a dancing figure of Bacchus, crowned with a laurel wreath and holding a bunch of grapes. Ogiński is famous for establishing the canal system which connected the Black Sea with the Baltic via a network of rivers.

The Baroque Nieborów Palace

Between 1771 and 1945 Nieborów belonged to the aristocratic Radziwiłł family. Their magnificent furnishings and extensive collection of art can be seen throughout the palace's rooms and corridors.

The collection includes Antoine Pesne's portrait of Anna Orzelska, the daughter of August II Mocny who was renowned for her beauty *(see p25)*. The antique head of Niobe, carved in white marble, is a Roman copy of

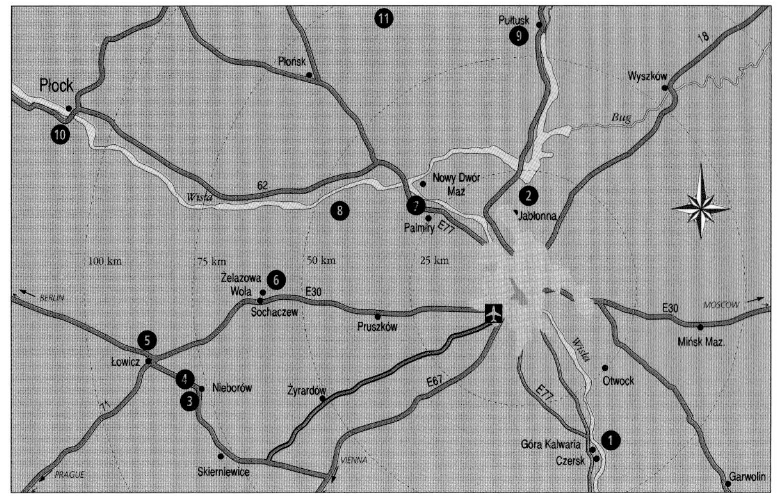

the Greek original, which dates from the 4th century BC. The head was extolled by the poet Konstanty Ildefons Gałczyński, and was presented to Princess Helena Radziwiłł by Empress Catherine II.

Temple of Diana, Arkadia Park

Arkadia ❹

85 km (53 miles) W of Warsaw. *from Śródmieście Station to Mysłaków.* *May–Oct: 10am–4pm; Jun–Aug: 10am–6pm.*

ROMANTIC Arkadia Park, situated between the towns of Nieborów and Łowicz, was established in 1778 by Princess Helena Radziwiłł.

The intention was to create an idyllic landscape of trees and lakes, together with picturesque buildings. Several pavilions were designed by Szymon Bogumił Zug and Henryk Ittar. The park is currently overgrown, but is still a delightful area in which to stroll. Among its buildings are the Temple of Diana, the Priest's Sanctuary, Burgrave House with its stone arch, the Gothic House, the Sybil Grotto and the aqueduct. Some of the park walls incorporate fragments of the original sculptures and stonework from the Renaissance bishop's palace, which once stood in the town of Łowicz.

Remains of a Gothic building in Arkadia Park

Łowicz ❺

81 km (50 miles) W of Warsaw. *from Śródmieście or Central Station.* **Łowicz Regional Museum** *(046) 837 39 28.* *10am–4pm Tue–Sun.*

THIS SMALL town dates from the 13th century, and was originally the centre of one of the oldest Polish castellanies (counties). For several centuries Łowicz was the residence of the archbishops of Gniezno, who were also the primates of Poland. Their legacy comprises several ecclesiastical buildings.

The most outstanding among these is the medieval **Collegiate Church**, which was reconstructed in the 17th century. The church is filled with magnificent works of art and tombs. A notable tomb is that of Jakub Uchański, the primate of Poland who died in 1581. It is in a chapel rebuilt in 1782–3 in an early Neo-Classical style to a design by Efraim Schroeger. The tomb features a 16th-century alabaster statue by Jan Michałowicz of Urzędów.

It is worth visiting Łowicz on the feast of Corpus Christi (which is in either late May or early June) to see the ceremonial procession in which many of the women wear traditional folk costume.

By the market square is a series of buildings, including a former monastery and the Seminary for Missionaries, which houses the **Łowicz Regional Museum**. The museum has a collection of folk art, and in the vaults of the former chapel (designed by Tylman of Gameren in 1689–1701) is a collection of Baroque art and murals by Michelangelo Palloni. A small *skansen* (open-air museum) behind the chapel features two period farmhouses with original furnishings.

Żelazowa Wola, the birthplace of Frederic Chopin

Żelazowa Wola ❻

52 km (32 miles) W of Warsaw. *(046) 863 33 00.* *from Zachodni Station.* *Apr–Oct: 9:30am–5:30pm Tue–Sun; Nov–Mar: 10am–4pm Tue–Sun.*

POLAND'S MOST renowned composer, Frederic Chopin, was born in this manor house on 1 March 1810. At that time the house was a thatched cottage, occupied by Chopin's parents, Mikołaj and Justyna.

The house was opened as a museum in 1931, under the administration of the Chopin Society in Warsaw. The society rebuilt the house, furnishing it in the original 19th-century manner. They assembled a collection of memorabilia associated with the composer to form the museum's exhibits. The surrounding park was planted with a wide range of trees and shrubs, donated by various Polish regions.

During World War II many artefacts were looted by the Nazis. They also banned performances of Chopin's music, and even destroyed portraits of the composer.

Following refurbishment, the house was reopened to the public in 1949, on the 100th anniversary of the composer's death.

Chopin concerts are held on the terrace at the side of the house, on most weekends between May and October.

About 11 km (7 miles) northwest of Żelazowa Wola is Brochów, a village on the edge of Kampinos National Park. Here, in the Renaissance church, Chopin's parents were married and Frederic Chopin was baptized.

Palmiry ❼

25 km (16 miles) NW of Warsaw. *from Marymont and Zachodni stations.*

SITUATED in Kampinos National Park, Palmiry cemetery is a resting place for over 2,200 victims of Nazi executions, which were carried out here and in other forests within the Warsaw area.

By the entrance to the cemetery is an inscription bearing the words of an unknown prisoner of the Gestapo: "It is easy to talk about Poland, more difficult to work for her, even harder to die for her, but the hardest of all is to suffer for her."

Graves at Palmiry cemetery

From December 1939 to July 1944, prisoners were brought here and shot. These mass grave sites were subsequently planted with trees. Many well-known Varsovians were killed here, including Janusz Kusociński, the 10,000-metre gold medal winner at the 1932 Los Angeles Olympic Games.

Kampinos National Park ❽

Puszcza Kampinoska

On the northwest borders of Warsaw. *708, 712, 714 and 716 from Marymont and Zachodni stations. The best starting points are Dziekanów Leśny, Truskaw, Zaborów or Kampinos.*

Kampinos National Park

ESTABLISHED IN 1959, the Kampinos National Park comprises 35,500 hectares (88,000 acres) of a large forest to the northwest of Warsaw.

Although the forest consists mainly of pine, the area also includes about 1,000 species of trees, shrubs and other plants. The indigenous wildlife features beavers, elks, cranes and rare black storks. Until recently, there were even lynxes. One of the park's most unusual features is its tree-covered inland dunes.

Several marked trails provide very enjoyable day-long rambles through the park.

Interior of the Gothic-Renaissance Collegiate Church in Pułtusk

Pułtusk 9

60 km (37 miles) N of Warsaw.
from Zachodni Station.

PUŁTUSK'S SETTING on the River Narew is one of the loveliest to be found in Mazovia. Its Old Town occupies a large island, and features an ornate town hall with a brick tower, and one of the largest market squares *(rynek)* in Europe. At the northern end of the market square is the Gothic-Renaissance Collegiate Church of the Virgin Mary. The main nave's arched vaulting is the work of one of Venice's greatest architects, Giovanni Battista.

On the opposite side of the market square is the castle. Originally Gothic, the castle was subsequently destroyed and rebuilt several times. Following its reconstruction during the 1980s, the castle is now home to the Polish Expatriates House (Dom Polonii). The house is mainly used by Polish émigrés, but is open to everyone. It provides elegant rooms for overnight accommodation, and its restaurant serves traditional cuisine that is highly recommended. There are also sports facilities.

Epitaph in Pułtusk's Collegiate Church

Płock 10

110 km (68 miles) NW of Warsaw. *from Zachodni Station.* **Mazovian Museum** *(024) 262 44 91.* *mid-May–Sep: 9am–4pm Tue–Thu & Sun, 10am–5pm Fri–Sat; Oct–mid-May: 9am–3pm Wed–Fri, 9am–4pm Sat–Sun.* **Diocesan Museum** *(024) 262 26 23.* *Wed–Sun.*

THE FOCAL POINT of this city is its cathedral hill, where most of the historic sights are located. Płock has been the seat of the Mazovian bishops since 1075, and for a few hundred years after 1138 it was also the residence of the Mazovian and Płock princes.

The city's principal attraction is the Mazovian Museum (Muzeum Mazowieckie), which has the finest collection of Secessionist artefacts in Poland. These include several rooms that are furnished exactly as they would have been during the Secessionist era.

The Renaissance cathedral was built in the 16th century, by Giovanni Cini and Bernardino Zanobi de Gianotis, on the site of an earlier Romanesque church. The cathedral was subsequently refurbished by the Venetian architect Giovanni Battista. The richly decorated interiors contain several Renaissance and Baroque tombs. There are also a number of Secessionist-style frescoes.

Close to the cathedral is the Diocesan Museum (Muzeum Diecezjalne), which has a wide range of religious exhibits.

Opinogóra 11

100 km (62 miles) N of Warsaw. *(023) 671 70 25.* *to Ciechanów then by local bus.* **Museum** *10am–4pm Tue–Sun.*

OPINOGÓRA is a small Neo-Gothic palace which is set within a Romantic, landscaped park. The palace was built in 1843, when it was given as a wedding present to Count Zygmunt Krasiński (1812–59). Krasiński is one of Poland's greatest Romantic poets, alongside Adam Mickiewicz and Juliusz Słowacki.

The design of the palace has been attributed to the eminent French architect Eugène Emmanuel Viollet-le-Duc. In the 19th century, he was also responsible for the restoration of Nôtre Dame in Paris.

The palace is home to the Museum of Romanticism (Muzeum Romantyzmu), which includes restored interiors and various items that once belonged to Zygmunt Krasiński. Additional exhibits can be seen in a neighbouring building.

The park is also worth a visit, and contains the parish church. Built between 1874 and 1885 in a Neo-Classical style, the church was designed by Wincenty Rakiewicz. The vaults of the church contain the Krasiński family mausoleum, where Zygmunt Krasiński was laid to rest.

Main entrance to Płock Cathedral

Three Guided Walks

Warsaw is an ideal city to explore on foot, as the major attractions in the city centre are within a short walk of each other. In addition, the entire Old Town and New Town are closed to traffic, and several more parks, squares, arcades and the River Vistula are within easy reach.

One attractive walking itinerary is the Royal Route, along which you will find historic palaces, churches and monuments. This runs south from the Old Town, roughly parallel to the Left Bank of the Vistula *(see pp112–25)*. Or, if you have time, try one of the three walks described on the following six pages. The first takes you through the districts between the Royal Route and the Left Bank. The second leads through parks near the riverside in Powiśle district, while the third takes you through the Saska Kępa district, on the Right Bank of the Vistula. This includes Skaryszewski Park, and residential areas with striking modern architecture from the 1920s and 1930s.

Urn on the terrace of the Ostrogski Palace

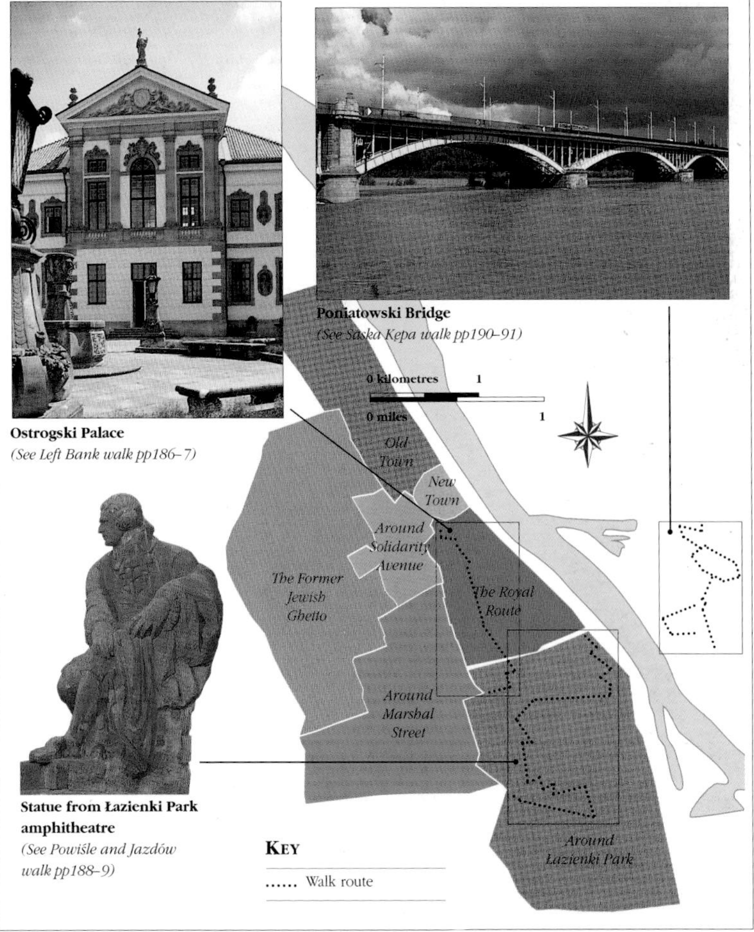

Poniatowski Bridge
(See Saska Kępa walk pp190–91)

Ostrogski Palace
(See Left Bank walk pp186–7)

Statue from Łazienki Park amphitheatre
(See Powiśle and Jazdów walk pp188–9)

◁ **Skaryszewski Park, on the Saska Kępa walk**

A Walk Along the Left Bank

THIS WALK WILL TAKE you along the crest of the escarpment, parallel to the River Vistula, along its Left Bank. It leads through the gardens of several palaces and monasteries and across the Military Museum's grounds and the Frascati residential district, to the Three Crosses Square. A short distance further on is Łazienki Park.

View from Mariensztat Square ②

Kazimierzowski Palace ⑤

From Castle Square to Kazimierzowski Palace
Start your walk at Castle Square. From here, turn towards the River Vistula and descend the steps by the bell tower of St Anna's Church ① to the Mariensztat district. At the end of a narrow passage you will reach Sowia Street. Alternatively, after descending the steps, you can walk across Mariensztat Square ②. Sowia Street leads into Furmańska. Continue along this street, taking time to notice the former Carmelite gardens and park, at the rear of Namiestnikowski Palace ③.

The next right turn takes you into Karowa Street. Climb halfway up the steps to the level of a spiral road, and pass under the arches of the 19th-century viaduct, with its statue of the Mermaid of Warsaw ④. Then take the path that runs along the crest, at the rear of the University. The green expanse of Kazimierzowski Park ⑤ stretches below this point.

From Kazimierzowski Park to Powiśle Station
Walk on through Kazimierzowski Park and cross over Oboźna Street; then follow the escarpment. From this vantage point, you will be able to see Dynasy Park. Continue walking and you will join Bartoszewicza Street. At the end of this street there is a flight of steps that takes you down to a footbridge over Tamka Street. This brings you to the back of Ostrogski Palace ⑥, which is now the home of the Frederic Chopin Museum. If you look down from the footbridge, you will see a square with a fountain at its centre. This marks the location of an underground

Mermaid of Warsaw statue ④ on top of the 19th-century viaduct

pool, in which the legendary Golden Duck of Warsaw *(see p19)* guarded a hoard of treasure. The treasure was hidden in dungeons under Ostrogski Palace, and according to the legend, its finder would be allowed to keep it after fulfilling

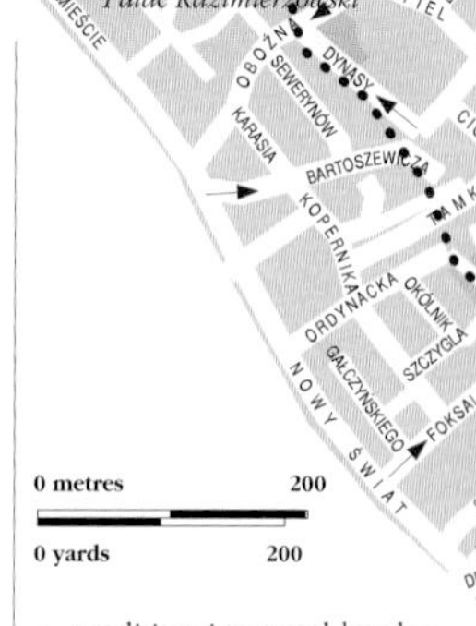

a condition imposed by the Golden Duck. The condition was to spend 1,000 ducats, entirely for the finder's benefit and within 24 hours. The legend tells that one man succeeded in finding the treasure. He amused himself with his wealth, according to the condition, until he was down to the last ducat. At the final moment of his allotted

Bust from the Ostrogski Palace ⑥

24 hours, he gave this single ducat to a beggar and so was denied the remaining hoard.

Once you have passed Ostrogski Palace, climb the steps to the park at the rear of the Academy of Music ⑦. Many years ago, a circus stood here, which was famous for its wrestling competitions. In 1966, the present Academy of Music was built in its place. Continue by following the wall on the left, behind which lie the gardens of the Sisters of Charity ⑧. From the crest of the escarpment, you can observe the nuns tending their gardens, remote and totally shielded from the noise of nearby city life. On your right, behind the iron railings, you should be able to see the pink and white edifice of Zamoyski Palace ⑨. Dating from 1877, the palace is surrounded by attractive gardens. Interestingly situated in the left wing of the palace is the Foksal Gallery, which exhibits contemporary art. Pick up the route again, and continue until you reach Jerozolimskie Avenue and Powiśle Station.

From Powiśle Station to Three Crosses Square

Before resuming the walk, make a detour to see the Powszechny Bank Kredytowy ⑩ at Aleje Jerozolimskie 2, which is a good example of postwar architecture.

Walk under the viaduct of Poniatowski Bridge ⑪, which is flanked by towers built in a Polish Renaissance style. It is the work of architects Stefan Szyller and Mieczysław Marszewski, and when built in 1914, was Europe's longest reinforced-concrete construction. From the underpass, you emerge in the grounds of the Polish Military Museum ⑫, where many weapons and vehicles from World War II are exhibited. Leave by the southern gate and walk through Na Książęcem Park until you cross the footbridge over Książęca Street. To your left stretches an 18th-century park with its original pavilions. Continue along the escarpment, passing the house of the architect Bohdan Pniewski *(see pp110–11)*, which he had built for his family. It is a fine example of modern, functional architecture. Currently it houses a branch of the Earth Sciences Museum ⑬.

From this point, the path along the escarpment becomes Na Skarpie Street. Walk on until you reach the right turn into Bolesława Prusa Street. Here you will see the YMCA, which houses the Theatre Buffo ⑭. Continue past the Sheraton Hotel and turn right into Three Crosses Square ⑮.

Zamoyski Palace, viewed from the escarpment ⑨

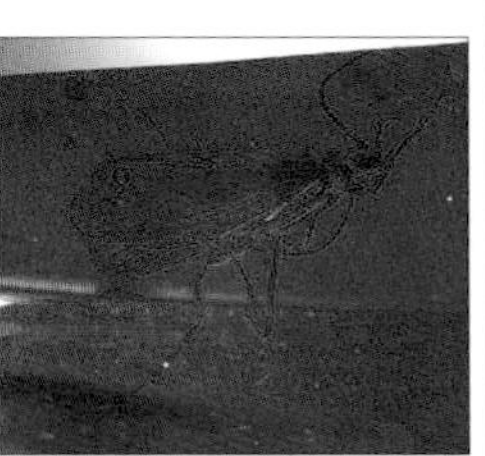

Insect in Baltic amber from the Earth Sciences Museum ⑬

Key

- • • • Walk route
- Viewpoint
- Bus stop

Tips for Walkers

Starting point: *Castle Square.*
Length: *3 km (2 miles).*
Getting there: *Take bus nos. 116, 122, 175, 195, 503 to Castle Square (Plac Zamkowy).*
Stopping-off points: *Cafés and restaurants at the Sheraton, Prusa Street, Tsubame on Foksal Street and the Literacka in Castle Square.*

A Walk in Powiśle and Jazdów

MOST OF THIS WALK passes through the parks and attractive greenery of Jazdów and Powiśle. Before World War II Powiśle was an industrial district; after the war the large Rydz-Śmigły Park was created from the ruins. Continuing on past the Polish Parliament (Sejm), the walk takes in the 19th-century Ujazdowski Park. The final stretch of the walk passes the entrance to Łazienki Park *(see pp162–3)* and the Botanical Gardens *(see p160)*, both just to the south of Agrykola.

From Poniatowski Bridge to Rydz-Śmigły Park

Holy Trinity Church ②

This walk begins at the western end of Poniatowski Bridge. From the tram stop at Wisłostrada, walk down the steps on the south side of the bridge to reach Wioślarska Street. As you walk down this street, with the River Vistula to your left, you will pass (on the right) the Neo-Classical pavilion that was first erected in the mid-19th century as an abattoir. It now houses the office of the Asia and Pacific Museum ① *(see p89)*.

By the museum turn right into Ludna Street, walk as far as the next junction, and then turn left into Solec Street. At the end of this street you will see Holy Trinity Church ②. This small Baroque church was built between 1699–1726. The interiors were largely destroyed in World War II, and have subsequently been restored. But the 17th-century figure of Christ miraculously survived destruction, and is an object of special veneration. A monastery was also built here for the Trinitarian Order, which was dissolved in 1795. These former monastery buildings are now home to the Warsaw Archdiocese Museum ③.

From the church turn right down Gwardzistów Street and take the first left into the park. Continue through the park until you reach Bolesław Prus Avenue, a wide tree-lined road that links the district's green spaces. On this avenue stands the dramatic "Sappers' Memorial" ④, which takes the form of concrete pillars "shooting" into the air. It was designed by Stanisław Kulon in 1975.

Continue along the same avenue towards the top of the Escarpment and Rydz-Śmigły Park. In the middle of this park is a viewing terrace ⑤, built in a Socialist Realist style in the Communist era. It provides delightful views of the Vistula and the city below.

View of the Sappers' Memorial ④

From Rydz-Śmigły Park to Ujazdowski Park

From the viewing terrace, you can choose between two routes to continue the walk, one which takes you along the district's streets, and one that continues through parks.

To take the street route, walk downhill away from the terrace along Frascati Street. No. 2 in this street is an imposing modern building, completed in 1939 for the Chamber of Industry and Commerce and designed by Zdzisław Mączeński. It is now the Foreign Ministry ⑦. Turning left at the end of Frascati Street takes you into Wiejska Street, featuring other Parliament buildings, and the site of the 19th-century Ujazdowski Hospital, which was destroyed in World War II ⑨.

To take the park route from the Rydz-Śmigły viewing terrace, turn left into Na Skarpie Street. The houses that

line this street were built for prominent Communist Party officials. Then continue along the rear of the buildings which house both chambers of Parliament, the Sejm and the Senate ⑥. On the left are prefabricated timber houses *(domki fińskie)* ⑧. These

The Senate in session ⑥

Prefabricated Russian-built house on Na Skarpie street ⑧

were "presented" to Warsaw by the Soviet Union in 1945–6, during a severe shortage of housing in the city. Only a few of these original 350 houses remain. At the end of Na Skarpie, cross Górnośląska Street using the footbridge, turn right, and walk

0 metres 200

0 yards 200

along Górnośląska Street to its intersection with Wiejska and Piękna Streets. Here you join the street route. The two routes are linked midway by a path from Wiejska Street under the bridge that connects the Sejm with an office block.

Beyond the hospital, walk along Piękna Street, and continue past Jazdów Street, and then past John Lennon Street to reach the northern gate of Ujazdowski Park.

Ujazdowski Park to Agrykola

Turn left through the park's Piękna Street gate. Statues in the park include Pius Weloński's *The Gladiator* ⑩, *Eve* by Edward Wittig ⑪ and the Paderewski Memorial ⑫. At the southern gate of the park, turn left and walk to the footbridge to cross Trasa Łazienkowska. On the far side is Ujazdowski Castle ⑬, which now houses the Modern Art Centre *(see p159)*. The castle was built above a stronghold that pre-dates the founding of Warsaw's Old Town. Take the steps behind the castle and the path along Piaseczyński Canal to reach Myśliwiecka Street. Turn right to come to Agrykola Street and the former Guardhouse at the entrance to Łazienki Park ⑭ *(see pp162–3)*. From here you can enter the park, or continue along Agrykola to King Jan III Sobieski's monument ⑮ *(see p160)*. Beyond, past the entrance to the Botanical Gardens is Na Rozdrożu Square, the end of this walk, where there are buses to the centre.

Eve **by Edward Wittig ⑪**

Ujazdowski Castle ⑬

The plain façade of the former guardhouse in Łazienki Park ⑭

Key

- ••• Walk route
- Viewing point
- Main bus route

Tips for Walkers

Starting point: *Poniatowski Bridge.*
Length: *4 km (2.5 miles).*
Getting there: *Buses 101, 102, 111, 117, 158, 303, 517, 521. Tram lines 7, 8, 9, 12, 22, 24, 25 alighting at the Wisłostrada stop.*
Stopping-off point: *Qchnia Artystyczna restaurant in Ujazdowski Castle.*

A Two-Hour Walk in Saska Kępa

SASKA KĘPA is one of Warsaw's most attractive districts. It is divided from Praga-Północ district by Kamionkowskie Lake and Skaryszewski Park, and from central Warsaw by the River Vistula. Historically, the river was even wider than its current 500 m (1,600 ft), and frequent floods converted Saska Kępa into an island *(kępa)*. August III (elector of Saxony and king of Poland) used this "island" from time to time as a picnic spot, and it is from this that it derived the name Saska (Saxon).

The Neo-Classical Toll House ①

Kamionek District

Beginning at the Neo-Classical Toll House ① on Grochowska Street, walk south towards the Church of Our Lady of Victories ②, which is immediately visible in the distance. Although construction of this church began in 1929, it is still not finished. The parish of Kamionek, created in the 13th century, is the oldest parish on this side of the Vistula. The first election of a Polish king was held here in 1572, when Henryk Walezjusz was elected.

The Three Days' Battle against the Swedes was fought here in 1656. This, and numerous later battles, are commemorated by a stone monument, which is dedicated to the soldiers of various nationalities and creeds who were buried in the former graveyards surrounding the church.

From the church, walk in the direction of Kamionkowskie Lake ③, originally a tributary of the Vistula. Following the curve of the lake leads to Zieleniecka Street.

Skaryszewski Park

Walking around the lake and continuing south along Zieleniecka Street leads to Skaryszewski Park ④, which is also known as Paderewski Park. Designed by Franciszek Szanior and laid out between 1905 and 1922 in a Secessionist and early Modernist style, this is one of the most beautiful parks in Warsaw.

Following the edge of the lake – a favourite place for anglers – you will reach a memorial ⑤ to the crew of the *British Liberator 961*, from 178 Squadron RAF. This plane was shot down over the city during the Warsaw Uprising in 1944, while dropping supplies to the Armia Krajowa (Home Army). The memorial was unveiled in 1988 by Margaret Thatcher (then British prime minister).

Within the park you can also see several sculptures dating from the 1918–39 interwar period. Among the finest are *The Dancer* by Stanisław Jackowski ⑥, *The Bather* by Olga Niewska ⑦ and Henryk Kuna's *Rhythm*. There is also a statue of Colonel Edward House ⑧, advisor to US President Woodrow Wilson during World War I and a staunch supporter of Poland. This monument was recently recast, as the original was destroyed by the Communists. First unveiled in 1932, it was funded by the pianist and statesman Ignacy Paderewski. A bust of Paderewski stands by the path near the park gate leading onto Rondo Waszyngtona ⑨. Across this large square is a bust of the first president of the USA, George Washington ⑩ unveiled in 1989.

***The Bather* ⑦**

Washington Memorial ⑩

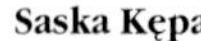

Saska Kępa

Continue south from Rondo Waszyngtona along Francuska Street, which is the main shopping thoroughfare of Saska Kępa. This street and the surrounding district were almost entirely developed between 1918 and 1939.

The street's Modernist-style houses ⑪ are generally only a few storeys high and are set among green shrubbery.

At the corner of Obrońców Street, you can take a detour from the route by turning left past spacious villas from the 1930s. Take the third on the left, Nobla, and turn right at the end of this street to reach the Church of Our Lady of Perpetual Succour ⑫.

This church was built over a long period between 1938 and 1956, and was designed by Piotr Lubiński, Józef Łowiński and Jan Bogusławski. The appearance of its façade was influenced by the style of provincial churches during the Middle Ages. The nave is surprisingly high, while the ceiling is supported by concrete columns and arches.

Leaving the church, retrace your steps along Obrońców Street to return to the main walk route. Cross Francuska Street, then turn right into the narrow Katowicka Street. This street features several avant-garde villas which date from the late 1920s and the 1930s.

One particularly interesting house is at No. 7a Katowicka Street. Built in 1938 for the Avenarius family, it was designed by Jerzy Szanajca, Stanisław Barylski and Bohdan Lachert. The house boasts a glass-fronted concrete staircase, which is covered with a flat, perforated concrete roof.

Interior of the Church of Our Lady of Perpetual Succour ⑫

At No. 11 Katowicka Street stands the two-storey Villa Lachert ⑬, which Bohdan Lachert designed as his private residence. Constructed in 1929, it is based on the design principles that were established by the renowned 20th-century Modernist architect Le Corbusier.

Other buildings that line this street boast interesting decorative features dating from the 1940s. Several of the villas currently belong to the German Embassy.

When you come to the end of Katowicka Street, at the corner of Walecznych Street, turn left and continue until you come to the Miedzeszyński Embankment, which runs alongside the River Vistula. From here, there is a good view across the river, including buildings in the low-lying Powiśle district on the opposite bank. Beyond Powiśle, you will also have an excellent view of the many rooftops and spires that characterize the centre of Warsaw.

Tenth Anniversary Stadium

Turn right when you come to the eastern end of Poniatowski Bridge ⑭ and continue back towards Saska Kępa, heading away from the river. The twin towers of the Poniatowski Bridge were rebuilt in 1988, following the original, turn-of-the-century design by Stefan Szyller.

Passing underneath the bridge you will be faced by the massive Tenth Anniversary Stadium ⑮. It was built in 1954–5 to mark the tenth anniversary of the end of World War II and the first decade of Communist rule. The architects were Jerzy Hryniewiecki, Marek Leykam and Czesław Rajewski. Rubble from the wartime destruction of Warsaw was used to construct the foundations of the stadium.

Soon after the stadium was completed in 1955, it was used to stage the opening ceremony of the World Festival of Youth. After years of isolation imposed by Communism, it was the first opportunity for Poles to meet people from all over the world, and these visitors appeared highly exotic to local citizens. In later years the stadium gradually fell into disrepair, but after 1989 a new role emerged for it: the stadium became Eastern Europe's largest open-air market, known as the "Saxon Fair". Traders from across the whole of Europe and even from Asia travelled to the market to buy and sell a wide range of merchandise.

***The Relay* ⑯**

Continuing past the stadium you will come to the Socialist Realist statue entitled *The Relay* ⑯. From here it is a short walk back to Rondo Waszyngtona, where there are numerous bus and tram connections running to central Warsaw.

The avant-garde Villa Lachert in Katowicka Street ⑬

Key

••• Walk route

Main bus stops

Tips for Walkers

Starting point: *Zamoyski Street by the toll houses and the Church of Our Lady of Victories in Kamionek.*
Length: *5 km (3 miles).*
Getting there: *Tram no. 6 arrives at the begining of the walk, while tram no. 25 has a stop within 100 m (100 yards). Return from Rondo Waszyngtona by trams 7, 8, 9, 12, 22, 24 and 25 or buses E-5, 101, 102, 111, 117, 158, 303, 509, 517, 521.*
Stopping-off points: *During the summer a café is open within Skaryszewski Park, which also has plenty of benches and delightful spots in which to sit. Otherwise there are numerous cafés and bars in Rondo Waszyngtona and along Francuska Street.*

Travellers' Needs

Where to Stay

Until quite recently it was difficult to find accommodation in Warsaw, and hotel standards were far behind those of Western Europe. Many new hotels have opened since 1989, but these are mostly deluxe and very expensive. They also tend to be part of international chains, and therefore do not reflect local tradition. With a few exceptions, mid-price hotels are fairly anonymous but comfortable, and are at least centrally located. A growing range of budget-priced options, typically converted from workers' hostels, office buildings, barracks and student halls of residence, are mainly located in the suburbs, and there is still a shortage of inexpensive accommodation in the city centre. The hotel listings on pages 200–203 cover a range of options, with hotels listed by area and in order of price. Accommodation can also be arranged in private houses *(see p197)*, many of which are centrally located. Some booking agencies also handle property rentals.

Youth hostels and camp sites provide other inexpensive options *(see pp196–7)*, although their facilities can be limited, and locations are not usually very convenient.

Porter at the exclusive Bristol Hotel

The elegantly restored reception area at the Bristol Hotel

Where to Look

Warsaw is a sprawling city, so the city centre *(śródmieście)*, close to the main tourist attractions and the best shops and restaurants, is the most convenient place to stay. Although this part of town has a large number of hotels, they are not concentrated in any particular areas. An ideal location is around Krakowskie Przedmieście and Plac Piłsudskiego (Piłsudski Square). This is Warsaw's most historic part, and is only a short walk from the Old Town (Stare Miasto).

Accommodation in this area is mainly provided by international chain hotels, of varying standard, or by large, plain hotels that are aimed at foreign business travellers, often from the ex-Soviet countries, who come to trade in Warsaw's markets. There are only a few hotels in the city that still have original interiors and their own unique atmosphere. A prime example of one that does possess these qualities is the exclusive Bristol Hotel, which has beautifully restored Secessionist-style interiors. There are much cheaper hotels in the same area, but they usually need modernization. Small roadside hotels and motels in the suburbs have a friendly atmosphere, and are often set in pleasant gardens. However, staying in the suburbs involves a time-consuming journey to reach the centre of Warsaw.

Booking Ahead

In planning a visit to Warsaw, it is advisable to book your hotel in advance. Finding accommodation on arrival may be difficult, especially in June and July, from September to November, and during religious holidays. During these periods, hotel reservations should be made several weeks ahead.

The grand and stately setting of the restaurant at the Polonia Hotel

The modern hotel lobby of the Mercure

Facilities

Hotel rooms in Poland tend to be rather small as a rule, though those that have been refurbished and modernized usually have *en suite* showers or bathrooms. Most of these hotels are equipped with televisions in each room, and some also have videos. There is generally a laundry service at most hotels.

The more expensive hotels also offer 24-hour room service and have a mini-bar in each room. Some hotels are able to accommodate pets, should you be taking them on your visit to Warsaw.

Guests are usually asked to vacate their rooms by midday when checking out. But, if you are departing later, you may leave luggage with the hotel's concierge. The majority of hotel staff in Warsaw speak English or German.

Discounts

Prices in all of Warsaw's more comfortable hotels are quite high, and are quoted in US dollars. Hence in the hotel listings *(see pp200–203)*, the price categories are given in dollars. However, many hotels, including the more exclusive ones, offer weekend discount packages and special rates for children. Various discounts are also offered by hotels belonging to international chains, such as the Intercontinental and Forum. Sometimes discounts can be negotiated in advance with the hotel, especially if visiting outside the peak seasons of summer and autumn. Prices are charged per room, and discounts are rarely offered for single occupancy of a double room – and in Warsaw there are relatively few single rooms available.

Hidden Extras

Most hotels quote prices that include both VAT (which is currently fluctuating between 7 and 22 per cent) and service. In Poland it is not customary to tip staff, except in the capital's more exclusive hotels.

A choice of set breakfast menus, and Swedish-style buffets, are a standard feature of most hotels. Some hotels charge extra for breakfast, whether served in the room or in the hotel restaurant – check this when you book in.

Most hotels have direct dial telephones in the rooms for the use of guests. Bear in mind, however, that international calls from hotels usually prove expensive, as they incur a high surcharge. Public telephones are significantly cheaper, and also offer international direct dialling. Public phones are easily found throughout the city centre, and work using phone cards *(see p242)*. These are readily available from newsagents and kiosks.

Disabled Visitors

Only a few of Warsaw's hotels provide adapted rooms and facilities for aiding the disabled visitor. Detailed information on hotels that offer wheelchair access can be found on page 244.

The National Council for the Disabled (Krajowa Rada Osób Niepełnosprawnych) can also be contacted for further advice on hotels, as well as specific information on sightseeing in Warsaw, and throughout Poland *(see p244)*.

Travelling with Children

Warsaw is generally a child-friendly city *(see pp232–3)*, and most hotels welcome children warmly.

Many offer a reduced price for children, while some hotels provide free accommodation for children up to the age of three. In a few cases this even extends up to the age of 14, so long as the child is travelling with its parents. It is best to enquire about any discounts that are available when making the reservation.

It is also common for children to share their parents' room, often for no extra charge. Hotels are used to this, and will generally provide a folding bed for this purpose. Many hotel restaurants are very accommodating, though they may not offer a special children's menu, and highchairs are relatively rare. The biggest problem, however, is that it tends to be quite difficult to find a child-minder.

An opulent, if slightly faded, room in the Europejski Hotel

Directory

Useful UK and US Addresses

American Travel Abroad
250 West 57 Street
New York,
NY 10107.
(212) 586-5230.

Bogdan Travel
5 The Broadway,
Gunnersbury Lane,
London W3 8HR.
(020) 8993 9997.

LOT Polish Airlines
313 Regent Street,
London W1R 7PE.
(020) 7580 5037.

500 Fifth Ave.
New York,
NY 10036.
(800) 223-0593.

Polish Embassy (UK)
47 Portland Place,
London W1B 1JH.
(0870) 774 2700.

Polish Embassy (US)
2640 16 Street NW
Washington,
DC 20009.
(202) 234-3800.

Polish National Tourist Office (UK)
1st floor,
Remo House, 310–12
Regent Street,
London W1R 5AJ.
(020) 7580 8811, (020) 7580 6688.

Polish National Tourist Office (US)
275 Madison Avenue,
New York, NY 10016.
(212) 338-9412.
www.polandtour.org

Accommodation Agencies

Almatur
Kopernika 23.
Map 2 E4.
826 26 39.
Jun–Sep: Mon–Fri 9am-6pm.

Gromada Tours
Plac Powstańców,
Warszawy 2.
Map 2 D4.
827 92 51.

Mazurkas Travel
Nowogrodzka 24/26.
Map 6 D1.
629 12 49.

Długa 8/14.
Map 1 C2.
536 46 00.

Orbis Travel
Świętokrzyska 20.
Map 1 B5, 5C1.
826 16 80.

Syrena Unilevel
(accommodation in private properties)
Krucza 17.
Map 6 D2.
628 75 40.

Warsaw and National Accommodation Agency (Warszawska Informacja Noclegowa)
(telephone enquiries only)
641 53 66.
Mon–Fri 10am–5pm.
662 64 89.
Mon–Fri 5–11pm, Sat–Sun 10am–5pm.

Warsaw Tourist Information Centre (Warszawskie Centrum Informacji Turystycznej)
Plac Zamkowy 1/13.
Map 2 D2.
635 18 81.
Mon–Fri 9am–6pm, Sat, Sun 9am–6pm.

Apartments and Rooms to Let

These agents deal with leases that are usually of at least several months' duration.

Agencja Kaczmarczyk
Aleje Jerozolimskie 31/8.
Map 6 D1.
832 22 29.

Drągowski Properties (Drągowski Nieruchomości)
Jasna 10.
Map 1 C4.
827 30 02.

Marszałkowska 83.
Map 6 D3.
622 30 33.

Śliska 3.
Map 1 B5.
652 30 44.

Nobil House Agency (Agencja Nobil House)
Aleje Ujazdowskie 20
Floor 10.
Map 6 E2.
625 40 59.

Piotrowski Agency (Agencja Piotrowski)
Żurawia 24.
Map 6 D2.
621 47 46.

Marszałkowska 85.
Map 1 C4.
622 71 81, 622 71 82.

Strzelczyk Brothers (Bracia Strzelczyk)
Plac Konstytucji 4.
Map 6 D2.
625 66 61.

Marszałkowska 58.
Map 1 C4.
625 15 15.

Bonifraterska 16.
Map 3 B3.
635 30 65.

Unikat
Fabryczna 16/22.
Map 6 F2.
337 13 13.

Marszałkowska 83 m1.
Map 6 D2.
628 11 57.

Student Halls and Boarding Houses

Duet Medical Academy Students' Hall No. 1 (Dom Studenta Duet nr 1 Akademii Medycznej)
Batalionu "Pięść" 9.
836 03 71.

Grosik Students' Hall (Dom Studenta Grosik)
Madalińskiego 31/33.
849 23 02.

Hermes Students' Hall (Dom Studenta Hermes)
Madalińskiego 6/8.
849 67 22.

Oasis Students' Hall (Dom Studenta Oaza)
Madalińskiego 39/43.
849 24 01.

Youth Hostels

Karolkowa 53A.
632 88 29.
all year.

Międzyparkowa 4/6.
831 17 66.
Apr–mid-Nov.

Smolna 30.
827 89 52.
all year.

Camp Sites

Bitwy Warszawskiej 1920 r 15/17.
823 37 48.
Apr–Oct.

Park Kultury Powsin.
648 48 11.
May–Oct.

Żwirki i Wigury 32.
825 43 91.
Apr–Oct.

Apartments and Rooms to Let

The number of rooms available to let in Warsaw has risen considerably in the last few years. They offer an inexpensive and popular option, particularly when located near the town centre. An average price for a night in a private house or flat is $18 for one person, and $22 for two. However, these prices do not include extras such as breakfast.

Agencies usually offer a wide choice of accommodation, and some offer longer term lets. When making a reservation you should specify the range of facilities required, and the preferred district. Praga-Północ (Praga-North) and other outlying housing estates are not recommended. One exception is Ursynów Natolin, which is linked to the town centre *(śródmieście)* by Warsaw's underground metro service.

Agencies expect to be paid in cash, and issue a receipt which is then presented to the landlord. Bank transfers can be arranged, but only for longer term rentals.

Accommodation in student halls is sometimes available in the summer, coordinated by the **Almatur** agency.

Youth Hostels

Warsaw has three youth hostels which are open all year, with another two open only during peak season. They are all relatively clean, and mainly offer dormitory-style accommodation. Bookings should be made two or three days prior to arrival. The busiest periods are Fridays and Saturdays, but also during spring and autumn, when hostels are taken over by school trips. Hostels close between 10am and 4pm. You should check in before 10pm as arriving any later may be problematic. Prices are below $10 per night for a bed in a communal room. Hostels offer discounts if you have an **IYHF** (International Youth Hostel Federation) card.

Camp Sites

Most camp sites are located on the outskirts of Warsaw; the only exception is the site at Żwirki i Wigury. Facilities are fairly standard, though in addition to space to pitch a tent, or park a caravan or camper, they also provide chalet accommodation. Camp sites are usually open from April until October. One camp site which is open for tents throughout the year is at Grochowska Street. This is near the Warsaw to Moscow trunk road, 8 km (5 miles) east of the town centre. The city's most attractive camp site is Powsin. Only open for the main tourist season, Powsin is set in a forest, close to the Botanical Gardens. Information on Warsaw's camp sites, and their facilities, is available from the **Warsaw Tourist Information Centre (Waszawskie Centrum Informacji Turystycznej)**.

Suite of rooms at the Karat Hotel, near Łazienki Park

Using the Listings

The hotels included on pages 201–3 are listed in order of price, from the cheapest to the most expensive. The symbols summarize the facilities at each hotel:

- rooms with shower and/or bathroom
- 1 single room
- rooms for more than two persons or with space for an additional bed
- 24 24-hour room service
- TV TV in every room
- rooms for non-smokers
- rooms with a scenic view
- all rooms air-conditioned
- gymnasium
- swimming pool
- business facilities: including information service, fax, desk and telephone in the room; conference room
- facilities for children; cots available
- wheelchair access
- lift
- P car park
- garden or terrace
- bar
- restaurant
- tourist information
- credit cards welcome

AE American Express
DC Diners Club
MC MasterCard
V VISA
JCB Japanese Credit Bureau

Price categories for a double with bathroom or shower per night, including breakfast, service and 7 per cent VAT:

- $ up to $40
- $$ $40–75
- $$$ $75–110
- $$$$ $110–145
- $$$$$ over $145

Warsaw's Best: Hotels

THE NUMBER OF HOTELS in Warsaw has increased considerably over the past few years. New luxury hotels have been built, while many older establishments have also been refurbished and modernized. The standards of service and range of facilities have generally improved, although there are still exceptions. The selection of hotels on these two pages (all of which have been reviewed in the listings section) offer a very enjoyable, albeit expensive, stay in Warsaw.

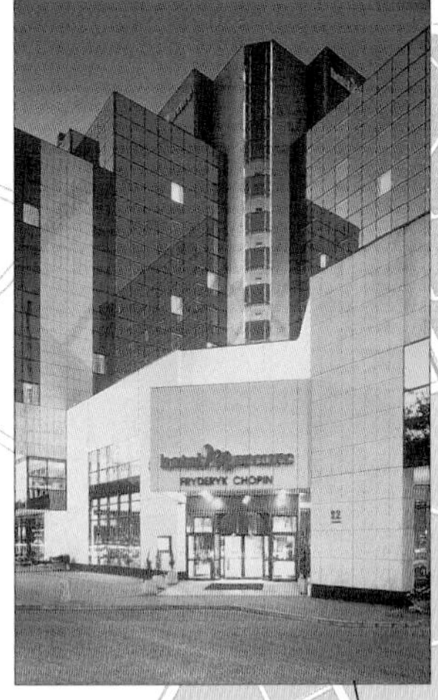

Mercure-Fryderyk Chopin
This contemporary hotel offers French cuisine in Le Balzac restaurant, and an international menu in Le Stanislaus (see p202).

The Former Jewish Ghetto

Holiday Inn
Having opened in 1989, this was Warsaw's first international standard hotel (see p202).

Marriott
Various restaurants, as well as business and sports facilities have helped establish this deluxe hotel as one of the most popular (see p202).

Jan III Sobieski
This features a modern interpretation of traditional Varsovian architecture (see p202).

Europejski
With a mid-19th-century façade, this is the city's oldest hotel. The restaurant and patisserie are also well established (see p202).

Bristol
Following extensive renovation, this is Warsaw's most luxurious hotel, combining modern facilities with beautiful Secessionist interiors (see p202).

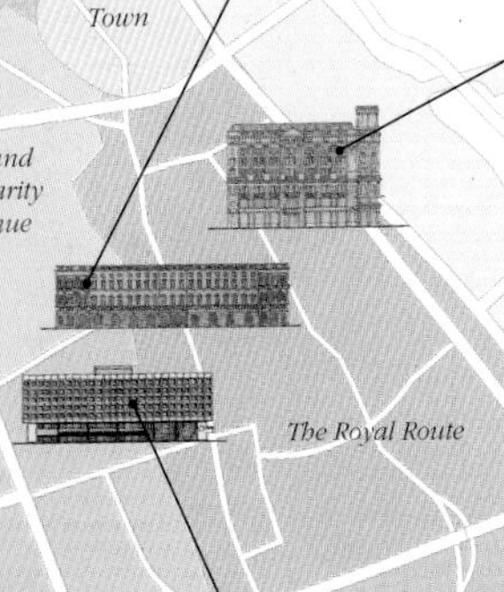

Sheraton
This deluxe venue is the latest international chain hotel to open in Warsaw (see p203).

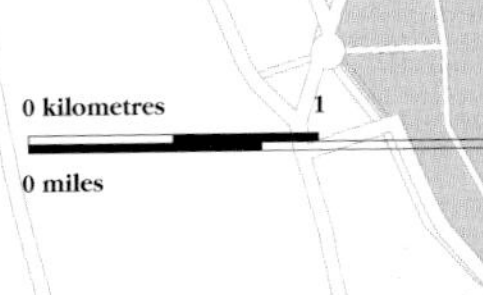

Sofitel Victoria
With its renowned restaurant, the Sofitel Victoria also has attractive modern interiors (see p203).

Choosing a Hotel

THIS CHART is a quick reference guide to the hotels that we have reviewed on the following pages. They are a selection of the best hotels in and around Warsaw, in respect of value, location, facilities and service. The selection takes in a wide range of hotels right across the price spectrum, and there should be a choice to suit all needs. For information on other types of accommodation see pages 194–7.

Hotel	Price	Number of Rooms	Double Rooms Available	Business Facilities	Facilities for Children	Recommended Restaurants	Shops Nearby	Quiet Location	24-Hour Room Service
City Centre *(see pp201–3)*									
Mazowiecki	$$	54	●				●		●
Belwederski	$$$	51		●	●			●	●
Gromada Centrum	$$$	236		●	●		●		●
Harenda	$$$	45		●	●		●		●
Karat	$$$	37	●	●	●			●	
Maria	$$$	24	●		●				●
Metropol	$$$	182		●			●		●
Parkowa	$$$	44		●	●			●	
Polonia	$$$	234		●	●		●		●
Warszawa	$$$	126					●		●
Europejski	$$$$	238	●	●	●	●	●		●
Grand	$$$$	385		●	●		●		●
MDM	$$$$	120		●	●	●	●		●
Solec	$$$$	137		●	●				●
Bristol	$$$$$	206	●	●	●	●	●		●
Holiday Inn	$$$$$	336	●	●	●		●		●
Jan III Sobieski	$$$$$	414	●	●	●	●	●		●
Marriott	$$$$$	525	●	●	●	●	●		●
Mercure–Fryderyk Chopin	$$$$$	250	●	●	●	●	●		●
Novotel Warszawa Centrum	$$$$$	733		●	●		●		●
Sheraton	$$$$$	352		●	●	●	●	●	●
Sofitel Victoria Warsaw	$$$$$	365	●	●	●	●	●		●
Further Afield *(see p203)*									
Agra	$	40	●					●	●
Felix	$$	234	●						●
Gromada	$$$	127	●	●	●				●
Hotel IBiIB	$$$	44	●	●					
Zajazd Napoleoński	$$$	24							
Vera	$$$$	161	●	●	●	●			●
Novotel	$$$$$	278			●	●			●
Beyond Warsaw *(see p203)*									
Eden	$$	52	●	●					●
Konstancja	$$$	44	●	●	●	●		●	●

Price categories for a double room with bathroom or shower including breakfast, service and 7 per cent VAT. Hotel prices in Warsaw are quoted in US dollars:

$ under $40
$$ $40–$75
$$$ $75–$110
$$$$ $110–$145
$$$$$ over $145

Business Facilities
Including a telephone in the room, plus information service, fax and conference facilities.

Facilities for Children
Including cots or folding beds in the rooms.

Recommended Restaurants
Restaurants near to the hotel that have excellent reputations for their cuisine, and unusual or historic settings.

CITY CENTRE

Mazowiecki

Mazowiecka 10. **Map** 2 D4. *827 23 65.* FAX *827 23 65.* ***Rooms:*** *54.* AE, DC, MC, V. $$ *www.mazowiecki.com.pl*

Originally a garrison hotel, this has been open to the public for the last few years, but has not really developed beyond its military origins. The staff still cultivate manners reminiscent of army barracks, with a receptionist who rarely smiles. Smells from the kitchen hit you as soon as you cross the threshold. Only a few rooms have bathrooms. However, the hotel has competitive rates, and is close to the city centre.

Belwederski

Sulkiewicza 11. **Map** 6 E4. *840 40 11.* FAX *840 08 47.* ***Rooms:*** *51.* AE, MC, V. $$$ *www.hotelbelwederski.pl*

This eight-storey building was renovated and refurbished in the late 1990s. The top floors give onto fine leafy views across the Łazienki Park, and it is well located near Belveder Palace. In front of the hotel lies the direct route to the Old Town and Wilanow. The hotel is owned by the military, but civilians are welcome. At weekends discounts of up to 30 per cent operate.

Gromada Centrum

Plac Powstańców Warszawy 2. **Map** 2 D3. *827 92 51.* FAX *625 21 40.* ***Rooms:*** *236.* AE, DC, MC, V, JCB. $$$ *www.gromada.pl*

The hotel's former name, "Peasants' House" stems from the Communist era, when the government tried to forge better relations between industrial workers and peasants. The hotel still retains some of that character, as it continues to attract Polish country folk visiting the capital. Designed by Bohdan Pniewski, an outstanding architect of the mid-20th century *(see pp210–11)*, this is one of the more interesting examples of late 1950s design. Although the large lobby is quite gloomy, the rooms themselves have all been modernized.

Harenda

Krakowskie Przedmieście 4/6. **Map** 2 D4. *826 00 71, 826 00 72, 826 00 73.* FAX *826 26 25.* ***Rooms:*** *45.*

15. AE, MC, V, JCB. $$$ *hh@hotelharenda.com.pl*

Located above an antique shop and auction house, this small hotel is on the second floor of the former Tourist Hostel (Dom Turysty). The location is good, as Krakowskie Przedmieście is adjacent to the Old Town, and also happens to be one of the most beautiful streets in Warsaw's historic centre. Only a few rooms have a private bathroom, and double rooms are small. There is also dormitory-style accommodation, without a private bathroom. However, the conditions are more reminiscent of a camp site than a hotel. The Harenda features a restaurant, which has a good reputation, and an English-style pub.

Karat

Słoneczna 37. **Map** 6 E4. *601 44 11, 849 84 54.* FAX *849 52 94.* ***Rooms:*** *37.* AE, MC, V. $$$ *www.hotelkarat.pl*

This is a newly renovated hotel, in a residential street lined with picturesque villas, by the banks of the River Vistula and close to the Łazienki Park. Rooms are larger than average for Warsaw hotels, and prices are relatively low. Smart, white bathrooms are immaculately maintained.

Maria

Aleja Jana Pawła II 71. **Map** 3 A3. *838 04 62.* FAX *838 38 40.* TX *81 77 57.* ***Rooms:*** *24.* AE, MC, V, JCB. $$$ *www.hotel-maria.com*

This small hotel, set at the northern edge of the town centre, has a homely atmosphere which provides a welcome respite from the urban hustle. The proprietors and staff are unfailingly polite. The rooms are large and tastefully furnished, as well as being clean.

Metropol

Marszałkowska 99a. **Map** 6 D2. *629 40 01.* FAX *625 30 14.* ***Rooms:*** *182.* AE, DC, MC, V, JCB. $$$ *hotel.metropol@syrena.com.pl*

The Metropol is situated just a few minutes' walk from the Central Railway Station (Dworzec Centralny). Built in the 1960s, the Metropol is regarded by many as something of an architectural monstrosity but, on the plus side, it does have clean rooms with decent bathrooms, and the prices are attractively modest.

Parkowa

Belwederska 46/50. **Map** 6 E4. *694 80 00, 841 60 21.* FAX *41 60 29.* ***Rooms:*** *44.* AE, DC, MC, V, JCB. $$$

In its previous incarnation, the Parkowa was a garrison hotel, and was regarded as luxurious by officers of the former Warsaw Pact countries. It is now open to the general public, having undergone modernization, though staff continue the unhelpful attitudes fostered during the years of Communism. However, the hotel's location does make up for its shortcomings. Rooms on the upper floors provide views over the Russian Embassy gardens, as well as the Ministry of Defence grounds and Łazienki Park *(see pp162–3)*.

Polonia

Aleje Jerozolimskie 45. **Map** 2 E5. *628 72 41.* FAX *622 31 18.* ***Rooms:*** *234.* *147.* AE, DC, MC, V, JCB. $$$

Built between 1909 and 1913 in a distinctive Beaux Arts style *(see p136)*, the Polonia features some opulent interiors, particularly in the lobby and in its rather swanky restaurant. The ambience is similarly refined and voluptuous, and one can almost imagine Fred Astaire lolloping down the stairwell. During the immediate postwar period, the hotel provided accommodation for several embassies and other diplomatic agencies, and thus acquired an intriguing history. Unfortunately, the refurbishment that took place during the 1960s deprived the rooms of much of their character. However, the building is now due for further renovation, which may well herald the return of some of its austere charm. The Polonia is in a central location, by the Palace of Culture and Science (Pałac Kultury i Nauki).

Warszawa

Plac Powstańców Warszawy 9. **Map** 6 D1. *826 94 21.* FAX *827 18 73.* ***Rooms:*** *126.* AE, DC, MC, V, JCB. $$$ *hotel.warszawa@syrena.com.pl*

Dating from 1934, this was once the tallest building in Poland *(see p131)*, but was overtaken by the towering Palace of Culture and Science (Pałac Kultury i Nauki). Following postwar reconstruction, the building was converted into a hotel, though not all rooms include private bathrooms, so you can make new friends on the landing. The currency exchange counter offers some of the city's most reasonable rates.

Europejski

Krakowskie Przedmieście 13. **Map** 2 D3. *826 50 51.* FAX *826 17 11.* ***Rooms:*** *238.* *AE, DC, MC, V, JCB.* $$$$ *europej@orbis.pl*

Housed behind a Neo-Renaissance façade, this is Warsaw's oldest hotel, and it was built between 1855 and 1877. In 1939 it provided a refuge for King Zog of Albania, after he was overthrown by the Italians. However, having been rebuilt from its wartime ruins, the interiors have lost their former character. Rooms can be quite small, though all have mini-bars. The hotel has fallen into a somewhat dilapidated state in recent years, but is now being modernized. The restaurant has a good reputation, while the ground floor café serves pastries made on the premises, renowned as some of Warsaw's finest. Another coffee bar in the hotel, facing Krakowskie Przedmieście, also offers these famous pastries.

Grand

Krucza 28. **Map** 6 D2. *583 21 00.* FAX *621 97 24.* TX *81 34 22.* ***Rooms:*** *385.* *AE, DC, MC, V.* $$$$

This is a misnomer, as there is not much grandeur on offer in this large-scale building, which dates from the late 1950s. The rooms are blandly decorated, with those on the top floors providing the best views. The main attraction, for gamblers and sybarites, is the extensive gaming club which nestles in the Grand.

MDM

Plac Konstytucji 1. **Map** 6 D2. *621 62 11.* FAX *621 41 73.* TX *81 48 71.* ***Rooms:*** *120.* *AE, DC, MC, V, JCB.* $$$$

The MDM is an example of so-called Socialist Realism *(see p31)*. Following modernization, all rooms now have sparkling clean bathrooms en suite and pleasant furnishings. A small lobby leads to a large restaurant, the Ugarit, with interiors inspired by Syrian architecture. The hotel is near some very good shops and an interesting urban development of the 1950s, the Marshal Street Residential Quarter, which gave the hotel its name *(see p132)*.

Solec

Zagórna 1. **Map** 6 F2. *625 44 00.* FAX *621 64 42.* ***Rooms:*** *137.* *AE, DC, MC, V, JCB.* $$$$ *solec@orbis.pl,htp*

Adjacent to a park and the River Vistula, this two-storey hotel was built in the 1970s. The hotel's facilities include a shopping arcade together with a restaurant, a bar and some shops. Rooms are relatively modern, though nothing special. This is also one of the very few hotels in central Warsaw with its own garden, although this is quite small. Unfortunately, it is also situated by the busy and noisy Wisłostrada trunk road.

Bristol

Krakowskie Przedmieście 42/44. **Map** 2 D3. *625 25 25.* FAX *625 25 77.* ***Rooms:*** *206.* *AE, DC, MC, V, JCB.* $$$$$ *www.lemeridien-bristol.com*

The most exclusive hotel in Warsaw is listed as a national monument. Its beautiful Secession-style architecture was designed by the Viennese architect Otto Wagner the Younger. Since first opening in 1900, the hotel has received a great many celebrities. The restaurant has hosted former French president Charles de Gaulle and the Shah of Iran, Reza Pahlavi. Following extensive restoration, the Bristol was officially reopened in December 1992, by Lady Thatcher. Prices are high at this hotel, but it does offer a fine experience. The Malinowa restaurant serves Polish/French cuisine, while Italian food is served in the Marconi restaurant.

Holiday Inn

Złota 48/54. **Map** 5 B1. *697 39 99.* FAX *697 38 99.* ***Rooms:*** *336.* *AE, DC, MC, V, JCB.* $$$$$

Opened in 1989, the Holiday Inn was Warsaw's first Western-standard hotel, featuring a glazed lobby full of greenery, as well as restaurants, cafés and shops. Some of the rooms offer extra space, gained from triangular bay windows. The hotel is located by the Central Railway Station and the Palace of Culture and Science.

Jan III Sobieski

Plac Zawiszy 1. **Map** 5 B2. *579 10 00.* FAX *659 88 28.* ***Rooms:*** *414.* *AE, DC, MC, JCB.* $$$$$

Postmodernist elevations, mixed with avant-garde interiors, made this hotel a talking point when it opened in 1992 *(see p105)*. However, the building was soon accepted by locals, and has also blended into the city landscape. A spacious lobby is decorated with pink marble and colourful mosaics, while an open-plan restaurant includes an atrium and water feature. The hotel commemorates its namesake, King Jan III Sobieski *(see pp22–3)* with a marble statue, together with a selection of old paintings and framed copies of 17th-century drawings. Rooms are decorated with wicker, cherry wood and marble furniture. When making a booking, it is worth requesting a room overlooking the roof garden.

Marriott

Aleje Jerozolimskie 65/79. **Map** 2 E5. *630 63 06.* FAX *830 03 11.* ***Rooms:*** *525.* *AE, DC, MC, V, JCB.* $$$$$ *www.marriott.com*

The Marriott is a deluxe 40-floor tower, with spacious, elegantly furnished rooms occupying the 20 topmost floors. A grand lobby, extending from the ground floor to a mezzanine level, has marble, chrome and crystal glass features. Various restaurants span Polish, Italian, American and international cuisine, with cafés, a casino and several bars providing alternative options. The Panorama Bar, which is situated 140 m (460 ft) above ground level, offers amazing views of the city. Various function and conference rooms are also available.

Mercure–Fryderyk Chopin

Aleja Jana Pawła II 22. **Map** 3 A3. *620 02 01.* FAX *620 87 79.* ***Rooms:*** *250.* *AE, DC, MC, V, JCB.* $$$$$ *mercure@perytnet.pl*

This luxury hotel is part of the French Mercure chain, and it has more than its share of savoir faire. Rooms are furnished with elegant, modern furniture. The choice of restaurants comprises Le Balzac, specializing in French cuisine, and Le Stanislaus, which boasts an international menu. There is also a charming café/patisserie. The hotel is conveniently situated near the Central Railway Station.

Novotel Warszawa Centrum

Nowogrodzka 24/26. **Map** 5 B2. *621 02 71.* FAX *625 04 76.* ***Rooms:*** *733.* *AE, DC, MC, V, JCB.* $$$$$

Formerly the Forum, this is Warsaw's largest hotel. The rooms here are small, with rather uninteresting furniture dating from the Polish People's Republic. Some rooms do have mini-bars, and the newly refurbished bathrooms are very good. There is a large lobby on the ground floor, with cafés, restaurants, travel agents and other shops. Rooms situated above the 20th floor offer superb views over central Warsaw.

Sheraton

Prusa 2. **Map** 6 E2. *657 61 00.* FAX *657 62 00.* ***Rooms:*** *352.* *AE, DC, MC, V, JCB.* $$$$$ *www.sheraton.pl*

This is the city's most recently-built, deluxe hotel. Behind an impressive postmodernist façade, it has strikingly opulent interiors in an international style. An excellent location is combined with every amenity to make life more enjoyable, including a jazz bar that is renowned in Warsaw. The hotel is mainly geared to visiting VIPs and business people. The even more luxurious "Towers" section, which occupies the top floors, functions almost as a separate hotel, with superb suites and service.

Sofitel Victoria Warsaw

Królewska 11. **Map** 4 D5. *657 80 11.* FAX *827 98 56.* ***Rooms:*** *365.* *AE, DC, MC, V, JCB.* $$$$$ *sofitel@victoria.pl*

In the late 1970s this was Warsaw's most exclusive hotel. However, since the 1989 democratic elections, several luxurious hotels have opened up, leaving the Sofitel Victoria a little lower in the league table. Nevertheless, all rooms are equipped with mini-bars and modern bathrooms, and are newly furnished. Amenities include some very pleasant restaurants, a café, and a spacious lobby, overlooking Piłsudski Square – one of the largest squares in Warsaw, named after Marshal Piłsudski *(see p30)*, and bordered by the National Theatre (Teatr Wielki Narodowy) and Saxon Gardens (Ogród Saski).

Further Afield

Agra

Falęcka 9/11. **Map** 6 D5. *849 38 81.* ***Rooms:*** *40.* *AE, DC, MC, V.* $

Inexpensive rates are the main advantage of this hotel, formerly a student hall of residence belonging to the Agricultural Academy (Szkoła Główna Gospodarstwa Wiejskiego). In line with student hostels, bathrooms are shared by two rooms. There is also a cellar bar.

Felix

Omulewska 24. *810 97 72, 810 06 91.* FAX *813 02 55.* ***Rooms:*** *234.* *AE, MC, V.* $$

The Felix plays host to many tour groups from different countries, especially from former Soviet states. Converted from what was once a workers' hostel, modest rooms are reflected in equally modest prices.

Gromada

17 Stycznia 32. *567 46 00.* FAX *846 15 80.* ***Rooms:*** *127.* *AE, DC, MC.* $$$ *airport@gromada.pl*

This is a new hotel belonging to the Gromada Company, which also owns the Gromada Centrum *(see p201)*. Being situated near Okęcie Airport, the hotel is 30 minutes' bus ride from the city centre. The rooms are clean, and each has a private bathroom and television. Adjacent to the hotel is a less expensive motel of brick bungalows and wooden chalets.

Hotel IBiIB

Ul Trojdena 4. *623 27 44.* FAX *658 28 71.* ***Rooms:*** *44.* *AE, DC, MC, V, JCB.* $$$

This hotel has the quiet and cloistered atmosphere one might expect from an establishment which tends to be popular with visiting academics. Its beautiful location and renowned standards of service often result in a full house, so be sure to book well in advance.

Zajazd Napoleoński

Płowiecka 83. *815 30 68.* FAX *815 22 16.* ***Rooms:*** *24.* *AE, DC, MC, V.* $$$ *www.napoleon.waw.pl*

Although Napoleon never actually resided here, he must at least have passed by the area with his Great Army of marching troops when beginning his doomed campaign to seize Moscow. The Napoleonic legacy is reflected in the hotel's interiors, which are modelled on a Polish manor house, and are Neo-Classical in style.

Vera

Bitwy Warszawskiej 1920 roku 16. *822 74 21.* FAX *823 62 56.* ***Rooms:*** *161.* *AE, DC, MC, V, JCB.* $$$$ *vera@orbis.pl*

Built in 1980, the hotel's architectural style, standards and prices are similar to those of the Novotel and Solec. Located by Warsaw's Western Railway Station (Dworzec Zachodni), the hotel is a 15-minute bus ride from the centre of Warsaw.

Novotel

1 Sierpnia 1. *846 40 51.* FAX *846 36 86.* ***Rooms:*** *278.* *in summer.* *AE, DC, MC, V.* $$$$$ *nov.airport@orbis.pl*

Situated in a tree-lined avenue leading to Okęcie Airport, this is one of several chain hotels built in Poland during the 1970s. The hotel's size and design are similar to those of the Vera and Solec hotels. The garden features a truly fine swimming pool.

Beyond Warsaw

Eden

Janki, Mszczonowska 43. *720 43 20.* ***Rooms:*** *52.* *AE, DC, MC, V.* $$

The Eden is a small hotel with a pleasant, homely atmosphere and a popular restaurant. It is situated on the main road to Katowice, near a large shopping centre in Janki.

Konstancja

Konstancin Jeziorna, Źródlana 6/8. *756 43 25, 756 46 74.* FAX *756 43 67.* ***Rooms:*** *44.* *AE, DC, MC, V.* $$$

Located about 20 km (12 miles) from Warsaw, the Konstancja is within the spa town of Konstancin-Jeziorna. It is surrounded by a park, featuring twin saline water towers, creating a unique microclimate. Barbecues and horse riding are available.

For key to symbols *see p197*

RESTAURANTS, CAFÉS AND BARS

THE RESTAURANT SCENE has flourished in Warsaw ever since the return of private ownership, following the 1989 democratic elections. While the quality and quantity of the city's restaurants continues to increase, Warsaw already has a surprisingly international choice of cuisines. This ranges from French, Italian, Spanish, British and Greek, to Japanese, Chinese, Vietnamese and Mexican; not to mention vegetarian. Naturally, there are many restaurants serving traditional Polish food, while Modern Polish cuisine, featuring imaginative updates of traditional dishes, is also emerging in the city. Although prices are generally on the increase, eating out in Warsaw still represents excellent value for Western tourists, with the city also providing a good choice of inexpensive venues. Meanwhile, cafés and bars are booming, with an ever wider selection of venues on offer. These pages provide guidelines on deciding where to eat and drink, with individual listings on pages 214–19.

Vegetarian platter

The Chopin Restaurant in Jan III Sobieski Hotel *(see p219)*

RESTAURANTS

WHILE an international range of cuisine, spanning Mediterranean, Asian and South American, can easily be enjoyed in Warsaw, hotel restaurants tend to serve traditional Polish food. This ranges from the hearty and rustic, to the more sophisticated. Modern Polish (classics updated with a range of international techniques and ingredients) is the forté of more expensive restaurants, such as Fukier, the Malinowa in the Bristol Hotel, and the Chopin restaurant in the Jan III Sobieski Hotel.

Various restaurants also provide highly atmospheric interiors. In the Old Town for instance, Bazyliszek resembles an 18th-century hunting lodge, while Swiętoszek is housed in an intimate, brick-vaulted cellar.

The city's restaurants usually stay open from 11am or noon until 11pm, and often later. Booking in advance is recommended.

CAFÉS, BARS AND PUBS

WARSAW has a great choice of cafés and patisseries, serving tempting cakes accompanied by speciality coffees, hot chocolate or lemon tea.

Particular favourites include the Krokodyl café in the Old Town Market Square, Café Blikle, Wedel's café, the Hotel Europejski's patisserie, and Café Bristol, which has beautiful Secession-style interiors. In the summer, café tables spill out onto numerous squares and pavements throughout the city.

Bars and pubs are ideal for sampling vodka, especially as Poland produces the world's largest range of clear and flavoured vodkas, including lemon, pepper, honey and cherry styles. English and Irish-style pubs are also established in the city, offering an impressive range of beers.

Alfresco terrace of a café in the New Town

Fast Food and Snacks

The city centre has an abundance of self-service cafeterias as well as fast-food outlets. These span the usual range of McDonald's, Burger King and Pizza Hut, as well as inexpensive Chinese, Vietnamese and Polish food. Many delicatessens and grocery stores also sell sandwiches and rolls. During the summer, ice-cream vans operate throughout the city.

The Ugarit Restaurant, which specializes in Arabic food ***(see pp216–17)***

Vegetarian Food

A few restaurants specialize in vegetarian food, while salad bars are also emerging. Additionally, many eateries offer meatless dishes. Some classic Polish dishes, like *pierogi* (ravioli) and *mizeria* (cucumber and soured cream salad) are ideal vegetarian choices. Asian and Italian restaurants also offer a wide selection of vegetable-based main dishes and side plates.

Montmartre Restaurant in Nowy Świat Street ***(see p218)***

Prices and Tips

Prices can vary enormously in the city's restaurants. The least expensive three-course meal (without drinks) usually costs around 25 złotys ($6) per person. However, in a luxurious restaurant the bill can easily reach ten times as much. Another consideration is that prices do not always include VAT, which may be stated separately on the menu. If a dish is not priced, then the cost should be established before you order (though this may also mean that the dish is temporarily unavailable). Many restaurants offer fixed-price menus or buffets, which are often good value.

As imported wines and spirits can be very expensive (and they are always more than Polish drinks), it is worth checking the price before you order. Even soft drinks can drastically increase the bill.

Credit cards are usually accepted in more expensive restaurants, but they can rarely be used in bars, pubs, cafés and the cheaper eateries. It is customary in Warsaw to leave a ten per cent tip.

Candlelight adds charm to some of Warsaw's best restaurants

Using the Listings

Key to symbols in the listings on pages 214–19.

- V vegetarian dishes
- live music
- outdoor eating
- good wine list
- ★ highly recommended
- credit cards accepted
- $ under $7
- $$ $7–$14
- $$$ $14–$25
- $$$$ over $25

Warsaw's Best: Restaurants and Cafés

THE CITY'S comprehensive range of restaurants and cafés spans traditional and modern Polish food and drink, as well as the pick of the world's most interesting cuisines. Numerous restaurants and cafés in central Warsaw also provide historic and beautiful settings, such as a vaulted cellar, a burgher's house or even Secessionist splendour and elegance.

Pożegnanie z Afryką
"Out of Africa" is a café serving some of the city's finest coffee (see p214).

Café Bristol
As well as excellent coffee and cakes, this café offers light lunches. The Secessionist interiors create a delightful Viennese atmosphere (see p215).

The Former Jewish Ghetto

Café Blikle
Having been carefully restored, this historic café is one of the city's most fashionable meeting places, offering a range of renowned cakes and pastries (see p214).

Casa Valdemar
A magnificent clay oven, used to prepare Castilian roasts, is a feature of this celebrated Spanish restaurant (see p218).

0 kilometres 1
0 miles 0.5

Fuks
Among Warsaw's growing number of vegetarian restaurants, this is one of the most popular (see p219).

Fukier
An exquisite burgher's house in the Old Town Market Square provides an idyllic setting for Modern Polish dishes, served in a traditional atmosphere (see p214).

Malinowa
This elegant Secessionist dining room has received many distinguished guests, and is now highly regarded for its modern interpretations of classic Polish cuisine (see p215).

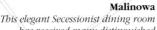

Tsubame
Having provided the city with its first sushi bar, Tsubame is also one of the finest Oriental restaurants, serving elegant Japanese dishes (see p215).

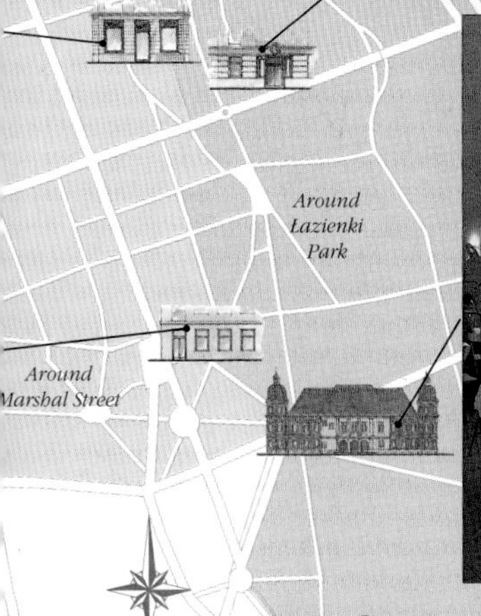

Qchnia Artystyczna
This postmodernist restaurant within the Modern Art Centre, where concerts as well as exhibitions are held, offers delightfully eccentric interiors and an interesting menu (see p217).

Belvedere
With its sublime location, an historic orangerie in the Łazienki Park, this restaurant offers superb Modern Polish and French cuisine (see p218).

What to Eat in Warsaw

Rye bread

Polish cuisine, which has Slav origins, was also influenced by neighbouring countries such as Russia, Lithuania, Belarus, Ukraine and Germany. Similarly, the Jewish population added various dishes, while French and Italian princesses who married Polish kings introduced their own native specialities. Under Communism, when shortages were a fact of daily life, Polish cuisine regressed. However, Warsaw's finest chefs are now reviving and updating traditional dishes. Meals often begin with soup, followed by a meat dish (beef, pork, poultry or game), served with potatoes, buckwheat *(kasza)* or dumplings, and vegetables such as wild mushrooms, beetroot and cabbage. Typical desserts include stewed fruit and cheesecake.

Pickled cucumbers

Wild mushrooms

Mushrooms in cream

Side Dishes

Served as side dishes or on their own as snacks (typically with a glass of vodka) are marinated cultivated or wild mushrooms, and pickled cucumbers with dill.

Hors d'Oeuvres

Among the most popular *hors d'oeuvres* are carp Jewish-style, herring in soured cream, and smoked eel.

Potato pancakes
These are pancakes made from grated raw potatoes, served hot with cream and salt or sugar, or with a sauce.

Hare pâté – a traditional Polish speciality

Herrings
A very popular hors d'oeuvre is herring served with a cream and apple and onion sauce.

Bean and herring salad

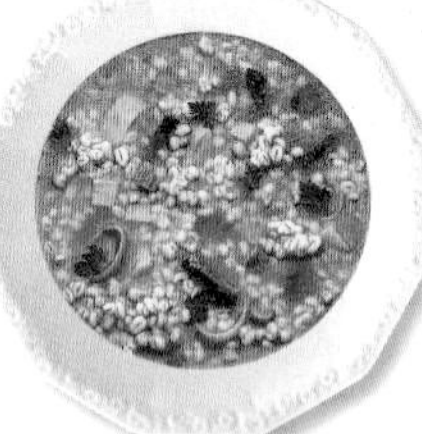
Krupnik
This soup is prepared from pearl barley and potatoes in a meat or vegetable stock.

Tripe Warsaw-style
Tripe, often served with meatballs, is a local speciality frequently featured on menus.

Borsch
This soup is made from beetroot and served hot. Lithuanian borsch is a cold variation.

Żurek
Made using white sausage, this is an unusual but tasty fermented "sour" soup.

Mushroom soup
"Whitened" by adding milk, this soup comes with dumplings or choux pastry peas.

Stuffed Cabbage Leaves
Stuffed with buckwheat or rice, and with the addition of meat or mushrooms, the cabbage leaves are baked in a tomato or mushroom sauce.

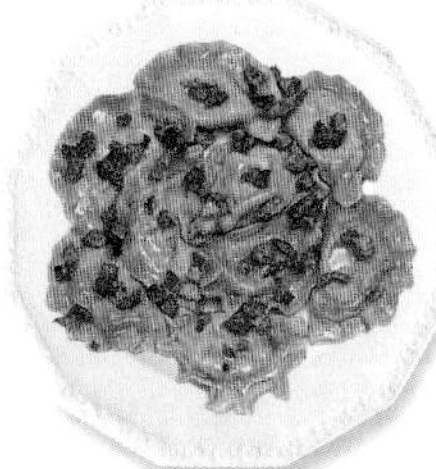

Pierogi
Usually prepared with a meat stuffing, or with sauerkraut and mushrooms, pierogi *may also be served with cheese.*

Bigos (Hunter's Stew)
This classic Polish dish includes sauerkraut, as well as fresh cabbage, cooked slowly with Polish sausages.

Breaded pork chops
These hearty chops are typically eaten with mashed potatoes and cabbage.

Beef Olives
Rolled pieces of beef are filled with a stuffing of sauerkraut and mushroom, meat, or streaky bacon and pickled cucumber.

Duck baked with apple
Game is popular in Poland, and this is one of the most typical duck dishes. It is usually served with roast potatoes.

Roast pork with prunes
Pork loin is a popular cut and a great favourite when stuffed with prunes to make this classic "Old Polish" dish.

Perch Polish-style
This is poached and garnished with melted butter, lemon wedges and chopped hard-boiled egg.

DESSERTS

Among the most popular desserts are cakes and pastries, including doughnuts filled with rose petal jam; poppyseed cake (especially at Easter and Christmas); and ginger cake made to a traditional medieval recipe.

Ice cream
Served with fruit, whipped cream or wafers, ice cream is always on the menu and comes in a wide variety of flavours.

What to Drink in Warsaw

Logo of Polish vodka distilleries

POLISH VODKA is internationally renowned for its excellent quality. The vast range available includes clear vodkas, generally distilled from rye, with flavoured styles ranging from dry to sweet, and from fruity to herbal and spicy. Imported drinks, such as Cognac, Scotch whisky, gin and wine, carry much higher duties than Polish drinks, so prices can be astronomical. Beer is also enjoying a boom in popularity, with English and Irish-style pubs opening throughout Warsaw. Meanwhile, the range and quality of Polish beer have improved dramatically over the past few years, and are now on a par with imported brands. Among soft drinks, Poland excels in fruit juices such as blackcurrant, raspberry and cherry, while several mineral water brands are sourced from Polish spa towns.

Żywiec, one of Poland's most historic and popular beer brands

POLISH VODKA

VODKA HAS long been established as Poland's national drink, and there are hundreds of brands of vodka on the market. Unlike neutral tasting "international" vodka, Polish vodka has a distinct character. It should be served chilled, and sipped to appreciate the depth of flavours.

Vodkas are divided into clear and flavoured varieties. Among clear vodkas, the most famous is Wyborowa. It has a rye flavour and subtle sweetness, which is derived entirely from the distillation process, and not from the use of additives. Kosher vodkas are also produced, in accordance with kosher regulations. Deluxe vodka brands have emerged over the past few years, including Chopin, which features a portrait of the composer on the label. Belvedere is another such brand, and is named after the palace in Warsaw.

Label on Żubrówka bottle

Flavoured vodkas are infusions of fruit, herbs and various other ingredients. One of the most original is Żubrówka, flavoured with a herb called bison grass. This grass, which grows only in the Białowieża National Park in Eastern Poland, is a favourite foodstuff of the European bison, which are still to be found roaming there.

Another unique Polish vodka is Goldwasser, which includes flakes of gold leaf, in accordance with the original 16th-century recipe. It is usually drunk as a *digestif*, after a meal.

Vodka is rarely served without food. Before a meal, it will be accompanied by a range of hors d'oeuvres (referred to as *zakąski*), such as salt herring fillets, pickled mushrooms, dill cucumbers, Polish sausage and rye bread. These salty, spicy flavours balance the vodka, while encouraging the next round.

Clear vodkas

Premium Vodka, distilled in Poznań

Wyborowa, the most famous export brand

Flavoured vodkas

Żubrówka, flavoured with bison grass

Goldwasser, which includes gold leaf

BEER

Brok

Żywiec

EB

Okocim

BREWERIES were among the first businesses to take advantage of Poland's transformation into a free-market economy in 1989. The result has been a dramatic improvement in the quality of Polish beers, which are predominantly lagers. The choice of brands has also become much broader, with the establishment of various regional and "boutique" breweries.

Among the most popular beer brands are Żywiec, Brok, Heweliusz, EB, and Okocim.

Okocim label

Żywiec label

The bar of a typical Warsaw pub

Polish beer now competes successfully in terms of quality with imported beers, including Irish, German, Dutch, Danish and Czech brands, which are readily available.

The recent emergence of themed pubs, as well as various new bars, has also helped to boost beer's popularity *(see pp214–19)*.

MEAD

ONE OF POLAND'S most historic drinks, mead is still prepared according to traditional recipes. Mead is created from fermented honey, diluted with water, and flavoured with spices and hops, though precise recipes are usually shrouded in secrecy.

The strength of mead usually ranges from 9–18 per cent alcohol by volume, with the strength and character of the mead determined by the ratio of honey to water. Different ratios have their own official terminology. *Półtorak* (meaning "two-thirds") indicates a ratio of two parts honey to one part water. This style of mead, the strongest and the sweetest, is also widely considered to be the finest quality. *Dwójniak* means equal parts honey and water, *trójniak* is one part honey to two parts water, while *czwórniak* refers to one part honey to three parts water.

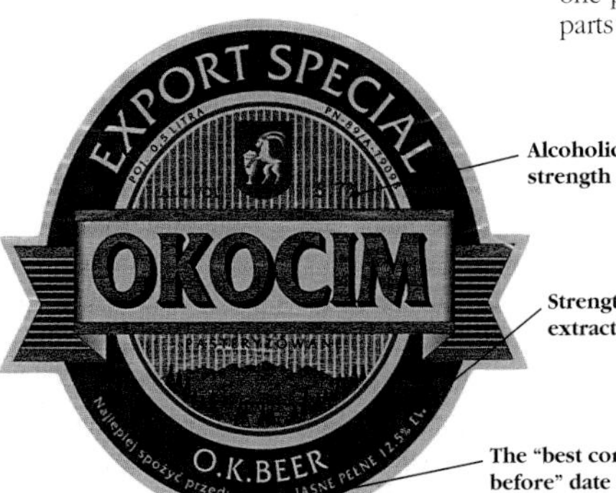

Deciphering an Okocim beer label

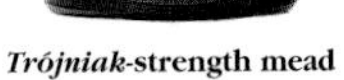
Trójniak-strength mead

Choosing a Restaurant

THE RESTAURANTS AND CAFES in this guide have been chosen primarily for their fine food, although some may get a mention for great value or their ambience. This chart highlights some factors which may influence your decision when choosing a restaurant, while full reviews appear on pages 214–19. Establishments are listed by area of the city, and alphabetically within each price category.

		Attractive Location	Tables Outside	Polish Specialities	Late Opening	Vegetarian Specialities
Old Town *(see p214)*						
Maharaja-Thai	$$$	●	■		■	●
Rycerska	$$$	●	■	●	■	
Dom Restauracyjny Gessler	$$$$	●		●	■	●
Fukier ★	$$$$	●	■	●	■	●
Tsarina	$$$$	●			■	●
New Town *(see p214)*						
Pożegnanie z Afryką ★	$	●				
Pod Samsonem	$$	●	■	●	■	
Nove Miasto	$$$	●	■	●		●
Around Solidarity Avenue *(see p214)*						
Prohibicja	$$	●	■		■	●
Pekin	$$$					●
Barbados	$$$$	●	■	●	■	●
Der Elefant	$$$$	●	■		■	●
El Popo	$$$$	●			■	●
La Bohème	$$$$	●	■	●	■	●
The Royal Route *(see pp214–15)*						
Europejska	$$	●	■			
Pod Baryłką	$$		■		■	
Café Blikle ★	$$$	●	■	●		●
Chianti	$$$	●			■	
Harenda	$$$	●	■		■	
Literacka	$$$	●	■			●
Café Bristol ★	$$$$	●				●
Malinowa ★	$$$$	●		●		●
Nowy Świat–Café	$$$$	●	■	●		
Tsubame ★	$$$$				■	●
Around Marshal Street *(see pp216–17)*						
Batida	$					●
Krokiecik	$					●
Café Brama	$$				■	
Capriccio	$$$	●	■	●	■	
Dong Nam	$$$					●
Ha Long	$$$	●			■	●
Mekong	$$$				■	●
Sportowy Champions Bar	$$$	●		●	■	
Ugarit	$$$		■	●	■	●
Chicago Grill	$$$$				■	
Lila Weneda	$$$$			●	■	●
Parmiggiano	$$$$					●

Price categories refer to a three-course meal for one, half a bottle of house wine and all unavoidable extra charges such as service tax (in US dollars).

$ under $7
$$ $7–14
$$$ $14–25
$$$$ over $25

★ Means highly recommended

Attractive Location
Restaurants in unusual or historic settings, or with an outstanding view

Tables Outside
Food is served outdoors in fine weather.

Polish Specialities
Restaurants that have a good selection of traditional dishes.

Late Opening
Last orders accepted at or after 11:30pm.

Vegetarian Specialities
Restaurants that have a good selection of vegetarian dishes.

	Price	Attractive Location	Tables Outside	Polish Specialities	Late Opening	Vegetarian Specialities
U Szwejka	$$$$	●	●	●	●	●
The Former Jewish Ghetto *(see p217)*						
99	$$$$		●			●
Caryca Katarzyna	$$$$		●		●	●
Le Balzac	$$$$					
Restauracja Warszawa Jerozolima	$$$$			●	●	
Around Łazienki Park *(see pp217–18)*						
Czytelnik	$	●		●		
Da Elio	$$		●	●		●
Klub Aktora	$$$	●		●	●	
Belvedere ★	$$$$	●	●	●	●	●
Casa Valdemar ★	$$$$	●	●		●	●
London Steak House	$$$$	●	●		●	
Montmartre	$$$$		●		●	
Qchnia Artystyczna ★	$$$$	●	●	●	●	●
Studio Buffo	$$$$		●	●		●
Other Districts *(see pp218–19)*						
B-40	$	●	●		●	
Zielona Gęś	$		●		●	
Boston Port	$$		●			
Rong Vang	$$					●
Amigos	$$$		●		●	
Le Cedre	$$$		●			●
Mibella	$$$		●	●	●	●
Positano	$$$		●			●
Chopin	$$$$		●	●		●
Flik	$$$$	●	●	●		●
Santorini	$$$$		●			●
Shogun	$$$$					●
Zajazd Napoleoński	$$$$		●	●	●	
Further Afield *(see p219)*						
Pod Złotym Linem	$$$	●	●	●		
Trattoria	$$$$		●		●	●

The photographs and descriptions on pages 208–9 illustrate some of Poland's most popular dishes.

Old Town

Maharaja-Thai

Szeroki Dunaj 13. **Map** 1 C1 & 3 C4. *635 25 01. noon–midnight daily.* V AE, DC, MC, V. $$$

This was the first Thai restaurant in Poland. It has an interesting interior, and somewhat passive service, but the food is very good indeed. The chef has, out of necessity, substituted the usual Thai coconut milk with cow's milk and the speciality straw mushrooms with oyster mushrooms but, thanks to a skillful and inventive use of ginger, garlic, lemon, peppers, herbs and various types of curry, the resulting dishes have a truly Thai flavour. The best among them are lemon-flavoured chicken soup, green curry chicken, fried fish, Thai minced pork omelette and stuffed chicken wings.

Rycerska

Szeroki Dunaj 9/11. **Map** 1 C1 & 3 C4. *831 36 68. noon–11pm daily.* V AE, MC, V. $$$

While the restaurant and the menu have remained in the style of the early 1970s, the cuisine represents a decent standard, and the atmosphere is very pleasant. Rycerska serves an interesting, old-fashioned Polish white borsch, known as *żurek*, as well as tasty herrings, rustic dishes of suckling pig roasted in beer and turkey in mulled-wine sauce. Among the fish dishes, look out for the appetizing boiled carp in lemon sauce.

Dom Restauracyjny Gessler

Rynek Starego Miasta 21. **Map** 4 D4 & 6 D1. *11am–until the last guest leaves daily.* V AE, DC, MC, V. $$$$

The food is not the best in Warsaw, but the interior never fails to impress, particularly the cellar, built in the style of an 18the-century country inn, supposedly brought over from a small village called Wojtkowice Stare. It is full of arts and crafts, and the effect is enchanting. Many traditional Polish dishes are served.

Fukier

Rynek Starego Miasta 27. **Map** 4 D4 & 6 D1. *831 10 13, 831 58 08. noon–until the last guest leaves daily.* V AE, DC, MC, V. $$$$ ★

Here you will find excellent cuisine served in some of Warsaw's most beautiful surroundings. The oak floors, tables, together with the aroma of herbs, candles and flowers, create a wonderful atmosphere. Fukier serves mainly Polish cuisine at its most creative, enriched with French and other European influences. The menu includes such dishes as pig's trotters in aspic, carpaccio of ceps, *żurek* (fermented soup) with ceps and white sausage, calf's liver with balsamic vinegar, asparagus, carp baked in cream with ceps and haunch of venison. Among the desserts are wonderful poppy-seed cake, lemon sorbet with vodka and delightfully fluffy cheesecake.

Tsarina

Jezuicka 1/3. **Map** 4 D4 & 6 D1. *635 74 74. noon–midnight daily.* V AE, DC, MC, V. $$$$

The restaurant has succeeded in bringing the world of Russian fables to life. Five large private dining rooms and five small rooms make up the restaurant, to which you summon waiters using an ebony telephone. The discreet staff are dressed in Tsarist military uniform. The Russian menu includes caviar, pelmeni and fine soups, delicately seasoned. *Condé Nast Traveler* rates this as one of the world's top 50 restaurants.

New Town

Pożegnanie z Afryką

Freta 4/6. **Map** 1 C1 & 3 C4. *11am–8pm daily.* $ ★

The most delectable aromas in town emanate from this tiny café. It is connected with a shop, and both offer a huge selection of excellent coffees. Only coffee is sold here, unless you count wafer cakes, but there is neither space nor need for anything else. The quality of coffee served outclasses anything else you may get in town; a visit here is an adventure in itself.

Pod Samsonem

Freta 3/5. **Map** 1 C1 & 3 C4. *831 17 88. 10am–11pm daily.* V AE, DC, MC, V. $$

Recommended for anyone on a budget, this is a favourite meeting place for cost-conscious, though outstanding representatives of Warsaw intelligentsia. The restaurant offers unpretentious service, clean surroundings, and a combination of Polish and Jewish cuisine. Their specialities include minced liver, also known as "Jewish caviar", stuffed carp and escalopes. For dessert, the cardinal peaches come highly recommended.

Nove Miasto

Rynek Nowego Miasta 13/15. **Map** 1 C1 & 3 C4. *831 43 79. 10am–midnight daily.* V $$$$

Set on the New Town Market Square, this mostly vegetarian restaurant is decorated in bright colours and comfortably furnished. The extensive menu features a range of unusual salads, vegetarian *pierogi* and, for fish eaters, pasta with tuna and crab. All the dishes are subtly flavoured with herbs and spices, and are presented with flair. Enjoy the live music indoors, or dine outside when the weather is fine.

Around Solidarity Avenue

Prohibicja

Podwale1/3. **Map** 2 D2, 4 D4. *635 62 11. noon–midnight daily.* V AE, DC, MC, V. $$

This small restaurant with a café and bar is popular for its tasty, unpretentious food, as well as the chance of bumping into one of the establishment's owners. Wojciech Malajkat, Bogustaw Lind, Mark Kondrat and Zbigniew Zamachowski are all Polish film stars who have cooperated on this new venture.

Pekin

Senatorska 27. **Map** 1 C2 & 4 D5. *827 48 04. noon–11pm daily.* V AE, MC, V. $$$

Pekin offers some of the best Far Eastern dishes in town. Although inexpensive, the service can be poor. Chinese music is piped into the restaurant and an excellent choice of fish is offered, along with several types of prawns, tasty duck and a variety of vegetarian dishes. For dessert, the banana fritters are unrivalled. The range of beer and spirits is reasonably priced.

Barbados

Wierzbowa 9. **Map** 1 C3 & 3 C5. *827 71 61. 1pm–midnight Mon–Thu, 1pm–1am Fri, 5pm–1am Sat, 3pm–midnight Sun.* V AE, DC, MC, V. $$$$

A wide choice of starters in this large restaurant offers several prawn dishes. Lovers of Polish cuisine can try borsch with dumplings or wild-mushroom soup. Recommended main dishes include sliced duck with pear and potatoes in a wine and juniper sauce, or veal cutlets in garlic. Several main fish courses include trout stuffed with fresh herbs in a herb and butter sauce. After dinner, DJs spin the decks in the main area and open mezzanine on Thursday through to Sataurday.

Der Elefant

Plac Bankowy 1. **Map** 1 B3 & 3 C5. *624 79 05. 10:30am–1:30am daily. AE, DC, MC, V.* $$$$

The Elefant offers some of the best pub food in town, as well as a terrific atmosphere, and Irish and German beers. Grilled meat, such as steaks, kebabs, large spicy hamburgers *(pleskawica)* and sausage, are all served with chips. There are also tasty hot mussels served with cold sauces and deep-fried Camembert with cranberries.

El Popo

Senatorska 27. **Map** 1 C2 & 4 D5. *827 23 40. noon–until the last guest leaves daily.* $$$$

One of two Mexican restaurants in Warsaw, El Popo features live Mexican music in a colourful Aztec setting, complemented by a warm and cosy atmosphere. It serves Mexican favourites from the tradi-tional fajitas and tortillas in many different combinations to specialties such as sizzling prawns in garlic or the unusual turkey in chocolate.

La Bohème

Pl Teatralny 1. **Map** 1 C2 & 3 C5. *692 06 81. 11am–until the last guest leaves daily. AE, DC, MC, V.* $$$$

A dual venue with a café and restaurant, handily located next to the National Theatre. The European menu focuses mainly on French and Italian food. Lobster is a speciality, served in several different ways. Game is also recommended. Opposite the square is the restaurant shop, where takeaway versions of the day's dishes are for sale.

THE ROYAL ROUTE

Europejska

Europejski Hotel, Krakowskie Przedmieście 13. **Map** 2 D3 & 4 D5. *826 50 51. 11am–10pm (midnight in summer) daily. AE, DC, MC, V.* $$

This large café-restaurant, also known as Przy Ossoliúskich offers an engaging atmosphere. Once a favourite meeting place in Warsaw, it has retained many loyal patrons, particularly for breakfast.

Pod Baryłką

Garbarska 5/7. **Map** 2 D2 & 4 D5. *826 62 39. noon–midnight daily.* $$

This is one of Warsaw's nicest pubs. It has a pleasant, cosy interior, with a quiet atmosphere. The food includes grilled ham and cheese sandwiches and pretzels to nibble with a choice of 11 draught beers.

Café Blikle

Nowy Świat 33. **Map** 2 D5 & 6 D1. *826 66 19. 8am–11pm Mon–Fri, 9am–11pm Sat, 10am–11pm Sun. DC, MC, V.* $$$ ★

Café Blikle is a fashionable meeting place that is helping to resurrect Warsaw's café society. Here you will find a buzzing, lively café, with many well-known Poles. The frozen yogurt and sorbets are excellent, and its famous "hollow-cheek" doughnuts are truly delicious. The café offers tempting breakfasts and good teas, with such enticements as herring dumplings, patés with minced apricots, nuts and prunes, and vegetarian rolls.

Chianti

Forsal 17. **Map** 2 E5 & 6 D1. *828 02 22. noon–11pm daily.* $$$

An ideal choice for a romantic dinner. Stone walls and colourful plasterwork, the aroma of basil and rosemary, as well as good piped music, creates the atmosphere of an Italian town. With a large choice of mainly pasta dishes, it is worth trying the aubergine baked with mozzarella and parmesan, or penne with salmon in a white sauce. Tiramisu is recommended for dessert.

Harenda

Krakowskie Przedmieście 4/6. **Map** 2 D3 & 4 D5. *8am–3pm daily. 826 29 00.* $$$

Large, fashionable and always buzzing, this is the favourite spot for Warsaw's liberals, foreigners and better-off students. You can have a three-course meal here, but the menu is not ambitious – the main attraction of the evening is baked potatoes. The range of beers includes Guinness, Heineken and Żywiec.

Literacka

Krakowskie Przedmieście 87/89. **Map** 1 D2. *828 89 95. 10am–until the last guest leaves daily.* $$$

Situated in the legendary Dom Literata (Writer's House), the Liter-acka has an atmospheric café on the ground floor, but the restaurant in the cellar is not recommended. The desserts, such as apple fritters and vanilla custard, are delicious.

Café Bristol

Hotel Bristol, Krakowskie Przedmieście 42/44. **Map** 2 D3 & 4 D5. *625 25 25. 8am–11pm daily. AE, DC, MC, V* $$$$ ★

This is an exclusive, Viennese-style café, and an excellent place for breakfast, lunch or an elegant snack at any time of the day. The interior is beautiful and stylish, complemented by professional, charming staff. Apart from delicious sweets (mousses, cream cakes, eclairs, ice creams), there are also excellent hot and cold snacks, salads, patés, club sand-wiches, pancakes and lasagne. Coffee and other drinks are expen-sive, but light dishes and sweets will not ruin an average budget.

Malinowa

Hotel Bristol, Krakowskie Przed-mieście 42/44. **Map** 2 D3 & 4 D5. *625 25 25. 6pm–until the last guest leaves daily. AE, DC, MC, V.* $$$$ ★

Malinowa is renowned as the most exclusive restaurant in Warsaw. It employs world-class chefs, includ-ing Mrs Małgorzata Marchewka, whose speciality of suckling pig with bison grass won a Silver Medal at the 1st European Cup Competition for Regional Cuisine, held in 1995 at Poitiers. The restaurant's interior, which evokes the 1920s and 1930s, is luxurious and stylish. Prices, as you might expect, are very high, but the food is not only excellent but also beautifully presented. There are very exciting interpretations of classic dishes and innovative use of speciality ingredients, evident in some superb desserts.

Nowy Świat Café

Nowy Świat 63. **Map** 1 D5 & 6 D1. *826 58 03. 9am–10pm (11pm in summer) daily.* $$$$

For many years this was one of Warsaw's favourite restaurants. It is large, always full, and offers a rich selection of sweets and Austrian-style dishes. As well as

For key to symbols *see p205*

being a great place to eat, it also has the latest newspapers. The expensive but tasty menu here is full of Austrian flavour. Velvety garlic soup, served within a large crusty roll features as a starter, as well as chicken soup with spinach roulade. For main courses, pork dishes with fine cabbage, or Viennese Goulash with bread and onion dumplings are popular. Finish off with a traditional apple strudel with vanilla ice-cream and whipped cream. The coffee is excellent.

Tsubame

Foksal 16. **Map** 3 E5 & 6 D1. *826 51 27.* *noon–midnight daily.* $$$$ ★

This authentic Japanese restaurant offers a full range of fascinating cuisine, and includes the first sushi-bar in Poland, where you can taste specialities such as raw seafood served on a bed of rice, wrapped in a black ribbon of *nori* seaweed. Prices are high, but it offers an unforgettable experience for the gourmet. Excellent sushi provides a wide range of choice, with omelette, mackerel, tuna, salmon, yellowtail, red salmon roe, prawns, three types of mussels, octopus and squid. Other dishes include *maki* – attractive rolls made of rice and various ingredients, such as cucumber, pickled plums, pickled fibres of the campyo gourd or strips of avocado. They can be accompanied by a garnish of pickled ginger and washed down with hot sake. The tea is also very good.

Around Marshal Street

Batida

Nowogrodzka 1/3. **Map** 5 B2. *621 45 34.* *8am–4pm Mon– Fri, 8am–4pm Sat.* $

Batida is a snack-bar attached to a shop, and is modelled on a typical Parisian *croissanterie*, with the best French bakery in Warsaw. The hot dishes are quite good on the whole, but a major attraction is provided by the good coffee and cakes. At Batida, you will find a plethora of tarts, meringues, eclairs, buns and French croissants.

Krokiecik

Zgoda 1. **Map** 2 D5 & 6 D1. *827 30 37.* *9am–9pm Mon–Sat, 11am–7pm Sun.* $

This self-service bar, which has survived many changes of fortune, is an ideal place for a quick and inexpensive meal. The café includes Hungarian influences in its repertoire, and you are likely to find fantastic fried cabbage or mushrooms here, as well as pancakes *(krokiety)*, soups, including borsch (beetroot soup) and *bogracz* (goulash soup), plus Chinese-style chicken. And for dessert, there are tasty cold pancakes with fruit and whipped cream.

Café Brama

Marszałkowska 8. **Map** 6 D3. *625 09 10.* *2pm–until the last guest leaves daily.* $$

Located by the Variety Theatre (Teatr Rozmaitości), Café Brama has a Modern European style, with a nonchalant, bohemian setting. The menu is limited but excellent, with tasty dishes from the grill and a range of alcoholic beverages. Minimalist interiors give a tasteful backdrop, and the live progressive jazz in the evening enhances the dining experience.

Capriccio

Koszykowa 54. **Map** 5 B2. *630 88 51.* *noon–until last guest leaves daily.* *AE, DC, MC, V.* $$$

This new venture, which opened in 2002, is good example of a typical Italian restaurant and has a good central location. It also features some traditional Polish dishes. Diners can choose from specialities that include sole in saffron sauce, and wild duck breast in caramel sauce. There is also a good selection of Italian and other wines. The cosy atmosphere is augmented by live music three nights a week. Service is courteous without being overbearing, and the restaurant is willing to stay open until late.

Dong Nam

Marszałkowska 45/49. **Map** 6 D2. *621 32 34.* *noon–11pm daily.* $$$

The best Thai and Vietnamese cuisine in Poland are served at Dong Nam, which also provides the appropriate atmospheric interiors. Four containers on each table are filled with soy sauce, a bitter-sweet fruit sauce, sharp fruit sauce and a dark mixture of chillies which should be used sparingly. The green curry pork is excellent, while other good dishes include fish coated in red curry sauce with coconut milk, a black soup with seafood, and Hormok-style seafood served in the form of small soufflés with a frothy white sauce and coconut milk. The *pad thai* is also good, while an inferno on the palate is guaranteed by chicken *gai pad phet*, or a *tom yum* soup with chicken and lemon grass. Dong Nam's wine list, although not extensive, is reasonably priced.

Ha Long

Emilii Plater 36. **Map** 1 B5 & 5 C2. *620 15 23.* *11am–10pm.* *AE, DC, MC, V.* $$$

Two small, air-conditioned rooms with fitted carpets, an aquarium and several attractive graphics on the walls successfully create the atmosphere of a small, Far Eastern restaurant. The Chinese and Vietnamese cuisine includes duck prepared in a variety of ways, such as with sizzling king prawns or Sichuan-style, as well as the true Peking duck. The latter is not just a single dish but a full menu; it constitutes a magnificent Chinese feast which must be ordered 24 hours in advance. Soup delicacies include crab, prawns and eel, while best of all are the "sour pike" soups.

Mekong

Wspólna 35. **Map** 5 C2. *621 18 81.* *noon–11pm daily.* *AE, DC, MC, V.* $$$

Mekong offers Chinese cuisine in the most beautifully furnished oriental restaurant in Warsaw. The food smells exceptional, building up expectations, while soy sauce stands ready on each table. However, attempts to serve more ambitious cuisine are not always successful and often are underwhelming. Wines and spirits are pricy, but the green tea is a delight and far less expensive.

Sportowy Champions Bar

Marriott Hotel, Aleje Jerozolimskie 65/79. **Map** 2 E5 & 5 C1. *630 51 19 & 630 74 19.* *11am–midnight daily.* *AE, DC, MC, V.* $$$

This smart bar is expensive, but offers quality food in a comfortable setting. Sportowy serves the quintessential American meal, which includes the best hamburgers in Warsaw (Marriottburgers). The restaurant's menu includes sophisticated hamburgers and hot dogs, hot and cold sandwiches, as well as a selection of Austrian desserts. There is a good range of draught beer, including EB and Beck's.

Ugarit

MDM Hotel, Plac Konstytucji 1. **Map** 6 D2. *621 62 11 ext. 185.* *7am–midnight daily.* $$$

Ugarit offers the best Arab cuisine in Warsaw, at quite reasonable prices. Its marble interior, with columns and a high ceiling, creates the impression of a railway station. Meat dishes, cooked in a charcoal oven, include lamb and veal kebabs, shish-kebabs, chicken, ribs and giblets. Best of all are the starters: hummus, *muttabal* (smoked, puréed aubergines), vegetarian "Syrian steak", *basturma* (spiced meat sausage) and the warm *marija* (kebab in a roll).

Chicago Grill

Marriott Hotel, Aleje Jerozolimskie 65/79. **Map** 2 E5 & 5 C1. *630 51 75.* *6–10:30pm daily (Mon–Fri during Jul–Aug).* AE, DC, MC, V. $$$$

This is Warsaw's only up-market restaurant that specializes in traditional American cuisine. The Chicago Grill serves marinated steaks and barbequed ribs, with draught EB and Beck's.

Lila Weneda

Marriott Hotel, Aleje Jerozolimskie 65/79. **Map** 2 E5 & 6 C1. *630 51 76.* *6:30am–2:30pm Mon–Fri, 6:30am–10:30pm Sat, 6:30am–5pm Sun.* AE, DC, MC, V. $$$$

This smart and comfortable restaurant is suitable for lunch or early dinner, but not ideal for a romantic evening. It offers an excellent buffet lunch, which is free to children of up to eight years of age, and before 11pm there is a different "theme buffet" each night (Indian, Polish, Mexican, Oriental, seafood and American). The menu includes fantastic fried mushrooms in blue cheese sauce, Lebanese grilled chicken, leg of lamb with mint sauce and variety of very tasty potato dishes. You will also find American-style club sandwiches, rarely seen in Poland, and a selection of draught beers.

Parmiggiano

Hotel Marriott, Aleje Jerozolimskie 65/79. **Map** 2 E5 & 6 C1. *630 50 96.* *noon–10:30pm daily.* AE, DC, MC, V. $$$$

Parmiggiano is the best Italian restaurant in town, and offers a wide selection of tasty dishes, from antipasti, through pastas, risotto, fish and meat dishes, to delicious tiramisu for dessert. There is a friendly atmosphere and the service is excellent. The chef's specialities include tagliatelle in basil sauce, spaghetti carbonara, risotto with wild mushrooms, swordfish in tomato sauce, veal escalopes with sage *(saltimbocca)* and saddle of lamb with olives. But leave room for the desserts.

U Szwejka

MDM Hotel, Plac Konstytucji 1. **Map** 6 D2. *621 62 11 ext 495.* *10am–1am Mon–Fri, 10am–2am Sat–Sun.* $$$$

Noisy and full of atmosphere, here you will find the best pub food in town. Alongside a variety of beers, the chef's specials include grilled meat, such as *pleskawica* (a large, spicy minced steak with herb butter), served with excellent chips. Hot fried mussels are also a speciality, as are cold mussels, marinated and sprinkled with grated sheep's' cheese. Deep fried Camembert with cranberry sauce is another excellent choice on the menu. There are a number of draught beers, including Budweiser.

The Former Jewish Ghetto

99

Jana Pawła II 23. **Map** 1 B4 & 5 B1. *620 19 99.* *noon–11pm Fri, noon–midnight Sat.* AE, MC, DC, V. $$$$

This restaurant is located within the Atrium Commercial centre. The modern interiors are decorated with wood and metalwork features. The menu itself specializes in grilled dishes. A bread oven allows dishes to be traditionally cooked over a spit. International dishes include hot starters, such as goat's cheese tart. A good fish dish to try is the perch served with buckwheat in a mussel sauce.

Caryca Katarzyna

Chmielna, 132/4. **Map** 2 D5, 5 B2. *No phone.* *noon–11pm Mon–Fri, Sat 6pm–11pm.* $$$$

This was the first Russian restaurant in Warsaw. It offers many delicacies, from the world-renowned *bliny* (buck-wheat pancakes) with caviar, or Russian-style kulebyak, to special-ties such as smoked Russian sturgeon or imperial sturgeon baked in a caper sauce. Quick and polite waiters outfitted in the uniforms of the czar's officers serve customers while Russian ballads enhance the quiet, low-key atmosphere. Its decor includes 18the century icons and aims to provide and elegant atmosphere. Although not required, evening dress is highly recommended at this restaurant frequented by Warsaw's businessmen.

Le Balzac

Hotel Mercure, Jana Pawła II 22. **Map** 1 A2 & 3 A3. *620 02 01.* *noon–4pm, 6–10:30pm Mon–Fri (& Sat in winter).* $$$$

Le Balzac serves good quality French cuisine, while the atmosphere and guests are typical of a hotel. This is a very expensive but luxurious place, which is ideal for business lunches. The menu offers a large variety of fish and seafood, and exemplary frogs and snails. There is a tempting morel *velouté* and a fabulous confit of duck.

Restauracja Warszawa Jerozolima

Smocza 27. **Map** 3 A4. *838 32 17.* *noon–midnight daily.* MC, V. $$$$

Located in the cellars of the Business Club, this lively restaurant serves Jewish/Polish cuisine. The music is loud and features karaoke versions of Israeli, Eastern European and Polish hits. Even the waiters sing! Specialities include stuffed carp Jewish-style, goose livers served on a bed of cherries and toast, and baked lamb in red wine. All the wines are from Israel.

Around Łazienki Park

Czytelnik

Wiejska 12a. **Map** 6 E2. *628 14 41 ext. 304.* *9am–4pm Mon–Fri.* $

The self-service canteen-bar of the Czytelnik publishing house is open to the employees as well as the general public. It serves inexpensive bar food and lunches, and reasonable coffee and cakes. It is quite an elitist place, however, where local people come, not so much to eat (for the food is mediocre), but to see famous writers, editors and theatre people.

Da Elio

Żurawia 20. **Map** 6 D1. *629 06 02.* *11am–11pm daily.* $$

This buzzing Italian restaurant does not possess the most attractive decor, but is comfort-

For key to symbols *see p205*

able. It serves delicious pizzas, lasagne, cannelloni, *vitello tonnato* and *bistecca alla pirata*. Their ice creams and sorbets are delicious. To accompany your meal, there is a very good selection of Italian wine, which is all the better for being inexpensive.

Klub Aktora

Aleje Ujazdowskie 45. **Map** 6 E2. *628 93 66.* *noon–until the last guest leaves daily.* $$$

The former legendary SPATiF, this restaurant was renowned as the meeting place of Poland's cinema, theatre and literary circles. The food was not bad and the drinks were affordable. Now it is just a faint shadow of its former self: prices have risen and the food is mediocre, but you can still spot some well-known Polish faces here.

Belvedere

Łazienki Królewskie. **Map** 6 E5 & 6 F4. *841 22 50 & 841 48 06 (bookings).* *noon–until the last guest leaves daily.* $$$$ ★

With tables set among exotic plants of the former conservatory, this is probably the most expensive restaurant in Poland. It offers two main specialities. The first is the classic Polish menu, such as *żurek* (fermented soup) with gammon and mushrooms, roast sirloin prepared to the old recipes of Tremo (master chef at the court of King Stanisław August Poniatowski), saddle of venison in prune sauce and raspberry ravioli. The second is a French menu with all the embellishments, such as truffles, foie gras, caviar and oysters. The servings are small, but delicious and elegant.

Casa Valdemar

Piękna 7/9. **Map** 6 D2. *628 81 40 & 628 45 43.* *noon–until the last guest leaves daily.* $$$$ ★

This luxurious Spanish (Castilian) restaurant, with its tastefully furnished interior, combines elegance with panache, spiced with a little exuberance. It offers a splendid atmosphere and delicious food. Pride of place is given to various herb-scented dishes, cooked in the clay oven, including lamb, suckling pig, poultry, Spanish sausages and tortillas. Besides the classic gazpacho, there is also a sensational *ajo blanco* – a thick cold soup made with ground almonds and garlic; it is seasoned with oil and white sherry vinegar and includes whole green grapes.

London Steak House

Aleje Jerozolimskie 42. **Map** 2 E5 & 5 C1. *827 00 20.* *11am–midnight daily.* $$$$

This restaurant offers excellent grills and a selection of English food, in a setting that is reminiscent of a pub, but with higher prices. It serves a delicious roast beef with Yorkshire pudding, a stylish T-bone steak, steak Diane, as well as tasty potatoes and quite good soups. Żywiec is the draught beer.

Montmartre

Nowy Świat 7. **Map** 2 D5 & 6 D1. *628 63 15.* *11am–until the last guest leaves daily.* $$$$

Montmartre is an excellent French restaurant without aspiring to great elegance. Prices are expensive but not excessive compared with other restaurants offering a similar menu. Their appetizing dishes include green salad with hot chicken giblets, spicy Marseillais fish soup, calf kidneys in vermouth sauce, *côte de boeuf* (grilled beef ribs), frogs, snails, fresh oysters and a Parisian délicacy, champagne fried oysters – all luxurious and expensive, but also unforgettable. Hot apple tart in caramel sauce, with vanilla ice cream, makes an ideal dessert.

Qchnia Artystyczna

Modern Art Centre (Centrum Sztuki Współczesnej), Ujazdowski Castle, Aleje Ujazdowskie 6. **Map** 6 E2. *625 76 27.* *noon–midnight daily.* $$$$ ★

This is one of the most original restaurants in town, with an eccentric interior in what is claimed to be a postmodernist style. With a witty menu, good atmosphere and excellent company (the centre hosts many exhibitions, shows, concerts, symposiums and modern art workshops), it only lacks an excellent chef and proper execution to elevate it to the top of the Warsaw restaurant.list. A good tip is to choose the vegetarian dishes, which are reasonably priced.

Studio Buffo

Konopnickiej 6. **Map** 6 E2. *626 8907 (bookings).* *noon–11pm Mon–Fri, 1–11pm Sat–Sun.* $$$$ ★

This restaurant attracts artists connected with the Studio Buffo Theatre, as well as the city's politicians from the nearby Sejm and Senate. Straightforward interiors, ash tables, benches and chairs complement the Polish and international menu. Among the specialities are fish soup, lamb, stuffed pork knuckle, chicken liver shashlik and delicious Russian-style pierogi, with a recipe supplied by by politician Jacek Kuroń. The son of this renowned Polish politician, Maciej Kuroń, runs the restaurant and is known countrywide in his own right through his popular TV programme, Masterchef.

Other Districts

B-40

Most Poniatowskiego. **Map** 6 F1. *10am–until the last guest leaves daily.* $

This pub has an unusual location, housed in one of the pillars supporting Poniatowski Bridge on the Praga side of the River Vistula. It serves beer, vodka and coke, and is the meeting place of "rockers" and Harley-Davidson fans. The regulars are not especially keen on tourists, but if you have arrived in Warsaw on a Harley-Davidson, this is where you will make friends.

Zielona Gęś

Aleje Niepodległości 177. **Map** 5 C4. *825 20 26.* *9am–2am Mon–Fri, 9am–5am Sat, Sun.* $

This cowboy-style bar is "the" meeting place for fans of country music. It has a rancho-style decor, and offers a selection of grilled meats in keeping with the style, as well as salads and toasted sandwiches to enhance the atmosphere.

Boston Port

Okolska 2. *844 03 15.* *11am–8pm Mon–Fri, noon–7pm Sat, Sun.* $$

This small, modest, self-service bar concentrates on the food of the northeast coast of the United States. Dishes include a delectable New England fish chowder, which is prepared with five different varieties of fish. The restaurant also does a surprisingly good home-made corned beef and roast Virginia ham, while European specialities include *filet mignon* cooked in port and veal Marsala.

Rong Vang

Broniewskiego 74. *834 51 51.* *10:30am–10pm daily.* $$$

Rong Vang specializes in Vietnamese cuisine, has a cosy, lively atmosphere and moderately priced food. Interesting dishes include "moon-gazing carp", Tonkin duck, frogs fried in pastry, eel soup, coconut chicken, pork with bean sprouts, fried rice with prawns or crab and steamed vegetables with bamboo shoots. The namesake for the restaurant is a rather rubbery rice tart, positiviely stuffed with dry fruit.

Amigos

Aleje Jerozolimskie 119. **Map** 2 E5 & 5 C1. *629 39 69.* *noon–midnight daily.* $$$

The clientele is not particularly exciting at this American-style steak house and the prices are high, but the food is excellent. Tuna salad, sweet roast ribs, roast pork in garlic sauce and Boston steak are all tasty, while the bar offers a large selection of expensive spirits and a variety of international cocktails. In addition to American food, the restaurant now also serves some Mexican dishes. Draught beers include an excellent Czech lager.

Le Cedre

Aleja Solidarności 61. **Map** 1 A3 & 3 C5. *818 52 60.* *11am–until the last guest leaves daily.* V $$$

At Le Cedre, Greek and Mediterranean cuisine is delivered with pleasant service. Although off the main tourist route, it is worth visiting for its many interesting and tasty mutton dishes. Also worth trying are *shawarma* (meat with onion and tomatoes in a sesame sauce), grape leaves filled with rice and vegetables, or frog in the chef's secret sauce.

Mibella

Kasprowicza 56. *834 23 78.* *11am–midnight daily.* V $$$

This unpretentious place, offering good food and a pleasant atmosphere, is the best restaurant in this part of town. The menu offers calf livers braised in cream, chicken nuggets served with three different sauces and the classical *pfefferstek*. In the winter, a selection of hot punches, beer with spices, mead and wine are served.

Positano

Wołoska 74a. *848 24 55* & Witosa 31 (Panorama Building). *642 87 11.* *noon–11pm daily.* V $$$

One of only a few pizzerias in town, Positano includes two small but pleasant sections offering thin crisp pizzas with tasty embellishments. They also offer delicious *lasagna al forno* and salads. Other branches of the Positano chain are located at Kasprowicza 30 (tel: 834 48 10) and Aleje Krajowej Edukacji Narodovej 14 (tel: 649 44 64).

Chopin

Hotel Jan III Sobieski, Plac Zawiszy 1. **Map** 5 B2. *658 44 44 ext. 1008.* *6:30am–10:30pm daily.* V $$$$

This expensive restaurant, set in a modern hotel, has a tasteful interior, with an atrium and verdant plants. The "Royal Table" dishes, prepared according to old Polish recipes, include excellent venison fillets à la Jagiellon as well as a rich selection of dishes from all around the world, including Austrian *tafelspitz*, Florentine veal, Alpine pork knuckle, Mexican *puntas de filete*, spicy Thai salad and Nile perch in balsamic sauce. Some are delicious but the quality is inconsistent. The fried ice cream is a must for dessert.

Flik

Puławska 43. **Map** 6 D4. *849 44 06.* *10am–until the last guest leaves daily.* V $$$$

Flik has the most affordable prices of all the luxury restaurants. It offers an excellent view over Morskie Oko Park while the menu provides well-prepared Polish meals such as: black pudding with apples; sauerkraut soup with potatoes; pork knuckle cooked in beer; bliny (buckwheat pancakes) with caviar; chopped spring onions, hard boiled egg and thick cream; foil-baked potatoes, caviar and prawns. Flik also offers the best *pierogi* (ravioli) in town, with cream cheese, cabbage, mushrooms, meat or strawberries. In the summer, there is a grill and outdoor dining in a pleasant garden. Good wines are served at decent prices.

Santorini

Egipska 7 (in Saska Kępa). *672 05 25.* *noon–11pm, daily.* V $$$$

Slightly out of the city centre, this Greek restaurant is an excellent place for a romantic dinner. Even though the office building exterior is not promising, the interior transports you a few hundred kilometres south to a the sunny setting by the Aegean Sea. Cold *meze* (starters) include excellent olives, feta cheese, hummus, stuffed vine leaves and cooked beetroot in garlic paste. All are served with warm dips as well as Greek wine like retsina.

Shogun

Migdałowa 12. *648 19 19.* *noon–10pm Tue–Fri, 2–10pm Sat–Sun.* V $$$$

This luxurious Japanese restaurant in the outlying Natolin district is incredibly expensive and visited mainly by the bosses of large international electronic and car companies. Its speciality is sukiyaki – an interesting Japanese fondue.

Zajazd Napoleoński

Płowiecka 83. *815 30 68.* *1pm–until the last guest leaves daily.* V $$$$

Set in a country manor house, this restaurant offers tasty Polish and French cuisine using frogs, snails, wild mushrooms, cream asparagus, veal knuckle braised in honey, rolled fillets of venison, roast duck and veal escalope in cep sauce. For dessert, try vanilla ice cream smothered in hot raspberries. Only the overly ornate decor may take the edge off your appetite.

FURTHER AFIELD

Pod Złotym Linem

In Wierzbica, past Serock, en route to Olsztyn. *782 74 73.* *8am–9pm (10pm in summer) daily.* $$$

This relatively inexpensive, top restaurant offers a huge variety of fish: tench, crucian carp, zander, catfish, trout, carp, eel and pike. The fish is mainly fried, braised in cream or served in cold jelly. A speciality is the eel in dill sauce.

Trattoria

Villa Park Wesoła Hotel, ul.1. Praskiego Pułku 89, Wesoła. *773 61 30.* *11am–until the last guest leaves daily.* V $$$$

One of three restaurants in the Villa Park Wesoła Hotel, the Trattoria is an upmarket Italian restaurant. On offer are modern takes on traditional Italian fare as well as all the mainstays of this Mediteranean cuisine - Parma ham, tomato and mozzarella salads, spaghetti, and veal dishes. Desserts include crêpes and hot, caramelised bananas. Well-presented food and modern décor.

For key to symbols *see p205*

Shopping in Warsaw

Shopping has become a completely different experience in Warsaw, ever since privatization dawned in 1989. After years of shortages, which encompassed foodstuffs as well as various consumer goods, it is now possible to buy virtually anything in Warsaw. Many Western retailers have opened branches here, and international brand names are increasingly available. Polish manufacturers and retailers, spurred on by this competition, are now beginning to match the quality and range of imported goods. A growing number of department stores, shopping arcades, and pedestrianized areas in the city are ideal for leisurely browsing, while a traditional bustling atmosphere draws bargain hunters to the bazaars and markets.

Polish ceramics

Opening Hours

Shops in central Warsaw are usually open from 11am until 7pm Monday to Friday, and from 9am until 2pm or 3pm on Saturdays. Delicatessens and many of the supermarkets often open earlier, and stay open until 8 or even 10pm in the evenings.

Department stores and large shopping centres also have longer opening hours, while each district in Warsaw has at least one or two shops that are open 24 hours a day. Large shopping centres tend to open on Sundays, as do many of the souvenir shops during the tourist season.

On the last Sunday before Christmas and Easter virtually all of the city's shops stay open for shoppers who need to make a few last-minute purchases. In the centre of Warsaw, shops are at their busiest on Saturdays and during the afternoon, so aim to shop early in the day if you want to avoid the crowds

How to Pay

Not surprisingly, cash is the preferred method of payment in Poland. Although certain shops used to accept hard currency from tourists, this no longer applies, so all transactions are now handled in the national złoty.

A traditional paper cut-out

Do not be surprised if shop assistants ask you for the exact sum when you pay for goods, as a shortage of change seems to be a constant problem. Many retail outlets, particularly the department stores, accept cheques, but only from Polish bank accounts.

Ballantine's, a spirit shop specializing in whisky

Fukier decoration located on Mokotowska Street

Western-owned as well as Polish shops selling luxury goods and souvenirs take all the more popular credit cards. Look out for the logos of accepted credit cards, which are usually prominently displayed.

All prices in Poland include VAT, which can be reclaimed when taking goods bought in shops displaying a "Tax-Free" sign out of the country. There are several duty-free shops inside Okęcie Airport.

Sales

The phenomenon of sales has been known in Poland for only a few years. Initially only large department stores and Western-owned shops offered seasonal price reductions. Polish-owned stores were slower to adopt this new pattern of trading, particularly as the word "sale"

A fashion boutique on Chmielna Street

was previously associated with the cut-price and sub-standard goods that used to clutter many shops during the Communist era.

Now, however, sales are an accepted part of the shopping calendar. As in most other European countries, sales are usually held twice a year, just after Christmas and during the summer months.

Department Stores and Shopping Centres

Warsaw has several department stores of a very good standard, which provide a comprehensive range of merchandise to satisfy even the most fervent shopaholics. Moreover, a number of stores in the city have recently been refurbished, making them much more attractive and user-friendly.

Marshal, a popular clothes shop on Nowy Świat

The most popular department store among locals is **Galeria Centrum** with its Polish and international branded fashion, shoes, accessories and cosmetics. The **Empik Salon Megastore "Junior"** stocks international publications, books, records, and prestigious cosmetics *(see p222)*. Foodstuffs are available from the nearby **Sezam**, which is also on Marshal Street (Marszałkowska).

The best place to go when shopping for children and expectant mothers is a department store called **Smyk** *(see p132)*, which stocks everything from children's and baby clothes and equipment, to maternity dresses and toys.

Also worth visiting is the **Arka** shopping centre on Bracka Street. This occupies an attractive Secessionist building, which was formerly the Jabłkowski Brothers' department store *(see p131)*. Its range of boutiques offers clothes, shoes and cosmetics, as well as interior design items.

Among Warsaw's modern, purpose-built shopping centres are **Promenada** and **Panorama**, which provide a choice of individual shops, cafés and dining areas. After a day's shopping at Promenada you can see an evening film at its Ster Century or Atomic Swiat Rozrywki multiplexes.

Markets

Many of Warsaw's locals consider markets to be the only place to shop, if you are looking for low prices.

The largest of Warsaw's markets is the **Saxon Market** (Jarmark Saski), held at the Dziesięciolecie Stadium. This once impressive sports venue is now one of the biggest open-air markets in Europe. Street vendors and Russian traders offer an astonishing range of goods. The market may be closing down within a few years, however.

A market frequented by locals is at **Defilad Square**, next to the Palace of Culture and Science. A good place to buy fresh fruit and vegetables is the **Mirowski Halls** (Hale Mirowskie). The Banach Halls and Marymoncki Halls also have fresh produce markets, which were established in the late 1990s. Extending along both sides of John Paul II Avenue, you will find a vast assortment of foodstuffs, including meat and dairy produce. Warsaw's most famous food market is at **Polna Street**. This long-standing institution, where it has always been possible to find international delicacies, survived even the Communists' attempts to regulate trade. The original shabby kiosks have been replaced by a new purpose-built building.

Modern interior of Panorama

Where to Shop

Warsaw's shops offer a wide selection of internationally established designers and brand names, as well as Polish specialities such as amber jewellery, Silesian crystal glass, leathergoods, tableware, folk art and contemporary art. Several department stores provide "one-stop shopping", while plenty of boutiques, bookshops, galleries and souvenir shops are also excellent for browsing. The greatest concentration of shops is within the Old Town, the New Town, Nowy Świat Street and around Marshal Street.

Polish Folk Art

Polish handicrafts and folk arts are renowned for their quality and beauty. Among the most popular items are embroidered tablecloths, pottery, leathergoods, painted wooden Easter eggs *(pisanki)* and Christmas tree decorations fashioned from straw. Other specialities are colourful paper cut-outs of rustic motifs, naive art such as paintings on glass and carved religious figures.

The **Cepelia** retail chain specializes in folk art, with beautiful hand-woven kilims, textiles, wickerwork, and leathergoods such as the unique moccasins *(kierpce)* produced by Polish highlanders from Zakopane, in the south of Poland.

Folk Art and Handicrafts in Chmielna is one of the best shops in the Cepelia chain. **Folk Art and Crafts Gallery,** on Plac Konstytucji at the far end of Marshal Street, is also well worth visiting.

Contemporary Arts and Crafts

Numerous art galleries and interior design shops throughout the city provide a comprehensive choice of items of modern Polish and European design.

The finest handblown glass and crystal can be found in **Galeria MP**, located in the Old Town Market Square. In addition, the **Opera** shop in the New Town has a wide selection of attractive artefacts produced mainly by Polish artists and craftsmen. Fans of modern Italian design will find items from the Alessi range in **Gallery Aina Progetti**, on Krakowskie Przedmieście. The flamboyant interiors of **Magda Gessler Decoration**, on Mokotowska Street, provide an inspiring showcase for an extensive choice of top quality soft furnishings, glassware, pottery and other decorative items.

While Gdańsk is the capital of Poland's historic amber trade, Warsaw also has several galleries which specialize in amber jewellery and *objets d'art,* particularly in the Old Town and along the Royal Route.

Among central Warsaw's more prestigious contemporary art galleries are **Zapiecek** and **Plac Zamkowy**, both in the Old Town, **ZPAP** in Krakowskie Przedmieście and **Posters and Graphic Arts** on Hoża Street.

Original paintings are also available at far more affordable prices from stalls and street artists in the Old Town Market Square, on Nowomiejska Street and by the Barbican.

Antiques

While Warsaw has a growing number of antique shops, strict regulations limit the export of any works of art produced before 1945.

Antiques can only be exported with a special government licence, which is issued only in exceptional circumstances. This protectionist move followed the enormous losses suffered by Poland's art heritage during World War II.

Many good antique shops are located in the Old Town and along the Royal Route. Some of the best known among them are **Desa UNICUM** and **Rempex**. The Sunday **Antique Market** is held every week in Koło. It is worth arriving early for the best choice, as the market usually begins to wind down in the afternoon, at around 2pm. The **Saxon Market** *(see p191)* is also worth a visit, if you enjoy sifting through an assortment of bric-a-brac.

Books and Records

Although it is possible to buy guide books and illustrated books in English, German and French, these are still something of a rarity in Warsaw. The widest range of foreign-language books is available at the city's largest bookshops: **Empik Megastore, Empik "Junior"**, **Odeon**, **Leksykon** and the **Joseph Conrad Bookshop**.

Impressive selections of fiction and reference books can be found in **Bolesław Prus** and **Liber** bookshops, while the widest variety of books covering fine art is provided by the **Royal Castle** shop in Świętojańska Street.

Collectors of prints and books should visit the city's numerous second-hand book shops (look out for shop signs saying "Antykwariat"). A good "itinerary" is to follow the Royal Route, starting at **Kosmos** and **Logos** in Aleje Ujazdowskie (Ujazdowskie Avenue) and continuing to the Old and New towns, particularly via Nowomiejska and Freta streets.

Odeon and **By the Opera** have a considerable selection of records and a large stock of sheet music. Collectors' items can also be found in the small shops dotted around the centre of Warsaw.

Clothes and Shoes

The choice and quality of clothes and footwear has improved dramatically over the past few years. **Marks & Spencer** has opened a branch in Warsaw, and a range of denim jeans and jackets can now be found in two branches of **Levi Strauss**. Meanwhile, clothes designed by Warsaw's own growing band of young fashion designers are available in boutiques such as **Joanna Klimas** and **Grażyna Hase**.

Department stores also sell good quality, yet inexpensive designs manufactured in Poland, under their own label. **Galeria Mokotow**, a new up-market shopping centre, features a range of well-known names such as **Diesel, Lacoste, River Island**, **Esprit, Bata, Olsen, Wallis** and **Mothercare**.

Shops and boutiques in the city centre carry a range of brand names catering to most budgets. At the sophisticated end of the market are **Dantex** and **Lord**, while **Pod Papugami** and **Marshal** are mid-range outlets. **India Market**, selling a variety of Indian clothes, is relatively inexpensive and popular with the city's younger consumers.

Shoe shops include **Bata** and **Salamander**, as well as the ubiquitous **Adidas** stores.

Poland is renowned for the quality and design of leather-goods, including handbags, purses, jackets and belts. A good selection is available in **Pekar**, on Jerozolimskie Avenue and **Pantera** on Nowy Świat Street, as well as the eponymous boutique owned by the celebrated leather goods designer **Andrzej Kłoda**.

Perfumery

A comprehensive selection of the world's leading perfumes is available from **J Powierza**, which is located on Chmielna Street, as well as the **INA Centre**, which has two branches on Nowy Świat Street, and specializes in French perfumes.

Moreover, **Lancôme** and **Estée Lauder** have opened branches in Warsaw, which stock their full range of products.

Sothy's Cosmetics Shop is a convenient, centrally located store which can supply most brand name cosmetics. Cosmetics and toiletries, whether international or Polish brand names, are readily available from most pharmacies, larger supermarkets and department stores.

Food and Drink

The city centre has plenty of delicatessens where you can stock up on various supplies. Fresh fruit and vegetables can be bought at markets or from numerous stalls scattered around the centre. There are also shops and mini-supermarkets open 24 hours and seven days a week. Among the larger stores with a comprehensive selection are **Sezam**, **Rema 1000**, **Supersam**, Robert, Globi or Billa, several of which are open seven days a week.

The **Hypernova** supermarket is located in the newly-opened, Galeria Mokotow shopping centre. It stocks upmarket, quality produce and boasts a fine cheese counter as well as a large selection of cured meats.

The largest supermarkets tend to be on the outskirts of town, catering for shoppers who drive to do their weekly shopping. These include Globi, Billa, Leclerc Auchan, Carrefour, Geant and Robert.

Imported wines and spirits are expensive in Poland, and while there is no local wine production, there is a good selection of beer and vodka. The largest selection is stocked by **Alcoholic Drinks of the World**, while spirits, particularly whisky, are a speciality of **Ballantine's**. A large choice of coffees is available in **Farewell to Africa** (Pożegnanie z Afryką), a café which also has a shop.

Patisseries and Confectioners

Warsaw offers plenty of opportunities for anyone with a sweet tooth. The **Hortex** chain for instance, offers an array of cakes and gateaux at branches throughout the city. There are of course a great deal of smaller patisseries, many of which also have a café on the premises. Warsaw's "institutions" include **Blikle** *(see p124)*, which is famed for its doughnuts. Blikle has its main outlet on Nowy Świat Street, as well as branches on Hoża Street and Wilcza Street. Other specialities include a very good *sękacz* ("knobbly cake") at the **Pomianowski** patisserie, excellent cream slices at the **Hotel Europejski's** patisserie, and the best apple strudel at the **Bristol Hotel** café.

Zielona Budka ("Green Kiosk") specializes in ice cream and its range can be found throughout Warsaw.

For the finest chocolates try **Staroświecki firmowy E. Wedel** ("Old-fashioned Shop of E Wedel"), where a charming café specializes in hot chocolate and chocolate cake.

Pharmacies

In line with international practice, many types of medication and drugs can only be purchased with a doctor's prescription. However, many non-prescription drugs (under international brand names) are readily available over the counter at very competitive prices.

Each district in Warsaw has a 24-hour pharmacy. The city centre is served by a pharmacy in the **Central Railway Station** (Dworzec Centralny). Other convenient pharmacies are on Widok and Freta Streets.

Two of Warsaw's most attractive pharmacies feature splendid 19th-century interiors. There is a shop at No. 18 Nowy Świat Street where the decor is English Gothic, while at No. 19 Krakowskie Przedmieście, the interiors are Neo-Renaissance in style.

Florists

One of Warsaw's largest florists is **Tulipan** ("Tulip"), in Jerozolimskie Avenue, with another shop on Nowy Świat Street.

If you would like to send flowers, **Sonia Interflora**, at Andersa 26, delivers flowers to every country that is part of the Interflora network.

According to local superstition, a wedding bouquet ordered from **Glorioza** brings good luck to newlyweds.

Flower shops can also be found at various hotels, railway stations and the airport.

Directory

Department Stores and Shopping Centres (Domy Towarowe i Centra Handlowe)

Arka
Bracka 25.
Map 2 D5 & 6 D1.
☎ *692 14 00.*

City Center
Złota 44/46.
Map 1 B5 & 5 C1.
☎ *625 15 24.*

Panorama
Witosa 31.
☎ *640 14 00.*

Galeria Centrum
Marszałkowska 104/122.
Map 1 C5 & 5 C1.
☎ *827 72 11.*

Klif
Okopowa 58–72
Map 3 A5.
☎ *531 45 00.*

Promenada
Ostrobramska 75C
☎ *611 3952.*

Smyk
Krucza 50.
Map 2 D5 & 6 D1.
☎ *827 92 61.*

Bazaars and Markets (Bazary i Targowiska)

Defilad Square (Na placu Defilad)
Plac Defilad.
Map 1 C5 & 5 C1.

Market by Mirowski Halls (Przy halach Mirowskich)
Aleja Jana Pawła II.
Map 1 B4.

Polna Street (Na Polnej)
Polna.
Map 6 D3.

Saxon Market (Jarmark Saski)
Stadion Dziesięciolecia.
Map 4 F4.

Polish Folk Art (Folklor Polski)

Cepelia Folk Art and Handicrafts (Rękodzieło Ludowe i Artystyczne)
Chmielna 8.
Map 2 D5 & 6 D1.
☎ *826 60 31.*

Plac Konstytucji 5.
Map 6 D2.
☎ *621 26 18.*

Krucza 23/31.
Map 6 D2.
☎ *621 96 94.*

Marszałkowska 99/101.
Map 5 C1.
☎ *628 77 57.*

Folk Arts and Crafts Gallery (Galeria Sztuki Ludowej i Artystycznej)
Plac Konstytucji 2.
Map 6 D2.
☎ *621 66 69.*

Contemporary Arts and Crafts (Rękodzieło Artystyczne i Galerie Sztuki Współczesnej)

Aina Progetti
Krakowskie Przedmieście 17.
Map 2 D3 & 4 D5.

Art Gallery
Krakowskie Przedmieście 15/17.
Map 2 D3 & 4 D5.
☎ *828 51 70.*

Magda Gessler Decoration
Mokotowska 39.
Map 6 D2.
☎ *625 77 22.*

Galeria MP
Rynek Starego Miasta 9/11.
Map 2 D1 & 4 D4.
☎ *831 69 61.*

Opera
Freta 14.
Map 1 C1 & 3 C4.
☎ *831 73 28.*

Plac Zamkowy
Plac Zamkowy 1/13.
Map 2 D2 & 4 D4.
☎ *831 06 84.*

Posters and Graphic Arts (Galeria Grafiki i Plakatu)
Hoża 40. **Map** 6 D2.
☎ *621 40 77.*

Zapiecek
Zapiecek 1.
Map 2 D2 & 4 D4.
☎ *831 99 18.*

Antiques (Antyki)

Antique Market (Targ Staroci na Kole)
Obozowa 99.

Desa UNICUM
Nowy Świat 48.
Map 6 D1 & 2 D5.
☎ *826 44 66.*

Rynek Starego Miasta 4/6.
Map 2 D1 & 4 D4.
☎ *831 16 81.*

Nadine
Plac Trzech Krzyży 18.
Map 6 E1.
☎ *621 63 18.*

Rempex
Senatorska 11.
Map 1 C3.
☎ *826 60 09.*

Books and Records (Księgarnie)

Bolesław Prus Bookshop (Księgarnia im B Prusa)
Krakowskie Przedmieście 7.
Map 2 D3 & 4 D5.
☎ *826 18 35.*

By The Opera (Przy Operze)
Moliera 8.
Map 2 D3 & 4 D5.
☎ *826 46 48.*

Empik Salon Megastore "Junior"
Marszałkowska 104/122.
Map 1 C5 & 5 C1.
☎ *551 44 42.*
Nowy Świat 15–17.
Map 6 D1. ☎ *627 03 66.*

Joseph Conrad Bookshop
Aleje Jerozolimskie 28.
Map 2 D5 & 6 D1.
☎ *827 05 38.*

Kosmos
Aleje Ujazdowskie.
Map 6 E2. ☎ *628 65 82.*

Logos
Aleje Ujazdowskie.
Map 6 E2. ☎ *621 38 67.*

Leksykon
Nowy Świat 41.
Map 2 D5 & 6 D1.
☎ *826 45 33.*

Liber
Krakowskie Przedmieście 24.
Map 2 D3. ☎ *826 30 91.*

Odeon
Hoża 19. **Map** 6 D2.
☎ *621 80 69.*

Royal Castle (Zamku Królewskiego)
Plac Zamkowy 4.
Map 2 D2 & 4 D4.
☎ *657 22 64.*

Clothes and Shoes (Odzież i Obuwie)

Adidas
Aleje Jerozolimskie 56c.
Map 5 B2.
☎ *630 22 37.*

Andrzej Kłoda
Krakowskie Przedmieście 81.
Map 2 D3 & 4 D5.

Bata
Marszałkowska 87.
Map 6 D2.
☎ *629 15 94.*

Bytom
Galeria Centrum, Marszałkowska 104/122.
Map 1 C5 & 5 C1.

Dantex
Aleje Jerozolimskie 11/19.
Map 2 D5 & 6 D1.
☎ *621 67 94.*

Diesel
Galeria Mokotow, Wołoska 12.
Map 5 C5.
☎ *541 33 13.*

Esprit
Galeria Mokotow, Wołoska 12. **Map** 5 C5.
541 33 27.

Grażyny Hase
Marszałkowska 6 m. 2.
Map 6 D3.
628 21 59.

India Market
Hoża 5/7.
Map 6 D2.
629 61 68.
Krakowskie Przedmieście 14.
Map 2 D3.

Joanna Klimas
Chmielna 24/29.
Map 2 D5 & 6 D1.
826 75 75.

Lacoste
Galeria Mokotow, Wołoska 12. **Map** 5 C5.
541 31 81.

Levi Strauss
Chmielna 20.
Map 2 D5 & 5 B2.
827 27 61.
Aleje Jerozolimskie 51.
Map 5 C1.
621 75 71.

Lord
Marszałkowska 87.
Map 6 D2.
625 34 96.

Marks & Spencer
Al Jerozolimskie 52.
Map 5 C1.
652 05 29.

Marshal
Nowy Świat 49.
Map 2 D5 & 6 D1.

Mothercare
Galeria Mokotow, Wołoska 12. **Map** 5 C5.
541 32 23.

Olsen
Galeria Mokotow, Wołoska 12.
Map 5 C5.
541 33 27.

Pantera
Nowy Świat 21.
Map 2 D5 & 6 D1.
826 46 58.

Pekar
Aleje Jerozolimskie 29.
Map 2 D5 & 6 D1.
621 90 82.

Próchnik
Aleja Jana Pawła II 18.
Map 1 B5 & 5 B1.
620 34 16.

River Island
Galeria Mokotow, Wołoska 12. **Map** 5 C5.
541 33 62.

Salamander
Aleje Jerozolimskie 42.
Map 2 D5 & 6 D1.
827 02 67.

Wallis
Galeria Mokotow, Wołoska 12. **Map** 5 C5.
541 33 68.

Perfumery (Perfumerie)

Estée Lauder
Nowy Świat 47.
Map 2 D5 & 6 D1.
826 01 84.

INA Centre
Nowy Świat 45.
Map 2 D5 & 6 D1.
828 39 57.
Nowy Świat 30.
Map 2 D5 & 6 D1.
828 90 36.

J Powierza
Chmielna 18.
Map 2 D5 & 6 D1.

Lancôme
Mokotowska 55.
Map 6 D2.
622 94 28.

Sothy's Cosmetics Shop
Foksal 21.
Map 2 E5 & 6D1.
826 54 47.

Food and Drink (Sklepy Spożywcze)

Alcoholic Drinks of the World (Alkohole Świata)
Aleja Solidarności 84.
Map 1 A3.
838 52 40.

Ballantine's
Krucza 47a.
Map 6 D2.
625 48 32.

Farewell to Africa (Pożegnanie z Afryką)
Freta 4/6. **Map** 1 C1 & 3 C4.

Hypernova
Galeria Mokotow, Wołoska 12.
Map 5 C5.

Rema 1000
Krucza 50.
Map 6 D2.
827 08 68.

Sezam
Marszałkowska 126/134.
Map 1 C5 & 5 C1.
827 34 54.

Supersam
Puławska 2.
Map 6 D4.
825 24 74.

Patisseries and Confectioners (Cukiernie)

Blikle
Nowy Świat 35.
Map 2 D5 & 6 D1.
826 45 68.

Bristol Hotel
Krakowskie Przedmieście 42/44.
Map 2 D3.
625 25 25.

Hortex
Konstytucji pl. 7.
Map 6 D2.
628 76 78.

Marszatkowska 53 .
Map 6 D2.
621 53 15.

Hotel Europejski
Krakowskie Przedmieście 13.
Map 2 D3 & 4 D5.
826 50 51.

Pomianowski
Krakowskie Przedmieście 8.
Map 2 D3 & 4 D5.
826 77 25.

Staroświecki firmowy E. Wedel
Szpitalna 8.
Map 2 D5 & 6 D1.
827 29 16.

Zielona Budka
Puławska 11.
Map 6 D4.
849 89 38.

Pharmacies (Apteki)

Central Station (Na Dworcu Centralnym)
Aleje Jerozolimskie 54.
Map 5 C1.
825 69 846.

Kosma i Damian
Rynek Starego Miasta 17/19. **Map** 2 D1 & 4 D4.
831 17 84.

Other Pharmacies
Freta 13/15.
Map 1 C1 & 3 C4.
831 50 91.

Widok 19.
Map 2 D5 & 6 D1.
827 35 93.

Krakowskie Przedmieście 19.
Map 2 D3 & 4 D5.
826 18 03.

Nowy Świat 18.
Map 6 D1 & 2 E5.

Florists (Kwiacarnie)

Glorioza
Wilcza 19.
Map 6 D2.
629 63 86.

Sonia Interflora
Andersa 26.
Map 1 B1 & 3 B4.
831 11 65.

Tulipan
Aleje Jerozolimskie 21.
Map 2 D5 & 6 D1.
628 04 95.
Nowy Świat 19.
Map 6 D1.
826 44 58.

Entertainment in Warsaw

Warsaw has become a much livelier city over the past few years, and while not yet matching Paris or London in the diversity of entertainment on offer, there is still plenty to interest visitors. Two opera houses and the Philharmonia provide a programme that will please even the most discerning classical music lovers. Jazz fans can choose from several excellent clubs, while devotees of other types of popular music can enjoy a variety of venues, from palaces and museums to stadiums, pubs and clubs. Cinemas show major releases from around the world, usually in their original language with Polish subtitles, and English-language plays are also staged. Moreover, Warsaw holds various cultural festivals throughout the year, including music, film, theatre, art and jazz.

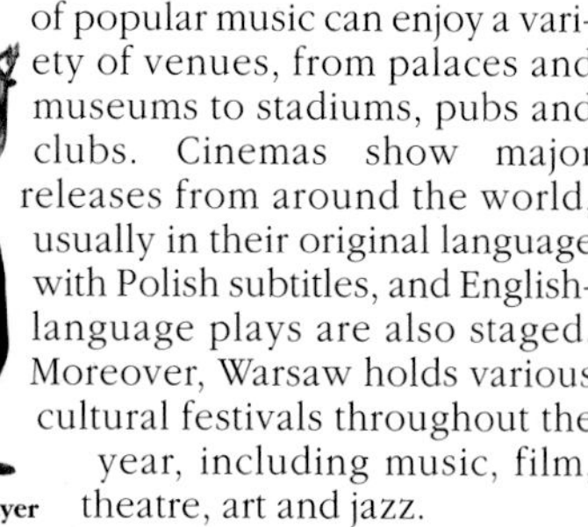

Saxophone player

A joint performance by José Carreras and Edyta Górniak at a charity concert

Practical Information

The most comprehensive and up-to-the-minute information on what is happening in Warsaw can be found in the monthly magazine *Kalejdoskop (Kaleidoscope)*, which is available from Ruch kiosks and other newsagents. *Kaleidoscope* has an English section with information on museums, galleries, exhibitions, theatre events, music and cinema. It also contains details of foreign culture centres, antique shops and auction houses, and has regular features on different aspects of life in the capital.

Additionally, there are a couple of English-language publications: *Warszawa What, Where, When* and *Welcome to Warsaw*. Both are published monthly, and are available free from many of the city's hotels. Together with features on topical events, both magazines provide comprehensive listings including museums and exhibitions, cinemas and theatres, as well as times of church services. The English-language weekly *Warsaw Voice* contains some listings. Warsaw's main tourist office *(see p237)* is also a good source of up-to-date entertainment information.

Numerous of the city's clubs, bars and restaurants also have free listings publications. The two best known are *City Magazine* and *Aktivist*. The latter is also available on the internet (www.aktivist.pl). A copy of the *Warszawa What, Where, When* publication can also be ordered online at www.what-where-when.pl

Performance in the Warsaw Concert Studio S1

A horse race at Służewiec Racetrack

Booking Tickets

Tickets for productions at all of Warsaw's theatres can be purchased up to two weeks in advance, at the theatre booking offices. Reservations can be made through the post or over the telephone, and all reserved tickets must be collected a short time before the performance is due to start.

Tickets to theatre productions, concerts and special events, together with festival passes, can also be purchased from **ZASP** booking offices. The company only charges a modest commission on its ticket transactions. Tickets can also be obtained through travel agencies that service visitors to Warsaw *(see p237)*.

Some travel agents, such as **Mazurkas Travel**, organize evening visits to concerts and the opera that include extra enticements, such as transport and a glass of champagne at the interval. Hotels also offer help booking tickets, either through the concierge or reception. In some cases, tickets may also be booked over the internet. Addresses of leading cultural institutions may be found using a search engine or by looking in the *Gazeta Wyborcza* newspaper's *What's On* section. Tickets for various theatres, including Ateneum, Polski, Roma, Buffo, Syrena and Współczesny can be reserved at http://www.bileteria.pl.

Ticket Prices

Ticket prices in Poland are generally lower than in Western Europe, although the cost of tickets to see world-class stars may be comparable. Important festivals, such as the Warsaw Autumn, the Mozart Festival and the Jazz Jamboree, attract major names, but ticket prices are affordable for the general public, due to generous sponsorship.

Cinema tickets are inexpensive, with theatre tickets cheaper than in many Western cities, though opera tickets can be quite expensive. In some instances, students can buy passes to sit in the gangways for a nominal fee.

Roulette table at Orbis Casino in the Victoria Hotel

Festivals

Warsaw is an established venue for various annual festivals *(see p52)* and competitions, where some of the world's finest performers can be seen. Opera lovers, for instance, can attend the annual Mozart Festival, which is held in June and July.

By far the largest number of festivals are held during the autumn months. If you are a fan of jazz music, the best time to come to Warsaw is in October, when you can attend the popular Jazz Jamboree concerts.

There are also classical music festivals at this time, including the Warsaw Autumn. Additionally, Renaissance and Baroque music is performed at the Festival of Early Music which is held in October.

Night Transport

The easiest and safest way of returning to your hotel after a night out is by taking a taxi. However, bogus taxi drivers tout for business, and you should either take a taxi from a rank or telephone for a radio taxi *(see p252)*. Licensed radio taxis are the least expensive option.

Daytime public transport services end at around 11pm, but night buses run every 30 minutes throughout the night. These buses stop at one central point on Emilii Plater Street, making it convenient to change bus routes. Tickets for night buses can be bought from the driver *(see p255)*.

Interior of the 18th-century Łazienki Theatre

Directory

Useful Addresses

Mazurkas Travel
Forum Hotel
Nowogrodska 24/26.
Map 6 D1.
☎ *629 12 49.*
Długa 8/14. **Map** 3 C4.
☎ *635 66 33.*
☎ *635 5182.*

Tourist Information
Plac Zamkowy 1/3.
Map 4 D4.
☎ *635 18 81.*

ZASP Booking Office
Aleje Jerozolimskie 25.
Map 2 D5.
☎ *621 94 54.*

Entertainment in Warsaw

WARSAW HAS long-standing theatrical and musical traditions. Many celebrated musicians have given concerts here, including Niccolò Paganini, Franz Liszt and Polish composers such as Stanisław Moniuszko. The greatest source of pride, however, is Frederic Chopin who studied and performed in Warsaw.

The first theatre open to the public, the Operalnia, was built in 1748, and the city now has a thriving repertoire of opera, ballet, musicals, cinema and concerts. In addition, Warsaw's programme of annual festivals includes organ music, jazz and street theatre.

Foreign-Language Performances

WARSAW IS PROUD of its **Jewish National Theatre**, which is unique in Europe. Performances are given in Yiddish, accompanied by translations into Polish and English. This provides an excellent opportunity to experience Jewish culture and a sense of Jewish life in Poland, which has all but vanished. The company's repertoire includes various plays and musicals based on several centuries of Jewish tradition.

English-language performances are staged by the Globe Theatre Group at the **English Theatre Company**, a venue that often plays host to British artists. Some of their productions are bilingual. Occasionally, other theatres offer English-speaking productions, while the **Espero** theatre company performs plays in the Esperanto language monthly.

Theatres

THE CITY'S long-standing theatrical tradition dates from the end of the 16th century when Warsaw became the capital of Poland.

Theatres are now free to choose from a wide range of classical and modern plays. During the Communist era, the choice of productions was always state-controlled.

Among the most popular venues with Varsovians are the **Powszechny**, **Ateneum**, and **Współczesny** theatres. They all employ the best actors and the best directors, and each opening night is a major social event. The **Polski**, **Dramatyczny**, **Rozmaitości**, **Nowy** and **Na Woli** theatres specialize in drama, while comedies are regularly staged at the **Kwadrat** theatre.

Teatr Studio is renowned for staging highly original works that frequently border on experimental theatre. Avant-garde productions, as well as audio and video art, can be seen at the Modern Art Centre (Centrum Sztuki Współczesnej, *see p159*).

Interesting productions are held at **Teatr Adekwatny** and **Teatr Maty**, featuring theatre groups from across the country.

Teatr Ochoty provides for audiences of a younger age group, while four other theatres also offer entertainment for children, usually in Polish *(see p233)*.

Opera and Ballet

WARSAW'S TWO opera companies are the National Opera, **Teatr Wielki**, which is based at the Grand Theatre, and the **Warsaw Chamber Opera** (Warszawska Opera Kameralna).

The National Opera is associated with the staging of monumental works, with huge casts and world-class soloists. The company's varied programme includes Polish operas, together with classics from other countries.

The Warsaw Chamber Opera, as its name suggests, mainly stages courtly Baroque operas. The company is particularly known for its productions of the music of Mozart. These performances form part of Warsaw's annual Mozart Festival *(see p53)*, and feature Mozart's work in its entirety, including his very early works.

The Warsaw Ballet Company is based at the Grand Theatre. Their performances alternate with the National Opera.

Musical Theatres

AMONG the wide choice of musical theatres to be found in Warsaw, one of the most popular is **Roma – Teatr Muzyczny**, which stages classical operettas and musicals.

For lighter musical entertainment, try **Rampa**, **Studio Buffo** or **Syrena**. These theatres stage musicals and reviews, as well as satirical cabarets and comedies, using established performers. Syrena's productions are generally more traditional than those of Rampa and Buffo, which aim at a younger audience. Various musicals based on Jewish life, which are performed in Yiddish, can be seen at the **Jewish National Theatre** (Teatr Żydowski). Musicals and revues are also included in the repertoires of other theatres.

Classical Music

THE MOST ESTABLISHED of Warsaw's concert halls is the **Philharmonic** (Filharmonia Narodowa, *see p131*). Its two auditoriums serve as venues for various classical music festivals, most notably the Warsaw Autumn *(see p54)*, and competitions such as the International Chopin Piano Competition *(see p54)* held every five years.

The Philharmonic also stages so-called Thursday Concerts, which are aimed at youth audiences, while on Sunday morning concerts of classical music are held for children.

Classical music can be heard in the **Polish Radio Concert Studio** (Studio Koncertowe Polskiego Radia), and also in the Academy of Music's concert hall. The Warsaw Music Society (Warszawskie Towarzystwo Muzyczne) also hosts concerts in Szuster Palace, while the Chopin Society organizes performances in the Ostrogski Palace.

Concerts in Palaces, Churches, and Museums

Many classical concerts are held in Warsaw's palaces, churches and museums. These historic settings, which often have excellent acoustics, provide a memorable experience for the audience.

Chamber music is a regular attraction at the **Royal Castle**, **Wilanów Palace** and venues within Łazienki Park, including the **Palace on the Water**, **Myślewicki Palace**, the **Theatre on the Island**, and the **Stanisławowski Theatre** in the **Old Orangerie**.

Among the museums providing concert venues are the National Museum and the Former Bank of Poland and Stock Exchange, which houses the John Paul II Art Collection. Concerts held at Staromiejski Dom Kultury and the Archdiocese Museum are also extremely popular.

Organ music can be enjoyed in various churches in Warsaw, but particularly at the following places: Holy Trinity Church (Przenajświętszej Trójcy), St John's Cathedral (katedra św. Jana), St Joseph's Church (św. Józefa), St Saviour's (Zbawiciela) and Holy Mary, Queen of the World (Matki Boskiej Królowej Świata).

During the summer, Chopin concerts are held in Żelazowa Wola and by the Chopin monument in Łazienki Park.

Cinemas

Most of Warsaw's cinemas are in the vicinity of Marshal Street (Marszałkowska). These include **Atlantic**, **Luna**, **Muranów**, **Bajka**, **Kinoteka** (at the Palace of Culture) and **Relax**, while the **Kultura** cinema is located on the capital's Royal Route.

A popular studio cinema in Warsaw that shows mainly Polish films is **Rejs**. Classic movies are screened at **Iluzjon**, while art-house films can be seen at the cinema in the Palace of Culture and Science. Many films are premiered in the conveniently situated, although somewhat dilapidated, Kultura. **Femina** was Warsaw's first "Multiplex" cinema, although others are currently available in the city centre.

Additionally, every autumn a film festival is held. At this, an international selection of films is usually previewed.

Music Clubs

The number of music clubs in Warsaw has increased considerably over the past few years, with the current total in excess of 50.

Followng the demise of the long-established Akwarium Jazz Club, the new leader of the scene is **Prohibicja**, a restaurant with live jazz and special events *(see p212)*. Other popular jazz venues are **Rynek Jazz Club, Swing Jazz Club, Stodoła** and **Riviera-Remont**. However, these jazz clubs also provide other popular music and hold discos. More varied repertoires are offered by **Empik Club Pub** and **Klub Giovanni**. Meanwhile, the **Irish Pub** specializes in country, folk and rock music, while the **Blues Bar** provides a wide range of blues music. Another popular pub in central Warsaw which offers live music is the **Piwnica pod Harenda**.

Nightclubs and Discotheques

Nightlife has greatly improved over the past few years. However, the most active venues still tend to be student discos, which means of course that the clientele is young. These discos include **Riviera-Remont**, **Stodoła**, **Park**, **Hades**, **Hybrydy-Vogue** and **Klub Medyka**.

Equally popular are the discos held at **Dziekanka, Bar u Pana Michała** and Underground Music Club. Additionally, **Ground Zero** offers a novel setting, being housed within a bunker that dates from the Stalinist era. Fans of techno music should try **Grota, Hades or Hybrydy-Vogue**.

Also popular to hang out in is Tam-Tam, a club with a folky-African decor, offering good music and some house music. Among the most exclusive and expensive nightclubs in Warsaw are **Stereo, Music Club, Scena, 2000, Cul-de-Sac, Tango, Yesterday** and **Orpheus**.

Gay and Lesbian Clubs

While there are not many gay and lesbian clubs in Warsaw, they are undoubtedly on the increase and no longer create a sensation when they open.

Among the casual venues where you can have a cup of coffee or a glass of beer are **Koźla Club** and the **Między Nami** café. Gay discos are also held at **Klub 69**, just off Marshal Street, and **Club Cocon** in the Old Town.

Sports

Warsaw offers sports enthusiasts a reasonable range of choices. Swimmers can use the pools at **Wodny Park's** "Warszawianka" or **Wodnik**, while tennis players can play on courts all the year round at **Solec**, the **Mera** sports hall or at the **Legia** sports stadium.

Football matches are also held quite regularly at the Legia stadium, with ice hockey and figure skating in **Torwar**. Speed skating is available at the **Stegny** track.

The best water sports facilities are provided outside the city on Zegrzyński Reservoir (Zalew Zegrzyński). Horse riding is offered by many out of town clubs, such as those in Kanie and Podkowa Leśna, with a round of golf available at the **First Warsaw Golf and Country Club**.

The surrounding countryside is also ideal for walking and cycling. These activities can be undertaken as part of an escorted group, with various groups meeting at weekends. Joining such a group is free, with the times and places of meetings advertised in newspapers and listings magazines *(see p237)*.

If you are a horse racing enthusiast, you can spend a very enjoyable Sunday at the **Służewiec Racetrack**.

DIRECTORY

FOREIGN-LANGUAGE PERFORMANCES

English Theatre Company
Szanajci 4/49.
619 98 17.

Espero
Galeria Nusantara, Nowogrodzka 18a.
Map 4 D1.
629 24 41.

Jewish National Theatre (Teatr Żydowski)
Plac Grzybowski 12/16. **Map** 1 B4.
620 62 81.

The Globe Theatre Group
Plac Grzybowski 6/2.
Map 1 B4.
620 44 29.

THEATRES

Ateneum
Jaracza 2.
Map 2 F4.
625 73 30.

Dramatyczny
Palace of Culture and Science.
Map 1 C5 & 5 C1.
656 68 44.

Kameralny (Scena Teatru Polskiego)
Foksal 16.
Map 2 E5 & 6 D1.
826 49 18.

Komedia
Północne Centrum Sztuki, Słowackiego 19a.
833 68 80.

Kwadrat
Czackiego 15/17.
Map 2 D4.
826 23 89.

Mały
Marszałkowska 122.
Map 1 C5.
827 50 22.

Narodowy
Plac Teatralny 3.
692 0604.

Na Woli
Kasprzaka 22.
632 24 78.

Nowy
Puławska 37/39.
Map 6 E5.
849 35 51.

Polski
Karasia 2.
Map 2 E4.
826 79 92.

Powszechny
Zamoyskiego 20.
818 25 16.

Rozmaitości
Marszałkowska 8.
Map 6 D3.
629 45 54.

Scena Prezentacje
Żelazna 51/53.
Map 1 A5 & 5 B1.
620 82 88.

Staromiejski
Jezuicka 4.
Map 2 D2 & 4 D4.
635 80 15.

Teatr Adekwatny
Biuro Obsługi Widzów, Kanonia 8/1.
Map 2 D2 & 4 D4.
831 85 67.

Teatr Ochoty
Reja 9.
Map 5 B3.
825 85 44.

Teatr Studio
Palace of Culture and Science.
Map 1 C5 & 5 C1.
620 21 02.

Współczesny
Mokotowska 13.
Map 6 D3.
825 59 79.

OPERA AND BALLET

Teatr Wielki
Plac Teatralny 1.
Map 1 C3 & 3 C5.
826 50 19.

Warsaw Chamber Opera (Warszawska Opera Kameralna)
Aleja Solidarności 76b.
Map 3 B5 & 1 A3.
831 22 40.

MUSICAL THEATRES

Rampa
Kołowa 20.
679 89 76.

Roma – Teatr Muzyczny
Nowogrodzka 49.
Map 5 C2.
628 03 60.

Studio Buffo
Konopnickiej 6.
Map 6 E2.
625 47 09.

CLASSICAL MUSIC

Academy of Music Dedicated to Frederic Chopin (Akademia Muzyczna im F. Chopina)
Okólnik 2.
Map 2 E4 & 6 D1.
828 19 10.

Frederic Chopin Fellowship (Towarzystwo im Fryderyka Chopina)
Okólnik 1.
Map 2 E4 & 6 D1.
827 54 71.

Philharmonic (Filharmonia Narodowa)
Sienkiewicza 10.
Map 1 C5 & 5 C1.
827 7479.

Polish Radio Concert Studio (Studio Koncertowe Polskiego Radia)
Woronicza 17.
645 52 52.

Warsaw Fellowship of Music
Pałac Szustra, Morskie Oko 2.
Map 6 E5.
849 56 51.

CINEMAS

Atlantic
Chmielna 33.
Map 2 D5 & 6 D1.
827 08 94.

Bajka
Marszałkowska 138.
Map 1 C4.
826 69 66.

Capitol
Marszałkowska 115.
Map 1 B3 & 3 C5.
827 35 00.

Femina
Aleja Solidarności 115.
Map 3 B5 & 1 A3.
620 18 10.

Iluzjon
Narbutta 50a.
Map 5 C5.
646 12 60.

Kinoteka
Palace of Cilture, Plac Defilad 1.
Map 1 C5 & 5 C1.
826 19 61.

Kultura
Krakowskie Przedmieście 21/23.
Map 2 D3 & 4 D5.
826 33 35.

Luna
Marszałkowska 28.
Map 6 D3.
621 78 28.

Multikino
Al Ken 60.
644 66 60.

Muranów
Andersa 1.
Map 1 B2 & 3 B5.
831 03 58.

Ochota
Grójecka 65.
Map 5 A2.
822 24 73.

Rejs
Krakowskie Przedmieście 21/23.
Map 2 D3.
826 33 35.

Relax
Złota 8.
Map 1 C5 & 5 C1.
828 38 88.

Silver Screen
Putawska 21/29.
Map 6 D4.
852 88 88.

Wars
Rynek Nowego Miasta 5/7.
Map 1 C1 & 3 C4.
831 44 88.

Wisła
Plac Wilsona 2.
Map 3 A2.
839 23 65.

Music Clubs

Blues Bar
Agrykoli 1.
Map 6 E3.
628 57 47.

Empik Club Pub
Nowy Świat 15/17.
Map 2 E5 & 6 D1.
625 10 86.

Harenda
Krakowskie Przedmieście 4/6.
Map 2 D3 & 4 D5.
826 31 37.

Irish Pub
Miodowa 3.
Map 1 C2.
826 25 33.

Klub Giovanni
Krakowskie Przedmieście 24/28.
Map 2 D3 & 4 D5.
826 92 39.

Piwnica pod Harenda
Krakowskie Przedmieście 4/6.
Map 2 D3 & 4 D5.
826 31 37.

Prohibicja
Podwale 1/3.
635 62 11.

Riviera-Remont
Waryńskiego 12.
Map 6 D3.
660 9123.

Rynek Jazz Club
Rynek Starego Miasta 2.
Map 2 D1 & 4 D4.
831 23 75.

Stodoła
Batorego 10.
Map 5 C4.
825 86 25.

Swing Jazz Club
Jana Pawta 52.
831 0843.

Viking
Mazowiecka 12.
Map 2 D4.
827 31 51.

Nightclubs and Discotheques

Bar u Pana Michała
Freta 4.
Map 1 C1 & 3 C4.
635 87 44.

Cul de Sac
Foksal 2.
Map 2 E5 & 6 D1.
827 87 07.

Dziekanka
Krakowskie Przedmieście 56.
Map 2 D3 & 4 D5.

Grota
Pl. Defilad 1.
Enter by the main entrance of the Palace of Culture.
656 63 15.

Ground Zero
Wspólna 62.
Map 5 C2.
625 39 76.

Hades
Aleja Niepodległości 162.
Map 5 C4.
849 12 51.

Hybrydy-Vogue
Złota 7/9.
Map 2 D5 & 5 C1.
827 66 01.

Klub Medyka
Oczki 5/7.
Map 5 C2.
628 33 76.

Loch
Rynek Starego Miasta 29/31.
Map 2 D1 & 4 D4.
831 02 63.

Orpheus
Hotel Marriott, Aleje Jerozolimskie 65/79.
Map 5 C2.
630 54 16.

Park
Aleje Niepodległości 196.
Map 5 C4.

Tango
Smolna 15
Map 2 E5 & 6 E1.
622 19 19.

Trend
Aleja Krakowska 171.
846 09 94.

Yesterday
Szkolna 2/4.
Map 1 C4.
826 99 81.

Gay and Lesbian Clubs

Club Cocon
Brzozowa 37.
Map 2 D1 & 4 D4.
831 95 39.

Klub 69
Piękna 28.
Map 6 D2.
816 14 79.

Koźla Club
Koźla 10/12.
Map 1 C1 & 3 C4.

Między Nami (Entre Nous)
Bracka 20.
Map 2 D5 & 6 D1.
827 94 41.

Sports

First Warsaw Golf & Country Club (Rajszewo)
Rajszew 70.
782 44 55.

Inflancka
Inflancka 8.
831 92 29.

Legia
Łazienkowska 3.
Map 6 F2.
628 13 60.

Mera
Bohaterów Września 6/12.
822 93 82.

Służewiec Racetrack (Tor Wyścigów Konnych)
Puławska 266.
843 14 41.

Solec
Solec 71.
621 68 63.

Stegny Skating Rink (Tor Łyżwiarski Stegny)
Inspektowa 1.
842 21 92.

Torwar
Łazienkowska 6a.
Map 6 F2.

Wodnik
Abrahama 10.
673 82 25.

Wodny Park (Warszawianka)
Merliniego 9.
845 0130.

Children's Warsaw

Warsaw offers many attractions for both children and teenagers, and you can easily spend several days in the city without any fear of your children getting bored. There are funfairs, playgrounds, puppet theatres and toy shops, as well as adventure parks and the zoo. Other options include riding in a horse-drawn carriage or a miniature train around the Old Town. There are also tourist attractions that are not specifically aimed at children, but which nevertheless appeal to them. For instance, children enjoy the view from the observation terrace at the Palace of Culture and Science *(see p135)*, while the Museum of Technology *(see p134)* is educational and entertaining.

Playing in the Warsaw snow

Practical Tips

Children are warmly welcomed in Poland, and numerous hotels will either offer a reduced rate for children, or even allow them to stay free of charge *(see p195)*.

Visitor attractions which usually charge admission fees, such as museums, theatres and the zoo, also offer special entrance charges for children. Additionally, many museums allocate certain days (during school holidays) when admission is free. Children are also eligible for reduced-rate tickets on public transport *(see p251)*, while those below the age of four usually travel free.

A carriage ride through the streets of the Old Town

Shopping

The best place for shopping with children in Warsaw is the Smyk department store *(see p132)*. Occupying five levels, Smyk provides most things that a child (from a baby to a teenager) will want or need. These include a wide range of toys and sports equipment, together with a variety of clothes and shoes.

Sign for Kidiland toy shop

Children's clothes are also available at **5 10 15**, and at **Panorama** department store, while **Świat Dziecka** (Children's World) has a good selection of clothes and toys for young children. When shopping specifically for toys, the widest choice is provided by **Baba Jaga** (The Wicked Witch) and **Disney**.

If you are near the New Town, it is worth going to **Kleofas**, which is in the area.

Shop Addresses

Baba Jaga
Marszałkowska 76. **Map** 6 D2.

Disney
Emilii Plater 47.
Map 1 B5 & 5 C2.

5 10 15
Bracka 22. **Map** 2 D5 & 6 D1.

Kleofas
Mostowa 32.
Map 1 C1 & 3 C4.

Panorama
Witosa 31.

Świat Dziecka
Puławska 2. **Map** 6 D4.

Museums

Many of Warsaw's museums are of great interest to children, as well as adults. This certainly applies to the Museum of Technology (Muzeum Techniki, *see p134*),

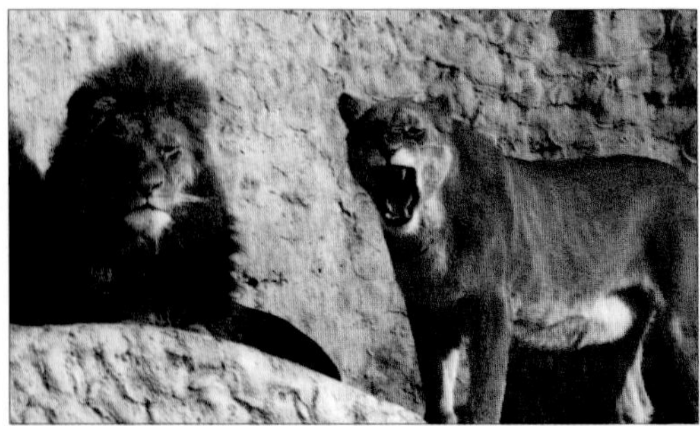

A lion and lioness in Warsaw's zoo

where numerous active displays and working models engage children's interest. The opening times for these museums are listed under the museum entries in this guide.

Theatres, Concerts and Circuses

Warsaw has three children's theatres, each with a repertoire that is aimed solely at the youngest members of the audience. These theatres are **Baj**, **Lalka** and **Guliwer**. Additionally, there are several theatres and opera houses that stage performances especially for children.

Classical music is particularly accessible to children at the Philharmonic (Filharmonia Narodowa), where special "child-friendly" performances are led by Aunty Jadzia. This entertaining, character can introduce children as young as two years old to the enchanting world of music.

Although Warsaw does not have a permanent circus, visiting circuses often pitch their tents in various parts of the city, providing shows at most times of the year.

Parks, Playgrounds and the Zoo

An ideal place to take children for a walk to escape the bustle of the city and to learn about wildlife is the Łazienki Park, where they can feed ducks, various birds and squirrels, and admire the colourful displays of peacocks' tails. Additionally, on Sunday mornings children can enjoy a pleasant ride on the ponies in the Łazienki Park.

An outing to one of the city's **Botanical Gardens** (Ogród Botaniczny) always provides a pleasurable expedition *(see p160)*. The main garden near Łazienki Park is open from May to October; another on the outskirts of town is open between April and October.

The **Zoo** (Ogród Zoologiczny, *see p174)* is situated on the picturesque right bank of the River Vistula.

Among Warsaw's many playgrounds and play centres, the most popular are **Hulakula**, Poland's largest family centre, **Orlando** in the Bródno district, and **Kolorado** in Jelonki. Both have fine attractions, including tunnels, slides and pools.

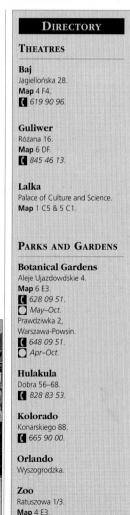

A typical performance at the Guliwer children's theatre

The "Choo-choo" miniature train which runs through the Old Town

Directory

Theatres

Baj
Jagiellońska 28.
Map 4 F4.
☎ *619 90 96.*

Guliwer
Różana 16.
Map 6 DF.
☎ *845 46 13.*

Lalka
Palace of Culture and Science.
Map 1 C5 & 5 C1.

Parks and Gardens

Botanical Gardens
Aleje Ujazdowdskie 4.
Map 6 E3.
☎ *628 09 51.*
◯ *May–Oct.*
Prawdziwka 2,
Warszawa-Powsin.
☎ *648 09 51.*
◯ *Apr–Oct.*

Hulakula
Dobra 56–68.
☎ *828 83 53.*

Kolorado
Konarskiego 88.
☎ *665 90 00.*

Orlando
Wyszogrodzka.

Zoo
Ratuszowa 1/3.
Map 4 E3.
☎ *619 40 41.*

E-2
E-3
116
122

Survival Guide

PRACTICAL INFORMATION

WARSAW HAS BECOME far more accessible to visitors over the past few years. New and refurbished hotels, restaurants and cafés have led the way in raising standards of service to Western levels, and broadened the choice considerably. Travel agents have also extended their range of services, while other considerations, such as public transport, currency exchange and shopping facilities, have greatly improved as well. All of the city's most popular attractions can easily be reached by public transport, while the centre of the city is best visited on foot. Although the cost of living in Warsaw is generally lower than in other European cities, prices in the finest restaurants and hotels are comparable. Warsaw is relatively safe, though as in any city visitors should be on their guard against thieves, and cars should only be left in guarded car parks.

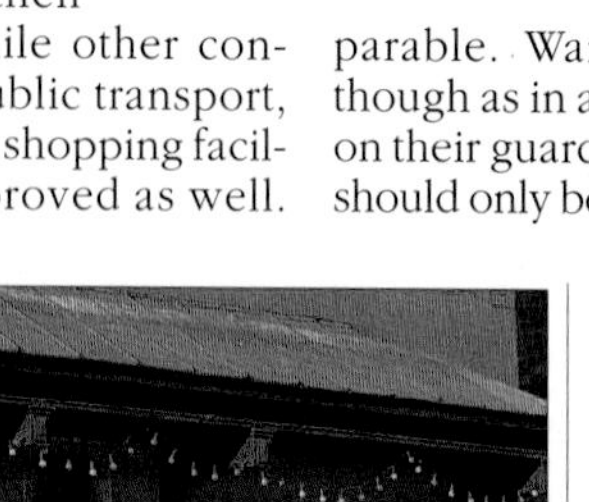

A carriage in the Old Town

The charming tourist information office in the Old Town

TOURIST INFORMATION

THE MOST COMPREHENSIVE tourist information office (Informacja Turystyczna) is located in Castle Square (Plac Zamkowy). They offer advice on visiting the city, as well as maps and guidebooks. Information on bed-and-breakfast accommodation is available from a kiosk in the Central Railway Station (Dworzec Centralny).

Anyone travelling further afield can purchase maps at the Atlas bookshop on Aleja Jana Pawła II (John Paul II Avenue). Hotels and guided tours in other Polish cities can be booked through **Orbis**.

ORBIS

Orbis logo

LANGUAGES SPOKEN

ENGLISH IS WIDELY spoken, particularly in hotels, restaurants, cafés, shops and other tourist venues, though it is less common at Polish railway stations. Many Varsovians speak at least some English, with German also often spoken as a second language. It should be possible, for instance, to get directions from local people in the capital, though not always at the first attempt.

WHEN TO VISIT

SPRING, SUMMER or early autumn are equally enjoyable times to visit Warsaw, and the month of May is often when it is at its best. However, this is also a favourite month for school trips, so the city is full of school children.

During the summer, the city has an abundance of fast food and ice cream stalls, while pavements and squares are lined with cafés, some offering live music and dancing.

OPENING HOURS

OPENING TIMES of museums and galleries are detailed in this guide. Generally they are closed on Mondays. However, there are exceptions, such as Wilanów, which is closed on Tuesdays. Most tourist attractions are usually open from 9am–5pm. However, out of season (from 1 October until 30 April) museum opening hours are shorter. Moreover, some locations, such as the Botanical Gardens and Arkadia Park in Nieborów, are closed during the winter.

Churches are open from early morning mass until the last evening mass (typically from 6am to 10pm). Monasteries have irregular visiting hours, but are usually open on Sunday afternoons.

Coach used by Mazurkas Travel

Delicatessens and food shops are usually open 7am–7pm from Monday to Saturday. Supermarkets have longer opening hours, sometimes until 10pm, and usually on Sunday mornings as well.

Department stores usually open from 9am to 8pm, with most other shops open from 10am to 7pm, Monday to Friday, and from 9am to 2pm on Saturday. All-night chemists, which are also open on Sundays, can be found in each district *(see p239)*. Banks in Poland are open 8am–6pm, from Monday to Friday.

Bars, cafés and restaurants set their own opening times. Restaurants tend to open at about noon and remain open, without an afternoon break, until late at night. In practice, they usually remain open until the last customers leave.

ZASP theatre booking office

Listings Magazines

Warsaw provides a wide range of cultural activities, with a variety of galleries and museums, as well as theatres and concert halls.

There are two English-language listings magazines: *Warszawa, What, Where, When*, and *Welcome to Warsaw*. Both are available free of charge and published once a month. They can be obtained from hotel reception desks and tourist offices. There are of course many Polish listings magazines, including the comprehensive *Warszawski Informator Kulturalny*. Theatre and concert tickets can be bought in advance from **ZASP** booking offices.

Admission Charges

Admission to museums is relatively inexpensive. In addition, each museum also operates its own system of reduced prices for children, students and senior citizens.

Admission is not charged when visiting churches or the cathedral, though a contribution can be left in the offertory box. This box is usually to be found in the porch.

Sightseeing

The easiest way to see Warsaw's sights is through the services offered by travel agents. **Mazurkas Travel** organize sightseeing tours of Warsaw with experienced guides, including visits to the Royal Castle *(see pp70–73)* and Wilanów Palace *(see pp168–71)*. Day trips to outlying attractions such as Żelazowa Wola, the manor house where Frederic Chopin was born *(see p182)*, and the Baroque Nieborów Palace, adjacent to the romantic park of Arkadia *(see p180)* are also available. More extensive trips can be arranged to other historic cities, such as Kraków and Gdańsk.

Budget travellers can join less expensive tours organized by **PTTK** (the Polish Tourist Organization). These include group walks around the city, as well as weekend excursions outside Warsaw.

One delightful option is a ride on the "choo-choo" miniature train. Its route runs from Castle Square, through the Old Town and New Town, and along the Royal Route. Alternatively, horse-drawn carriages can be found in the Old Town Market Square, for a leisurely tour of the city. English-speaking guides, walks and tours are available from the official agency, **Agencja Usług Przedwodnickich i Turystycznych**.

Admission ticket to Wilanów

Directory

Tourist Offices and Travel Agents

American Express
Sienna 39.
Map 1 B5 & 5B1.
581 51 00, 581 52 52.

Mazurkas Travel
Nowogrodzka 24/26.
Map 6 D1. 629 12 49.

Orbis
Bracka 16.
Map 6 D1. 827 71 40.

Guide and Tourist Services Agency (Agencja Usług Przedwodnickich i Turystycznych)
Sobieskiego 72–74.
657 21 78.

Logo of the Polish tourist office

PTTK
Litewska 11/13.
Map 6 D3.
629 39 47.

Kasprowicza 40.
834 54 43.

Tarczyńska 1/59.
Map 5 B2.
822 2517, 822 14 35.

Tourist Information Office
Plac Zamkowy 1/13.
Map 2 D2 & 4 D5.
635 18 81.

ZASP
Aleje Jerozolimskie 25.
Map 2 D5 & 6 D1.
621 94 54.

Security and Health

WARSAW'S STREETS are generally safe for tourists, and this applies especially within the central area, although sensible precautions should always be taken. Anyone suffering a minor health problem should seek advice at a pharmacy, while hotels can usually arrange a doctor's visit. British passport holders are entitled to free medical treatment in Poland, though it is best to take out insurance cover for every possible eventuality.

Personal Security

TOURISTS CAN VISIT most of Warsaw without anxiety, as it is very rare that tourists are attacked. However, as in all major cities, visitors should be aware of possible dangers, and should avoid taking unnecessary risks. Women are advised not to walk around unaccompanied late at night, and there are areas where visitors should either be on their guard, or avoid completely. This includes the Praga district, on the Right Bank of the Vistula, and particularly the area around Brzeska Street.

The atmosphere at the Eastern Station (Dworzec Wschodni) may be threatening, especially if travelling alone, and this also applies to Stadion Station and Różycki Market. Gambling at the market, such as the card and dice games, should be avoided, as they are run dishonestly. The most common street crime, however, is pickpocketing. Operating in gangs, the pickpockets often crowd unsuspecting victims. Handbags should be kept securely fastened, and always maintain a grasp of bags you are carrying. Also, do not carry valuables or your passport in trouser pockets (though carrying a form of identification is advisable). Extra care should always be taken at stations, and when travelling by train, tram or bus. Valuables should not be left unattended in cars, and it is safer to remove car radios if possible. Cars should be left in a guarded car park (which are becoming the norm). Western makes of car, such as BMW, Volkswagen Golf, Mercedes and Audi, are the ones most prone to theft. Public transport is best avoided late at night – it is safer to use official taxis, with a lit-up sign.

Sign outside police stations

Badge worn by traffic wardens

Policeman

Municipal policewoman

Municipal policeman

Beggars

BEGGARS HAVE BECOME a widespread sight in Warsaw. They are frequently encountered on the city centre's principal streets, many having arrived from neighbouring countries, such as Romania. While not dangerous, they can be extremely persistent. The best way to ward off unwanted advances is simply by saying a firm "no".

Police and Security Services

WARSAW IS PATROLLED by policemen and women, who belong to the various branches of the Polish police force. Private security firms also perform a similar role. Police officers patrol the city on foot and in clearly marked blue and white police cars. They are armed, and have the power to stop anyone they regard as suspicious.

Any criminal acts and related incidents should be reported immediately at a police station. The main police stations are indicated on the Street Finder maps *(see pp260–65)*.

Traffic police are principally concerned with driving offences and ensuring that traffic flows as smoothly as possible. They act decisively in any cases of drink-driving, since it is illegal in Poland to drive with any alcohol present in the bloodstream. Penalties for breaking this law are severe *(see p249)*, and random breath tests are conducted regularly. Similarly, penalties for speeding and parking offences are considerable. Anyone who is involved in a serious road accident is required by law to contact the traffic police, as well as calling for an ambulance and the fire brigade.

In addition to the regular police force, there are traffic wardens *(straż miejska)*, who enforce parking regulations.

Lastly, you may see private security guards, usually dressed in black uniforms, who frequently patrol private property, as well as many public events. Many were formerly employed in the police force.

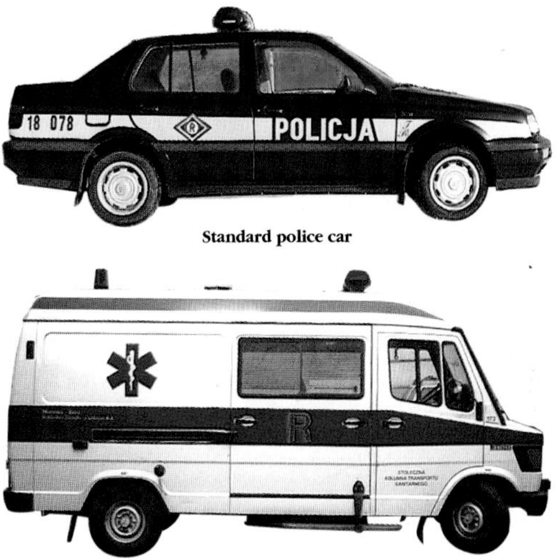

Standard police car

Warsaw ambulance

Health Care

Medical treatment can be obtained in Warsaw, either under the national health service or privately.

For minor health problems, there are pharmacies situated throughout the city. A selection of 24-hour pharmacies is also included on this page.

Do bear in mind that if you are taking any medication it is essential to travel with more than enough to last you for the duration for your trip; GPs will provide you with supplies on request.

First aid is provided free of charge in hospitals, while other types of hospital treatment may incur a charge. In more serious cases, or in the event of a medical emergency, the ambulance service is on call 24 hours a day. Hospitals with emergency casualty units are indicated on the Street Finder *(see pp260–65)*. However, it is advisable to take out fully comprehensive insurance, and to keep your policy documents with you. Visitors should also carry their passports to identify themselves to hospital staff, and obtain a receipt if payment is needed for any medical treatment.

Citizens of the following countries are entitled to free medical treatment in Poland: Belarus, the Czech Republic, Denmark, Finland, Sweden, Tunisia, UK, Ukraine, plus Mongolia, China and countries of former Yugoslavia.

APTEKA

Pharmacy sign

Lost Property

Great care should be taken with personal property at all times. Luggage should never be left unattended, particularly at the airport and at the rail and bus stations. Valuables should not be carried when sightseeing. Similarly, only take as much money as you think you will need, ideally using a money belt. Traveller's cheques are the safest method of carrying larger sums of money.

Although the chances of recovering lost property are usually minimal, any losses should still be reported to the city's Lost Property Office (Biuro Rzeczy Znalezionych).

Lost property should also be reported to the police and a reference number or official receipt obtained in order to make an insurance claim.

Lost or stolen passports should be reported straight away at your country's embassy in Warsaw *(see p244)*.

Directory

Emergency Services

Ambulance
999. *628 24 24.*

City Police
986.

Fire
998. *844 0071.*

Police
997.
112 (SOS from mobile phones.)

Medical Assistance

24-Hour Dental Clinic
Ludna 10. **Map** 6 F1.
625 01 02 & 625 01 05.

Pharmacy Information
911

24-Hour Pharmacies
Dworzec Centralny. **Map** 6 C1.
825 69 86.
Freta 13/15. **Map** 1 C1.
831 50 91.
Widok 19. **Map** 2 D5.
827 35 93.

Centralny Szpital Kliniczny WAM (Central Clinical Hospital)
Koszykowa 78.
684 31 72.

Informacja Medyczna (24-hour Medical Information Service)
9439.

Other Useful Numbers

Car Accidents
628 13 13.

City Information
General information on cultural events and local services.
629 84 89, 654 24 47.

Lost Property
Floriańska 10. **Map** 2 F1.
619 56 68.

Vehicle Assistance
981.

Wake-up Calls
917.

Banking and Local Currency

PKO Bank logo

Warsaw's banks and currency exchange facilities have become far more user-friendly to visitors since the democratic elections in 1989. Bureaux de change can be found easily throughout the city, and these frequently offer a more favourable exchange rate than banks. At the same time, credit cards and traveller's cheques are increasingly widely accepted, particularly by hotels, restaurants, travel agents and shops.

Sign for an exchange office

Banks and Bureaux de Change

Central Warsaw has plenty of banks offering a broad range of financial services. The usual opening hours are from 8am to 6pm. During the lunch hour (around 1–2pm) fewer tills generally operate, which obviously means that service is a little slower.

In addition to the exchange facilities provided by banks, there are bureaux de change all over the city. Rates vary between outlets, but bureaux de change generally offer better rates than banks.

Some bureaux de change offer a 24-hour service, but this option is usually reflected in a higher commission. One such bureau de change is located at the Central Railway Station (Dworzec Centralny). However, the station is a notorious low-life haunt late at night, and so it is not advisable to go there then.

Hotels also offer currency exchange, though their charges are usually higher. Currency should not be exchanged with "operators" in the street, as they are likely to be using counterfeit money.

Credit Cards

Credit cards, such as American Express, VISA and MasterCard, are increasingly accepted by local establishments – hotels, restaurants, nightclubs, car hire firms, travel agents, and more exclusive shops.

The logos of any accepted credit cards are usually displayed prominently by the entrance and at cash tills.

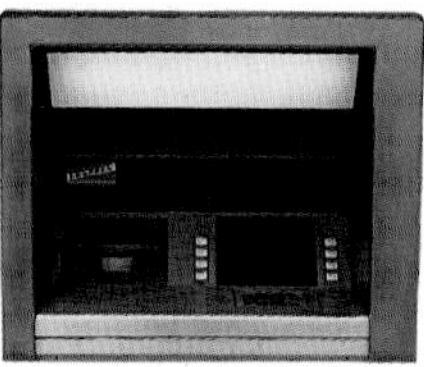
Bankomat cash dispenser

However, when paying by credit card it is advisable to ensure that no extra conditions apply, such as a minimum spend. Moreover, in privately owned shops a small discount is sometimes offered to customers who are able to pay in cash.

Major international credit cards can also be used to make cash withdrawals from banks. Additionally, American Express cards can be used to withdraw cash from the relevant Bankomat automatic service tills, as well as the American Express office.

Triangular pediment on the PKO SA Bank headquarters

Directory

Banks

BIG Bank Gdański SA
Karowa 20. **Map** 2 D3.
☎ *826 04 61.*

Bank Handlowy
Chałubińskiego 8.
Map 5 C2.
☎ *690 30 00.*
Aleje Jerozolimskie 65/79.
Map 5 A2.
☎ *830 06 76.*

Bank Polska Kasa Opieki SA (PKO SA)
Plac Bankowy 2. **Map** 1 B3.
☎ *531 10 00.*
Czackiego 21/23.
Map 2 D4.
☎ *661 30 17, 661 20 00.*

Bank Pnemysłowo Handlowy PBK SA
Nowy Swiat 6/12.
Map 6 D1.
☎ *661 77 77*
Jasna 8.
Map 1 C4 & 6 D1.
☎ *622 01 00.*

Narodowy Bank Polski
Plac Powstańców Warszawy 4.
Map 2 D4.

Bureaux de Change

American Express Travel
Sienna 39.
Map 1 B5 & 5 B1.
☎ *581 51 00, 581 52 52.*

Bilion
Piękna 11.
Map 6 D2.
☎ *625 14 25.*

Kantor
Rynek Starego Miasta 25.
Map 2 D2.
☎ *635 79 88.*

Podziemia Dworca Centralnego
Box 45. ☎ *630 29 66.*
Box 75. ☎ *630 29 90.*

Lost Credit Cards

Polcard, Dział Autoryzacji
For MasterCard and VISA.
☎ *515 30 00.*

Cash and Traveller's Cheques

The Polish unit of currency is the złoty, which literally means "golden", and it is generally abbreviated to "zł". There is also a smaller unit: the groszy. One hundred groszy are equivalent to one złoty. Traveller's cheques can be cashed in bureaux de change, as well as most hotels and many (but not all) banks. **American Express** and Thomas Cook are perhaps the best known brands, and both have offices in Warsaw.

Bank Notes

Bank notes are issued in denominations of 10, 20, 50, 100 and 200 złoty. All bank notes portray important Polish kings.

200 złoty

50 złoty

100 złoty

20 złoty

10 złoty

Coins

Coins are issued in these denominations: 1, 2, 5, 10, 20 and 50 groszy, and 1, 2 and 5 złoty. All coins feature an emblem of the Polish eagle on the reverse side.

5 złoty

2 złoty

1 złoty

5 groszy

10 groszy

20 groszy

50 groszy

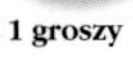

1 groszy

2 groszy

Bank Notes

Formerly bank notes featured celebrated Poles, such as Tadeusz Kościuszko, Chopin and the astronomer Copernicus. Notes from recent years feature Polish kings: Zygmunt I Stary (200 zł), Władysław Jagiełło (100 zł), Kazimierz Wielki (50 zł), Bolesław Chrobry (20 zł) and Mieszko I (10 zł).

Telephone and Postal Services

THE POLISH TELECOMMUNICATIONS AGENCY is called Telekomunikacja Polska, and the postal service is Poczta Polska. Various improvements have been made to both services in the past few years. However, queues in post offices can still be long and slow-moving, while finding a public telephone that works can also be a time-consuming endeavour.

Using the Telephone

THE BEST PLACE to find a public telephone in working order is in a post office. Hotels also provide public telephones in their lobbies. All modern phones are push-button, though older dial telephones are not uncommon.

There are no coin-operated public telephone boxes in Poland. All phones operate with the use of a telephone card *(karty)*, available at post offices or newspaper kiosks.

For intercity calls within Poland, there are three tariffs. The highest tariff is between 8am–6pm. From 6pm–10pm the charge is 25 per cent lower; while the charge is 50 per cent lower between 10pm–8am. Weekend calls are even less expensive. For international calls a single tariff applies for each country, regardless of the time of day.

A telephone kiosk

To make a call from a public phone, first check that on lifting the receiver there is a continuous tone. After dialling there is a short initial tone, followed by a longer intermittent tone. A short, rapidly repeating tone indicates that the number is engaged.

To ring Warsaw from the UK, dial 00 48 22, then the subscriber number. When calling the UK, dial 00 44, the city code (omitting the first 0) and then the subscriber number.

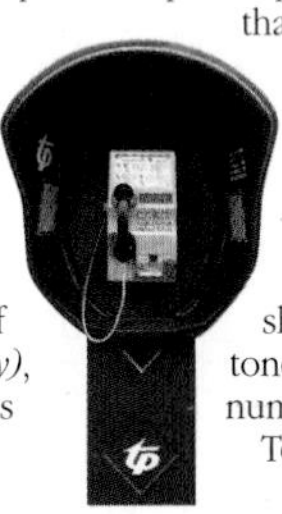

Accessing The Internet

WARSAW HAS plenty of public access to computers and the internet. Free internet access is often available at public libraries and there are several internet cafés which usually charge by the minute. Internet Cafés include Pub Internetowy (Piękna 68a) and Enigma (Al Solidarności 74a) which is open 24 hours.

One of the various types of telephone booths in the city

Using a Telephone Card

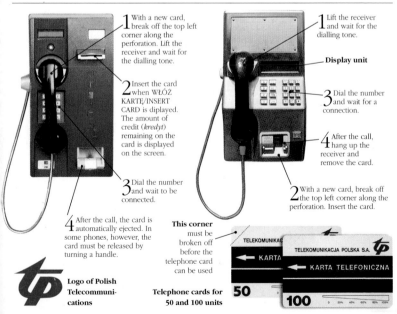

1 With a new card, break off the top left corner along the perforation. Lift the receiver and wait for the dialling tone.

2 Insert the card when WŁÓŻ KARTĘ/INSERT CARD is diplayed. The amount of credit (*kredyt*) remaining on the card is displayed on the screen.

3 Dial the number and wait to be connected.

4 After the call, the card is automatically ejected. In some phones, however, the card must be released by turning a handle.

1 Lift the receiver and wait for the dialling tone.

Display unit

3 Dial the number and wait for a connection.

4 After the call, hang up the receiver and remove the card.

2 With a new card, break off the top left corner along the perforation. Insert the card.

This corner must be broken off before the telephone card can be used

TELEKOMUNIKACJA POLSKA S.A.
KARTA TELEFONICZNA
50
100

Telephone cards for 50 and 100 units

Logo of Polish Telecommunications

Customers inside the main post office in Warsaw

Mobile Phones

Mobile telephone coverage is growing in Poland so if you have access to roaming facilities you should have no problem using your mobile in Warsaw. Remember to dial the Warsaw area code when making local calls. For other locations in Poland dial the appropriate area code followed by the subscriber's number.

Polish Postal Service logo

Postal Services

Post offices offer an increasingly comprehensive and varied range of services. There are post offices throughout the city, though Warsaw's main post office, **Poczta Główna**, is located on Świętokrzyska Street. It is open 24 hours a day, seven days a week. As well as the usual services – sending letters, packages, and telegrams, selling and mailing money orders (within Poland), and providing telephone directories – this post office also offers customers telex, fax, and telephone booths. It also provides a poste restante service. At a special counter, stamp collectors can also purchase commemorative sets of stamps.

Queues operate according to numbered tickets. On entering the post office, a ticket should be collected from a computerized machine. You must then wait until this number is displayed above a counter, indicating when and where you will be served.

Red letter box, used for mail for destinations outside the city

Posting Letters

Stamps are sold in newsagents' kiosks as well as in post offices, though newsagents will only sell stamps together with postcards. Around Warsaw, you will see green letter boxes, which are only for post destined within the city itself. For post to other destinations within Poland, and for all overseas mail, look for a red letter box. Deliveries within Poland usually take two or three days, while overseas post can take up to seven days. An express postal service is available for urgent deliveries, together with a special courier service (at a much higher price). International courier companies, such as **DHL**, also have offices in Warsaw.

Decorative Polish postal stamps

Useful Addresses

American Express
Sienna 39.
581 5100 or 581 5252.

DHL
Wirazowa 35.
0801 345 345.

Poczta Główna
Świętokrzyska 31/33. **Map** 1 C4.
826 60 01 or 827 0052.

Useful Telephone Numbers

- Local (Warsaw) directory enquiries: dial 913.
- National (Poland) directory enquiries: dial 912.
- International operator: dial 901.
- Warsaw city code: within Poland dial 01033 or 01044 then 22 and the local Warsaw number; from abroad dial 22.

To call overseas:

- Dial 0 and wait for signal. Dial 0 again and follow it with code of the country, the area code (minus the initial 0), followed by the subscriber number.

Additional Information

Disabled Travellers

Facilities for the disabled are still limited in Warsaw. Special lifts operate at air terminals and at metro stations, but access to most offices and shops is still difficult for those in a wheelchair. The numbers of cars parked on pavements throughout the city can also present serious obstacles.

There are, however, some hotels that have rooms specially equipped for the disabled *(see pp201–3)*. Among the many organizations that can provide assistance, the most established are listed below. Information for disabled travellers is available from the **Association for Assistance for the Blind and Deaf** and several companies offer specialized transport.

Useful Addresses

Association for Assistance for the Blind and Deaf (Towarzystwo Pomocy Głucho-Niewidomym))
Konwiktorska 9.
635 69 70.

Polish Association for the Blind (Polski Związek Niewidomych)
Konwiktorska 9.
813 33 83.

Polish Association for the Deaf (Polski Związek Głuchych)
Podwale 23.
831 40 71.

Polish Society for the Fight Against Disability (Polskie Towarzystwo Walki z Kalectwem)
Oleandrów 4/10.
825 98 39, 825 92 81.

Transport for Disabled People
Taxi service for disabled passengers.
919.
Tus – transport service for disabled people.
831 93 31.

Customs and Currency Regulations

Citizens of most European countries, and many outside Europe (including the US), need a passport valid for six months after the date of arrival, to enter Poland. Visitors from other countries must first obtain a visa.

There is no duty on purchases of personal items or gifts to the value of 70 Euros. Duty is charged on cigarettes and alcohol. A special permit is needed to export antiques. Firearms need special permission. You can bring unlimited foreign currency into Poland but a form must be completed on arrival, as you cannot depart with more money than you brought in.

An ISIC card

If you have any enquiries regarding imports and exports, contact the **Customs Information Office** 694 31 94.

Students

It is worth having a valid ISIC (International Student Identity Card) if you are visiting Warsaw. These are easily obtained on payment of a small fee from schools, colleges and places of further education, and can be renewed annually until you reach the age of 26. This entitles the bearer to reduced rates in museums and international students' hostels (which are open during holiday periods), as well as reduced fares on international rail and air travel. Reductions are not available, however, on Warsaw's public transport system. Holders of IYHF (International Youth Hostel Federation) cards are entitled to reduced charges at youth hostels *(see pp194–5)*. Eurocard holders may receive discounts in shops, bars, museums and exhibitions.

Television and Radio

Various satellite channels, such as CNN, Sky and MTV, are generally available to visitors staying in larger and more expensive hotels. These channels show news, films and other feature programmes in several languages. The most popular

Embassies and Consulates

Australia
Nowogrodzka 11. **Map** 5 B2.
521 34 44.

Austria
Gagarina 34. **Map** 6 F4.
841 00 81.

Canada
Matejki 1/5. **Map** 6 E2.
584 31 00, 584 33 01.

France
Puławska 17. **Map** 6 D4.
529 30 00.

Germany
Dąbrowiecka 30.
617 30 11.

Israel
Krzywickiego 24. **Map** 5 C3.
825 00 28.

Italy
Plac Dąbrowskiego 6.
Map 3 C5 & 1 C4.
826 34 71.

Russia
Belwederska 49. **Map** 6 E4.
621 34 53.

United Kingdom
Aleja Róż 1. **Map** 6 D2.
628 10 01.

USA
Al Ujazdowskie 29/31. **Map** 6 E2.
628 30 41.

television channels in Warsaw are broadcast in Polish. This includes stations 1 and 2, the city-wide channel WOT and the national POLSAT and TVN.

The most popular music programmes are broadcast by the "Trójce" station. Other stations for pop and rock music are Radio Z (107.5 FM), RMF (91.0 FM), Radio Kolor (103 FM) and Wa-Wa (89.8 FM).

However, the state-run Polish Radio (Polskie Radio) is the main broadcaster in Poland. Its two main stations are PR1, which is on 92.0 FM and PR2 on 102.4 FM. Other stations broadcasting in the Warsaw area include Radio Bis (102.4 FM), Radio Eska (102.0 FM), Radio dla Ciebie (101.0 FM), Rozgłosnia Harcerska (101.5 FM) and a Catholic radio station, Radio Maryja, which is on 96.5 FM.

The listings magazine *Warszawa What, Where, When*

Newspapers and Magazines

Foreign newspapers are readily available throughout Warsaw in hotel kiosks, certain bookshops *(see p222)* and the many Ruch kiosks.

Among the English-language publications produced in Warsaw are *Warsaw Voice* and *Warsaw Business Journal*. There are also monthly listings magazines, such as *Warszawa What, Where, When* (written in both English and German), *Welcome to Warsaw* (English), *Spotkania z Warszawa Kalejdoskop Kulturalny (Cultural Kaleidoscope)*.

Among Polish newspapers the most popular are *Życie Warszawy, Gazeta Wyborcza, Rzeczpospolita* and *Życie*.

***The Warsaw Voice*, the most popular English paper in Warsaw**

Electrical Appliances

Warsaw's electricity supply is 220 V. Plugs are the standard continental type, featuring two round pins.

A European travel adapter will enable you to use electrical appliances (this should ideally be purchased prior to your arrival in Warsaw).

Warsaw Time

Warsaw is one hour ahead of Greenwich Mean Time. During summer time, which runs from the end of March until the end of September, clocks go forward by 1 hour to daylight-saving time.

Places of Worship

Methodist Church (Kościół Ewangelicki Metodystyczny)
Mokotowska 12.
Map 6 D3. *628 53 28.*
11am Sun.

Mosque (Muzułmańskie)
Wiertnicza 103.
1pm (winter), noon (summer) Fri.
842 91 74

Polish Autocephalic Orthodox Church (Polski Autokefaliczny Kościół Prawosławny)
Aleja Solidarności 52.
Map 1 A3, 3 B5. *619 08 86.*
9am and 5pm Mon–Fri; 8am and 10am Sun.

Polish National Church (Kościół Polskokatolicki)
Szwoleżerów 2. **Map** 6 F3
841 37 43.
11am Sun.

Protestant Calvinist Church (Kościół Ewangelicko-Augsburski)
Plac Małachowskiego 1. **Map** 2 D4.
827 68 17.
10:30am Sun.

Protestant Reformed Church (Kościół Ewangelicko-Reformowany)
Aleja Solidarności 76a. **Map** 1 B3.
831 45 22.
10am Sun.

Seventh Day Adventists Church (Kościół Adwentystów Dnia Siódmego)
Foksal 8. **Map** 2 E5, 6 D1.
826 25 06.
9:30am–noon Sat; 5–6:30pm Sun.

Synagogue (Żydowskie)
Twarda 6. **Map** 1 B5, 5 B1.
620 43 24.
9:30am Sat.

Whitsuntide Church (Kościół Zielonoświątkowy)
Sienna 68/70. **Map** 1 A5, 5 B1.
624 85 75.
6pm Fri; 11am Sun.

A Roman Catholic priest conducting the celebration of Mass

Getting to Warsaw

Warsaw lies at the heart of Europe, and has excellent rail and air links with the rest of the continent. The airport is close to the city centre, and there are regular flights from major European cities, as well as from the USA, Southeast Asia and the Middle East. LOT Polish Airlines, the national carrier, offers flights from many countries. Poland's railway system is both efficient and inexpensive, with Warsaw's main station centrally located in the capital. The cheapest, though slowest, way to reach Warsaw is by coach. However, the number of motorways under construction in Poland means road travel, by coach or car, is also improving rapidly.

LOT aeroplane

Air Travel

Warsaw has direct air links with over 70 cities in 40 countries. These include daily connections with many European cities, and regular flights from North American cities such as Chicago, New York, Montreal and Toronto. There are no direct flights from Australia, but there are connections via Southeast Asia or several European cities, such as London and Paris.

Flights from London take 2 hours 15 minutes, from Paris 2 hours, and from New York about 9 hours 40 minutes.

Twenty-five airlines use Okęcie Airport, including **British Airways**, **Delta Airlines**, **Lufthansa** and **Air France**. In addition to international flights, **LOT** also offers internal flights to cities such as Poznań and Kraków.

Tickets

Apex tickets usually offer the best value, with savings of 30–40 per cent on the economy fare. However, these tickets must be booked up to one month in advance, and have a fixed return date. Bucket shops also offer reduced fares, while students, children and senior citizens usually qualify for discounts.

Airlines

Aeroflot
Aleje Jerozolimskie 29.
Map 6 D1.
☎ *628 17 10.*

Air France
Krucza 21.
Map 6 D2.
☎ *628 12 81.*

British Airways
Krucza 49.
Map 6 D1.
☎ *529 90 00.*

Delta Air Lines
Królewska 11.
Map 1 C4.
☎ *827 84 61.*

KLM
Krzywickiego 34.
Map 6 D2.
☎ *862 70 00.*

LOT
Aleje Jerozolimskie 65/79.
☎ *0801 30 09 52.*

Lufthansa
Warsaw Tower, Sienna 39.
Map 1 B5 & 5 B1.
☎ *0801 31 23 12, 338 13 00 (reservations).*

SAS
Warsaw Tower, Sienna 39.
Map 1 B5 & 5 B1.
☎ *850 05 00.*

LOT flight attendant at Okęcie Airport

Okęcie Airport

Okęcie is Warsaw's only airport handling international air traffic, and is conveniently situated just 6 km (4 miles) south of the city centre. The airport originally dates from 1933, but the present terminals were built in 1992, and have the capacity to handle approximately 3.5 million passengers annually.

The new airport building is easy to negotiate, with one terminal for international flights and an adjacent terminal for domestic flights.

Facilities at the airport include airline offices, travel agents, banks and currency-exchange counters, a post office, duty-free shops, souvenir shops, restaurants, cafés, bars and car hire.

The logo of City Line coaches, serving Okęcie from the city centre

City Connections

Regular bus services link Okęcie Airport with the centre of Warsaw and the outlying suburbs. Bus 175 operates between the airport and the city centre, with bus 188 operating between the airport and Praga. These are Warsaw City Transport buses, for which tickets are bought at newspaper kiosks, and cancelled in a ticket machine on boarding the bus. Taxis are available from the airport, with an information desk situated in the Arrivals Lounge. Visitors are strongly advised to pick a firm recognized by local authorities. It is best to avoid taxis waiting outside the terminal building, or drivers touting for business within it, as they are far more expensive than the standard firms. Currently three firms have been licensed by the city authorities: **Merc, MPT and Sawa-Taxi**. Radio taxis from the city can also be booked at the airport *(see p252)*. Due to its high running costs, the AirportCity bus service linking the airport with the city's principal hotels was discontinued in 1999. If you are travelling to a pre-booked hotel, you may be able to arrange to be collected by taxi at the airport by ordering a hotel taxi in advance when you make your booking, However, some hotels charge a very high mark-up on this, and their taxis are generally much more expensive than others.

Inside the terminal building at Warsaw's Okęcie Airport

Luggage trolley

LOT Airlines sponsored taxi

Warsaw's Air Links with Europe

Warsaw has good air links, not only with numerous European cities, but also with countries of the former Soviet Union and the Balkan states.

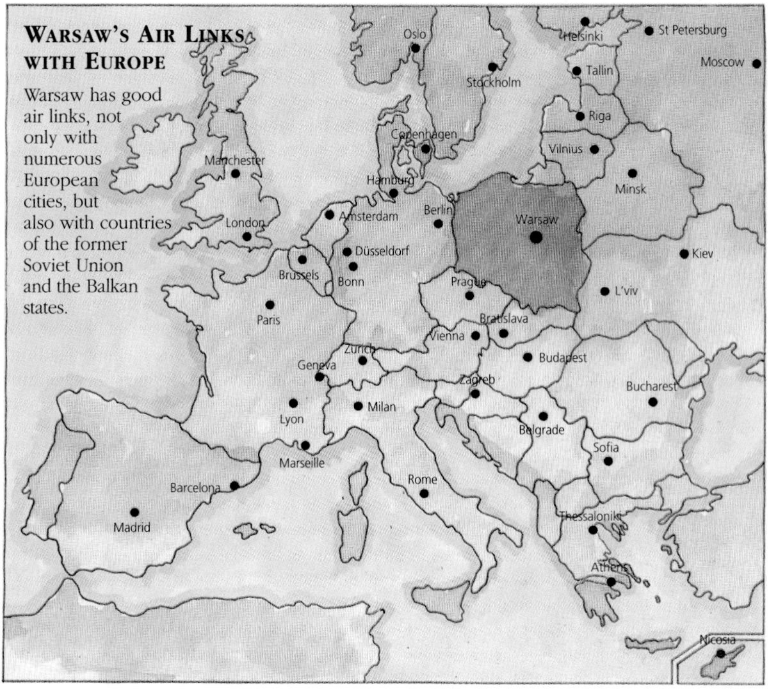

Travelling by Rail

Warsaw offers good international rail connections. The journey from the UK is relatively expensive but at just over 24 hours, it is quicker than a coach. Rail travel also offers the flexibility to stop off en route. Bookings can be made though **Trains Europe**.

Rail tickets within Poland are inexpensive, and Warsaw's central position makes the city an ideal base from which to explore the rest of Poland.

The extensive Polish railway network is operated by the state-owned PKP (Polskie Koleje Państwowe). The trains fall into several categories: express trains for long distance journeys with few stops; fast trains offering a greater number of stops; and local services which stop frequently.

Intercity trains also operate on principal routes. Intercity trains are more comfortable and faster than express services, but they also require seats to be reserved. A seat reservation should be arranged at the time of buying the ticket.

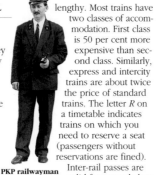

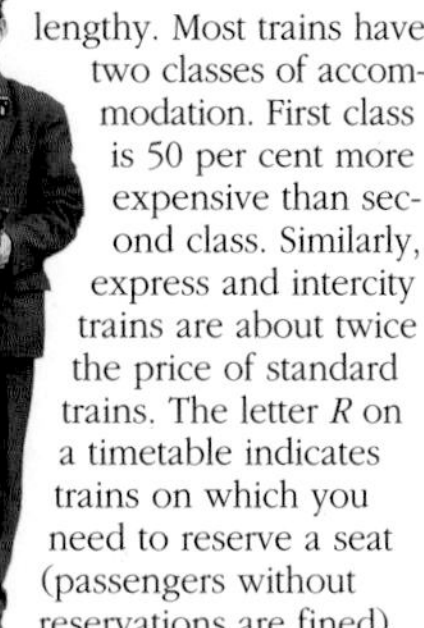
PKP railwayman

Ticket hall at the Central Railway Station

Trains Europe
☎ *0900 195 01 01.*

Buying Tickets

Tickets can be bought at railway stations or in advance from Orbis travel offices *(see pp236–7)*. When buying tickets at the station, allow at least half an hour before the departure time, as queues for tickets are often lengthy. Most trains have two classes of accommodation. First class is 50 per cent more expensive than second class. Similarly, express and intercity trains are about twice the price of standard trains. The letter *R* on a timetable indicates trains on which you need to reserve a seat (passengers without reservations are fined). Inter-rail passes are valid for second-class travel throughout Poland.

Railway Stations

Warsaw's Central Railway Station (Dworzec Centralny, *see p136)* is the largest and busiest railway station in the whole of Poland.

Most international trains pass through this station, which is located in the city centre by the Palace of Culture and Science. The station platforms are all below ground, with the main hall and ticket office situated on ground level. Passageways between the two levels contain a left luggage area, as well as 24-hour currency exchange counters, shops and some snack bars.

To the west of the city centre is Warszawa Zachodnia. This station is a departure point for many trains heading north and east, and is linked to the adjacent coach station. Similarly, trains heading west generally go from Warszawa Wschodnia, in the Praga district, to the east of the city centre.

Travelling by Coach

Coaches are the cheapest form of public transport – and quite probably the most reliable – whether you are travelling to Warsaw from other European countries, or travelling within Poland itself. Coaches offer the most comprehensive public transport network; the system reaches almost every town and even many villages. The state-owned company **PKS** (Państwowa Komunikacja Samochodowa) offers the largest number of potential destinations, with three types of service: local, intercity and long-distance. Warsaw has two PKS terminals: Warsaw Central, adjacent to the Central Railway Station, and Warszawa Zachodnia in the district of Ochota.

The privately owned coach company **Polski Express** is the principal alternative for those wishing to embark upon longer journies. Although the company offers fewer destinations than PKS, the coaches tend to be newer and more comfortable – and probably just that little bit more safe on the hair-pin bends – while journey times are usually faster and tickets are generally cheaper. Polski Express coaches operate from Okęcie Airport, but all services conveniently also stop adjacent to the Central Railway Station.

Polski Express coach

PKS
☎ *823 63 94.*
Polski Express
☎ *620 03 30.*

Zachodni coach station

Main Rail and Coach Stations

Gdańska
International, intercity and southern region suburban lines.

Śródmieście
East–west suburban line journeys depart from this station.

Central Station
International and intercity railway routes. Coach stop for long-distance and international services.

Główny
Central station for international and intercity routes.

Zachodni
International, intercity and suburban lines. Connected by subways with main coach terminal.

Zachodni
International journeys and all routes south and west. Connected by subways with the train station.

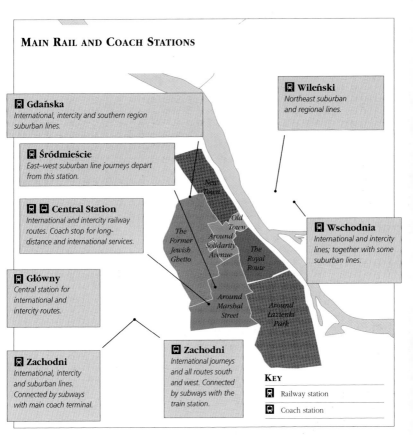

Wileński
Northeast suburban and regional lines.

Wschodnia
International and intercity lines; together with some suburban lines.

New Town
Old Town
The Former Jewish Ghetto
Around Solidarity Avenue
The Royal Route
Around Marshal Street
Around Łazienki Park

Key
Railway station
Coach station

Travelling by Car

Travelling to Warsaw by car offers the most flexiblility for your itinerary, and Poland is well-connected via international highways to many cities in the north of Europe. Poland imposes the usual restrictions on overseas drivers: a valid driving licence must always be carried, together with car registration documents, car stickers bearing initials that identify the country of origin, and a Green Card (an international certificate of insurance).

Within Warsaw, there are several car hire agencies, including international companies such as Hertz and Avis *(see p250)*. Prices are usually higher than in Western Europe, and it is also best to book at least a week in advance.

The minimum driving age in Poland is 17. Seat belts must be worn at all times. Children under the age of 12 are not allowed in the front passenger seat, and must sit in special seats with seat belts. Between 1 October and 1 March, all drivers are required by law to keep the car headlights turned on at all times, day and night. Speed limits indicated on road signs are shown in kilometres. Polish police continually monitor speed limits, and offenders are required to pay on-the-spot fines. Drink-driving laws are also strict, and the limit is so low that alcohol should be completely avoided when driving.

The price of petrol is relatively low in Poland, but apart from the main filling stations in Warsaw, credit cards are seldom accepted.

The Polish road system is extensive, but many roads are in poor condition, even in Warsaw. While parking is free outside the centre, car theft is common, so do only use guarded car parks if possible.

A road sign for the centre of Warsaw

Getting Around Warsaw

The centre of Warsaw is compact enough for visitors to explore on foot. Most areas beyond the centre can easily be reached using the city's bus and tram system. While Warsaw's underground system (metro) is being developed, currently it only links the Polytechnic in the city centre with the suburbs to the south, including Ursynów, the largest residential suburb. Beyond pedestrianized areas, a car is the best way to get around. Throughout this guide there are suggested routes for sightseeing, with tram and bus numbers indicated for each sight described. City maps which show bus and tram routes are available at Ruch kiosks, newsagents and tourist offices.

Driving in Town

Driving in Warsaw is becoming more demanding, and local drivers are not always the most courteous. While traffic jams do occur, they are usually only during rush hours (between 7–8am and 2–5pm). However, the roads are not always in good condition, with uneven surfaces and potholes not unknown, particularly outside the centre of Warsaw. Travelling by car is obviously the most convenient way to get around the city, particularly if you are planning to visit outlying attractions.

There are a number of car hire firms with branches in Warsaw. However, prices tend to be slightly more expensive than those in Western Europe. Major international companies, such as Avis, Budget, Europcar and Hertz, have offices at Okęcie Airport and in the centre.

How to Use a Parking Meter

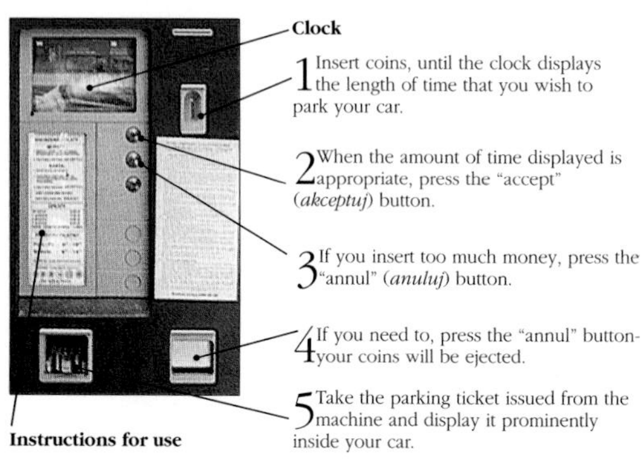

Clock
1 Insert coins, until the clock displays the length of time that you wish to park your car.
2 When the amount of time displayed is appropriate, press the "accept" (*akceptuj*) button.
3 If you insert too much money, press the "annul" (*anuluj*) button.
4 If you need to, press the "annul" button-your coins will be ejected.
5 Take the parking ticket issued from the machine and display it prominently inside your car.

Instructions for use

The Old Town and New Town are both closed to traffic, but are easy and enjoyable to explore on foot.

Parking

Parking is permitted on most Warsaw streets, which must be paid for, so long as there is no sign to indicate otherwise. Although the parking regulations in the city centre are fairly relaxed, there is a constant threat of break-ins and vehicle theft. Consequently, you are strongly advised always to leave your car in a guarded car park. There are several of these

City Information System

Warsaw has an extensive system of signs, plaques and street maps to guide visitors around the different districts of the city. The names of districts are shown against an orange background, while street names and sights are shown against a blue background. Symbols on posts indicate the location of the nearest telephone, tourist information centre, police station or toilet facilities. Special bronze signs are used in historic areas of the city.

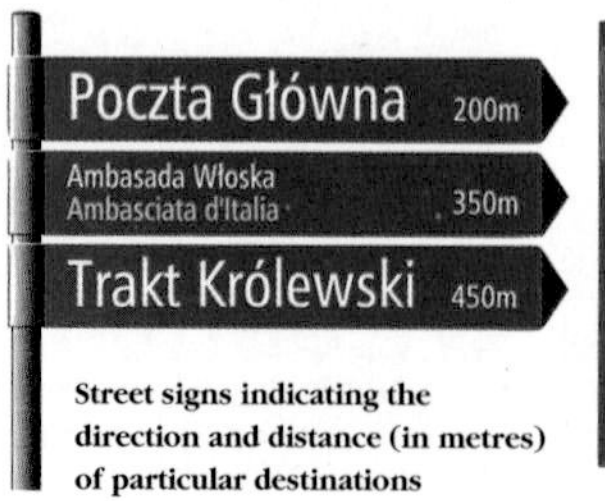

Street signs indicating the direction and distance (in metres) of particular destinations

Road sign giving directions to places nearby and to other districts

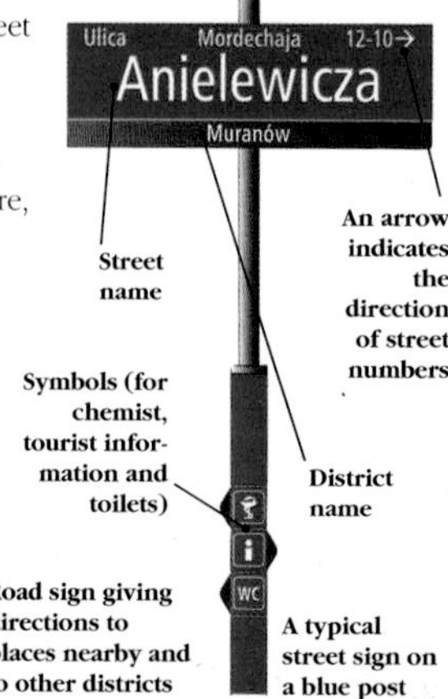

A typical street sign on a blue post

within central Warsaw, and they have been indicated on the Street Finder maps in this guide *(see pp256–65)*.

Parking Penalties

Despite relaxed parking regulations, if you park your car in a no-parking zone, you will have to pay a hefty penalty. A car that is parked dangerously and left unattended will be towed away by the vigilant traffic police. You will then have to reclaim your car, probably from a distant police compound. This can be extremely time-consuming and entails a fine (plus towing charges), which must be paid there and then.

Cars can also be wheel-clamped. In this case, you must telephone a traffic warden to remove the clamps, after the fine is paid (instructions are left on your car).

A wheel clamp

Warsaw Transport

The public transport system includes the extensive tram and bus network, while the metro is mainly used by commuters *(see p253)*. Buses and trams are inexpensive and frequent (operating between 5am and 11pm). Night buses augment the service, operating every half hour from a terminal behind the Palace of Culture and Science.

There is a flat-rate fare for bus, tram and metro journeys, regardless of distance. However, for fast buses (marked A–U) you need two tickets; for night buses you need three.

There are about 100 bus routes and 30 tram routes operating around Warsaw. Trams are most useful for short trips around the city centre.

Ruch kiosk, where public transport tickets are sold

Tickets

One type of ticket is valid for use on trams, buses and the metro. Tickets may be bought before boarding, and are available from all Ruch kiosks, newsagents and metro stations. As the majority of tickets are sold from kiosks, they can be difficult to purchase at weekends and during the evening, when the kiosks tend to be shut. It is often best to buy a pack of ten tickets at a time. One-day, group and family tickets are available. Tickets may also be purchased from the driver but these are slightly more expensive and you must have the correct change.

When travelling by tram and bus, passengers must "cancel" tickets, once on board, by punching them in a machine (on the metro, this is located on the station platform). It is important to always travel with a valid ticket, that is one which has been cancelled, as Warsaw has strict transport police, known as controllers. They operate in plain clothes, but carry identification. Fines must be paid on the spot, and are not negotiable. Routes most scrupulously controlled are trams between the Central Station and the market at the 10th Anniversary Stadium, and the No 175 buses. If you carry any luggage (including all but the smallest suitcase or backpack), you must buy an additional ticket – fines are also imposed for carrying luggage without a ticket. Children below the age of 4, and people over the age of 75, travel free.

Visitors sightseeing in Warsaw

Warsaw on Foot

Sightseeing in Warsaw is an enjoyable experience on foot, as many of the city's historic sights are within easy walking distance of each other, particularly in the Old and New Town. However, pavements can be in a state of disrepair, while pedestrianized areas are often cobbled. Wear comfortable shoes that can cope with this type of terrain. Also, take great care when crossing streets, even on zebra crossings, as drivers in Warsaw are not known for their willingness to stop for pedestrians.

Warsaw bus, with its distinctive red and yellow design

Getting Around by Taxi

Taxis provide the most efficient and comfortable means of travelling around Warsaw, and fares are not high by international standards. There are numerous reliable taxi firms based in Warsaw but, as in any major city, watch out for drivers who overcharge or take a circuitous route to your destination. It is best to either pre-book a taxi or take one from an official rank.

Types of Taxis

There is no official colour for taxis in Warsaw. However, all taxis feature a distinctive yellow and red stripe, together with the city's crest, an official number marked on the doors and a "taxi" sign on the roof. Most also display the name and telephone number of their company.

Warsaw's largest and most established taxi company is **MPT**, but there are plenty of other reliable companies that also provide a good level of service, among them **Korpo-Taxi**, **Super-Taxi**, **Tele-Taxi** and **Volfra-Taxi**.

The easiest way to hire a taxi is by phoning, as most companies offer an English-speaking telephonist. Taxis usually arrive in 10–15 minutes, and there is no booking fee. Some leading hotels provide their own car services, but these can be more expensive.

Warsaw taxi

Taxi Fares

When you start a journey by taxi, ensure that the meter has been switched on and is displaying the current minimum standard charge, above the word *opłata* ("fare"). Once you set off, the fare will increase after each kilometre travelled. Warsaw is divided into two zones, and taxi fares vary according to which one you travel through. Zone one covers the city centre, and journeys to districts outside this zone will be more expensive. It should be possible to negotiate a rate for a long journey, which should be done before you set off. Fares also operate at a higher rate during the night (from 10pm to 6am), as well as on Sundays and public holidays. Some taxis may have meters that pre-date the devaluation of the złoty. In these cases the driver converts the fare to its current equivalent. If you are concerned about the fare charged, ask for a receipt and check the amount with the taxi company concerned.

Taxi meter

How to Avoid Being Overcharged

Avoid using any cab that does not display the name of a recognized taxi company (listed on this page). The best place to find a taxi is at one of the many official taxi ranks, indicated by a blue sign. It is also possible to book taxis to collect you at a pre-arranged time. Most taxi companies employ telephone operators who speak English.

Taxi rank sign

Do not take taxis from drivers who solicit at Castle Square, the Central Railway Station or other main tourist locations. Only three taxi companies are authorized to operate at Okęçie Airport; MPT, Sawa-Taxi and Merc.

Radio Taxi Companies

Express-Taxi
877 0888.

Halo-Taxi
96 23.

Korpo-Taxi
96 24.

MPT-Radio Taxi
919.

OK Taxi
96 28.

Sawa-Taxi
644 44 44.

Super-Taxi
96 22.

Super-Taxi 2
96 61.

Lux-Taxi
825 79 99.

Taxi Plus
96 21.

Tele-Taxi
96 27.

Top Taxi
96 64.

Trans-Taxi
96 29.

Volfra-Taxi
96 25.

Wa Wa Taxi
96 44.

Getting Around by Metro

WARSAW'S METRO SYSTEM currently comprises one line. This operates between the city centre, from a station by Warsaw Centrum, near Al Jerozolimskie, and extends south for 12.5 km (8 miles) through districts such as Mokotów and Ursynów, before terminating at Kabaty. The metro is the fastest, most efficient means of transport to these areas. The metro line is being extended northwards to serve other parts of Warsaw. Some stations are under construction and due to open in the next decade.

Metro sign

USING THE METRO

METRO STATION ENTRANCES are indicated by yellow signs bearing a large red letter "M", with an arrow at the centre of the letter. Entrances include stairs and ramps, and at each station there is also a lift solely for the use of pensioners, disabled people and people travelling with small children. To use the lift, ask the station staff for assistance.

Tickets are available from the ticket office at each station. These are the same tickets that are used on trams and buses *(see p251)*.

Metro stations have a single platform, which is situated between the tracks, so that you can board a train going in either direction. The destination of the trains stopping on each side of the platform is indicated by a blue sign with an arrow and the name of the final stop on the line. To go towards Warsaw Polytechnic and the city centre, take the train from the platform marked "Centrum".

The edge of each platform is painted with an unbroken white line. For safety reasons, passengers are not permitted to cross this line until the train has come to a halt. When a train arrives the doors open and close automatically. A recorded warning sounds just before the doors close, and there is also an announcement of the next stop.

As a security precaution there are no litter bins on the metro, either in carriages or at stations. Used tickets and any other litter must be disposed of outside the stations. Smoking is forbidden anywhere in metro stations and in train carriages. Anyone who is found smoking is liable to pay a hefty fine.

Platform at Wilanowska station on Warsaw's metro system

TRAVELLING BY METRO

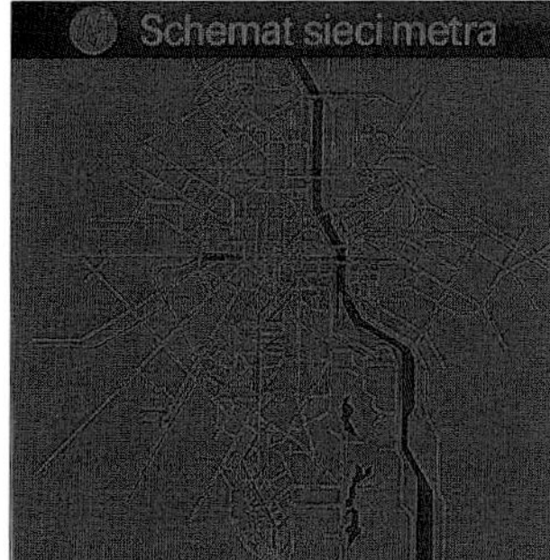

The metro system (including routes under construction). Maps are also displayed in metro carriages and on station platforms.

1 Before crossing the yellow line onto the platform, single tickets must be cancelled by punching the side of the ticket, using the red machines by the stairs to the platform. Daily, weekly and monthly tickets do not need cancelling.

2 An uncancelled ticket is not valid, and passengers found in the yellow zone with invalid tickets are liable to be fined. Keep cancelled tickets until you leave the station.

Machine for cancelling tickets

Sign showing tram connection

3 To reach your destination you may also need to use other means of transport. Look out for blue signs at metro station exits, which indicate tram and bus connections.

Travelling by Tram

THE TRAM SYSTEM is Warsaw's oldest form of public transportation. The first horse-drawn cars appeared on the streets of the capital in 1866, and were replaced in 1908 by the electric tram. Currently Warsaw's trams usually comprise two or three carriages, which fill up during the rush hours (approximately 7–8am and 2–5pm). Despite the crowds, trams still provide one of the city's fastest forms of public transport, taking the most direct routes along Warsaw's principal streets. Two of the most useful routes operate from Plac Zawiszy along Jerozolimskie Avenue then across the Vistula to the Praga district, and from Zbawiciela Square to Plac Bankowy (Bank Square) along Marshal Street. There are around 30 tram routes in total, which criss-cross the city on a grid pattern, running on either a north–south or east–west axis. Smoking is not permitted on trams.

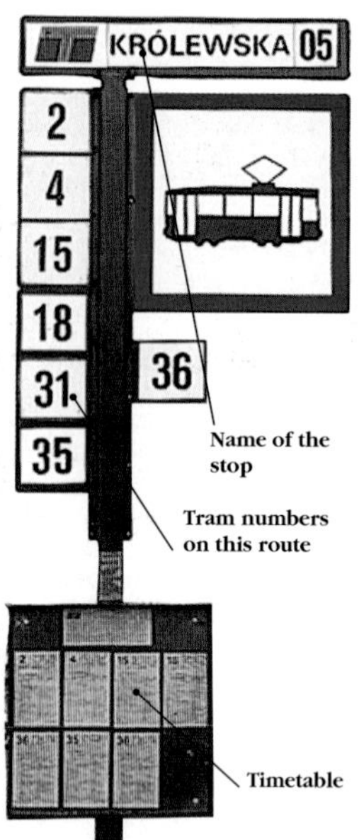

A typical Warsaw tram stop and timetable

Tram Tickets

ONE TYPE of ticket is valid for use on the metro, buses and trams throughout the city. Tickets may be bought prior to boarding a vehicle or from the driver, though the latter option works out slightly more expensive. Tram tickets are widely available from Ruch kiosks and similar outlets. There is a choice of single-journey, daily or weekly tickets. A single-journey ticket is valid for one journey only, no matter what the distance, but if you change tram routes you need to use another ticket.

On boarding the tram, a single-journey ticket must be cancelled by punching it in one of the small machines. Insert the end of the ticket marked with an arrow and the letter N. One-day and weekly tickets only need to be cancelled at the beginning of the first journey of the day or week, as appropriate. Anyone travelling who has not cancelled their ticket is liable to an on-the-spot fine imposed by plain-clothes controllers *(see p251)*. If you are carrying luggage you must cancel an extra ticket.

Municipal Transport Centre logo

Safety Precautions

IT IS WISE to observe sensible safety precautions when travelling on Warsaw's trams. Some routes, especially those most frequently used by tourists, are notoriously bad for pickpockets – the route that travels along Jerozolimske Avenue tends to be especially targeted. Take care to conceal your purse or wallet before boarding any tram, and in no circumstances keep money or valuables in an open bag or exterior coat pocket.

Warsaw Tours

A SIGHTSEEING TRAM called "Berlinka", marked with the letter T, operates on Saturdays, Sundays and public holidays. It departs every 40 minutes from 10am–5pm, and stops frequently (at the same stops as trams on a regular route) so the tour can be joined throughout the city. A conductor collects the fare, which is higher than usual, but the tour provides a great introduction to Warsaw.

Beginning at Narutowicza Square, the route follows Grójecka Street and Jerozolimskie Avenue, then crosses Poniatowski bridge to reach Praga. It returns via Śląsko-Dąbrowski bridge, Bank Square, Marszałkowska Street and Zbawiciela Square, before terminating at Narutowicza Square.

A Warsaw tram

Travelling by Bus

BUSES SERVE every district of Warsaw, as well as the outlying regions. Buses operate more extensive routes than trams, with over 100 routes in operation providing a frequent, if not particularly speedy, service. The majority of buses are state-owned, and on many routes relatively modern buses, sporting distinctive red and yellow paintwork, are in operation.

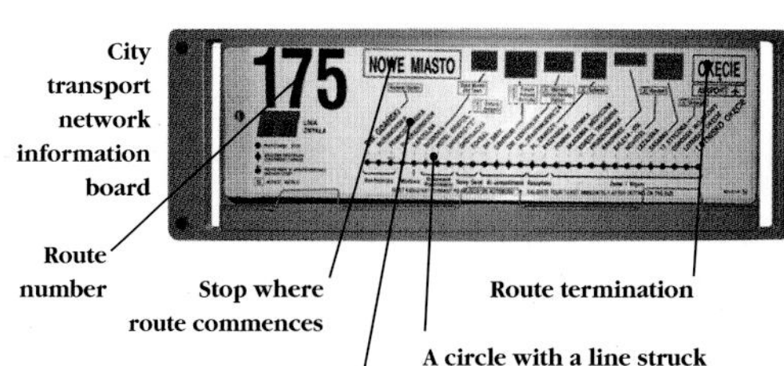

Bus Times and Routes

THERE ARE four principal types of public bus service in Warsaw: buses for travelling around the city centre; buses which link the centre with the outlying suburbs; night buses; and buses serving Warsaw's suburbs and further afield.

The four types can easily be distinguished by their route numbers and colours. Buses with black numbers from 101–199 operate within the city centre and stop frequently. Those with red numbers between 400–500 make fewer stops between the centre and the suburbs. Express buses are a subsection of this service, and are indicated by the letter E in front of the number. Night buses, which operate between 11pm and 5am, are numbered in black from 600–699, while green-line buses, serving the outskirts of the city, are numbered from 700 onwards.

All night bus routes are timed to meet at the same time at the junction of Emilia Plater and Świętokrzyska Street. A few private lines also operate from terminals at Marszałkowska Street in front of the Sawa department store, and in Jerozolimskie Avenue by the National Museum.

All bus stops display timetables of services that stop there. Frequency varies from 5–20 minutes.

Screen displaying date and time

Punch the ticket by placing it into the slot, striped side down.

Ticket-punching machine, found on buses and trams

Tickets

BUS TICKETS are the same as those used on trams and the metro. They may be purchased before you travel, and are available from Ruch kiosks, newsagents and metro stations. Tickets may also be purchased from the driver when boarding a bus, but these are more expensive and you need to tender the correct amount of money, as drivers do not give change. Single-journey tickets need to be cancelled on boarding the bus and are only valid for one journey on one vehicle, though this is regardless of distance. If you plan to use buses and trams frequently, it is well worth buying daily or weekly passes, which only need to be punched on the first trip. Tickets for groups are also available. Plain-clothes controllers check that your ticket has been cancelled, and hefty fines are imposed if you have not. Also bear in mind that an extra ticket must be used for each item of luggage, such as a suitcase or backpack. On private buses tickets can only be purchased from the driver when boarding.

Characteristic red and yellow Warsaw bus

Useful Routes

THE NUMBER 175 bus is ideal for getting around the city centre. The route links Krakowskie Przedmieście and Jerozolimskie Avenue with Warsaw's main railway stations and Okęcie Airport. It passes Warsaw University and the Royal Castle, and is handy for the Grand Theatre as well.

Routes 116, 122 and 195 are useful for travelling south of the city centre, as they continue along Miodowa Street, Krakowskie Przedmieście, Nowy Świat and Ujazdowskie Avenue, providing a fast link between the Old Town and Łazienki Park, passing Prymasowski Palace along the way.

Information

Duty Officer for ZTM Transport

995.

Street Finder

The black grid superimposed on the *Area by Area* map opposite shows which parts of Warsaw are covered in the *Street Finder*. The map references given throughout this guide for all sights, hotels, restaurants, shopping and entertainment venues refer to the numbered maps in this section. The key below lists the features indicated on the maps, including transport terminals, emergency services and tourist information points. All the major sights are clearly marked. An index of the street names on the maps follows on pages 258–9. Street names that include numbers are indexed under the first word; for example "3 May Street" will be found under "May".

Church of the Holy Spirit, seen from Freta Street

Pavement tables at a café in the Old Town

Old Town Market Square, lined with café tables

Key to Street Finder

- Major sight
- Other sight
- Other buildings
- Railway station
- Bus stop
- Coach terminal
- Metro station
- Parking
- Tram stop
- Hospital
- Police station
- Tourist information
- Church
- Synagogue
- Post office
- Railway line
- One way street
- Pedestrian street

Scale of Maps 1–2

0 m 200

1:10 000

0 yards 200

Scale of Maps 3–6

0 m 200

1:14 000

0 yards 200

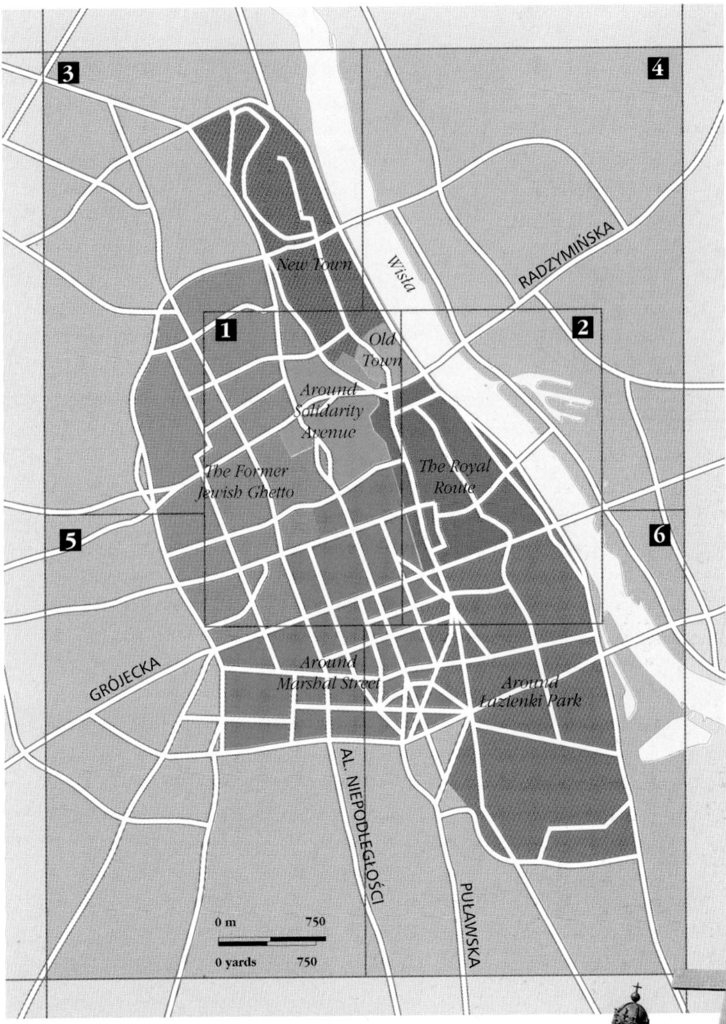

3
4
RADZYMIŃSKA
New Town
Wisła
1
2
Old Town
Around Solidarity Avenue
The Former Jewish Ghetto
The Royal Route
5
6
GRÓJECKA
Around Marshal Street
Around Łazienki Park
AL. NIEPODLEGŁOŚCI
PUŁAWSKA
0 m 750
0 yards 750

Fountain in the Saxon Gardens

Zygmunt's Column on Plac Zamkowy

Street Finder Index

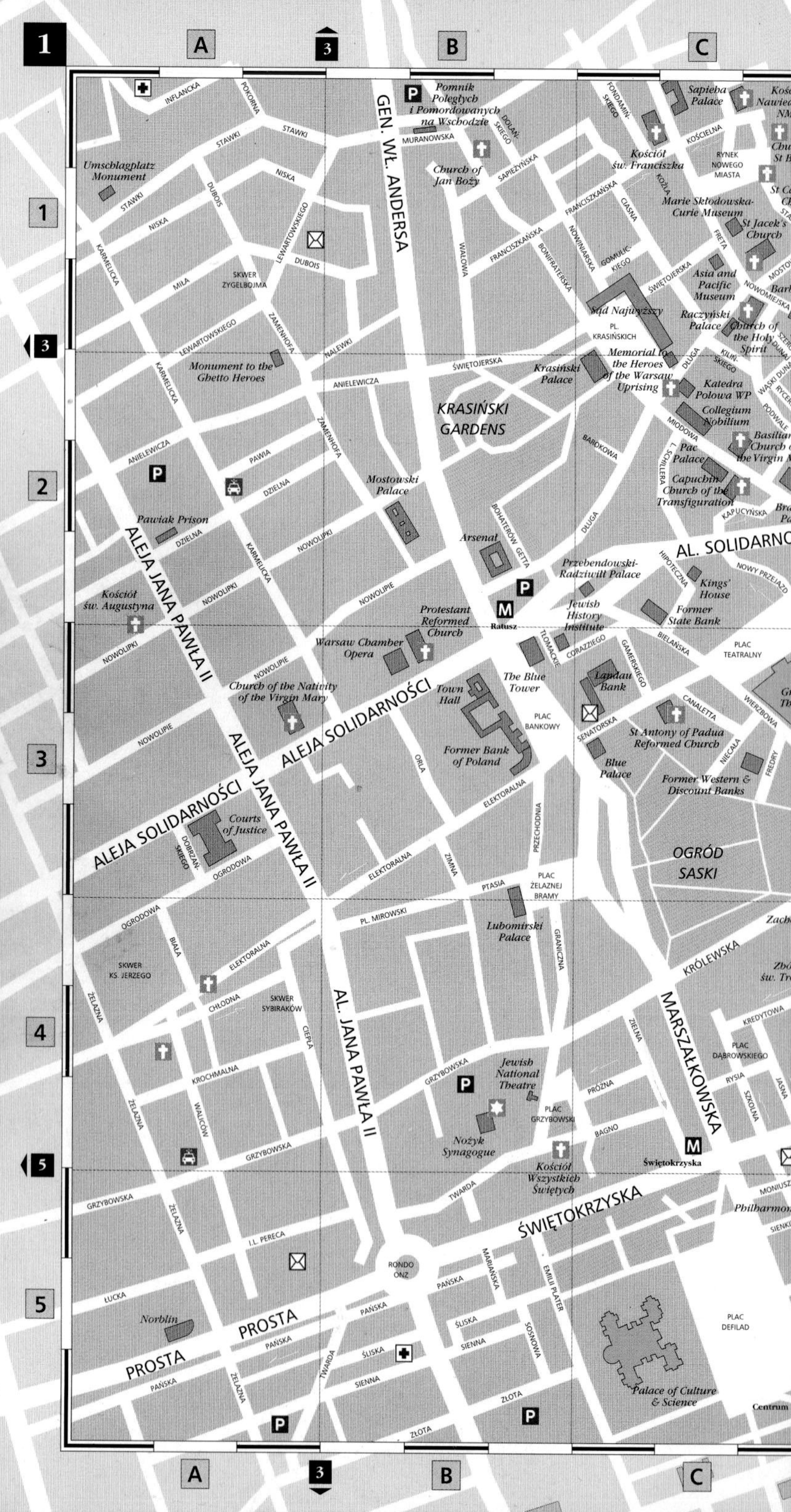

1
A
3
B
C
Pomnik Poległych i Pomordowanych na Wschodzie
Sapieha Palace
Kościół Nawiedzenia NMP
INFLANCKA
POKORNA
STAWKI
MURANOWSKA
DOLAŃSKIEGO
FONDAMINSKIEGO
KOŚCIELNA
RYNEK NOWEGO MIASTA
GEN. WŁ. ANDERSA
Umschlagplatz Monument
NISKA
DUBOIS
LEWARTOWSKIEGO
Church of Jan Boży
SAPIEŻYŃSKA
Kościół św. Franciszka
FRANCISZKAŃSKA
CIASNA
KOZLA
Marie Skłodowska-Curie Museum
St Jacek's Church
KARMELICKA
MIŁA
SKWER ZYGELBOJMA
WAŁOWA
BONIFRATERSKA
NOWINIARSKA
GOMULICKIEGO
ŚWIĘTOJERSKA
FRETA
Asia and Pacific Museum
Sąd Najwyższy
Raczyński Palace
Church of the Holy Spirit
PL. KRASIŃSKICH
ZAMENHOFA
NALEWKI
Monument to the Ghetto Heroes
Memorial to the Heroes of the Warsaw Uprising
Krasiński Palace
DŁUGA
KILIŃSKIEGO
Katedra Polowa WP
ANIELEWICZA
KRASIŃSKI GARDENS
Collegium Nobilium
MIODOWA
PODWALE
PAWIA
BAROKOWA
Pac Palace
Basilian Church of the Virgin Mary
DZIELNA
L. SCHILLERA
Mostowski Palace
Capuchin Church of the Transfiguration
2
KAPUCYŃSKA
Pawiak Prison
BOHATERÓW GETTA
Arsenał
AL. SOLIDARNOŚCI
NOWOLIPKI
Przebendowski-Radziwiłł Palace
HIPOTECZNA
Kings' House
NOWY PRZEJAZD
Kościół św. Augustyna
NOWOLIPIE
Protestant Reformed Church
Ratusz
Jewish History Institute
Former State Bank
Warsaw Chamber Opera
TŁOMACKIE
CORAZZIEGO
BIELAŃSKA
PLAC TEATRALNY
ALEJA JANA PAWŁA II
Church of the Nativity of the Virgin Mary
Town Hall
The Blue Tower
GAMERSKIEGO
Landau Bank
CANALETTA
WIERZBOWA
ALEJA SOLIDARNOŚCI
PLAC BANKOWY
SENATORSKA
St Antony of Padua Reformed Church
3
ORLA
Former Bank of Poland
Blue Palace
NIECAŁA
FREDRY
Former Western & Discount Banks
ELEKTORALNA
PRZECHODNIA
Courts of Justice
OGRÓD SASKI
DOBRZAŃSKIEGO
OGRODOWA
ZIMNA
PLAC ŻELAZNEJ BRAMY
PTASIA
PL. MIROWSKI
Lubomirski Palace
BIAŁA
SKWER KS. JERZEGO
GRANICZNA
KRÓLEWSKA
CHŁODNA
SKWER SYBIRAKÓW
ŻELAZNA
AL. JANA PAWŁA II
CIEPŁA
4
MARSZAŁKOWSKA
KREDYTOWA
ZIELNA
PLAC DĄBROWSKIEGO
KROCHMALNA
GRZYBOWSKA
Jewish National Theatre
PRÓŻNA
RYSIA
SZKOLNA
JASNA
WALICÓW
PLAC GRZYBOWSKI
Nożyk Synagogue
BAGNO
Świętokrzyska
Kościół Wszystkich Świętych
TWARDA
ŚWIĘTOKRZYSKA
MONIUSZKI
Philharmonic
I.L. PERECA
RONDO ONZ
MARIAŃSKA
EMILII PLATER
ŁUCKA
5
PAŃSKA
PROSTA
Norblin
ŚLISKA
SIENNA
SOSNOWA
PLAC DEFILAD
Palace of Culture & Science
ZŁOTA
Centrum

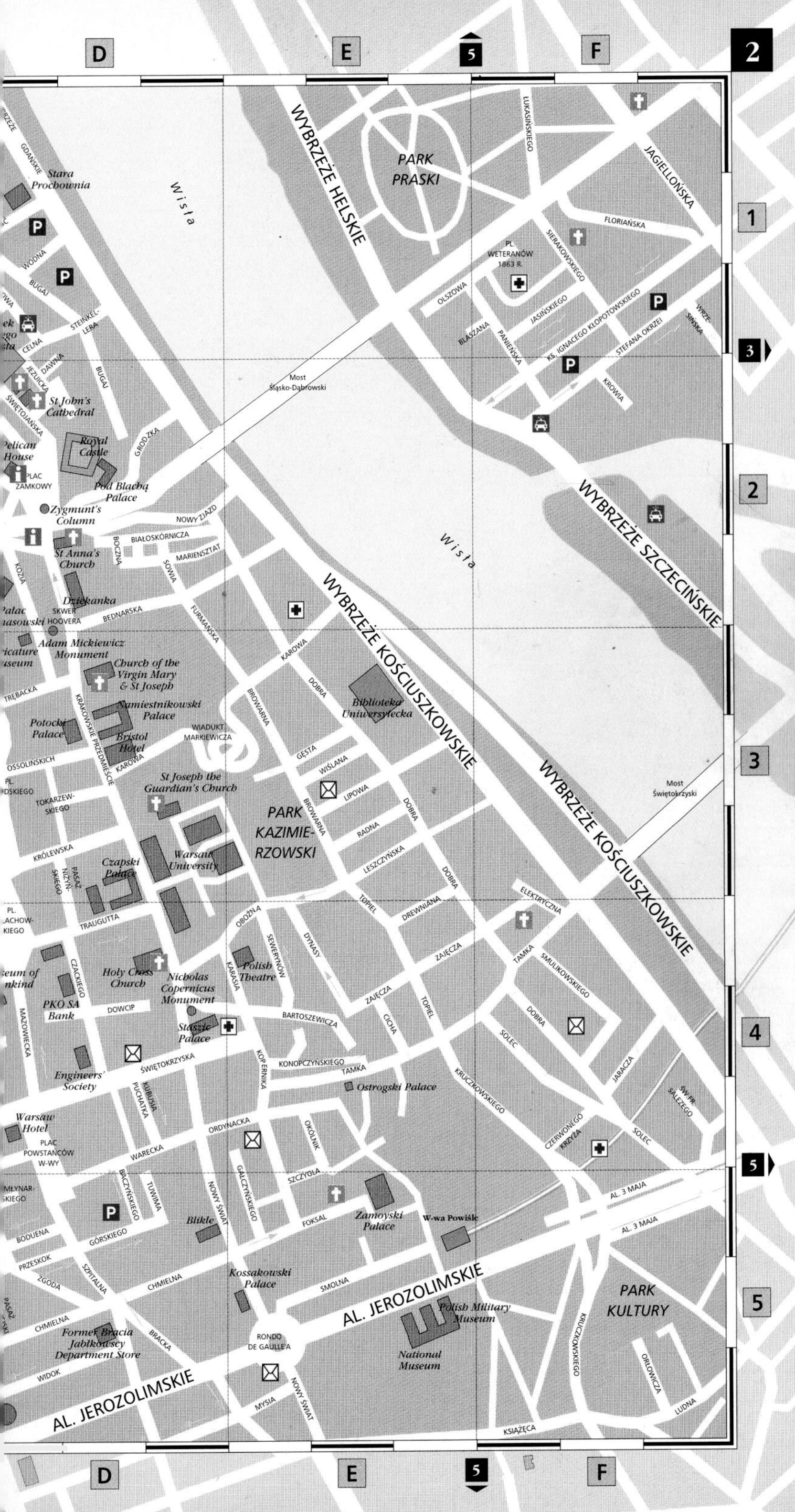

D
E
5
F
2
1
2
3
4
5
3
5
Wisła
Stara Prochownia
PARK PRASKI
WYBRZEŻE HELSKIE
JAGIELLOŃSKA
FLORIAŃSKA
ŁUKASIŃSKIEGO
SIERAKOWSKIEGO
PL. WETERANÓW 1863 R.
OLSZOWA
JASIŃSKIEGO
KS. IGNACEGO KŁOPOTOWSKIEGO
STEFANA OKRZEI
BŁASZANA
PANIEŃSKA
KROWIA
Most Śląsko-Dąbrowski
GDAŃSKIE
WODNA
BUGAJ
STEINKEL-LERA
CELNA
DAWNA
JEZUICKA
ŚWIĘTOJAŃSKA
St John's Cathedral
Royal Castle
GRODZKA
Pelican House
PLAC ZAMKOWY
Pod Blachą Palace
Zygmunt's Column
NOWY ZJAZD
BIAŁOSKÓRNICZA
BOCZNA
MARIENSZTAT
SOWIA
St Anna's Church
KOZIA
Dziekanka
SKWER HOOVERA
BEDNARSKA
FURMAŃSKA
Adam Mickiewicz Monument
Church of the Virgin Mary & St Joseph
TRĘBACKA
KRAKOWSKIE PRZEDMIEŚCIE
Namiestnikowski Palace
Potocki Palace
Bristol Hotel
KAROWA
WIADUKT MARKIEWICZA
OSSOLIŃSKICH
TOKARZEWSKIEGO
St Joseph the Guardian's Church
KRÓLEWSKA
Czapski Palace
Warsaw University
TRAUGUTTA
PARK KAZIMIERZOWSKI
WYBRZEŻE KOŚCIUSZKOWSKIE
WYBRZEŻE SZCZECIŃSKIE
Wisła
Biblioteka Universytecka
DOBRA
BROWARNA
GĘSTA
WIŚLANA
LIPOWA
RADNA
LESZCZYŃSKA
Most Świętokrzyski
TOPIEL
DREWNIANA
ELEKTRYCZNA
OBOŹNA
SEWERYNÓW
KARASIA
DYNASY
ZAJĘCZA
TAMKA
SMULIKOWSKIEGO
Polish Theatre
Holy Cross Church
Nicholas Copernicus Monument
CZACKIEGO
PKO SA Bank
DOWCIP
MAZOWIECKA
Staszic Palace
BARTOSZEWICZA
CICHA
SOLEC
KOPERNIKA
KONOPCZYŃSKIEGO
Engineers' Society
ŚWIĘTOKRZYSKA
KUBUSIA PUCHATKA
Ostrogski Palace
KRUCZKOWSKIEGO
JARACZA
ŚW. FR. SALEZEGO
Warsaw Hotel
PLAC POWSTAŃCÓW W-WY
ORDYNACKA
OKÓLNIK
WARECKA
CZERWONEGO KRZYŻA
NOWY ŚWIAT
SZCZYGŁA
GAŁCZYŃSKIEGO
BACZYŃSKIEGO
TUWIMA
AL. 3 MAJA
AL. 3 MAJA
Zamoyski Palace
W-wa Powiśle
Blikle
FOKSAL
BODUENA
GÓRSKIEGO
PRZESKOK
ZGODA
SZPITALNA
CHMIELNA
Kossakowski Palace
SMOLNA
AL. JEROZOLIMSKIE
Polish Military Museum
PARK KULTURY
CHMIELNA
Former Bracia Jabłkowscy Department Store
BRACKA
RONDO DE GAULLE'A
National Museum
KRUCZKOWSKIEGO
ORLOWICZA
WIDOK
AL. JEROZOLIMSKIE
MYSIA
NOWY ŚWIAT
KSIĄŻĘCA
LUDNA
D
E
5
F

3
A
B
C
1
2
3
4
5
BOGUCKIEGO
MARII KAZIMIERY
POTOCKA
MICKIEWICZA
MAŁOGOSKA
WYBRZEŻE GDYŃSKIE
PASKA
PLAC LELEWELA
SOLSKIEGO
BYTOMSKA
MYSŁOWICKA
DYGASIŃSKIEGO
GWIAŹDZISTA
K. PROMYKA
KOŹMIANA
BOHOMOLCA
ŻÓŁKOWSKICH
TUCHOLSKA
RYBIŃSKIEGO
GOMÓŁKI
DZIENNIKARSKA
SUŁKOWSKIEGO
SZCZEPANOWSKIEGO
KRECHOWIECKA
CIESZKOWSKIEGO
KĄTOWA
KARPIŃSKIEGO
SŁOWACKIEGO
KRASIŃSKIEGO
PL. SŁONECZNY
KANIOWSKA
SARMATÓW
SUZINA
FILARECKA
TOEPLITZA
PLAC WILSONA
JAKIELA
MUNKA
FORTECZNA
HAUKE-BOSSAKA
JAŚKIEWICZA
PRÓCHNIKA
KRASIŃSKIEGO
Church of St Stanisław Kostka
POGONOWSKIEGO
CZARNIECKIEGO
SZANIAWSKIEGO
ŚMIAŁA
KANIOWSKA
Warsaw Citadel & Independence Museum
CZUJNA
TROJAKA
KOSSAKA
KOCHOWSKIEGO
PL. HENKLA
NIEGOLEWSKIEGO
MIEROSŁAWSKIEGO
Kościół Dzieciątka Jezus
WYBRZEŻE GDYŃSKIE
Wisła
KS. J. POPIEŁUSZKI
WYSPIAŃSKIEGO
BRODZIŃSKIEGO
WIENIAWSKIEGO
KOZIETULSKIEGO
FELIŃSKIEGO
LECHONIA
PLAC INWALIDÓW
AL. WOJSKA POLSKIEGO
PLAC GWARDII
CUDNOWSKA
BITNA
SKAZAŃCÓW
GWARDII
FAWORY
ALEJA WOJSKA POLSKIEGO
PL. GRUNWALDZKI
OR-OTA
SZENWALDA
A. MICKIEWICZA
LEVITTOUX
MATYSIAKÓWNY
SOKOLICZ
J. ZAJĄCZKA
J. ZAJĄCZKA
KOKARDA
DYMIŃSKA
KRAJEWSKIEGO
JEZIORAŃSKIEGO
Most Gdański
RYDYGIERA
W-wa Gdańska
Royal Well
WENEDÓW
WYBRZEŻE GDAŃSKIE
KŁOPOT
BURAKOWSKA
BŁOŃSKA
Z. SŁOMIŃSKIEGO
SKWER BATALIONU CZATA 49
BONIFRATERSKA
PARK IM. J. KUSOCIŃSKIEGO
MIĘDZYPARKOWA
ZAKROCZYMSKA
PARK IM. R. TRAUGUTTA
BURAKOWSKA
RONDO ZGROMADZENIA AK „RADOSŁAW"
INFLANCKA
POKORNA
KONWIKTORSKA
WÓJTOWSKA
FONDAMIŃSKIEGO
Pomnik Poległych i Pomordowanych na Wschodzie
Sapieha Palace
KOŚCIELNA
Kościół św. Karola Boromeusza
POWĄZKOWSKA
STAWKI
MURANOWSKA
SAPIEŻYŃSKA
Kościół św. Franciszka
RYNEK NOWEGO MIASTA
Powązki Cemetery
OKOPOWA
Umschlagplatz Monument
NISKA
DZIKA
STAWKI
DUBOIS
LEWARTOWSKIEGO
Kościół św. Jana Bożego
GEN. WŁ. ANDERSA
CIASNA
KOZIA
St Jacek's Church
SPOKOJNA
DUBOIS
FRANCISZKAŃSKA
NOWINIARSKA
GOMULICKIEGO
ŚWIĘTOJERSKA
FRETA
KOLSKA
NISKA
KARMELICKA
MIŁA
SKWER ZYGELBOJMA
WAŁOWA
PLAC KRASIŃSKICH
Memorial to the Heroes of the Warsaw Uprising
STAWKI
LEWARTOWSKIEGO
ZAMENHOFA
NALEWKI
ŚWIĘTOJERSKA
DŁUGA
KILIŃSKIEGO
Monument to the Ghetto Heroes
ANIELEWICZA
Krasiński Palace
Collegium Nobilium
NISKA
SMOCZA
KRASIŃSKI GARDENS
BAROKOWA
MIODOWA
MIŁA
ALEJA JANA PAWŁA II
PAWIA
Mostowski Palace
Pałac Pac Palace
Capuchin Chu of the Transfigura
ESPERANTO
PASZYNA
Pawiak Prison
DZIELNA
NOWOLIPKI
BOHATERÓW GETTA
Arsenał
Przebendowski-Radziwiłł Palace
HIPOTECZNA
Kościół Brata Alber i św. Andrze
ANIELEWICZA
SMOCZA
KARMELICKA
Protestant Reformed Church
Ratusz
The Blue Tower
Jewish History Institute
BIELAŃSKA
PLAC TEATRAL
PAWIA
DZIELNA
Kościół św. Augustyna
NOWOLIPIE
Warsaw Chamber Opera
Town Hall
BELLOTTIEGO
NOWOLIPKI
SMOCZA
Church of the Nativity of the Virgin Mary
ALEJA SOLIDARNOŚCI
ORLA
PLAC BANKOWY
SENATORSKA
St Antony of Padua Reformed Church
CANALETTA
NIECAŁA
WOLNOŚĆ
OKOPOWA
NOWOLIPIE
Former Bank of Poland
Blue Palace
FREDRY
Former Western & Discount Ban
KACZA
Kościół Miłosierdzia Bożego
ŻYTNIA
ŻELAZNA
DOBRZAŃSKIEGO
Courts of Justice
ELEKTORALNA
PRZECHODNIA
OGRÓD SASKI
A
5
B
C

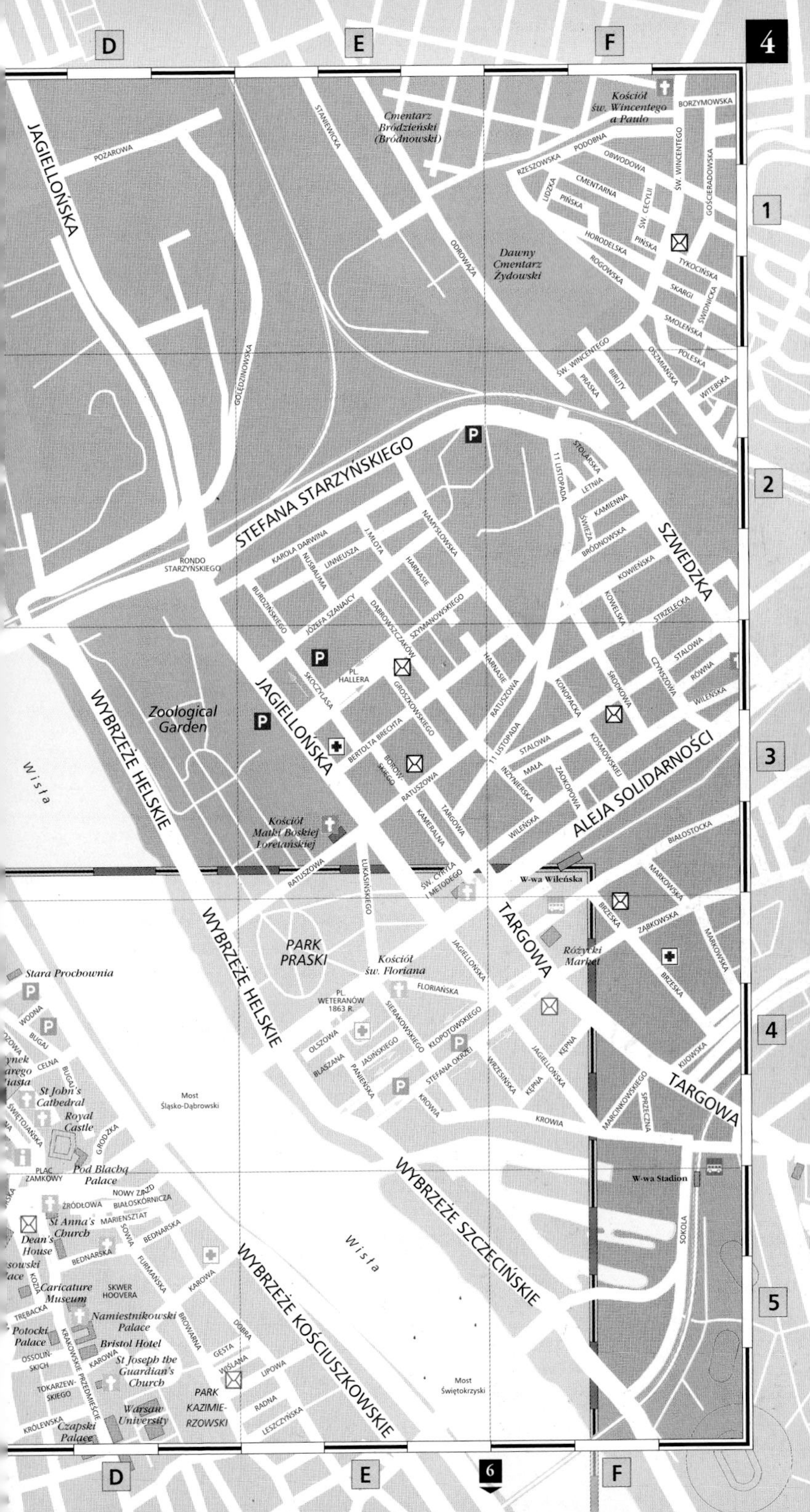
4
D
E
F
1
2
3
4
5
6
Kościół św. Wincentego a Paulo
Cmentarz Bródzieński (Bródnowski)
Dawny Cmentarz Żydowski
JAGIELLOŃSKA
STEFANA STARZYŃSKIEGO
RONDO STARZYŃSKIEGO
SZWEDZKA
Zoological Garden
WYBRZEŻE HELSKIE
Wisła
Kościół Matki Boskiej Loretańskiej
ALEJA SOLIDARNOŚCI
TARGOWA
W-wa Wileńska
Różycki Market
PARK PRASKI
Kościół św. Floriana
PL. WETERANÓW 1863 R.
Most Śląsko-Dąbrowski
WYBRZEŻE SZCZECIŃSKIE
WYBRZEŻE KOŚCIUSZKOWSKIE
W-wa Stadion
Most Świętokrzyski
PARK KAZIMIERZOWSKI
Stara Prochownia
St John's Cathedral
Royal Castle
Pod Blachą Palace
St Anna's Church
Dean's House
Caricature Museum
SKWER HOOVERA
Namiestnikowski Palace
Potocki Palace
Bristol Hotel
St Joseph the Guardian's Church
Warsaw University
Czapski Palace

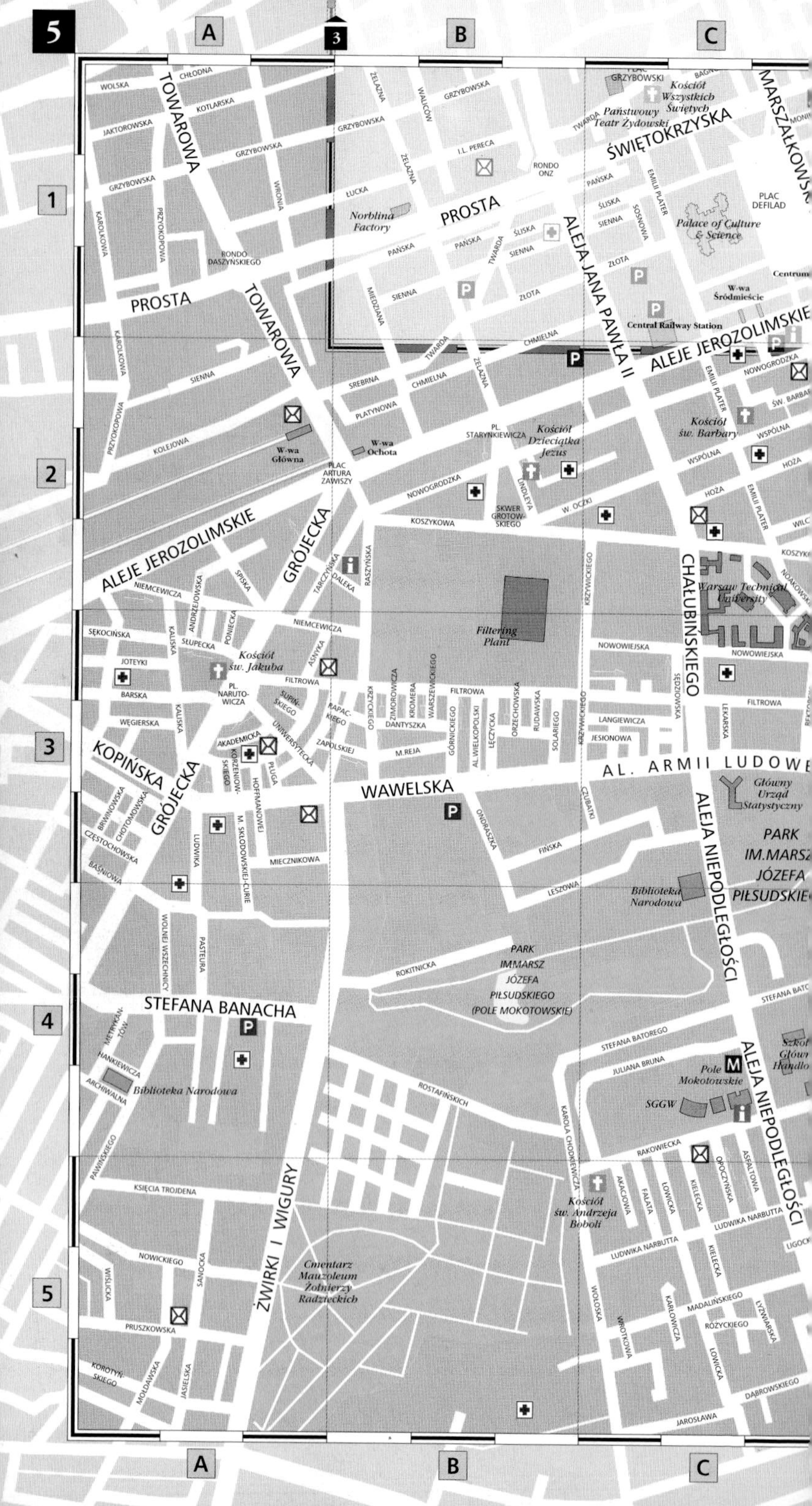

5
A
B
C
3
1
2
4
PROSTA
TOWAROWA
ŚWIĘTOKRZYSKA
MARSZAŁKOWSKA
ALEJA JANA PAWŁA II
ALEJE JEROZOLIMSKIE
GRÓJECKA
CHAŁUBIŃSKIEGO
KOPIŃSKA
WAWELSKA
AL. ARMII LUDOWEJ
ALEJA NIEPODLEGŁOŚCI
STEFANA BANACHA
ŻWIRKI I WIGURY
Kościół Wszystkich Świętych
Państwowy Teatr Żydowski
Norblina Factory
Palace of Culture & Science
PLAC DEFILAD
RONDO ONZ
RONDO DASZYŃSKIEGO
Central Railway Station
W-wa Śródmieście
W-wa Główna
W-wa Ochota
PLAC ARTURA ZAWISZY
Kościół Dzieciątka Jezus
Kościół św. Barbary
Warsaw Technical University
Filtering Plant
Kościół św. Jakuba
PL. NARUTOWICZA
Główny Urząd Statystyczny
Biblioteka Narodowa
PARK IMMARSZ JÓZEFA PIŁSUDSKIEGO (POLE MOKOTOWSKIE)
Pole Mokotowskie
SGGW
Kościół św. Andrzeja Boboli
Cmentarz Mauzoleum Żołnierzy Radzieckich

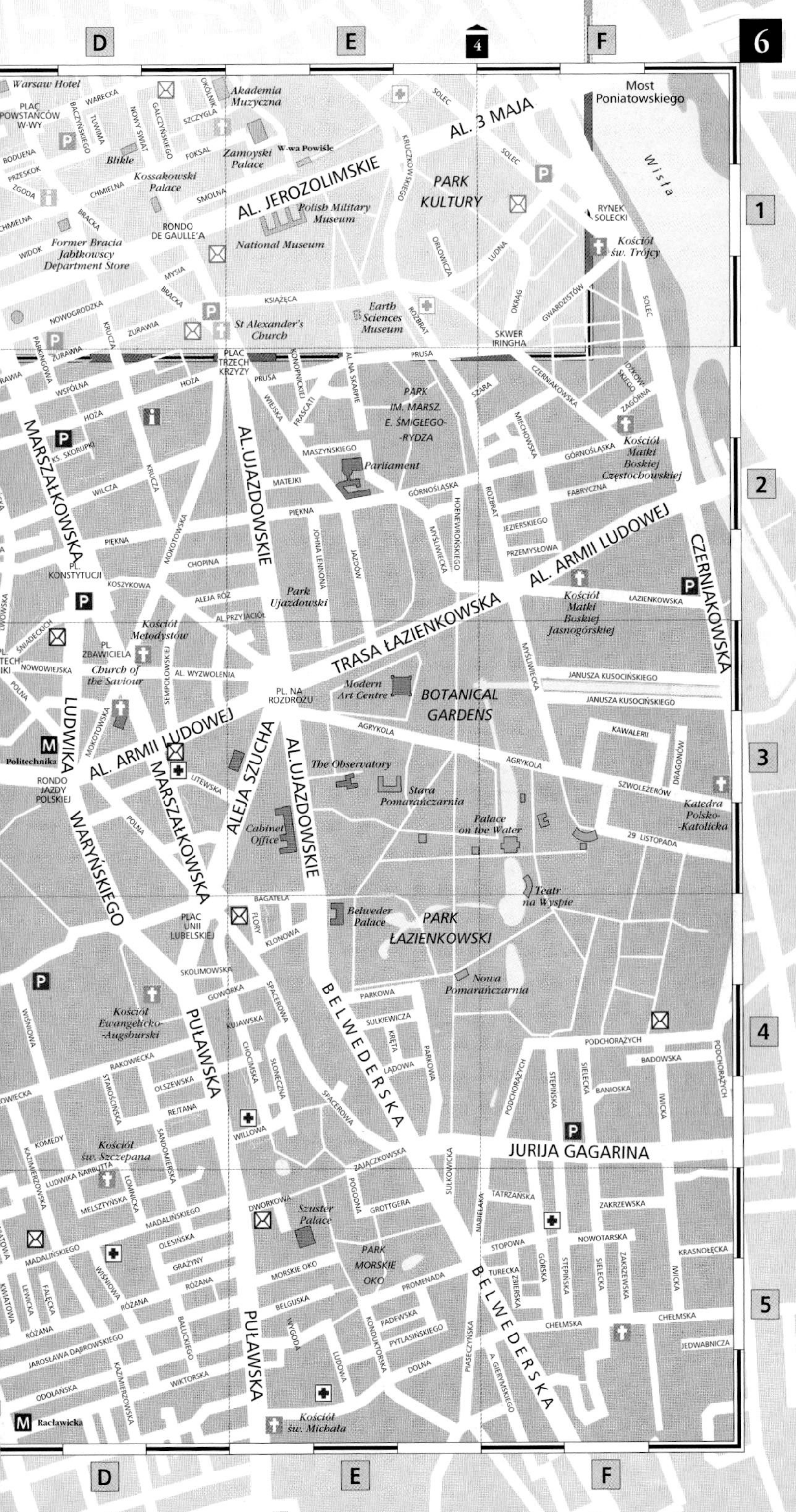
D
E
4
F
Warsaw Hotel
Akademia Muzyczna
Most Poniatowskiego
AL. 3 MAJA
Wisła
PLAC POWSTAŃCÓW W-WY
Blikle
Zamoyski Palace
W-wa Powiśle
AL. JEROZOLIMSKIE
PARK KULTURY
Kossakowski Palace
Polish Military Museum
RYNEK SOLECKI
RONDO DE GAULLE'A
National Museum
Kościół św. Trójcy
Former Bracia Jabłkowscy Department Store
Earth Sciences Museum
St Alexander's Church
SKWER IRINGHA
PLAC TRZECH KRZYŻY
PARK IM. MARSZ. E. ŚMIGŁEGO-RYDZA
MARSZAŁKOWSKA
Parliament
Kościół Matki Boskiej Częstochowskiej
AL. UJAZDOWSKIE
AL. ARMII LUDOWEJ
CZERNIAKOWSKA
PL. KONSTYTUCJI
Park Ujazdowski
TRASA ŁAZIENKOWSKA
Kościół Metodystów
Kościół Matki Boskiej Jasnogórskiej
PL. ZBAWICIELA
Church of the Saviour
PL. NA ROZDROŻU
Modern Art Centre
BOTANICAL GARDENS
LUDWIKA WARYŃSKIEGO
Politechnika
AL. ARMII LUDOWEJ
ALEJA SZUCHA
AL. UJAZDOWSKIE
The Observatory
Stara Pomarańczarnia
RONDO JAZDY POLSKIEJ
Cabinet Office
Palace on the Water
Katedra Polsko-Katolicka
Teatr na Wyspie
PLAC UNII LUBELSKIEJ
Belweder Palace
PARK ŁAZIENKOWSKI
BELWEDERSKA
Nowa Pomarańczarnia
Kościół Ewangelicko-Augsburski
PUŁAWSKA
JURIJA GAGARINA
Kościół św. Szczepana
Szuster Palace
PARK MORSKIE OKO
BELWEDERSKA
PUŁAWSKA
Racławicka
Kościół św. Michała
1
2
3
4
5
D
E
F

General Index

Page numbers in **bold** type refer to main entries.

A

B

C

D

L

M

N

T

Acknowledgments

DORLING KINDERSLEY would like to thank the following people whose contributions and assistance have made the preparation of this book possible.

CARTOGRAPHY
The Institute of Land Surveying and Cartography in Warsaw for the map of Warsaw; the Meteorological Institute in Warsaw for supplying meteorological data.

ADDITIONAL ILLUSTRATIONS
Marek Górka for the Palace on the Water; Dominik Bosekand for the Szuster Palace.

DESIGN AND EDITORIAL ASSISTANCE
Gillian Allan, Douglas Amrine, Vivien Crump, Guy Dimond, Paul Hines, Sarah Martin, Adam Moore, Lee Redmond, Harvey de Nick Ryder, Andrew Szudek.

PHOTOGRAPHY PERMISSIONS
The publisher would like to thank the following for their permission to photograph:
Central Archive of Historic Documents, Warsaw, Central Photographic Agency (PAP), Warsaw.

PICTURE CREDITS
Every effort has been made to trace the copyright holders. Dorling Kindersley apologizes for any unintentional omissions and would be pleased, in such cases, to add an acknowledgment in future editions.

The publisher would like to thank the following individuals, companies and picture libraries for kind permission to reproduce their photographs:

J BARANOWSKI (W Gomułka on plac Defilad).

JERZY BRONARSKI, ORLĘTA AGENCY (Royal Castle).

MACIEJ BRZOZOWSKI (Czeslaw Miłosz; the chamber in the Sejm, Polish Parliament).

PAWEL KOPCZYŃSKI (Warsaw on *Śmigus Dyngus*).

WOJCIECH KRYŃSKI AND TOMASZ PRAŻMOWSKI (Płock).

STEFAN KRZESZEWSKI (Senate Chamber in the Sejm).

J KUŚMIERSKI (baboons in the zoo).

DAMAZY KWIATKOWSKI (mass celebrated by the Pope).

JERZY MYSZKOWSKI (paintings by Bellotto).

ANDRZEJ PAWLISZEWSKI (Warsaw airport).

IRENEUSZ RADKIEWICZ (Lech Wałęsa).

HENRYK ROSIAK (the Marshal's mace).

WITOLD ROZMYSŁOWICZ (Dzierżyński's monument being destroyed).

JERZY SABARZ (Archdiocese Museum).
JAKUB SITO (Pułtusk).
MARIAN SOKOŁOWSKI (the Syrena car).

WOJCIECH STEIN (Cardinal Glemp; the Jazz Jamboree).

JANUSZ UKLEWSKI (Anna German).

TEODOR WALCZAK (horse races; lions in the zoo).

BARBARA WOŁOSZ (Natolin).

The publishers would also like to thank the following institutions:

Administration of the Main Post Office, Warsaw
Botanical Gardens, Warsaw
Czartoryski Museum, Kraków
Earth Sciences Museum, Warsaw
Frederic Chopin Society, Warsaw
Grand Theatre, Warsaw
Guild of Leather Crafts Museum dedicated to J Kiliński, Warsaw
Gulliver's Theatre, Warsaw
Handicraft and Precision Craft Museum, Warsaw
Historical Buildings Institute, Warsaw
Historical Museum of the City of Warsaw
Institute of Land Surveying and Cartography, Warsaw
Jewish Historical Institute, Warsaw
Jewish Theatre dedicated to Estera Kaminska, Warsaw
Literature Museum, Warsaw
LOT Polish National Airlines
Marie Skłodowska-Curie Museum, Warsaw
Museum of Fine Arts, Łódz
Museum of Mankind, Warsaw
National Museum, Warsaw
Nieborów and Arkadia Museums
Palace of Culture and Science, Warsaw
Palace on the Water, Warsaw
PAN Fine Art Institute, Warsaw
Pavilion X of the Citadel Museum, Warsaw
Polfilm advertising and photographic agency, Warsaw
Polish Military Museum, Warsaw
Pope John Paul II Collection, Warsaw
Poster Museum, Wilanów, Warsaw
Royal Castle, Warsaw
Technology Museum, Warsaw
Theatre Museum, Warsaw
Traffic Wardens Association, Warsaw
Union of Jewish Communes
Warsaw Chamber Opera
Wilanów Palace and Park, Warsaw
Xawery Dunikowski Museum within the Królikarnia, Warsaw.

Jacket:
Front – DK PICTURE LIBRARY: Dorota & Mariusz Jarymowiczowie bc; Hanna & Maciej Musial cbr, cbl; JAMES TRAVEL PHOTOGRAPHY main image.
Back – DK PICTURE LIBRARY: Hanna & Maciej Musial t, b.
Spine – JAMES TRAVEL PHOTOGRAPHY.

Phrase Book

Summary of Pronunciation in Polish

ą a nasal *"awn"* as in *"sawn"* or *"an"* as in the French *"Anjou"* but barely sounded

c *"ts"* as in *"cats"*

ć, cz *"ch"* as in *"challenge"*

ch *"ch"* as in Scottish *"loch"*

dz *"j"* as in *"jeans"* when followed by **i** or **e** but otherwise *"dz"* as in *"adze"*

dź *"j"* as in *"jeans"*

dż *"d"* as in *"dog"* followed by *"s"* as in *"leisure"*

ę similar to *"en"* in *"end"* only nasal and barely sounded, but if at the end of the word pronounced *"e"* as in *"bed"*

h "ch" as in Scottish "Loch"

i *"ee"* as in *"teeth"*

j *"y'* as in yes

ł *"w"* as in *"window"*

ń similar to the *"ni"* in *"companion"*

ó *"oo"* as in *"soot"*

rz similar to the *"s"* in *"leisure"* or, when it follows **p, t** or **k**, *"sh"* as in *"shut"*

ś, **sz** *"sh"* as in *"shut"*

w *"v"* as in *"vine"*

y similar to the *"i"* in *"bit"*

ź, ż similar to the *"s"* in *"leisure"*

Emergencies

Help!
pomocy!
pomotsi

Call a doctor!
zawołać doktora!
zawowach doctora

Call an ambulance!
zadzwonić po pogotowie!
zadzvoneech po pogotovee

Police!
policja!
poleetsya

Call the fire brigade!
zadzwonić po straż pożarną!
zadzvoneech po stras posarnAWN

Where is the nearest phone?
Gdzie jest najbliższa budka telefoniczna?
gjeh yest nlbleezhsha boodka telefoneechna

Where is the hospital?
gdzie jest szpital?
gjeh yest shpeetal

Where is the police station?
gdzie jest posterunek policji?
gjeh yest posterunek politsyee

Communication Essentials

Yes
Tak
tak

No
Nie
n-yeh

Thank you.
Dziękuję
jENkoo-yeh

No thank you.
Nie, dziękuję
n-yej jENkoo-yeh

Please
Proszę
prosheh

I don't understand.
Nie rozumiem
n-yeh rozoom-yem

Do you speak English? (to a man)
Czy mówi pan po angielsku?
chi moovee pan po ang-yelskoo

Do you speak English? (to a woman)
Czy mówi pani po angielsku?
chi moovee panee po ang-yelskoo

Please speak more slowly.
Proszę mówić wolniej
prosheh mooveech voln-yay

Please write it down for me.
Proszę mi to napisać
prosheh mee to napeesach

My name is . . .
Nazywam się . . .
nazivam sheh

Useful Words and Phrases

Pleased to meet you (to a man)
Bardzo mi miło pana poznać
bardzo mee meewo pana poznach

Pleased to meet you (to a woman)
Bardzo mi miło panią poznać
bardzo mee meewo pan-yAWN poznach

Good morning
Dzień dobry
jen-yuh dobri

Good afternoon
Dzień dobry
jen-yuh dobri

Good evening
Dobry wieczór
dobri v-yechoor

Good night
Dobranoc
dobranots

Goodbye
Do widzenia
do veedzen-ya

What time is it . . . ?
Która jest godzima?
ktoora yest gojeena

Cheers!
Na zdrowie!
na zdrov-yeh

Excellent!
Wspaniale!
wspan-yaleh

Shopping

Do you have . . . ? (to a man)
Czy ma pan . . . ?
che ma pan

Do you have . . . ? (to a woman)
Czy ma pani . . . ?
che ma panee

How much is this?
Ile to kosztuje?
eeleh to koshtoo-yeh

Where is the . . . department?
Gdzie jest dział z . . . ?
gjeh yest jawuh z

Do you take credit cards? (to a man)
Czy przyjmuje pan karty kredytowe?
chi pshi-yuhmoo-yeh pan karti kreditoveh

Do you take credit cards? (to a woman)
Czy przyjmuje pani karty kredytowe?
chi pshi-yuhmoo-yeh panee karti kreditoveh

bakery
piekarnia
p-yekarn-ya

bookshop
księgarnia
kshENgarn-ya

chemist
apteka
apteka

department store
dom towarowy
dom tovarovi

exchange office
kantor walutowy
kantor valootovi

travel agent
biuro podróży
b-yooro podroozhi

post office
poczta, urząd pocztowy
pochta, ooZHAWNd pochtovi

postcard
pocztówka
pochtoovka

stamp
znaczek
znachek

How much is a postcard to . . . ?
Ile kosztuje pocztówka do . . . ?
eeleh koshtoo-yeh pochtoovka do

airmail
poczta lotnicza
pochta lotneecha

Staying in a Hotel

Have you any vacancies? (to a man)
Czy ma pan wolne pokoje?
chi ma pan volneh poko-yeh

Have you any vacancies? (to a woman)
Czy ma pani wolne pokoje?
chi ma panee volneh poko-yeh

What is the charge per night?
Ile kosztuje za dobę?
eeleh koshtoo-yeh za dobeh

I'd like a single room.
Poproszę pokój jednoosobowy
poprosheh pokoo-yuh yedno-osobovi

I'd like a double room.
Poproszę pokój dwuosobowy
poprosheh pokoo-yuh dvoo-osobovi

I'd like a twin room.
Poproszę pokój z dwoma łóżkami
poprosheh pokoo-yuh z dvoma woozhkamee

I'd like a room with a bathroom.
Poproszę pokój z łazienką
poprosheh pokoo-yuh z wazhenkAWN

bathroom
łazienka
wazhenka

bed
łóżko
woozhko

bill
rachunek
raHoonek

breakfast
śniadanie
shn-yadan-yeh

dinner
kolacja
kolats-ya

double room
pokój dwuosobowy
pokoo-yuh dvoo-osobovi

full board
pełne utrzymanie
pewuhneh ootzhiman-yeh

guest house
zajazd
za-yazd

half board
dwa posiłki dziennie
dva posheewuhkee jen-yeh

key
klucz
klooch

restaurant
restauracja
restawrats-ya

shower
prysznic
prishneets

single room
pokój jednoosobowy
pokoo-yuh yedno-osobovi

toilet
toaleta
to-aleta

Eating Out

A table for one, please.
Stolik dla jednej osoby proszę
stoleek dla yednay osobi prosheh

A table for two, please.
Stolik dla dwóch osób proszę
stoleek dla dvooh osoob prosheh

Can I see the menu?
Mogę prosić jadłospis?
mogeh prosheech yadwospees

Can I see the wine list?
Mogę prosić kartę win?
mogeh prosheech karteh veen

I'd like . . .
Proszę
prosheh

Can we have the bill, please?
Proszę rachunek
prosheh raHoonek

Where is the toilet?
Gdzie jest toaleta?
gjeh yest to-aleta

Menu Decoder

baranina
mutton, lamb

barszcz czerwony
beetroot soup

bażant
pheasant

befsztyk
beef steak

bigos
hunter's stew (sweet and sour cabbage with a variety of meats and seasonings)

bukiet z jarzyn
a variety of raw and pickled vegetables

ciasto
cake, pastry

cielęcina
veal

cukier
sugar

cukierek
sweet, confectionery

dania mięsne
meat dishes

dania rybne
fish dishes

dania z drobiu
poultry dishes

deser
dessert

flaki
tripe

grzybki marynowane
marinated mushrooms

herbata
tea

jarzyny
vegetables

kabanos
dry, smoked pork sausage

kaczka
duck

kapusta
cabbage

kartofle
potatoes

kasza gryczana
buckwheat

kaszanka
black pudding

kawa
coffee

kiełbasa
sausage

klopsiki
minced meat balls

lody
ice cream

łosoś
salmon

łosoś wędzony
smoked salmon

makowiec
poppy seed cake

naleśniki
pancakes

piernik
spiced honeycake

pierogi
ravioli-like dumplings

piwo
beer

prawdziwki
ceps (type of mushroom)

przystawki
entrées

pstrąg
trout

rolmopsy
rollmop herrings

sałatka
salad

sałatka owocowa
fruit salad

sok
juice

sok jabłkowy
apple juice

sok owocowy
fruit juice

sól
salt

śledź
herring

tort
cake, gâteau

wieprzowina
pork

wino
wine

woda
water

ziemniaki
potatoes

zupa
soup

Health

I do not feel well.
Źle się czuję
zhleh sheh choo-yeh

I need a prescription for . . .
Potrzebuję receptę na . . .
potzheboo-yeh retsepteh na

cold
przeziębienie
pshef-yENb-yen-yeh

cough (noun)
kaszel
kashel

cut
skaleczenie
skalechen-yeh

flu
grypa
gripa

hayfever
katar sienny
katar shyienny

headache pills
proszki od bólu głowy
proshkee od booloo gwovi

hospital
szpital
shpeetal

nausea
mdłości
mudwosh-che

sore throat
ból gardła
bool gardwa

Travel and Transport

When is the next train to . . .?
Kiedy jest następny pociąg do?
k-yedi yest nastENpni pochAWNg do

What is the fare to . . .?
Ile kosztuje bilet do . . . ?
eeleh koshtoo-yeh beelet do

A single ticket to . . . please
Proszę bilet w jedną stronę do . . .
prosheh beelet v yednAWN stroneh do

A return ticket to . . . please.
Proszę bilet w obie strony do . . .
prosheh beelet v obye strony do

Where is the bus station?
Gdzie jest dworzec autobusowy?
gjeh yest dvozhets awtoboosovi

Where is there a bus stop?
Gdzie jest przystanek autobusowy?
gjeh yest pshistanek awtoboosovi

Where is there a tram stop?
Gdzie jest przystanek tramwajowy?
gjeh yest pshistanek tramvl-yovi

booking office
kasa biletowa
kasa beeletova

station
stacja
stats-ya

timetable
rozkład jazdy
rozkwad yazdi

left luggage
przechowalnia bagażu
psheHovaln-ya bagazhoo

platform
peron
peron

first class
pierwsza klasa
p-yervsha klasa

second class
druga klasa
drooga klasa

single ticket
bilet w jedną stronę
beelet v yednAWN stroneh

return ticket
bilet powrotny
beelet povrotni

airline
linia lotnicza
leen-ya lotna-yeecha

airport
lotnisko
lotn-yeesko

arrival
przylot
pshilot

flight number
numer lotu
noomer lotoo

gate
przejście
pshaysh-cheh

coach
autokar
awtokar

Numbers

0
zero
zero

1
jeden
yeden

2
dwa
dva

3
trzy
tshi

4
cztery
chteri

5
pięć
p-yENch

6
sześć
shesh-ch

7
siedem
sh-yedem

8
osiem
oshem

9
dziewięć
jev-yENch

10
dziesięć
jeshENch

11
jedenaście
yedenash-cheh

12
dwanaście
dvanash-cheh

13
trzynaście
tshinash-cheh

14
czternaście
chternash-cheh

15
piętnaście
p-yEntnash-cheh

16
szesnaście
shesnash-cheh

17
siedemnaście
shedemnash-cheh

18
osiemnaście
oshemnash-cheh

19
dziewiętnaście
jev-yENtnash-cheh

20
dwadzieścia
dvajesh-cha

21
dwadzieścia jeden
dvajesh-cha yeden

22
dwadzieścia dwa
dvajesh-cha dva

30
trzydzieści
tshijesh-chee

40
czterdzieści
chterjesh-chee

50
pięćdziesiąt
p-yENchjeshAWNt

100
sto
sto

200
dwieście
dv-yesh-cheh

500
pięćset
p-yENchset

1,000
tysiąc
tishAWNts

1,000,000
milion
meel-yon

Time

today
dzisiaj
jeeshI

yesterday
wczoraj
vchorI

tomorrow
jutro
yootro

tonight
dzisiejszej nocy
jeeshAYshay notsi

one minute
jedna minuta
yedna meenoota

half an hour
pół godziny
poowuh gojeeni

hour
godzina
gojeena

Days of the Week

Sunday
niedziela
n-yejela

Monday
poniedziałek
pon-yejawek

Tuesday
wtorek
vtorek

Wednesday
środa
shroda

Thursday
czwartek
chvartek

Friday
piątek
p-yAWNtek

Saturday
sobota
sobota

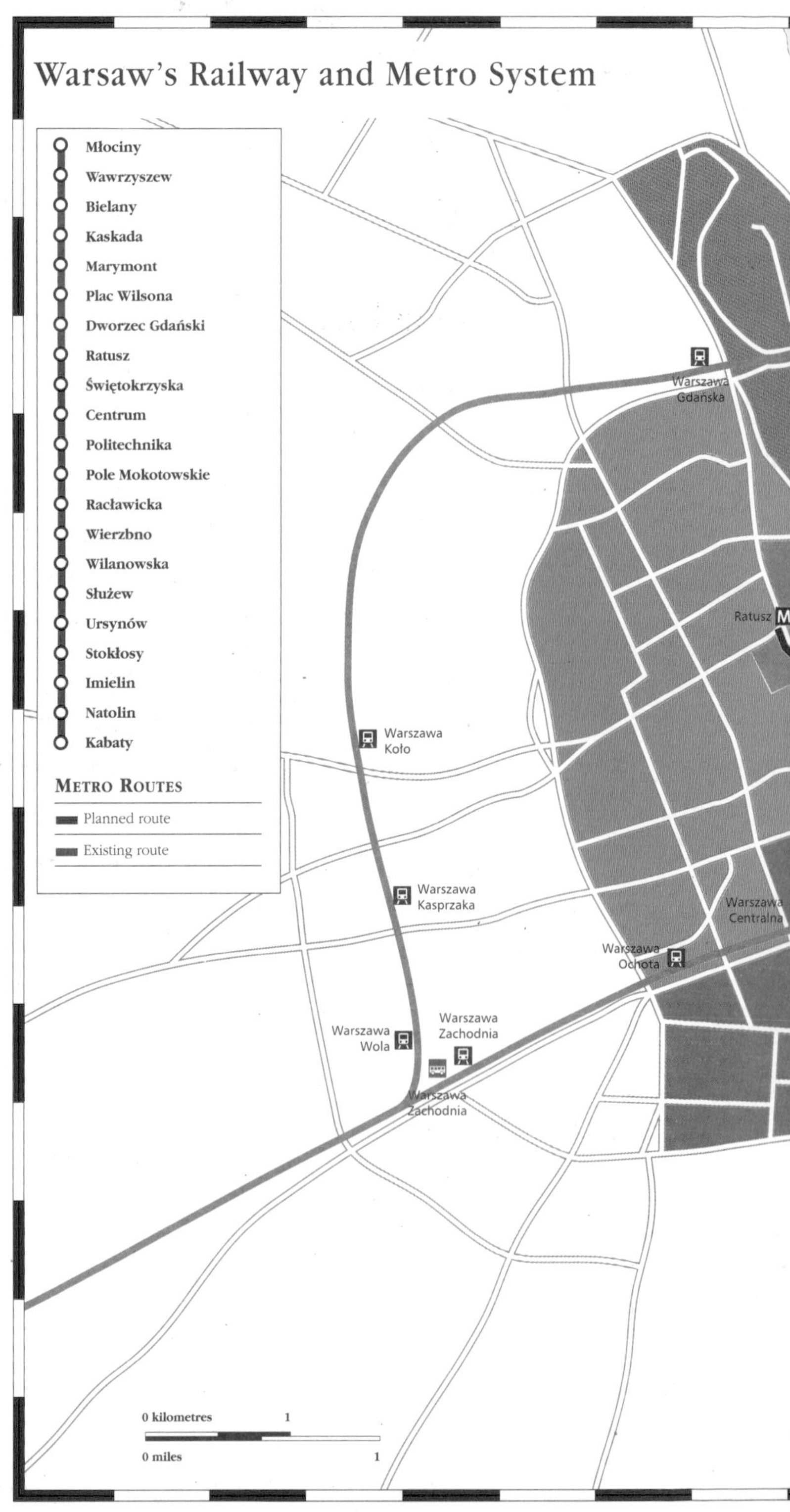

Warsaw's Railway and Metro System
Młociny
Wawrzyszew
Bielany
Kaskada
Marymont
Plac Wilsona
Dworzec Gdański
Ratusz
Świętokrzyska
Centrum
Politechnika
Pole Mokotowskie
Racławicka
Wierzbno
Wilanowska
Służew
Ursynów
Stokłosy
Imielin
Natolin
Kabaty
Metro Routes
Planned route
Existing route
Warszawa Gdańska
Ratusz
Warszawa Koło
Warszawa Kasprzaka
Warszawa Centralna
Warszawa Ochota
Warszawa Wola
Warszawa Zachodnia
Warszawa Zachodnia
0 kilometres
1
0 miles
1